HISTORIC PHOTOS OF
PENSACOLA

TEXT AND CAPTIONS BY
JACQUELYN TRACY WILSON

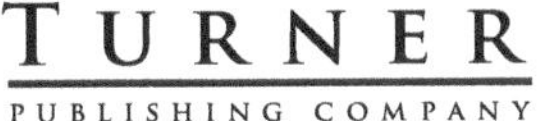

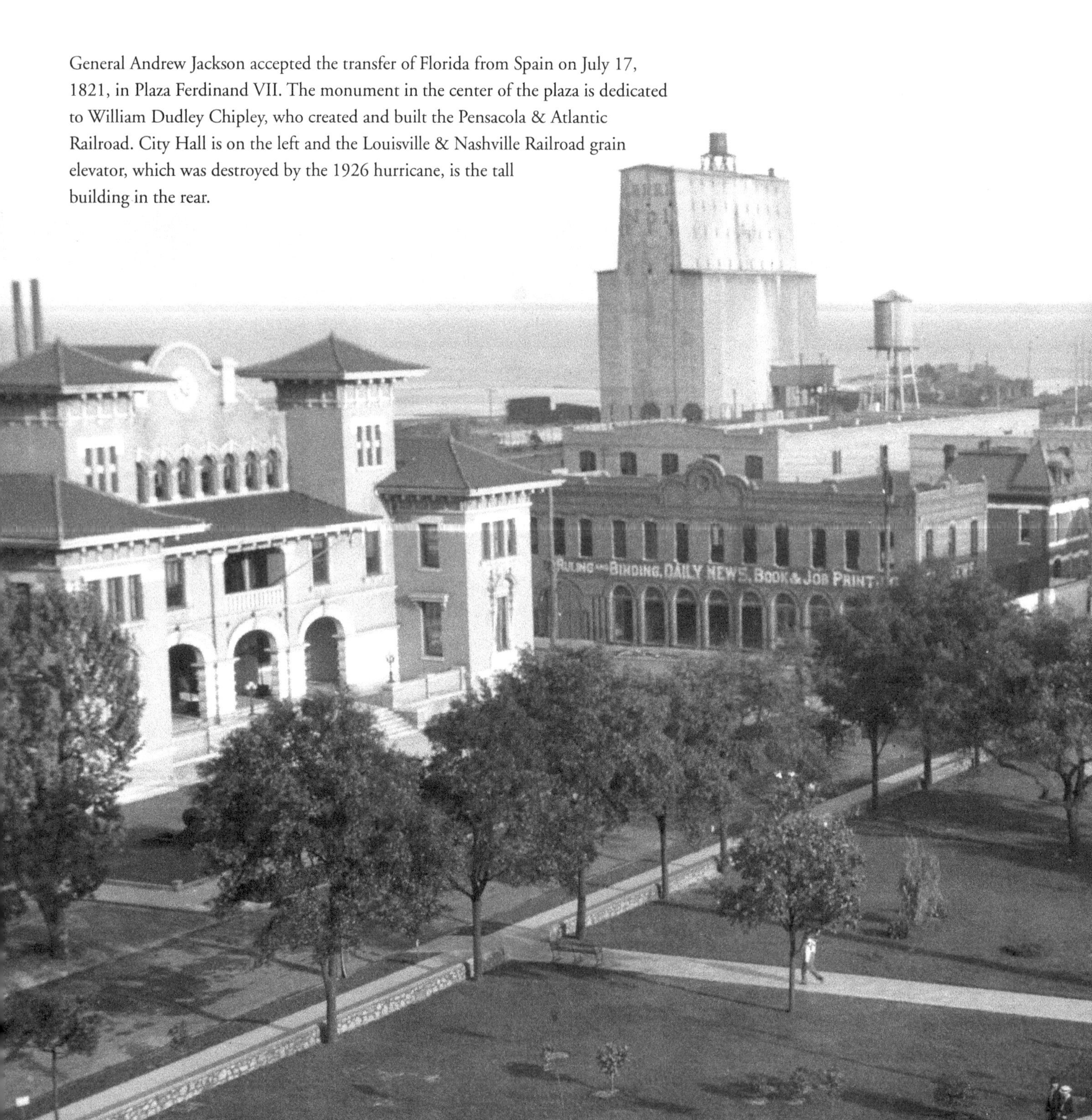

General Andrew Jackson accepted the transfer of Florida from Spain on July 17, 1821, in Plaza Ferdinand VII. The monument in the center of the plaza is dedicated to William Dudley Chipley, who created and built the Pensacola & Atlantic Railroad. City Hall is on the left and the Louisville & Nashville Railroad grain elevator, which was destroyed by the 1926 hurricane, is the tall building in the rear.

HISTORIC PHOTOS OF
PENSACOLA

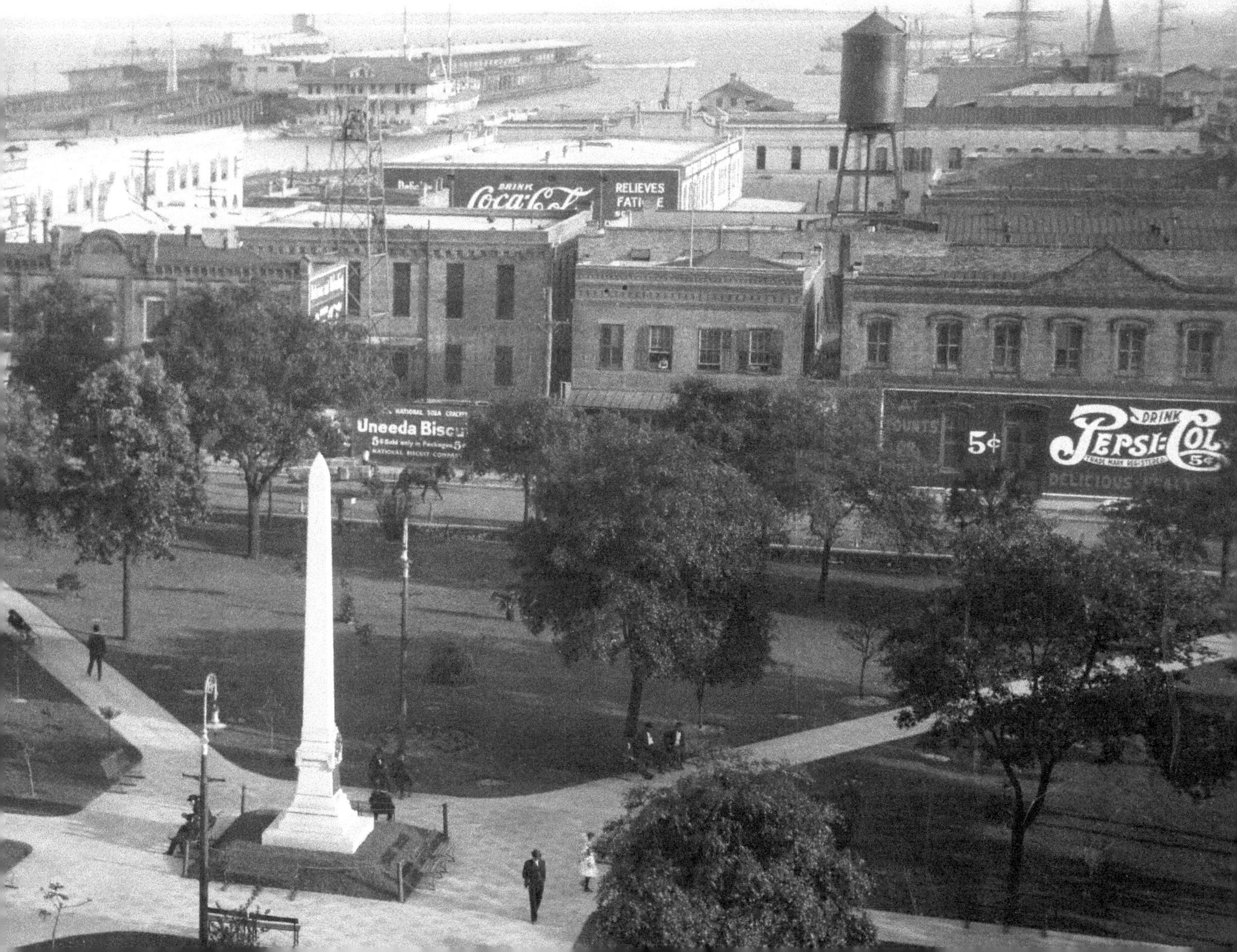

Turner Publishing Company
www.turnerpublishing.com

Historic Photos of Pensacola

Library of Congress Control Number: 2007941387

ISBN-13: 978-1-59652-426-2

ISBN 978-1-68442-003-2 (hc)

Contents

Margaret Wilkinson, Mary Turner, and Joan Simmons (left to right) pose with a pair of Navy wings and a Blue Angels jet during the Naval Aviation 50th anniversary celebrations at Pensacola in 1961.

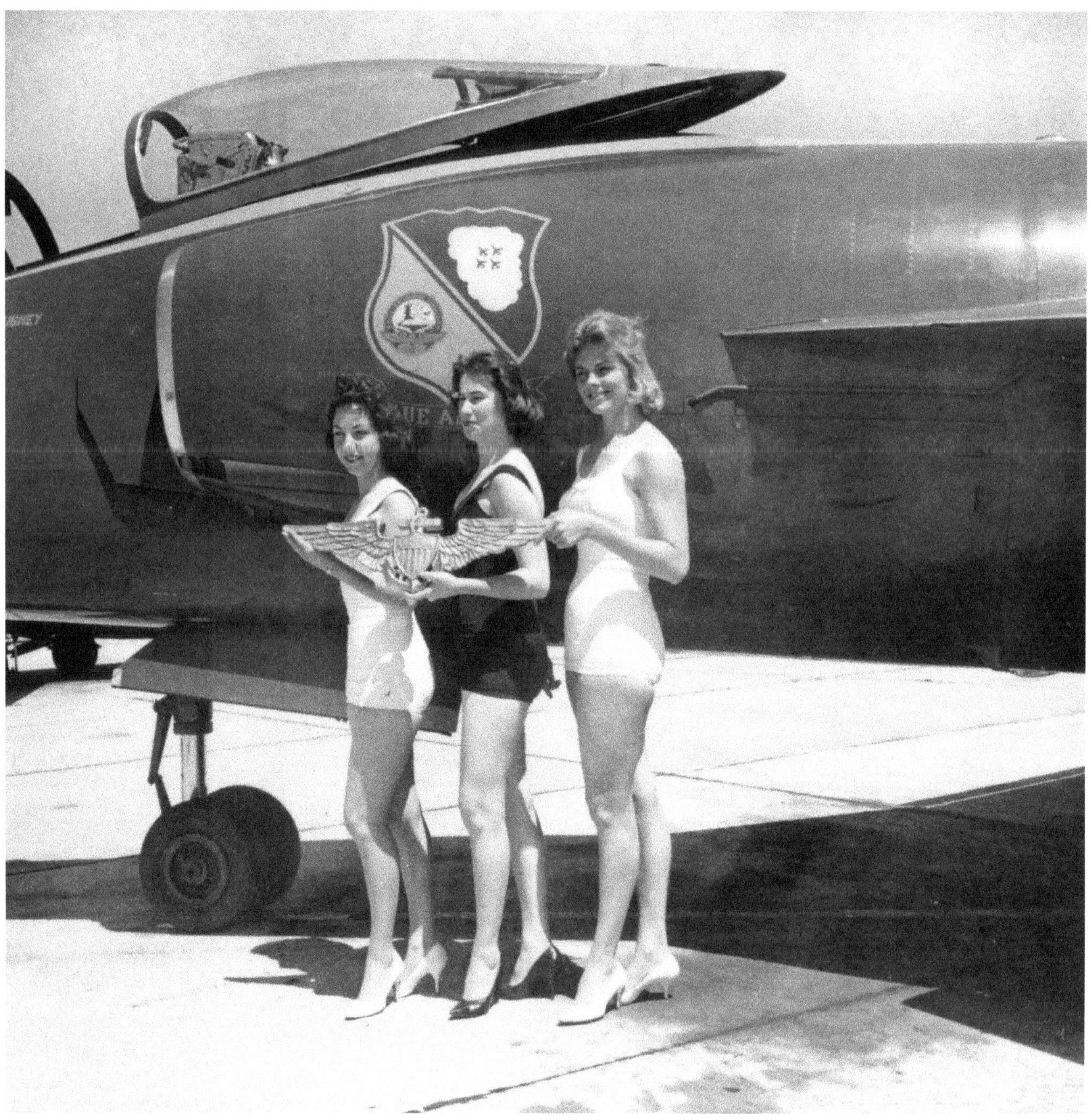

ACKNOWLEDGMENTS

This volume, *Historic Photos of Pensacola,* is the result of the cooperation and efforts of many individuals and organizations. It is with great thanks that we acknowledge the State Archives of Florida for their generous support.

As author, I would like to thank the Pensacola Historical Society for the use of their excellent research materials. Mr. David P. Ogden, historian and ranger for the Gulf Islands National Seashore, was an invaluable source for information about Fort Barrancas and the Navy Yard. Lieutenant Commander Donald T. McCloskey, USN (retired), offered me his vast knowledge of naval aircraft. The information they freely shared with me improved this book immensely.

Preface

Others have written wonderful books full of photos of Pensacola's past. I hope that my effort will be accepted for what it is intended to be, an addition to the story of the growth and development of a Southern city with a special place in history. As a native and lifelong resident of the greater Pensacola area, I hope that my personal knowledge and love of Pensacola has helped to add just that little something that may have been overlooked by others.

Photographs help to bring the past to life in a way that words alone cannot accomplish. They help the viewer understand a way of life that is foreign to them. Images capture moments of time, freezing minute details that may be overlooked elsewhere, aspects of the past that would otherwise be lost in the passage of time. Photographs also help cement our connections with the past. As a historian, I believe that we cannot understand the present without knowing the past that has shaped our environment. As an artist, I know that the visual can make a powerful, lasting impact on the viewer. Photographs are a wonderful aid for adding to our knowledge.

With the exception of cropping images where needed and touching up imperfections that have accrued over time, no other changes have been made to this collection of photographs. Their caliber and clarity are limited by the technology of the day and the ability of the photographer at the time they were made.

Pensacola has a long history filled with triumph and with tragedy. The photographs presented here capture some of these moments. The story begins with scenes of Confederate troops defending Fort Barrancas, which was recaptured by Union forces after the Confederate withdrawal from the city. Scenes of the bustling port city are followed by the stark images of a city almost totally destroyed by fire in December 1880. Throughout the book's pages are scenes from everyday life—triumphal parades, disasters, and people at play. And Pensacola's military bases, so important to the city, receive special focus. I hope you will enjoy these photographs and appreciate the full range of emotions many of them can evoke. Gaze amused at some of the dress styles, take pride in the city's accomplishments, understand the pain inflicted by wars. You will have the privilege of watching Pensacola grow and mature as you travel through these pages.

I wish that I could tell a much broader story than the one in this book, because Pensacola has so many stories to offer, but the scope of any single book must always be limited. Much of this book concentrates on the old core of Pensacola, the area found within the confines of Pensacola Bay, North Hill, Florida Blanca Street, and DeVilliers Street. Of course, no history of Pensacola is complete without a look at the Navy bases, the forts, and Pensacola Beach. As I look at old photographs, I want to know the story that was captured when the shutter clicked and the scene was burned onto film. With the use of newspaper clippings, city directories, conversations with knowledgeable people, and information in the archives of the Pensacola Historical Society, I have tried to find some of the stories hidden in these images. I hope you enjoy these stories as much as I do.

Confederate troops occupied Fort Barrancas from January 12, 1861, until they withdrew from Pensacola on May 10, 1862. These cannon overlooked the mouth of Pensacola Bay, controlling access to Pensacola's port. The shot furnace is in the upper-right corner of the photograph.

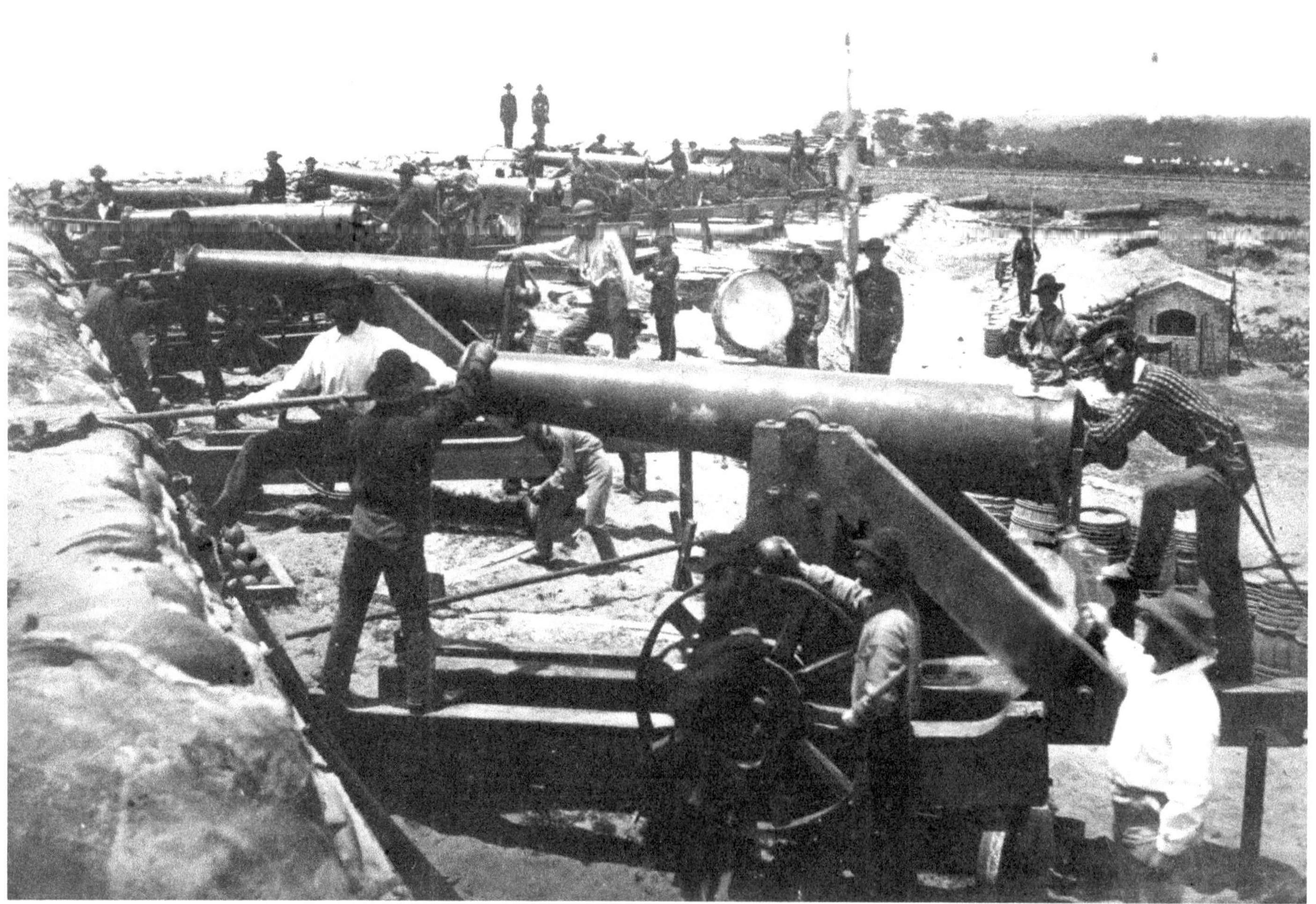

A City of Firsts

(1861–1899)

Pensacola was the first European settlement established in North America. Don Tristán de Luna y Arrelano arrived with 1,500 soldiers and settlers in 1559. Unfortunately, the settlement suffered after being ravaged by a hurricane and was abandoned two years later. A permanent European settlement was not established in Pensacola until 1698, but by 1861, Pensacola had become the largest city in Florida.

For many people, the beginning of the Civil War is associated with the shots fired at Fort Sumter, South Carolina, on April 12 and 13, 1861. Many historians have downplayed hostilities that took place in Pensacola prior to that date. At 11:00 P.M. on January 8, 1861, Confederate forces, under Colonel William H. Chase, fired upon the Union Army under the command of Lieutenant Adam J. Slemmer at Fort Barrancas, just west of Pensacola. On January 10, Lieutenant Slemmer moved his detail from Fort Barrancas to Fort Pickens on Santa Rosa Island, a position he felt would be easier to defend. The two forts engaged each other on November 22 and 23, 1861, firing 6,000 cannon balls across the mouth of Pensacola Bay. Because the forts sit just beyond the range of the cannons, very little harm was done to either fortification. Confederate troops pulled out of northwest Florida in 1862 and the Union Army regained control of Pensacola on May 10, leaving the forts virtually unscathed by the war. The Navy Yard, however, suffered heavy damage on November 22 and during another engagement on January 1, 1862. Confederate troops destroyed most of the buildings in the Navy Yard before withdrawing from Pensacola.

Pensacola grew around the waterfront. For many years, Pensacola could boast that it was the only natural deep-water port in the United States on the Gulf of Mexico. Fishing boats that harvested the abundance of fish in the local waters competed with cargo ships for dock space. Pensacola became known as the "Red Snapper Capital" of the world, and special boats, called Snapper Smacks, were devised to keep the deep-water fish alive in the days before ice was manufactured in the city and used to prevent spoilage. Fortunes were made when entrepreneurs realized that this port offered cheap transportation for the lumber they could cut from the dense forests of northwest Florida and southern Alabama. The port also attracted railroads, resulting in multiple lines serving Pensacola and the port.

Pensacola escaped the devastation suffered by many cities during the Civil War. However, an estimated nine-tenths of the city was destroyed on December 11, 1880, when a fire swept through the South Palafox business district. The citizens of Pensacola worked together to rebuild their city and make it better. The city endured extreme weather changes as the end of the century neared. The Great Blizzard of 1889 set record low temperatures and blanketed the city with several inches of snow. Snow covered the city again in 1894 and 1899.

Troops from Alabama, Mississippi, and Louisiana supplemented the Florida forces stationed at Fort Barrancas. The First Alabama Infantry Regiment was primarily responsible for manning the batteries at the fort. Their camp, pictured here, was behind the rear wall of the fort.

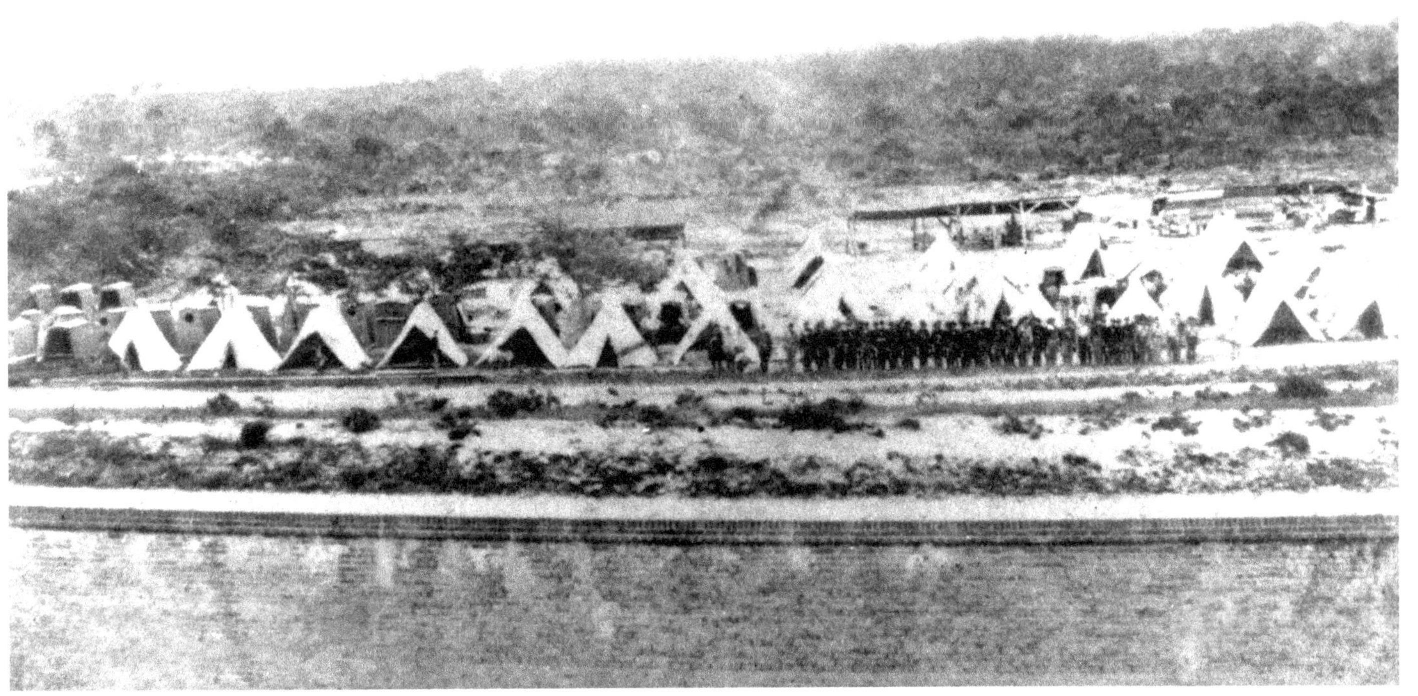

The 9th Mississippi was one of the first Confederate regiments to form in that state. They marched into Pensacola in April 1861 and camped near Fort Barrancas.

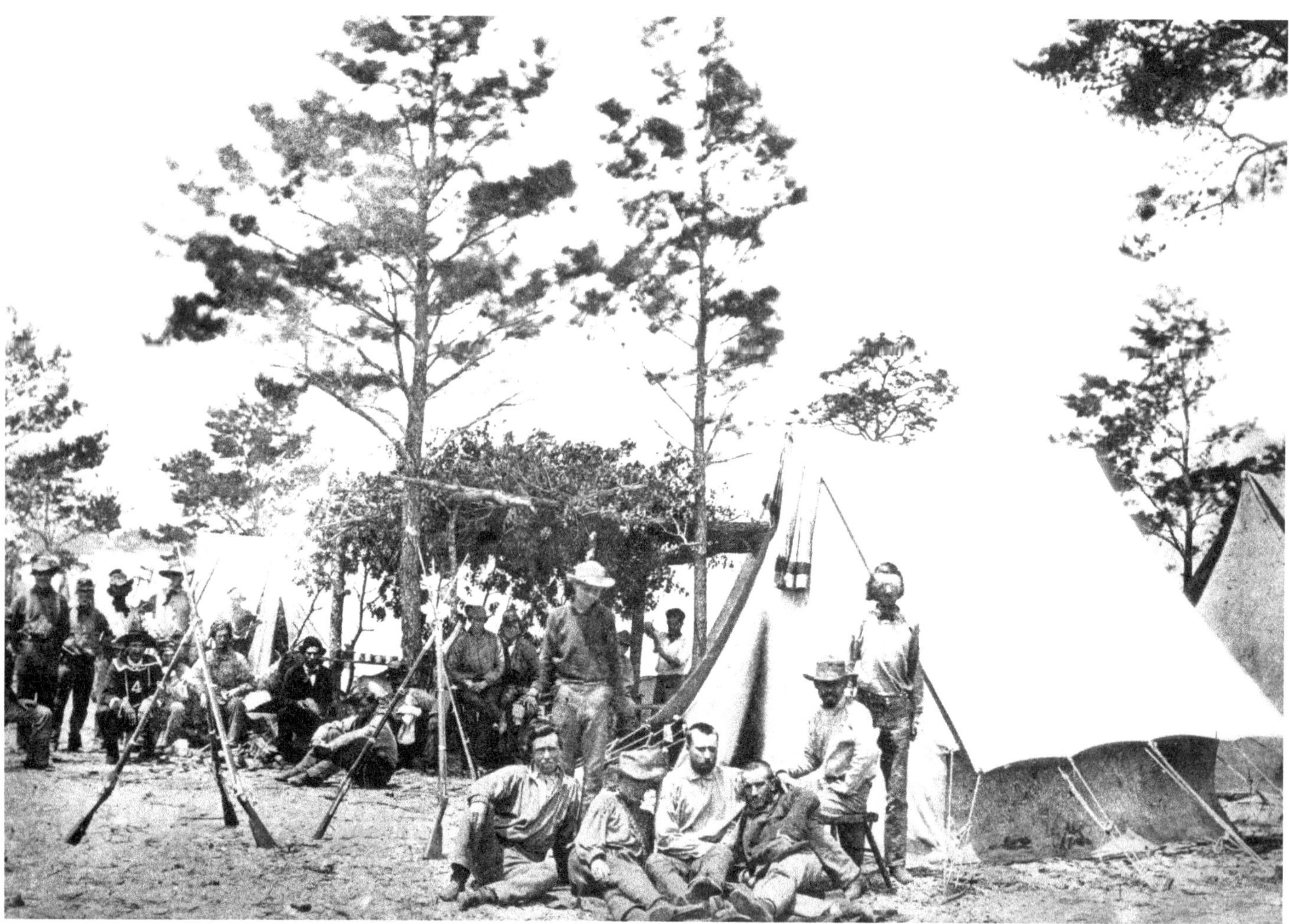

Along with cannons, Confederate soldiers used mortars to defend Fort Barrancas. Used to lob shells over walls and other obstacles, the mortar's range was controlled by the amount of gunpowder used with the round.

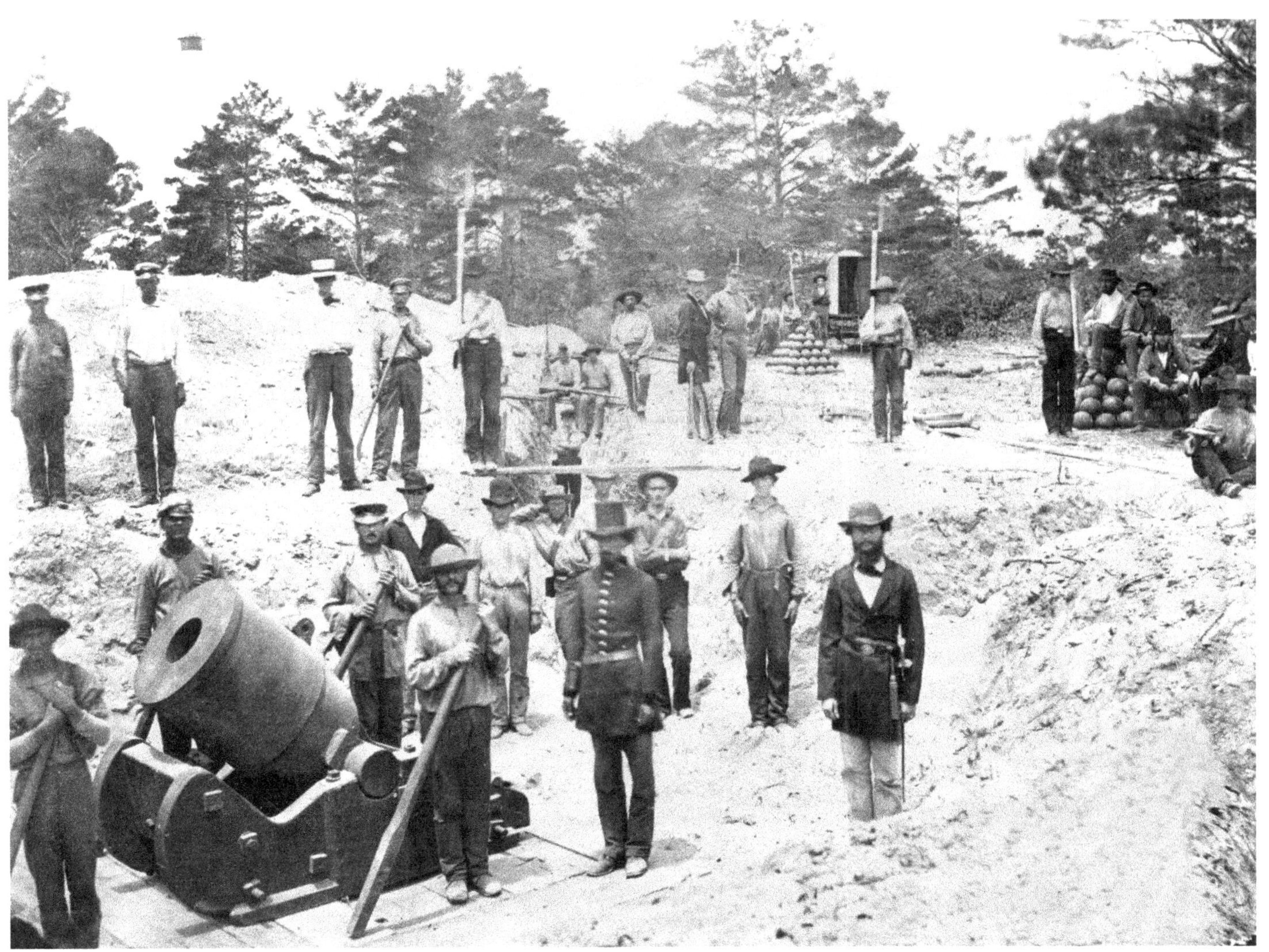

The original mission of ships stationed at the Pensacola Navy Yard was to patrol the Gulf of Mexico and the Caribbean to intercept pirates and slave ships. Some of the cannon used for defense of the yard are displayed in 1865. The steam engineering department, machine shop, and hospital are visible at the rear of the photograph.

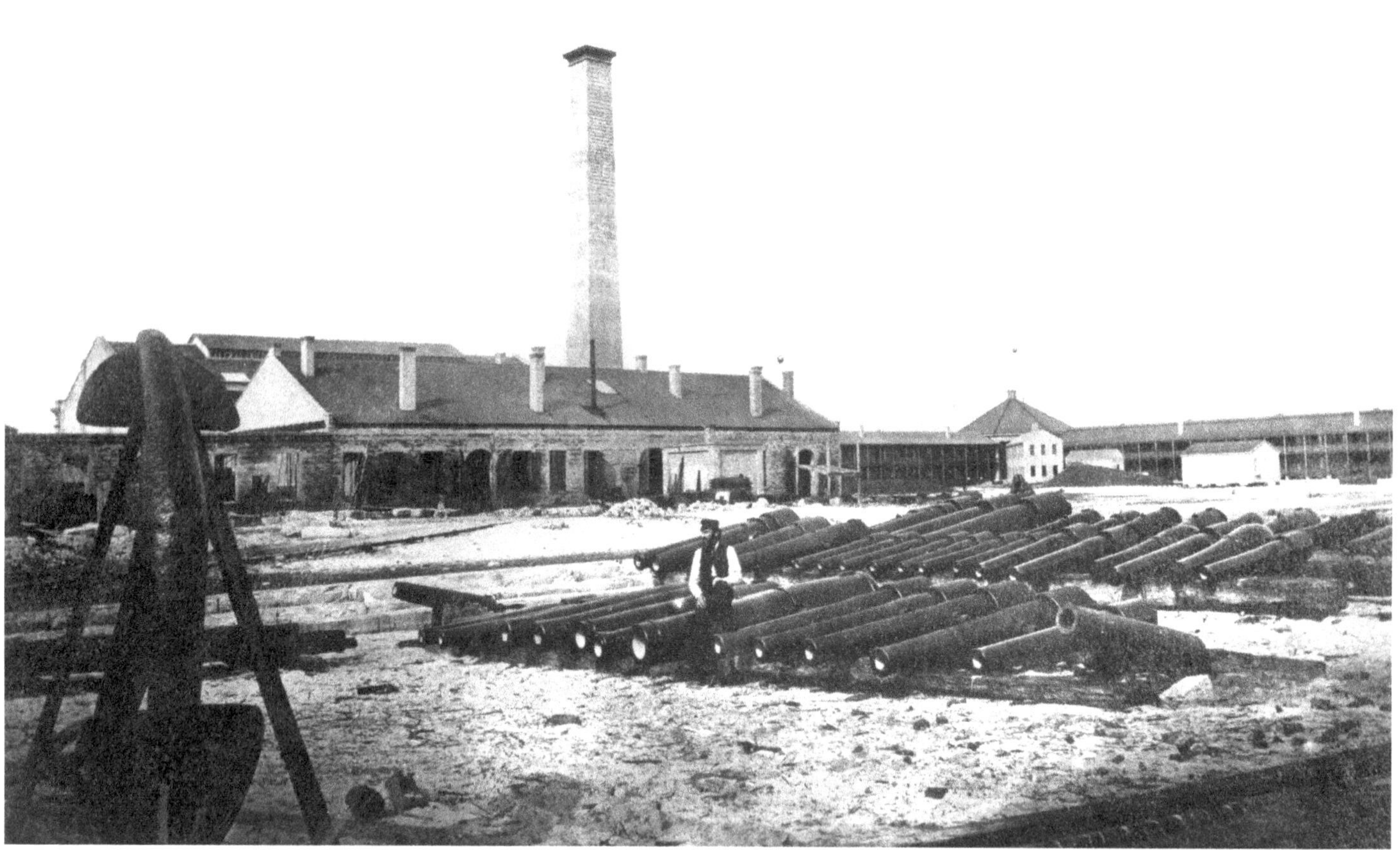

These Confederate troops camped beside Bayou Grande may be members of Company A of the Orleans Cadets, the first Confederate volunteer force to form in Louisiana. The Orleans Cadets organized on April 11, 1861, the day after Confederate troops demanded the surrender of Union forces at Fort Sumter, South Carolina.

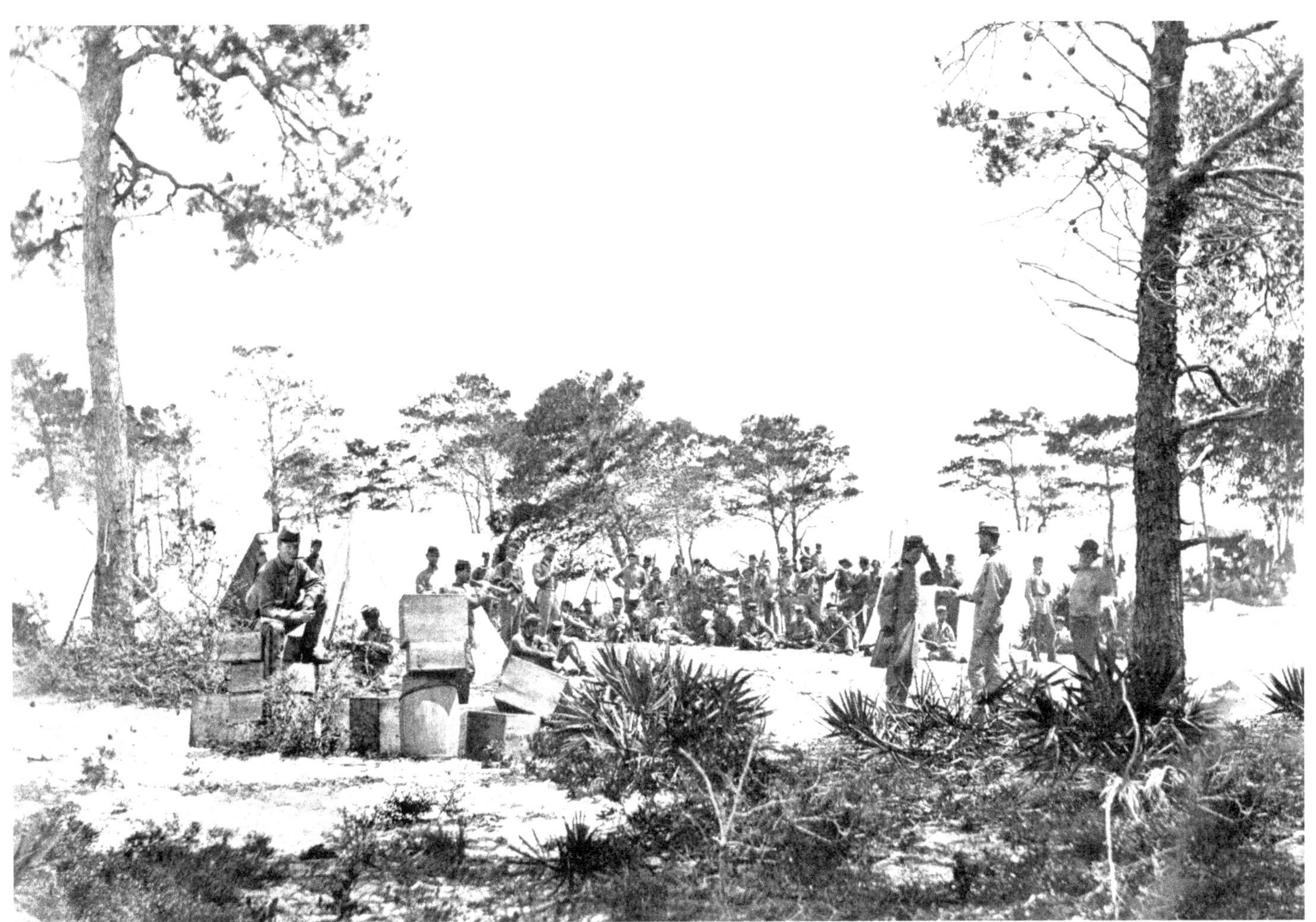

Stacked for storage, these cannon balls form sculptural displays at the Navy Yard in 1865. A ship's mast stands in the center of the display, and the steam-engineering department is at upper-left.

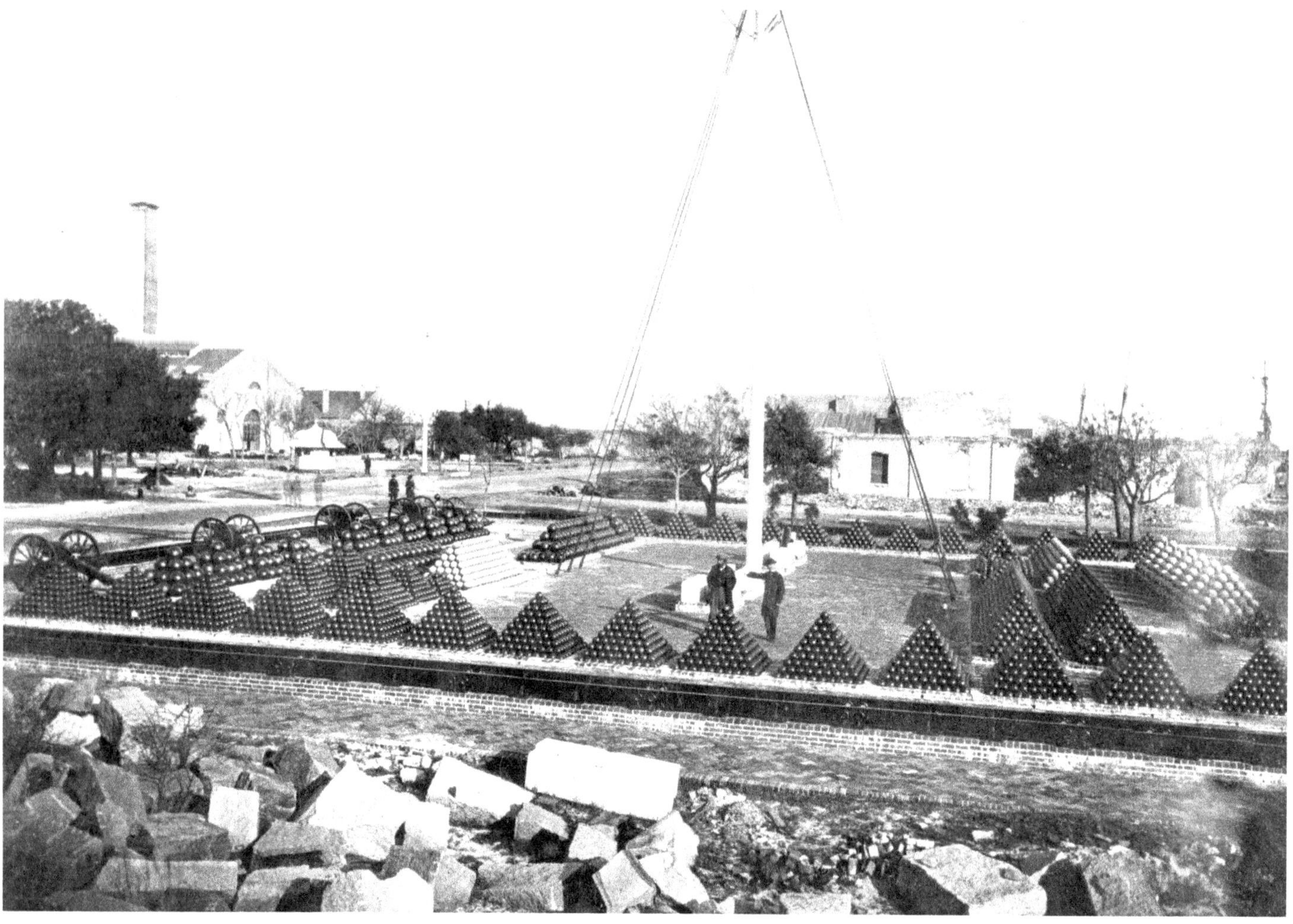

Union troops reclaimed the Pensacola military facilities after they were abandoned by the Confederacy in 1862. This view shows post–Civil War troops at leisure at Fort Barrancas in 1870.

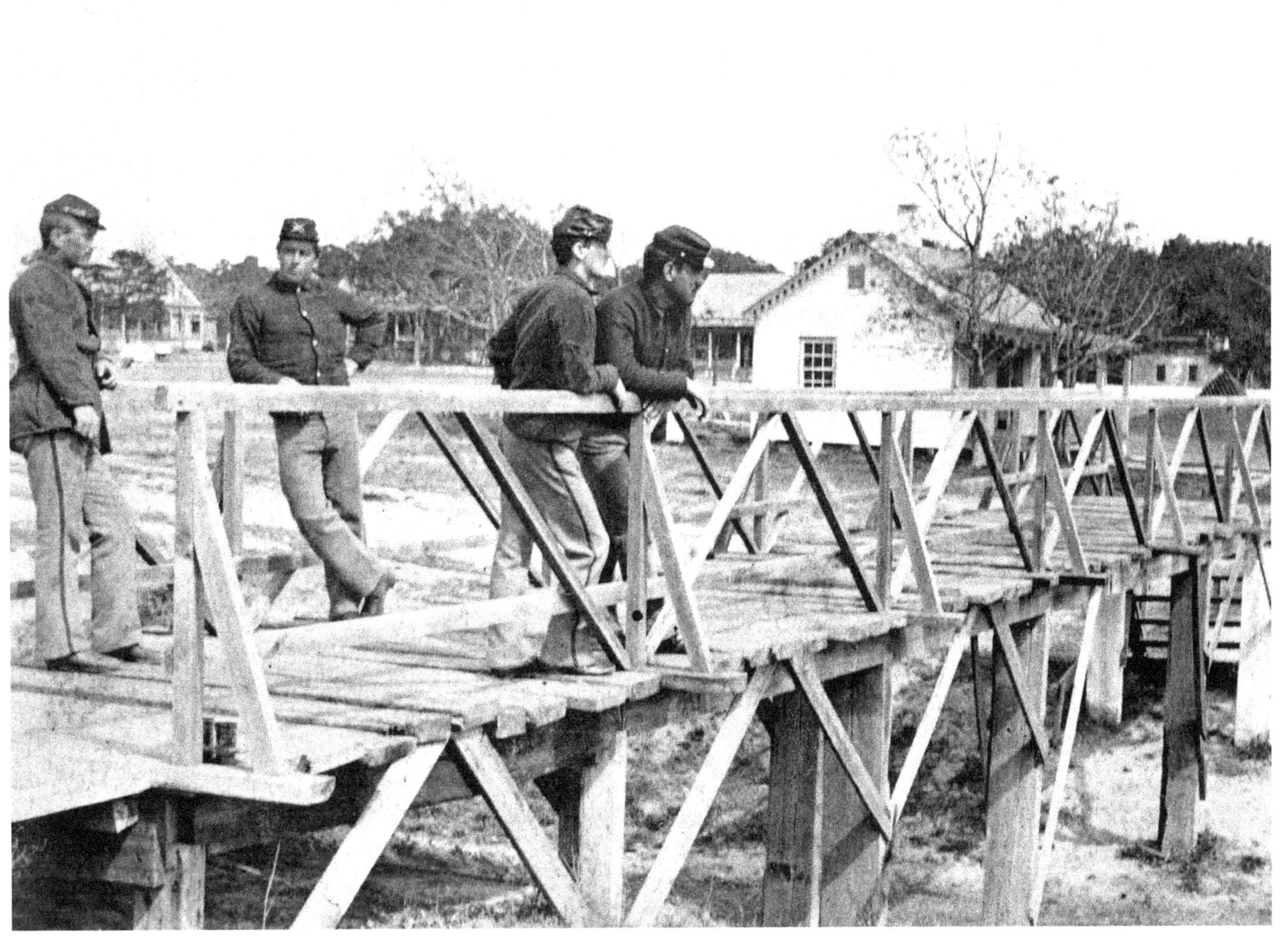

Yellow fever appeared in Fort Barrancas in the summer of 1875, brought to the area by the German ship *Von Moltke*. The majority of the personnel stationed at the fort transferred to Fort Pickens, but the post physician, Dr. George Miller Sternberg, and a small staff remained at the hospital to treat the ill. After Sternberg contracted the disease, Dr. James S. Herron came from Pensacola to care for the victims.

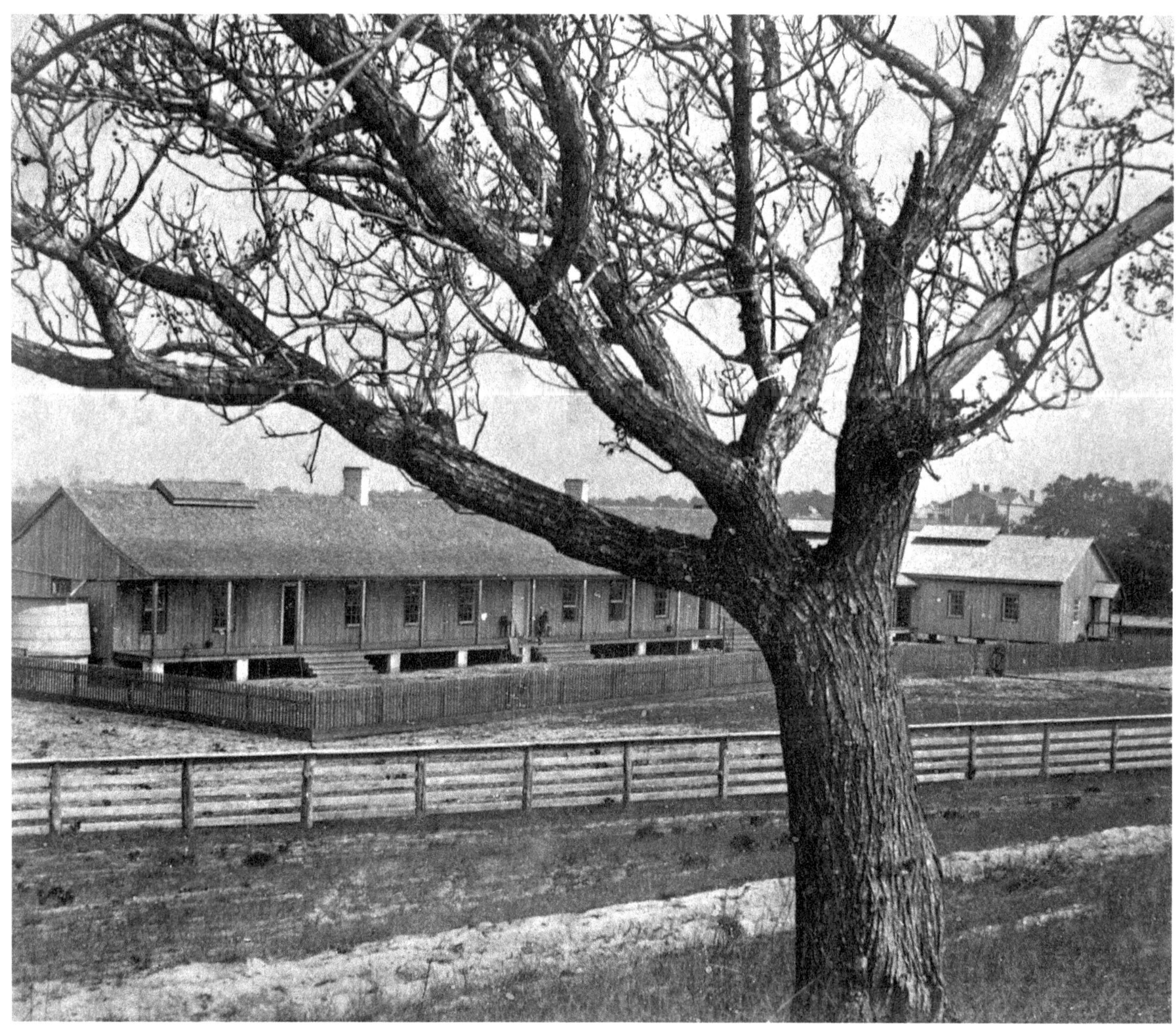

Members of the Kahn and Cohen families visit in front of the Kahn home on East Romana Street in 1870. Standing on the sidewalk are Lewis Kahn, Jake Kahn, and Gus Cohen. Mrs. Jake Kahn is on the porch and Lou Cohen and Mrs. Lewis Kahn are standing behind the fence.

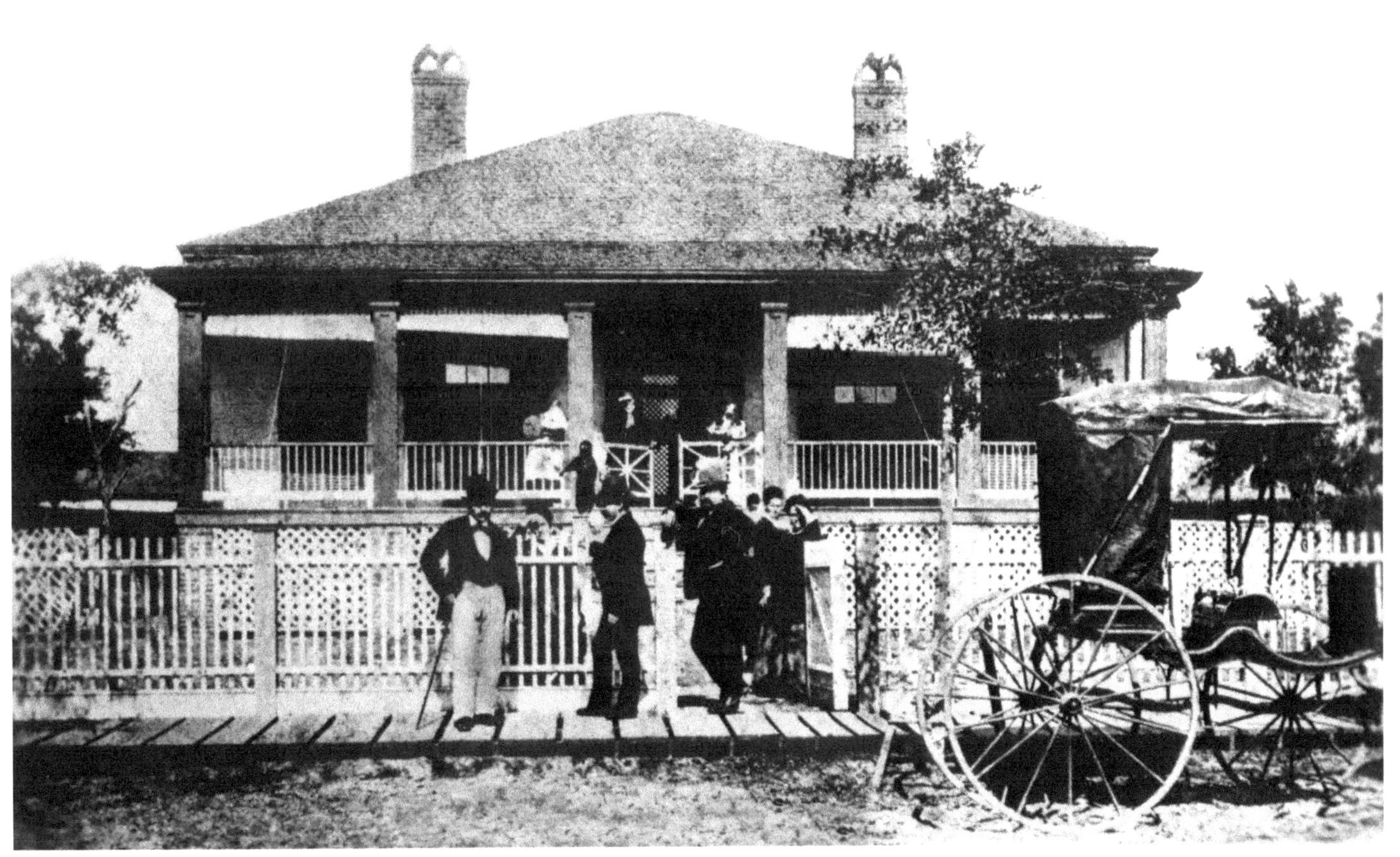

This spacious base housing was home to Captain Van Andress while he was stationed at Fort Barrancas around 1870. The deep porches and long windows helped to cool the home during hot, humid summers, and the latticework along the foundation helped to prevent wildlife from taking up residence under the house.

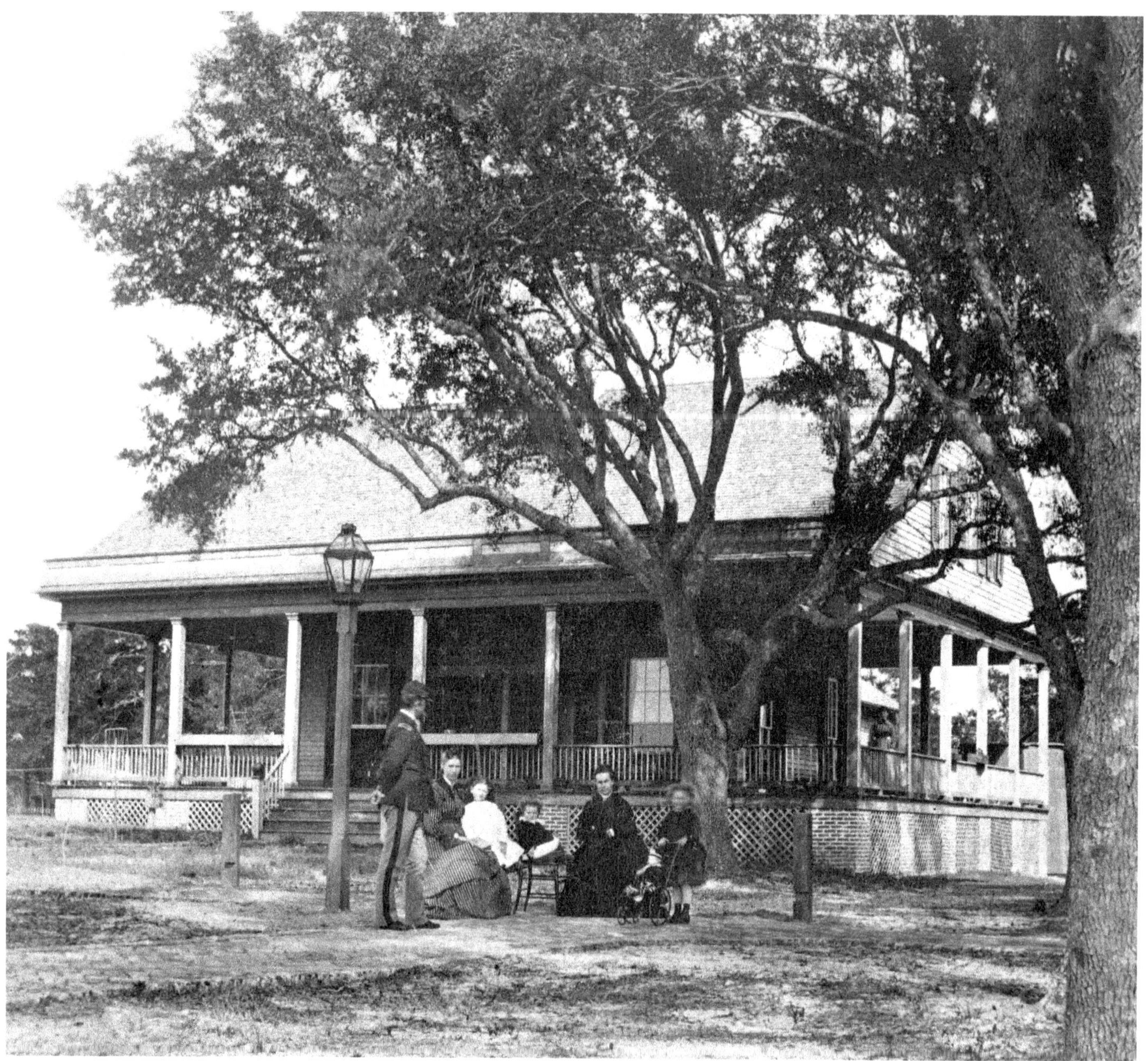

This 1871 view of downtown Pensacola faces northwest over the Pensacola skyline. The Masonic Temple is at upper-right and the steeples of the Methodist Episcopal Church and St. Michael's Catholic Church rise over North Palafox. The German Lutheran Church, at Garden and Baylen streets, is visible near the center of the picture. Most of the buildings on the west side of South Palafox were destroyed in the fire of 1880.

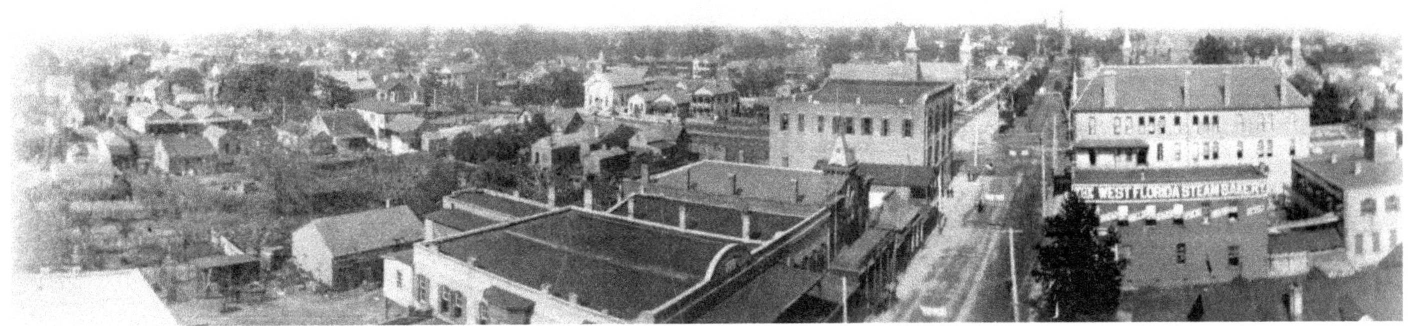

This variety store catered to the needs of a growing city. By the late 1800s, the downtown business district boasted wooden sidewalks and streetlights. The second story of buildings like this one often served as home for the business owner and his family.

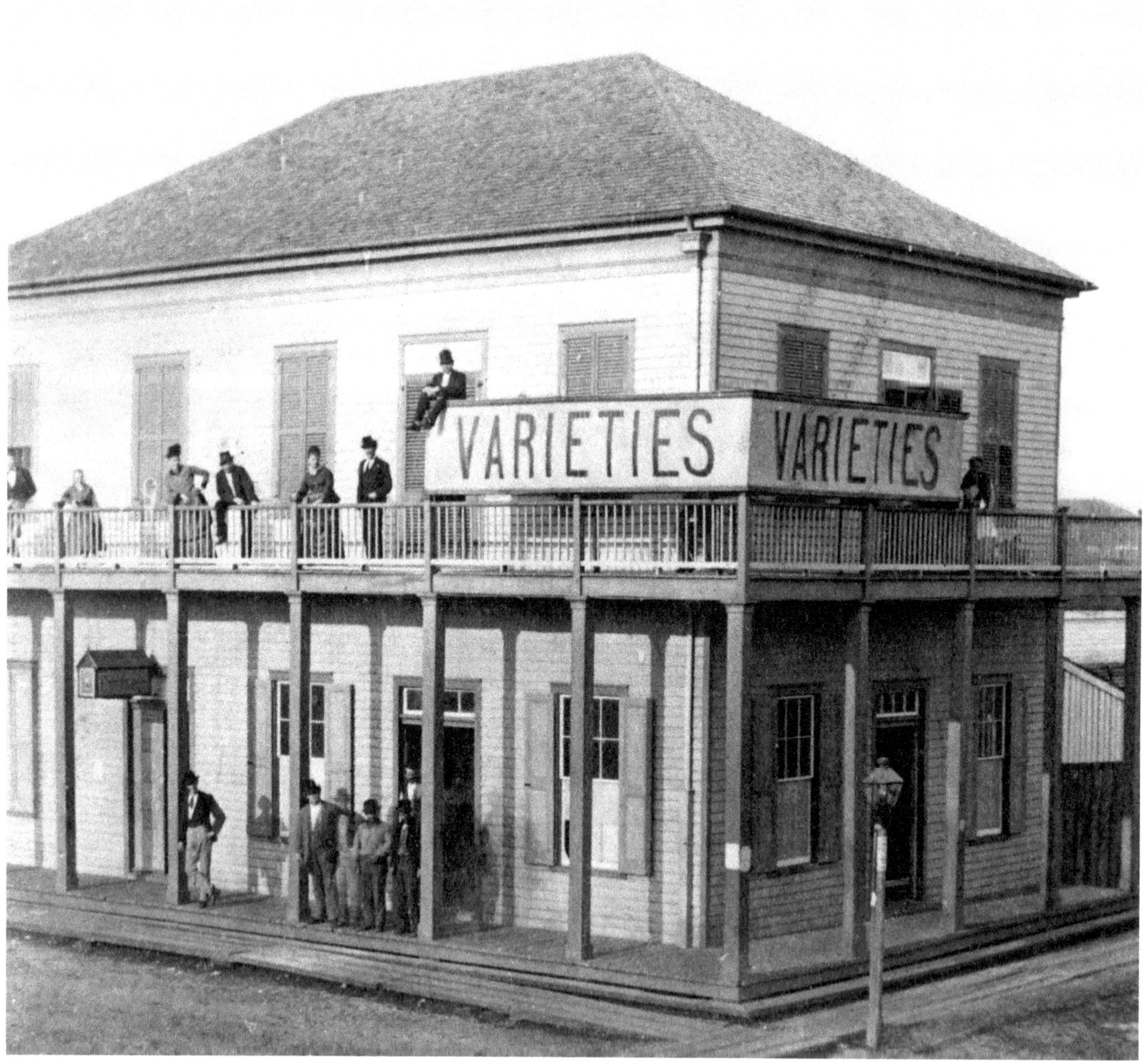

Based on plans drawn up by Admiral D. D. Porter, the *Barrancas* was built for the Navy's Quartermaster Department. Pictured here in the Pensacola harbor in November 1874, the steam-powered *Barrancas* ferried passengers and supplies to the forts that protected the mouth of Pensacola Bay.

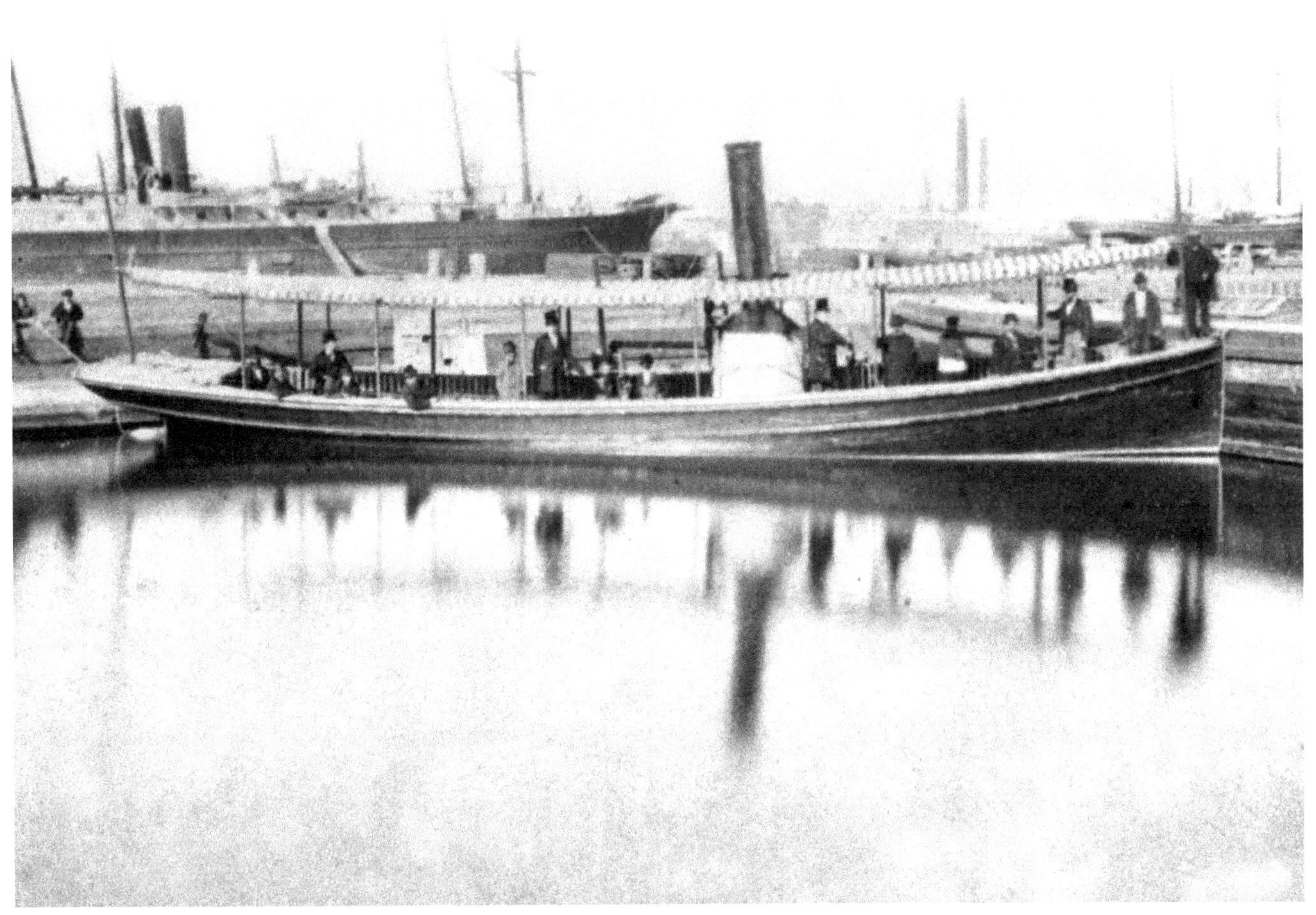

By 1876, the Pensacola business district had streetlights, but the roads remained unpaved. The sign on the store at right reflects the city's strong ties with its harbor and the ships that docked there.

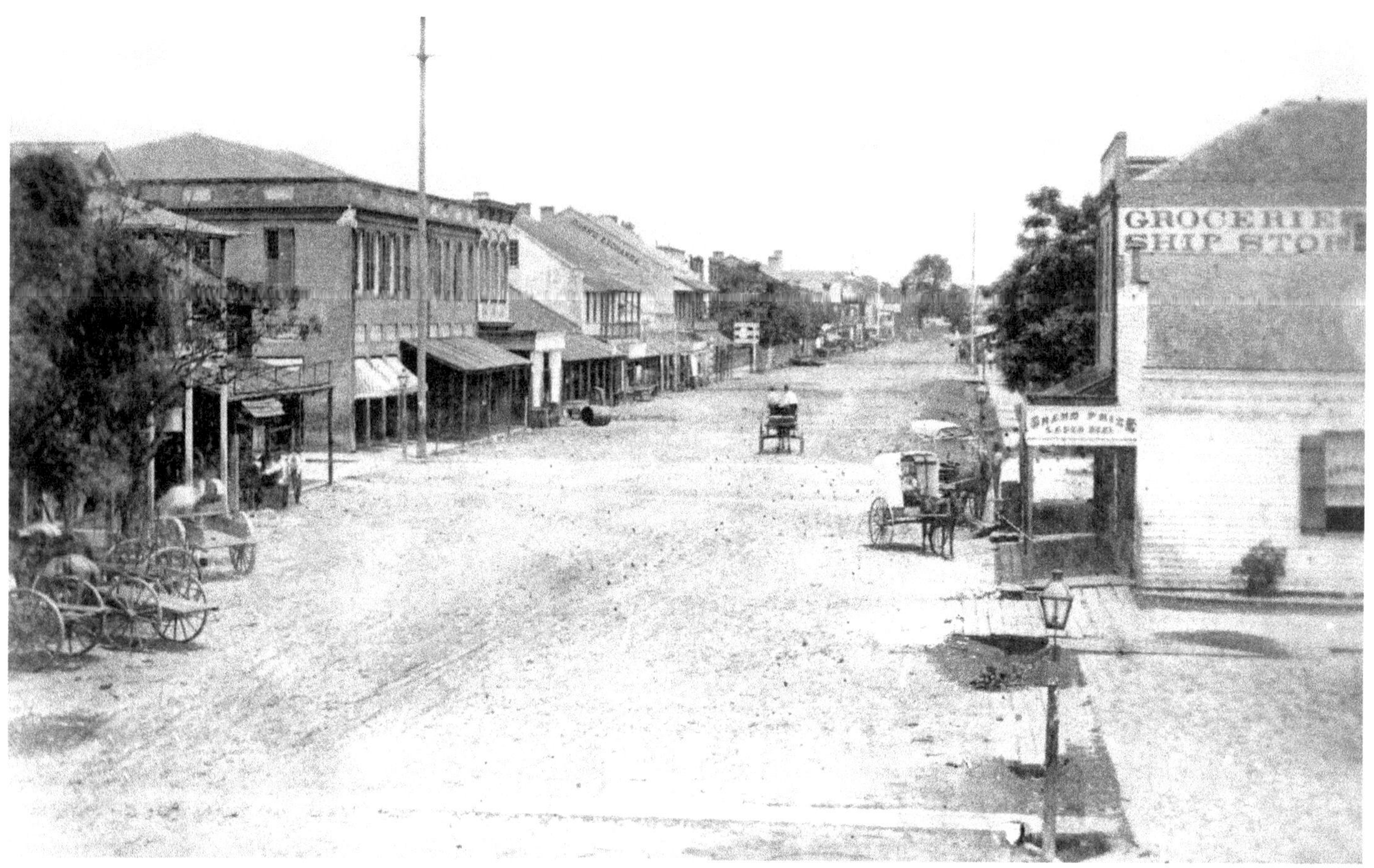

The Louisville & Nashville Railroad chartered the Pensacola & Atlantic Railroad Company March 4, 1881, to expand rail service east of Pensacola to Chattahoochee. This engine, built by the Rome Locomotive Works, was part of the Pensacola & Atlantic stock. The L&N Railroad obtained the majority of the Pensacola & Atlantic shares in 1885.

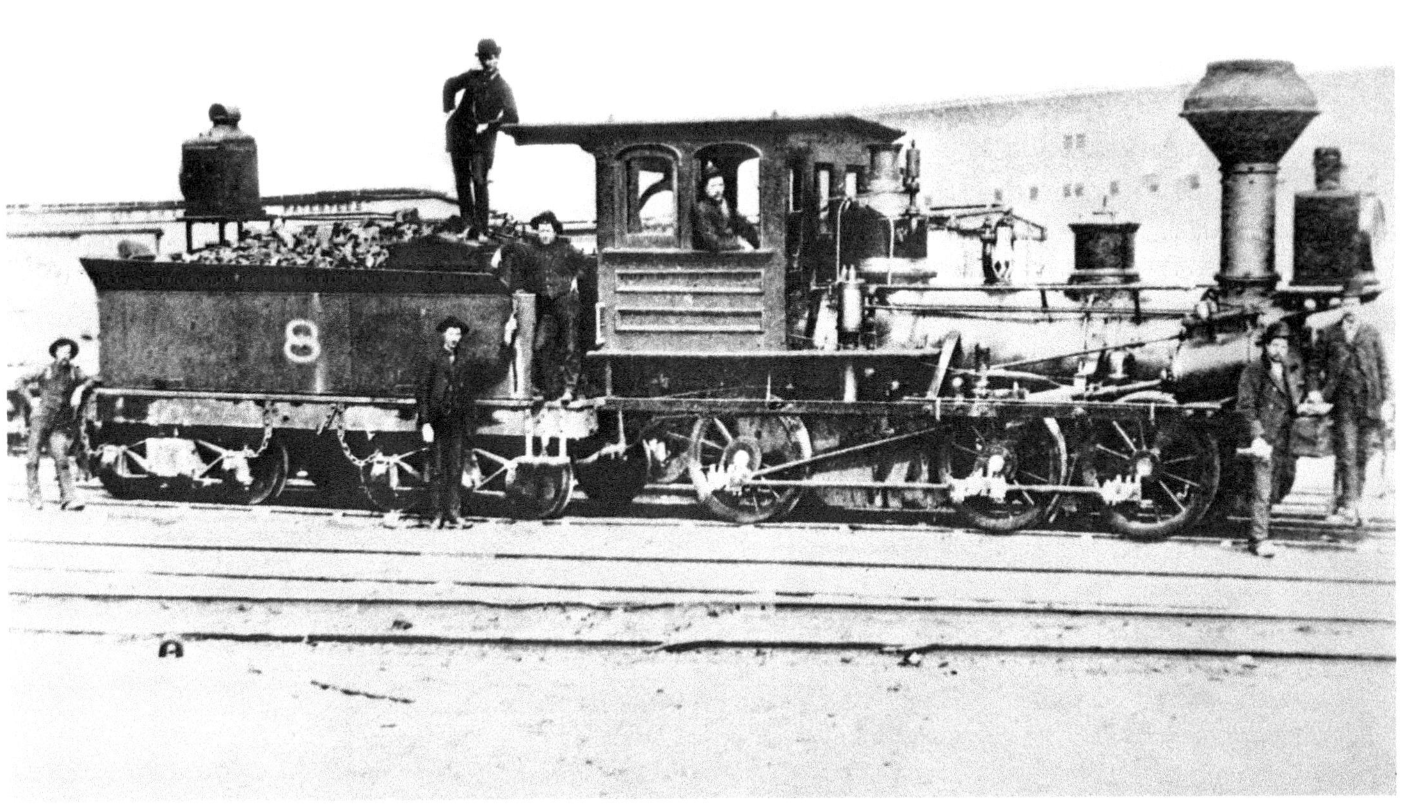

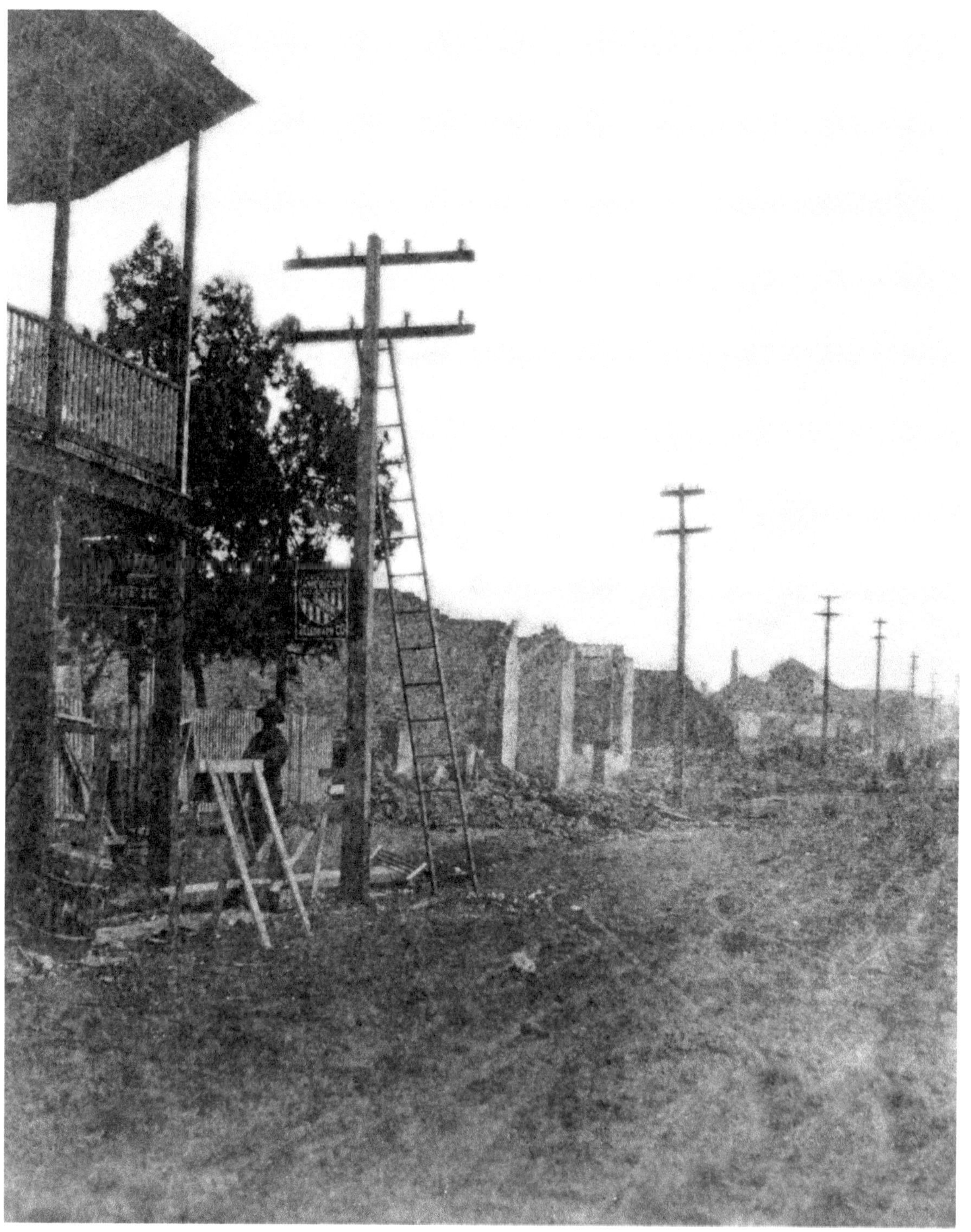

On December 11, 1880, a fire that began in a confectionery owned by Mrs. S. Damiana burned more than 100 buildings, destroyed most of the Pensacola business district, caused more than $1,000,000 in damages, and left 50 families homeless. At the time of the fire, Pensacola's only fire engine was undergoing repairs and was not in service. With no other fire departments within miles, citizens of Pensacola fought the fire with bucket brigades.

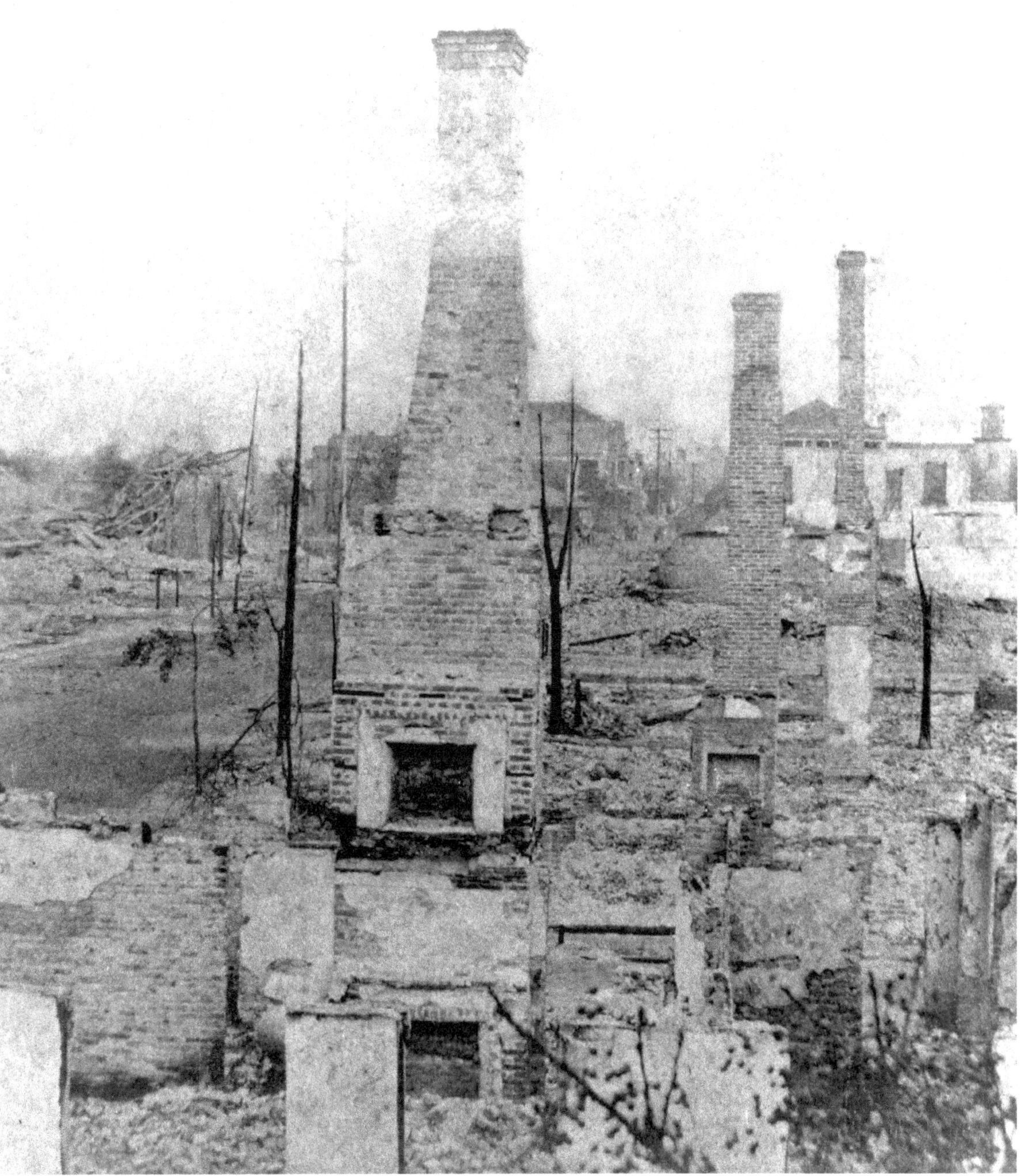

The 1880 fire destroyed nearly every building on South Palafox Street from Romana to Zarragossa streets. The destruction included both newspaper offices, the Customs House and Post Office, and all telegraph offices and drugstores. Mr. LaRue, the county clerk, managed to save the records stored in his office, but his home was destroyed. Mrs. S. Damiana, owner of the store where the fire began, died two days later from burns she suffered in the fire.

Cadets stationed at Fort Barrancas near the end of the nineteenth century proudly pose with a Gatling gun. The fort is also famous for housing some of the Chiricahua Apache tribe, including Chief Geronimo, for 18 months from 1886 until 1888.

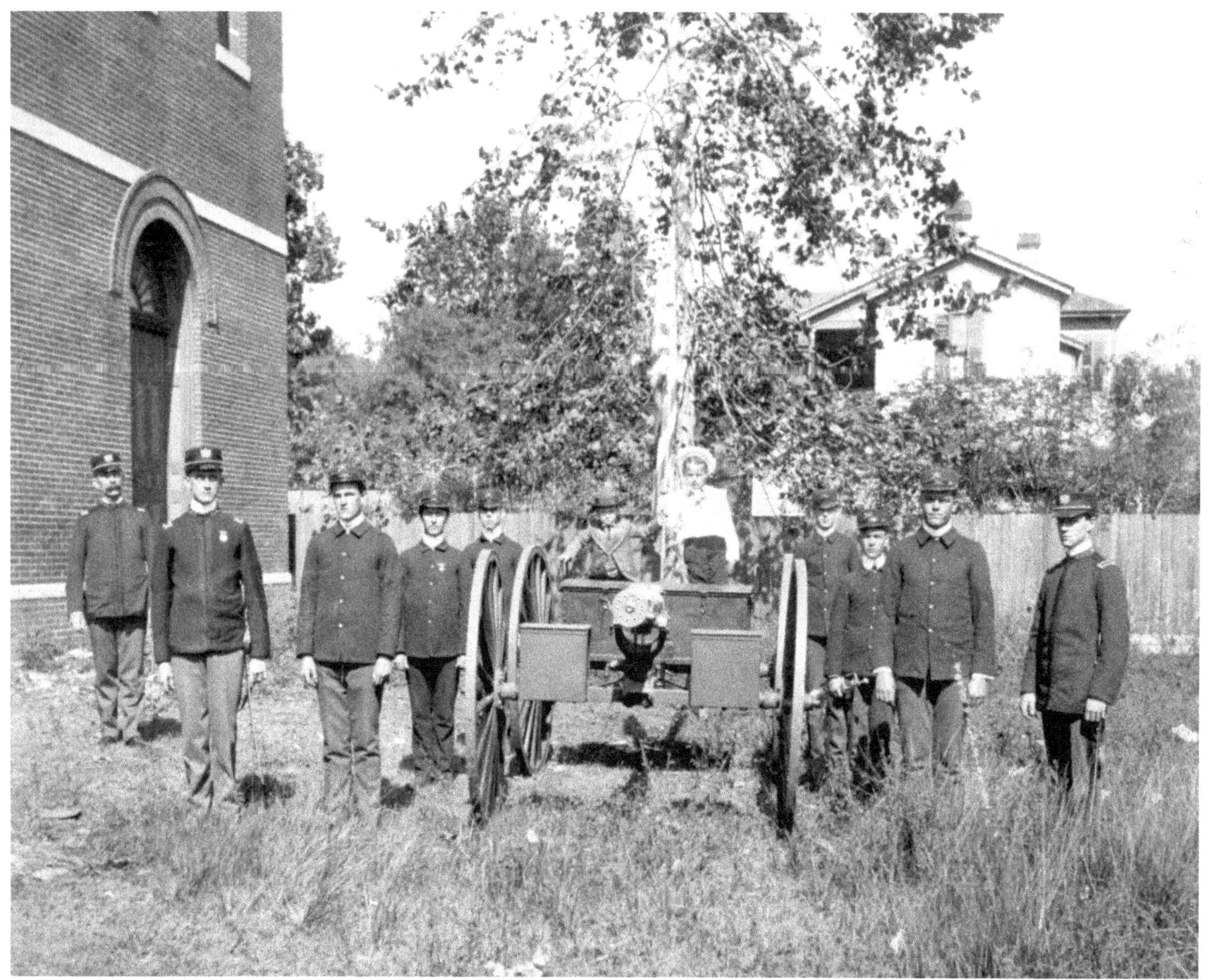

Francis C. Brent and his brothers began a general merchandise business after the Civil War. Located on the west side of South Palafox between Garden and Romana streets, the store's inventory included provisions, liquors, wines, and local produce. Francis later became president of the First National Bank, as well as president of the Pensacola Lumber Company.

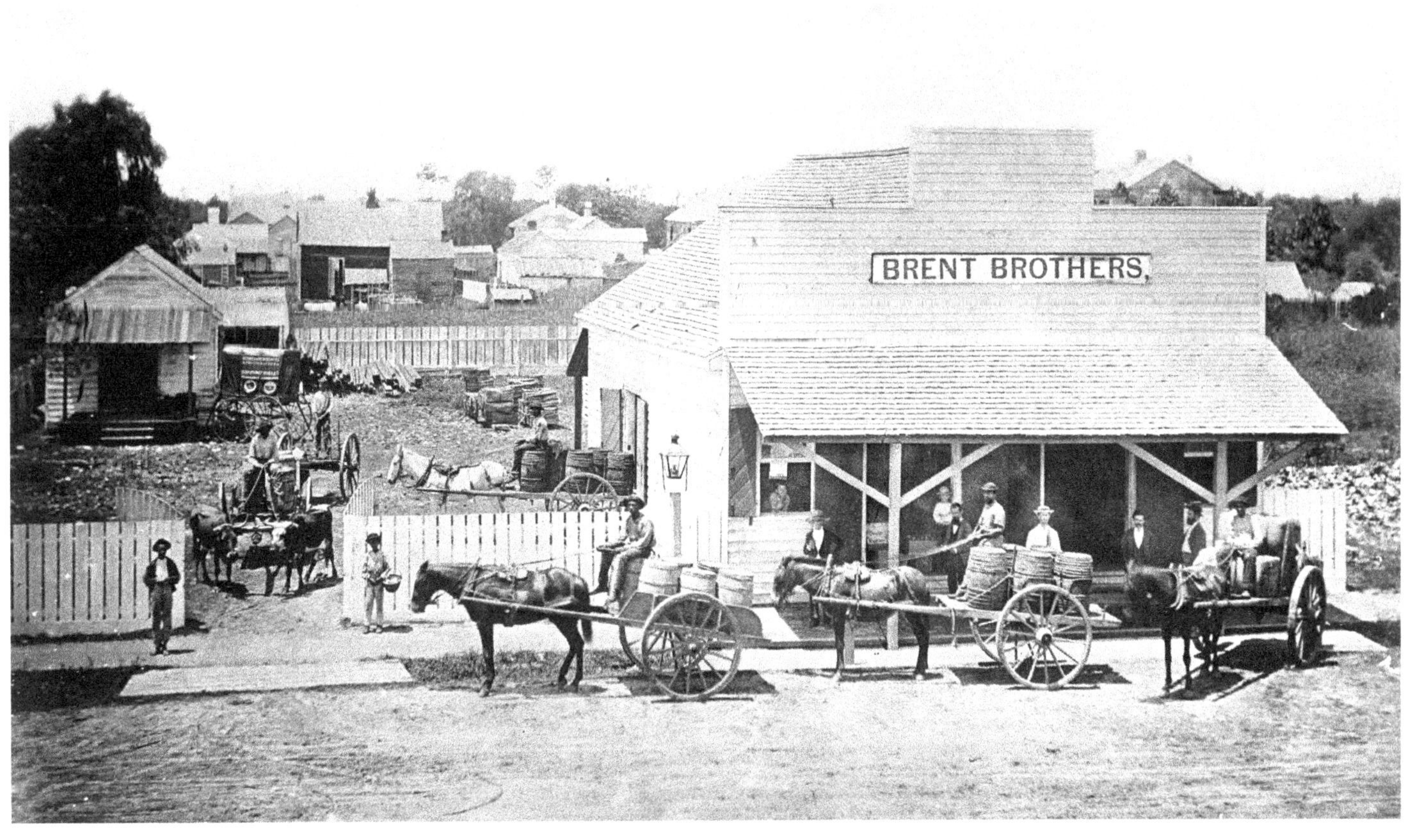

Plaza Ferdinand VII was named in honor of the king of Spain. The plaza's central location offers a convenient gathering place in downtown Pensacola. The U.S. Customs House and Post Office, at the corner of South Palafox and Government streets, is visible in the background. The building was destroyed in the 1880 fire.

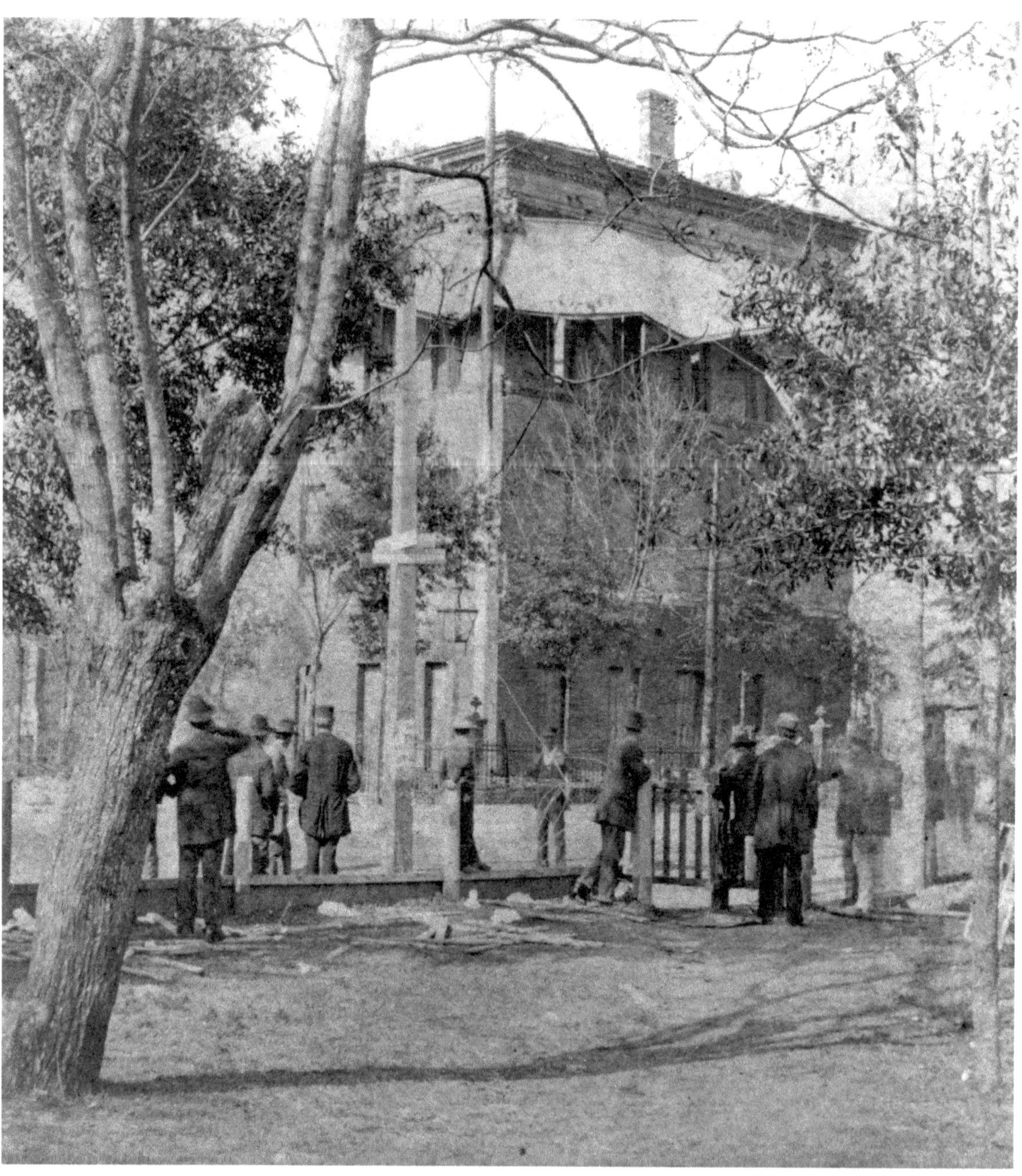

Looking beyond the northeast edge of Plaza Ferdinand VII, this photograph of ships in the harbor captures the importance of shipping to the Pensacola economy. Germania Hall, now Quayside Art Gallery, is visible at center. The wooden building at left stands on the site occupied today by the T. T. Wentworth, Jr., Florida State Museum.

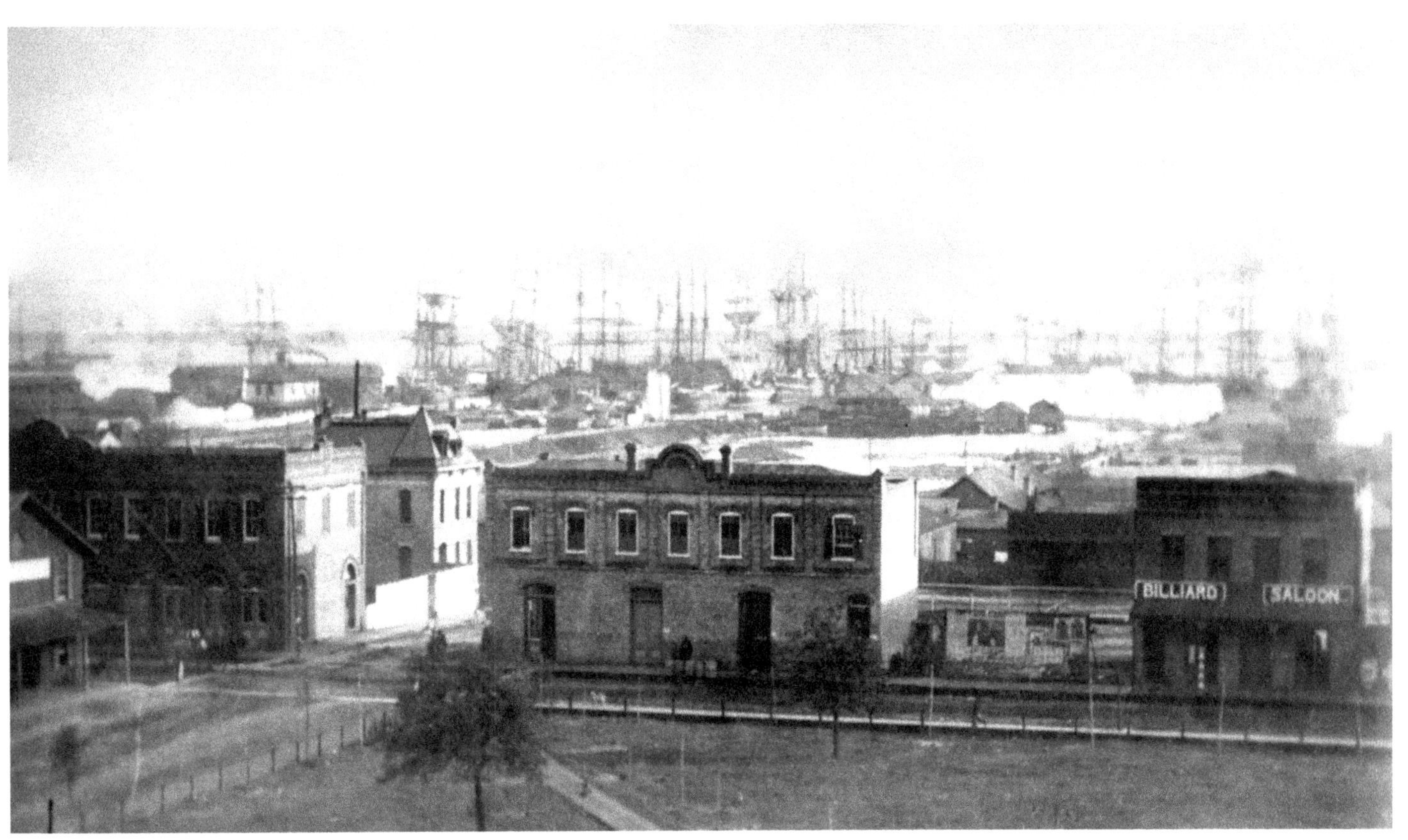

Pensacola rebuilt quickly after the 1880 fire. Dunn's Exchange, a restaurant owned by John Dunn, was one of the businesses destroyed in the fire. His new restaurant was located at 517-519 South Palafox.

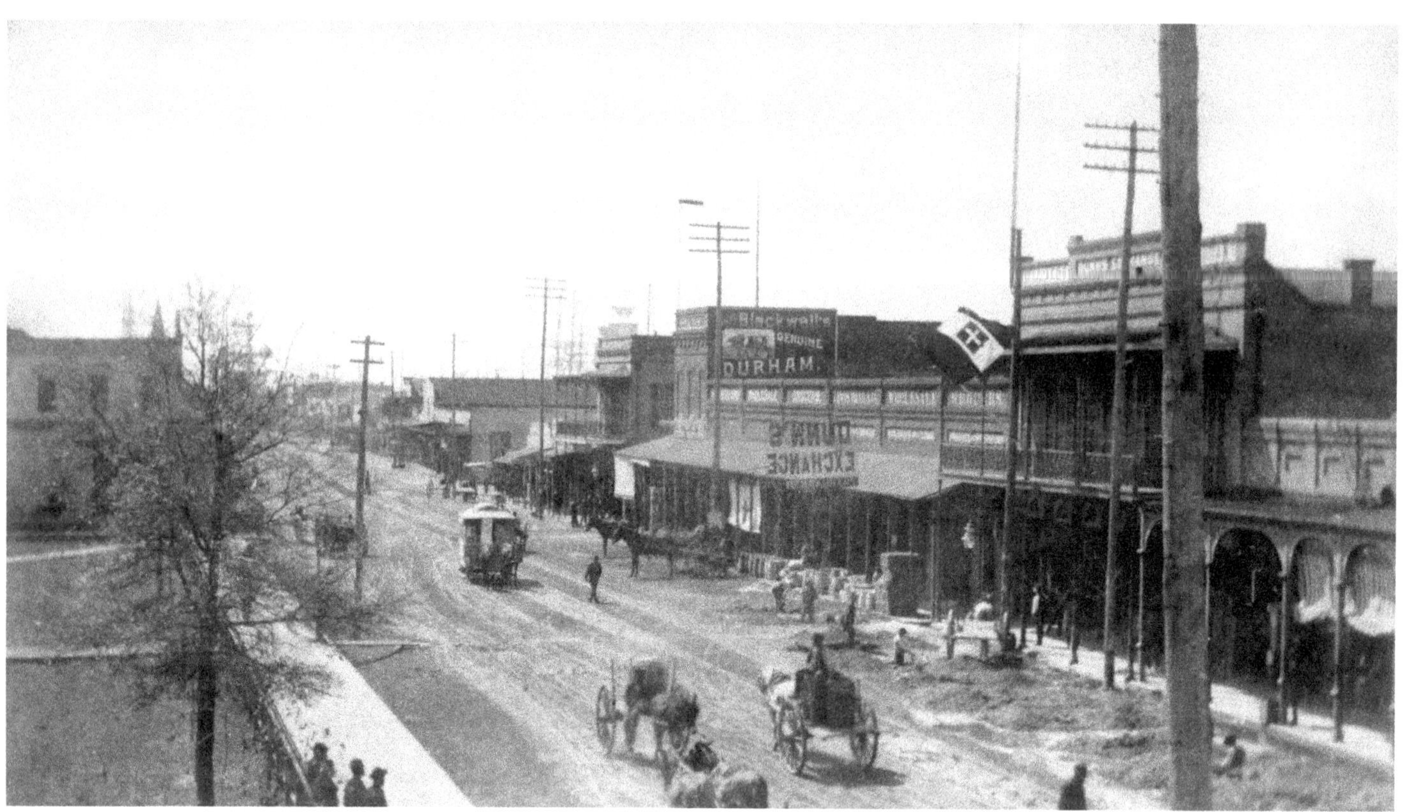

In 1883, a new Customs House and Post Office building arose on the site of the one destroyed in 1880. The Renaissance Revival–style building also contained offices for the district attorney and the district and circuit courts. In 1940, Escambia County accepted the building from the federal government and converted it into a county courthouse. County offices have now moved to a new building and the interior of the old courthouse is being restored to its original grandeur.

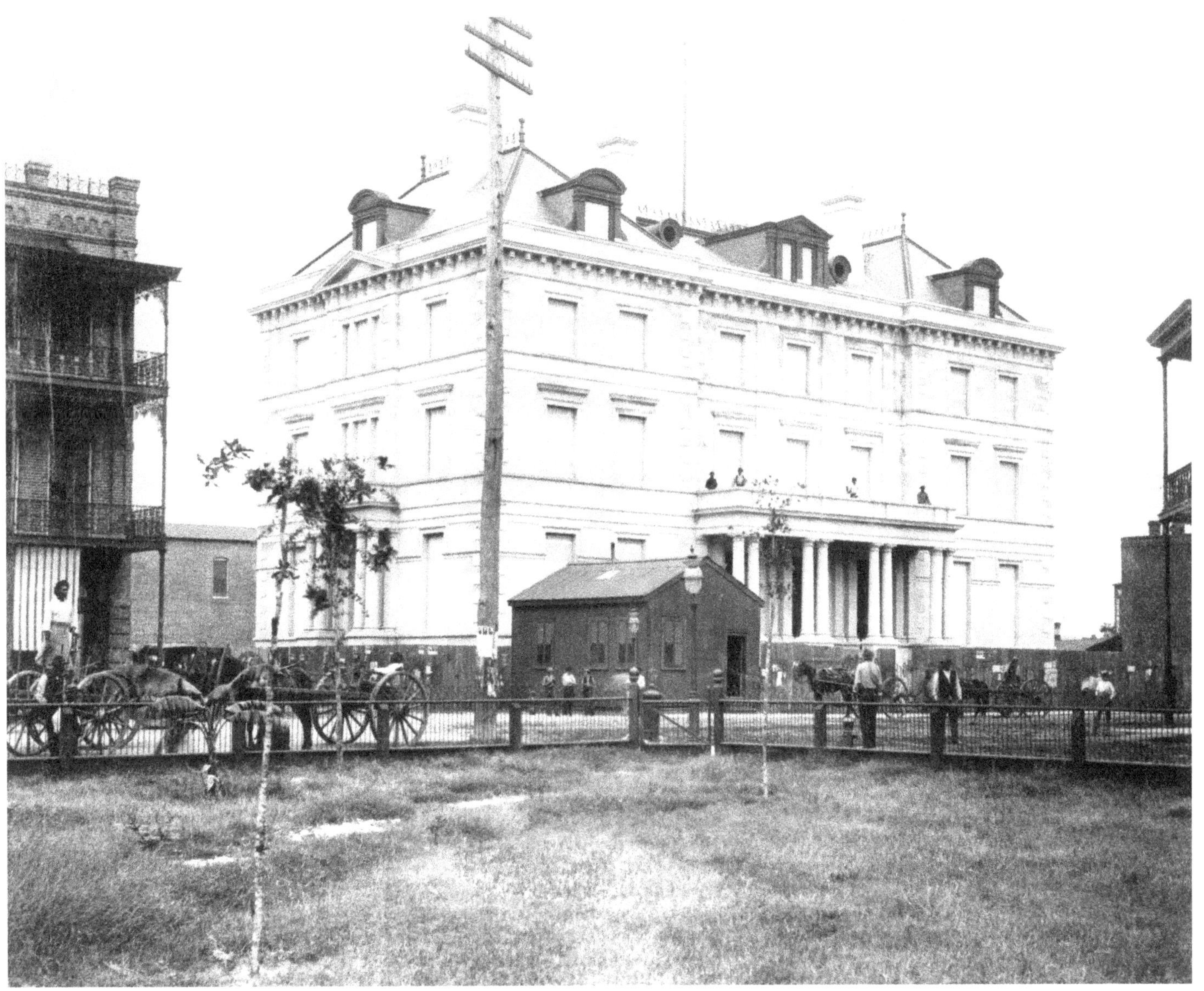

The E. E. Saunders Company, founded in 1883 by Eugene Edward Saunders and Thomas Everett Wells, had its own ice plant and cold storage facility. The many railroads that served Pensacola helped the E. E. Saunders Company to become the world's largest wholesaler of red snapper.

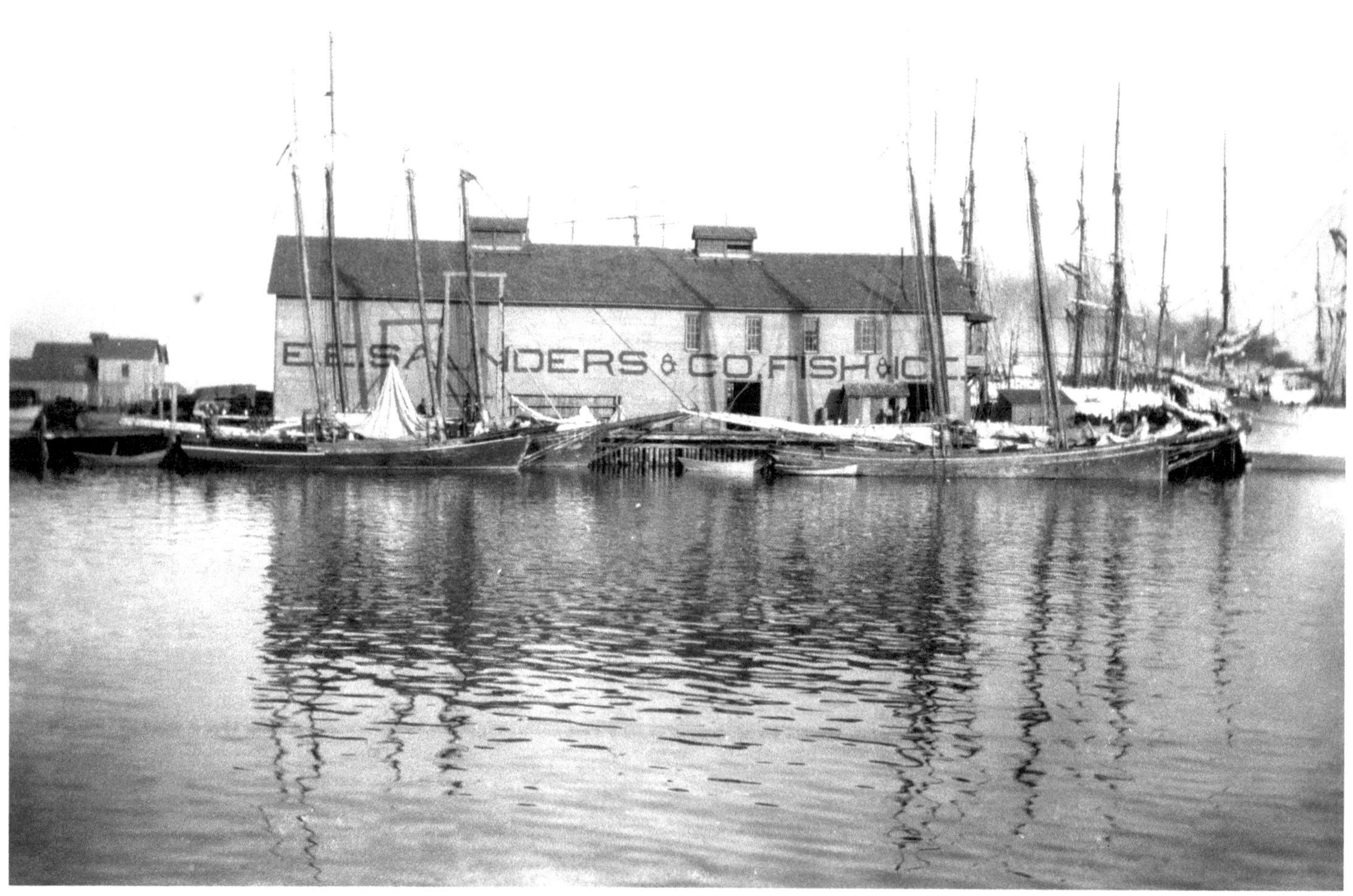

Professor Edward Wyer, a music teacher, bandleader, and composer, was bandmaster of the Creole division of the 3rd Battalion of the Florida State Troops and of the Escambia Rifles militia unit. Wyer's musical compositions included "Adjutant Ross's March," which was dedicated to the 3rd Battalion.

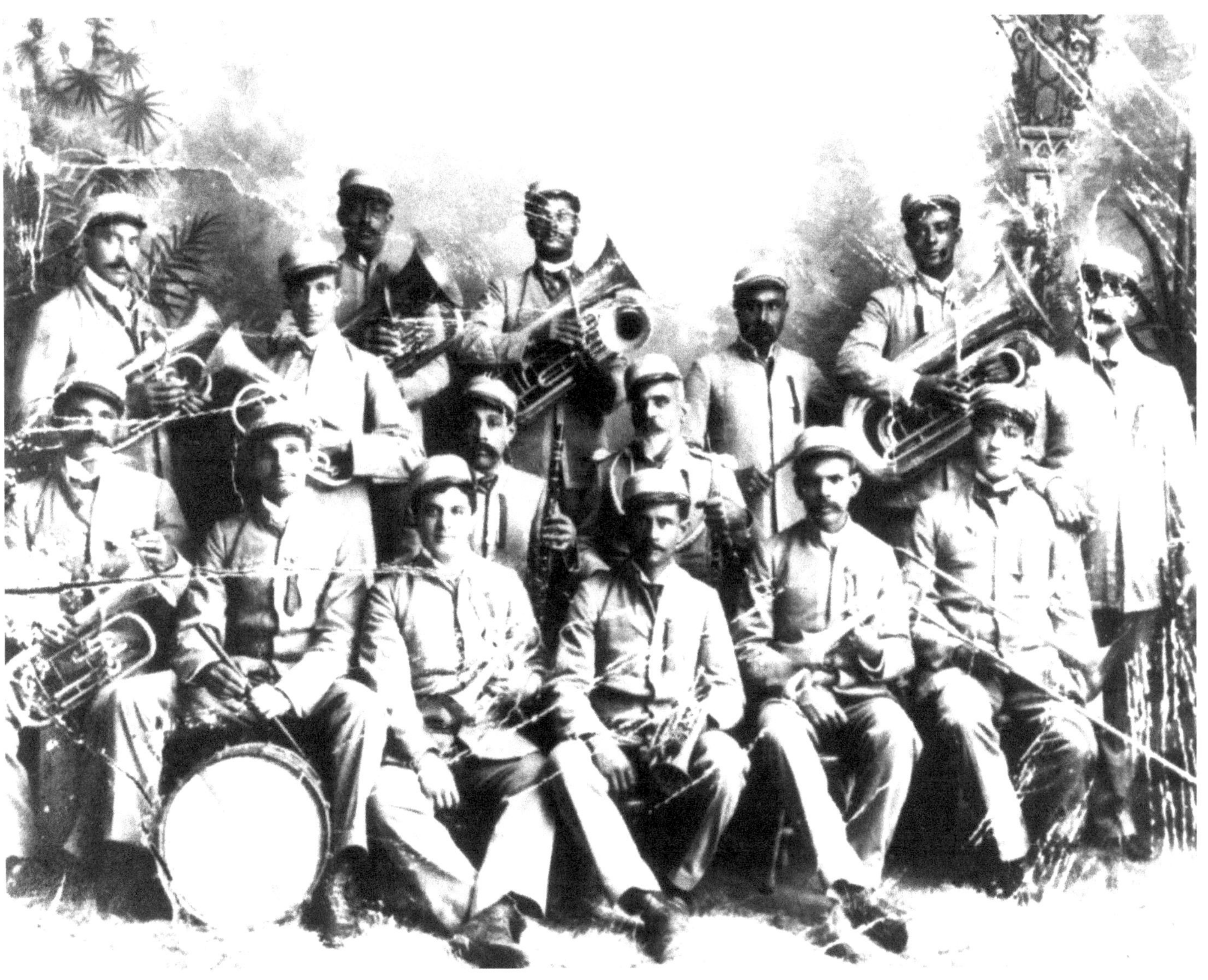

The Pensacola Fire Department acquired its first steam engine in 1878 and by 1893 it had grown to three companies. Station Number 1 was the Germania Hose Company on East Zarragossa, where the Quayside Art Gallery is now located. Number 2, the Florida Hose Company, was located on East Garden near the intersection of Jefferson. Company Number 3, the Washington Hose Company, was on West Zarragossa near Palafox Street.

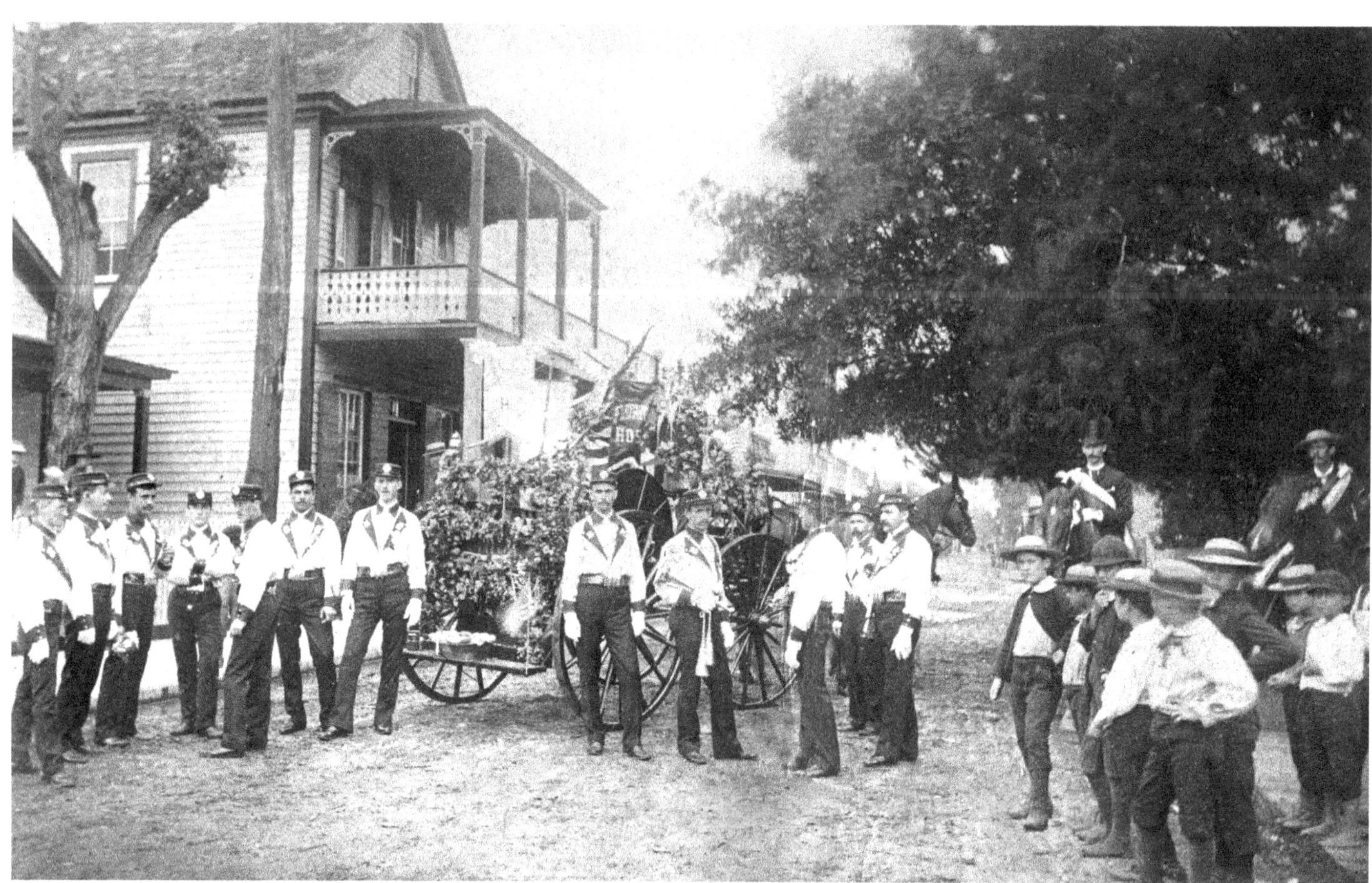

Father Fullerton, pastor of St. Joseph's Catholic Church, converses with Jack O'Donovan at the corner of North Palafox and East Garden streets in 1893. St. Michael's Catholic Church is visible on the left and the Escambia County Courthouse, with its clock tower, is on the right. The tall, chimneylike structure to the north (in the background) is the city's first water tower, which was located on North Hill.

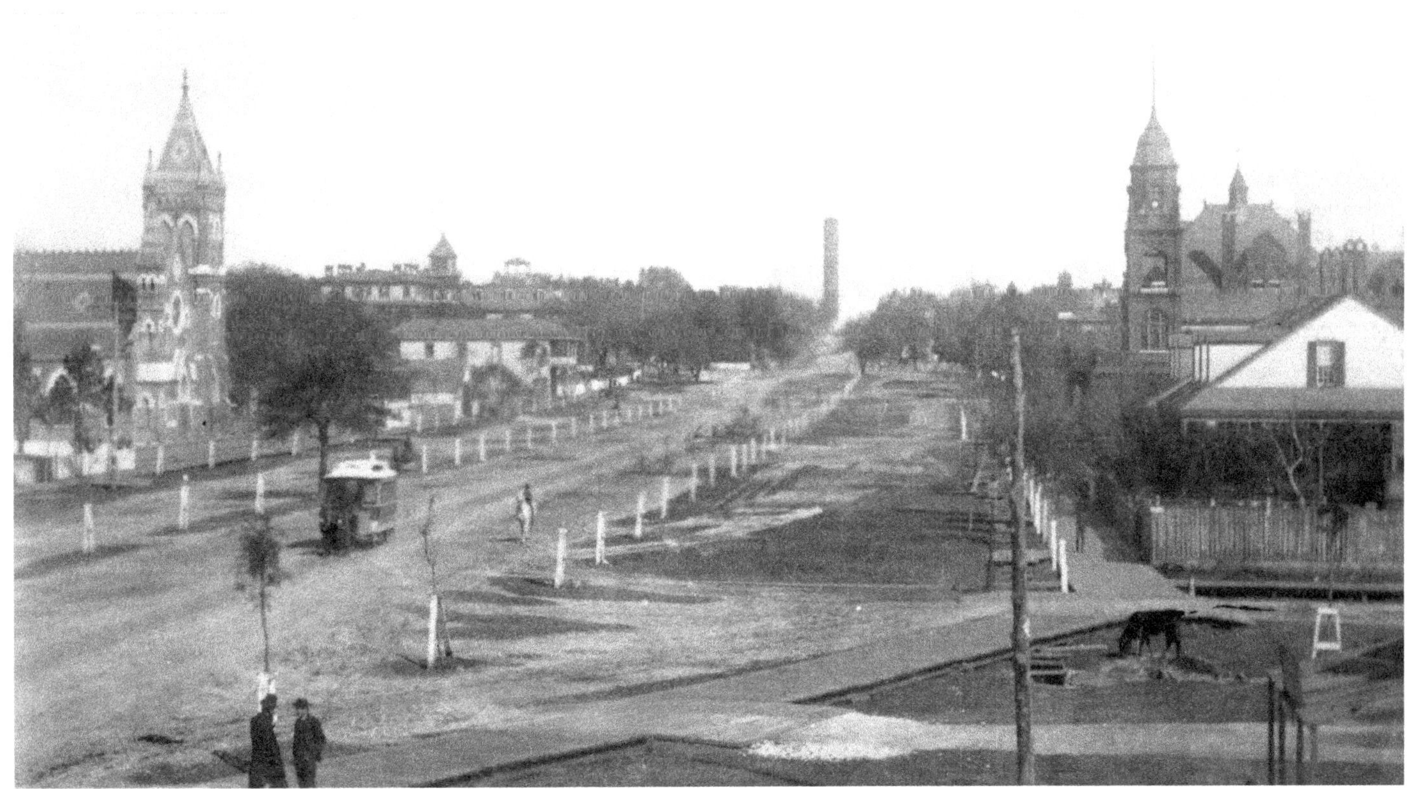

The Escambia County courthouse on North Palafox Street was built in 1883 at a cost of $32,000. The Armory, home of the 3rd Battalion Florida State Troops, was just north of the courthouse.

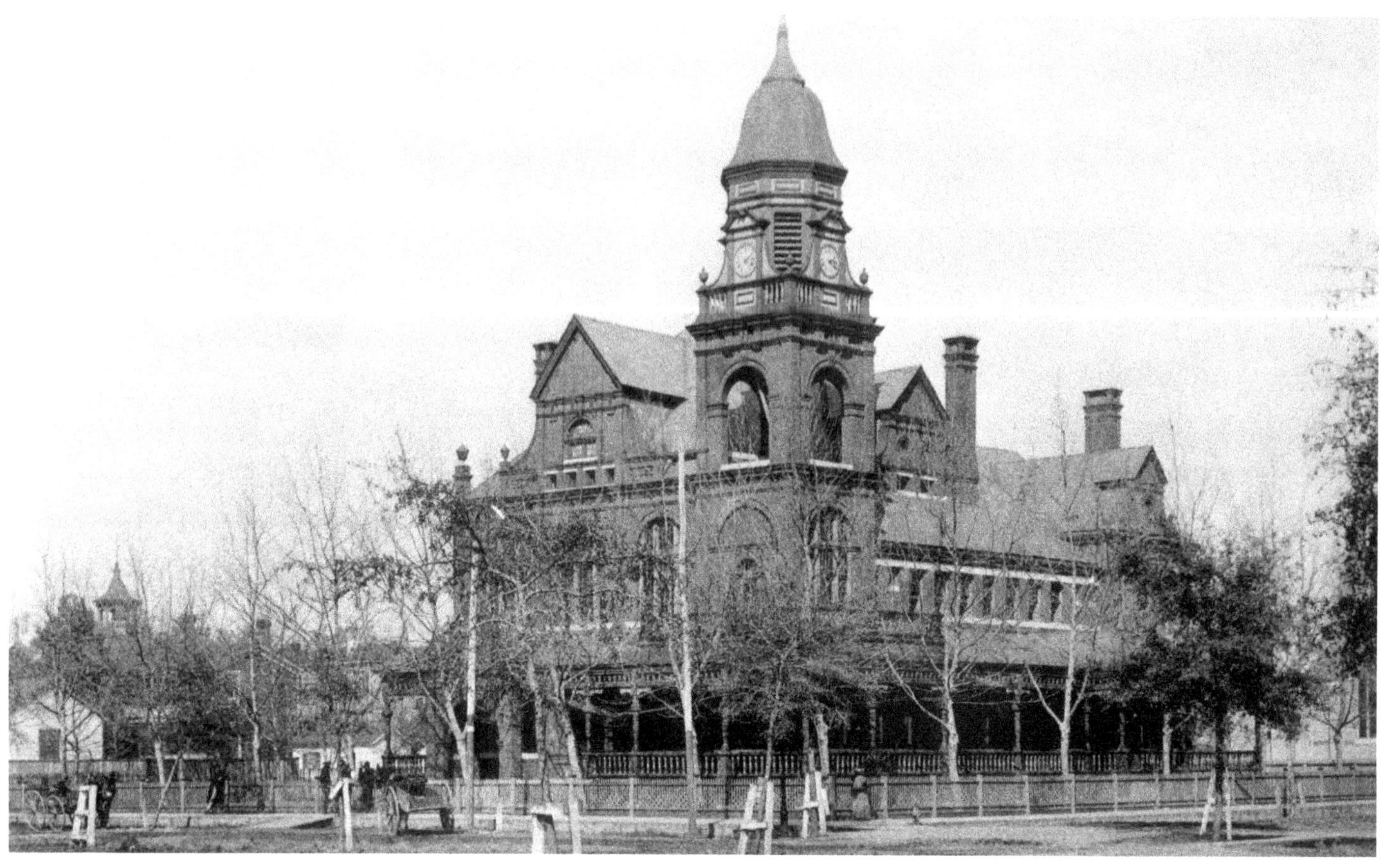

Pensacola's Methodist Episcopal Church, on the left, was established in 1821. Construction on this three-story Romanesque revival building began in 1881 and the first services were held in 1884, although the building was not completed until 1890. The building was sold in 1909 and the Hotel San Carlos was built on this site.

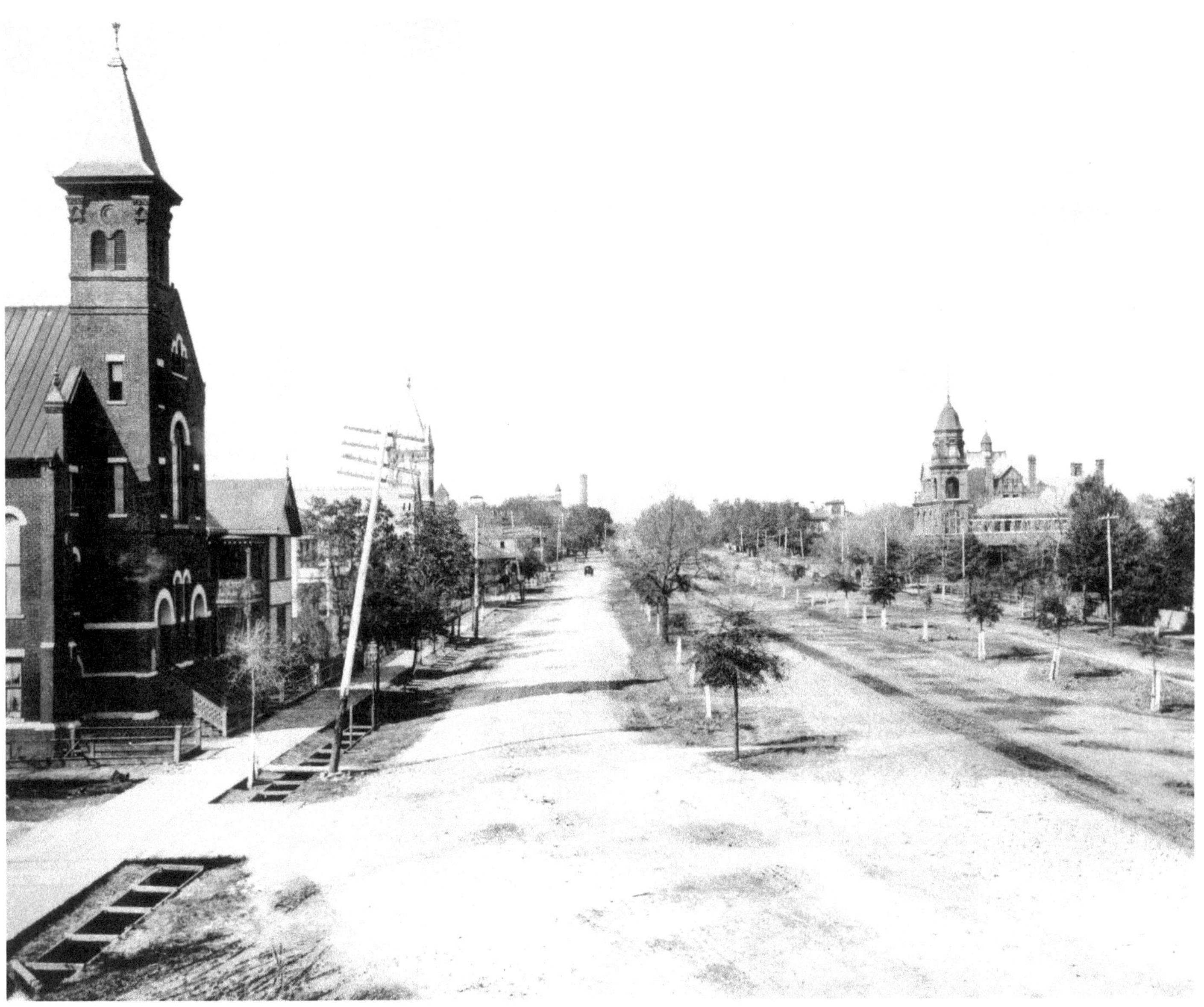

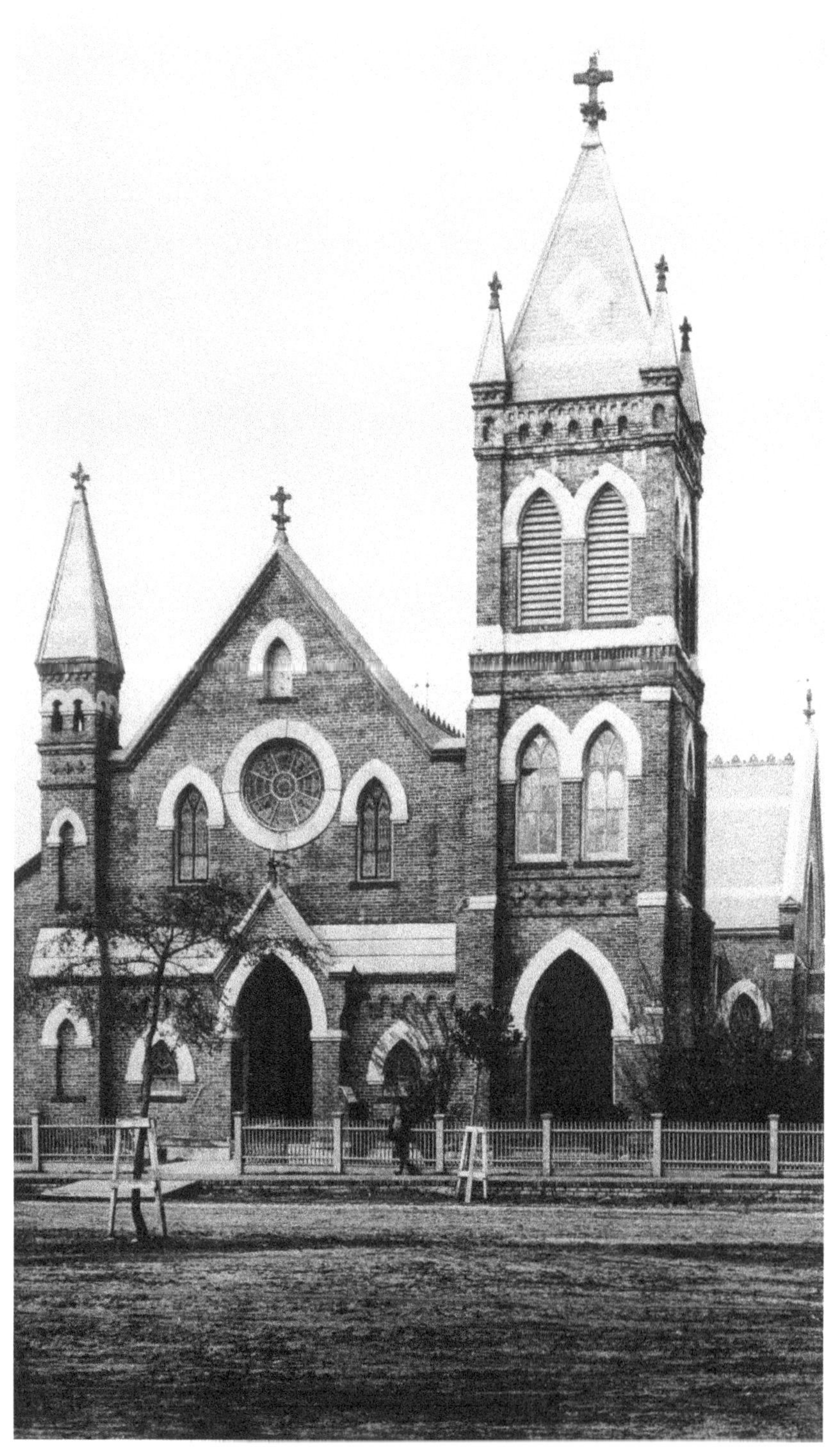

The original St. Michael's Church, located east of Plaza Ferdinand VII, was destroyed by fire during the Civil War. The church was rebuilt in its present location on North Palafox Street in 1885. Mass has been offered to the people of Pensacola since the first Spanish settlers landed in 1559.

A paved South Palafox, streetcar service, and new sidewalks welcomed visitors to the new Customs House and Post Office. The short wall around the building provided a convenient place for people to sit while they waited for appointments.

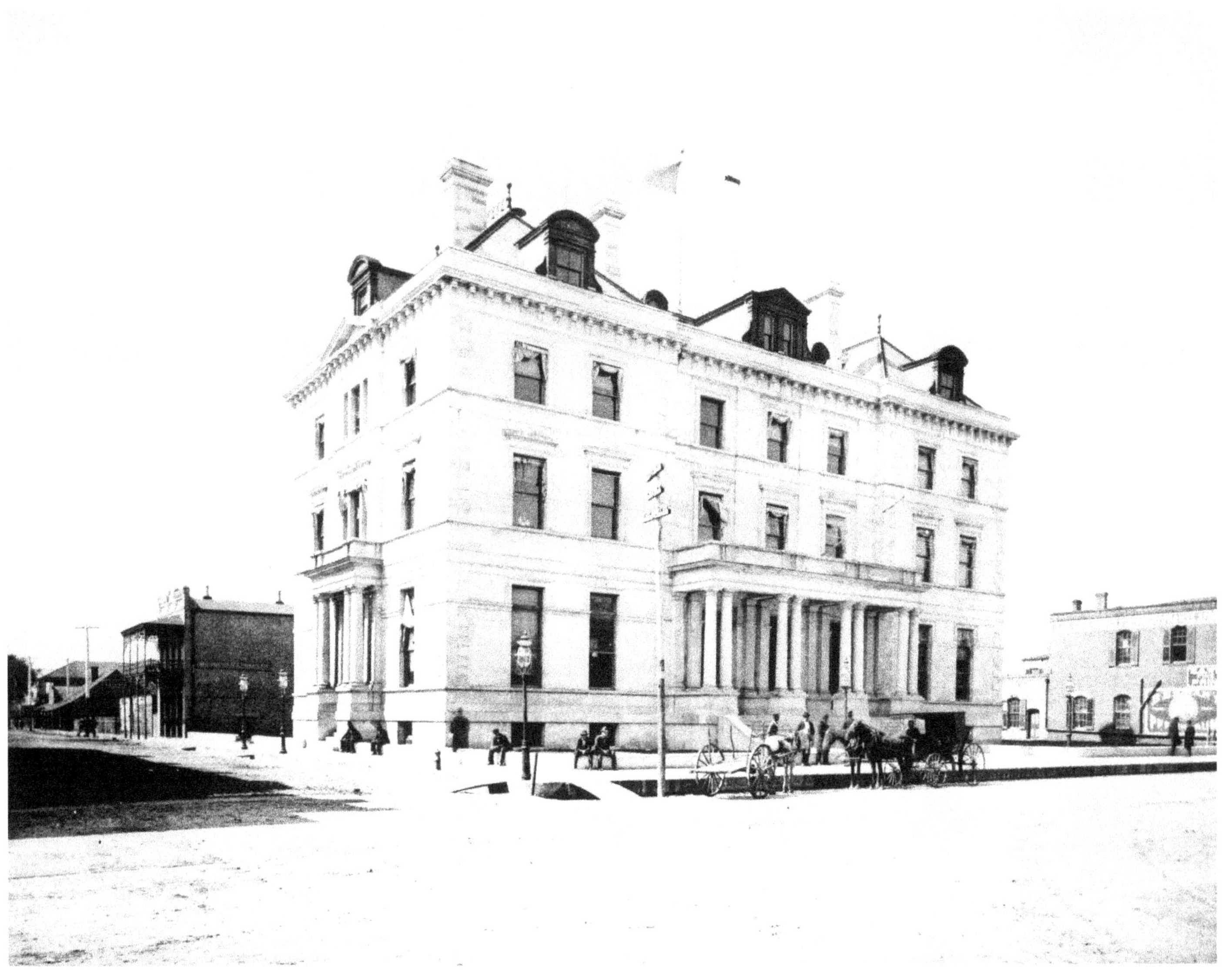

An extremely cold winter in 1894 blanketed the city with several inches of snow. Two men at the Navy Yard take advantage of the unusual event by engaging in a snowball fight.

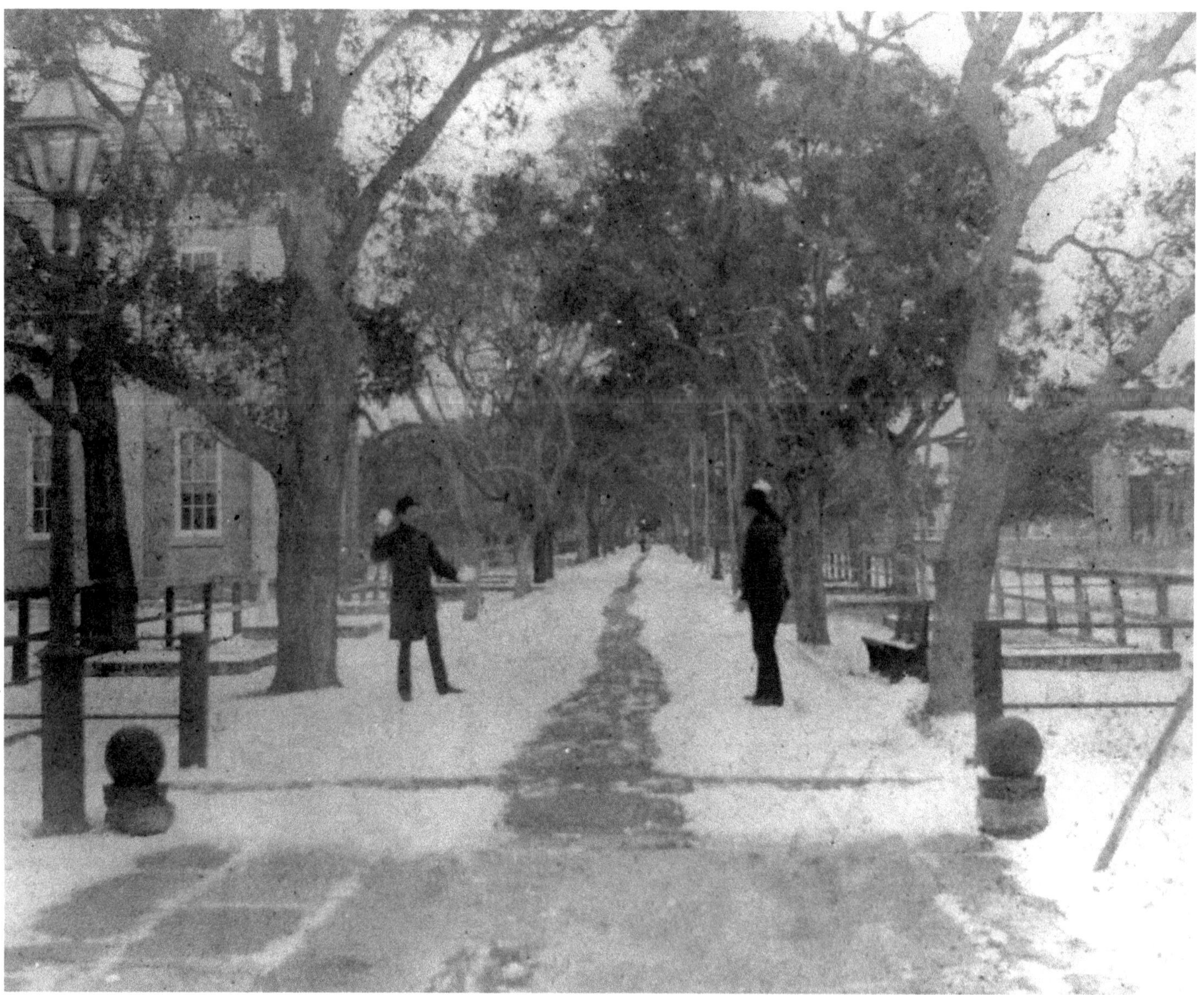

Erected around the turn of the century, this building was the home of the Masons for one hundred years, replacing their former lodge on East Zarragossa Street. The meeting rooms were on the third floor and the first and second floors were rented for professional offices and retail space. In 2000, the Masons moved to a new building on Longleaf Drive.

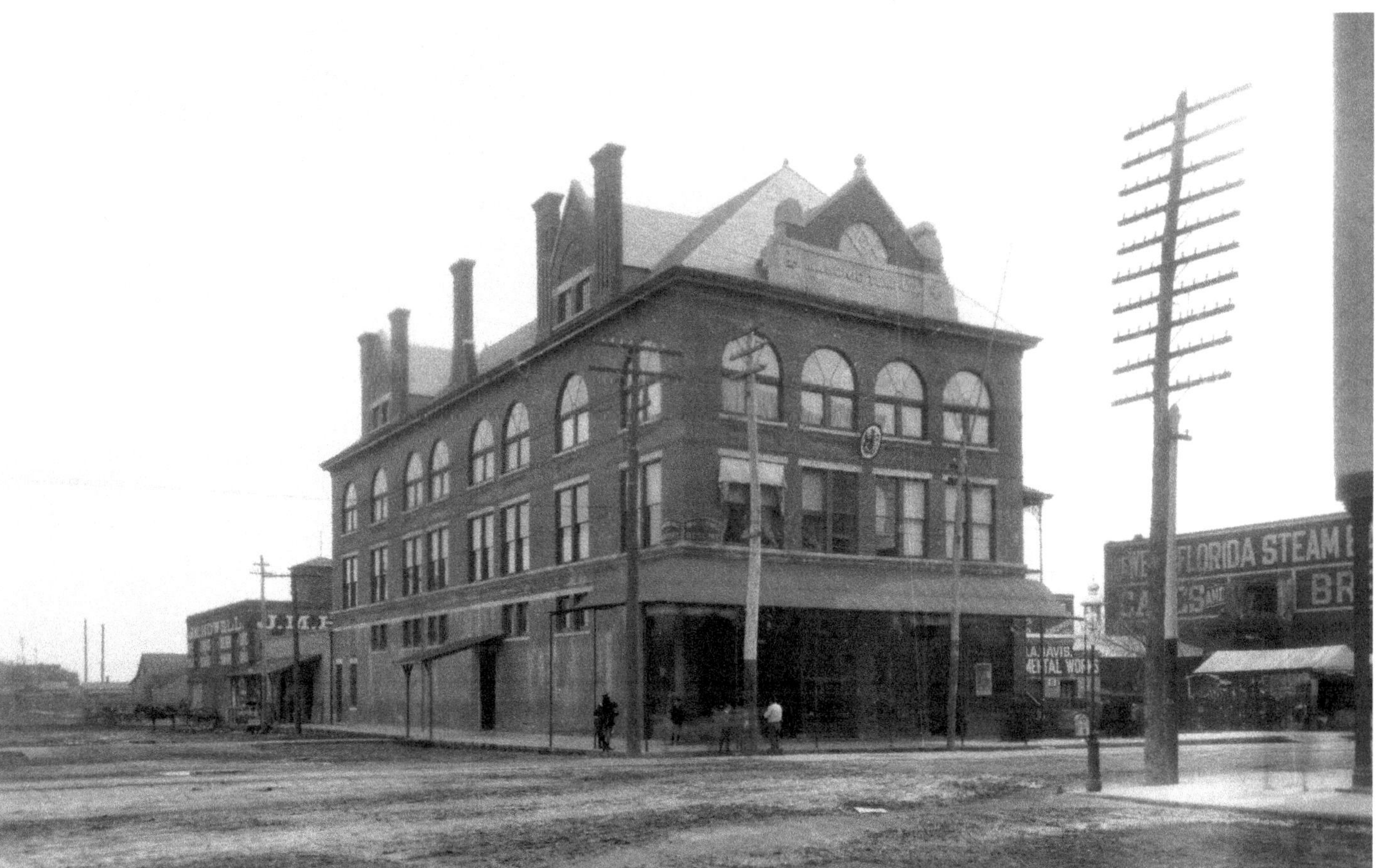

Built in 1871 on the west side of fashionable Seville Square, this was originally the home of Eban and Clara Barkley Dorr. It later became a Jewish school. Now owned by West Florida Historic Preservation, the Dorr House serves as the home for the president of the University of West Florida.

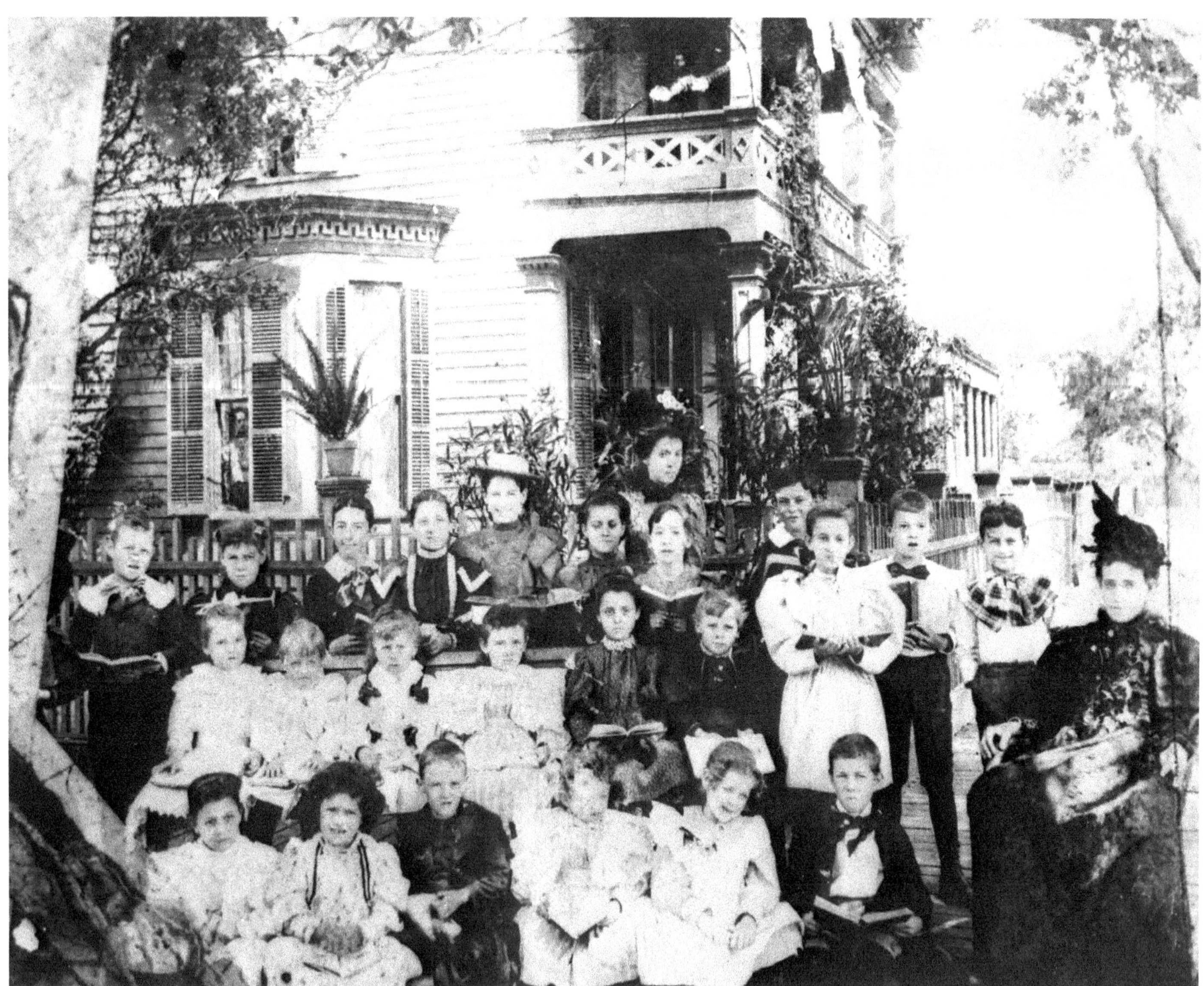

Begun in 1830 and completed in 1832, Old Christ Church is the oldest church in Florida that still sits on its original foundation. Services were held in this building until 1903, when the growing parish moved to their newly built church at the corner of North Palafox and Wright streets. During the Civil War, Union troops used the church building as a jail, hospital, and barracks. The building served as Pensacola's first public library and was home to the Pensacola Historical Society.

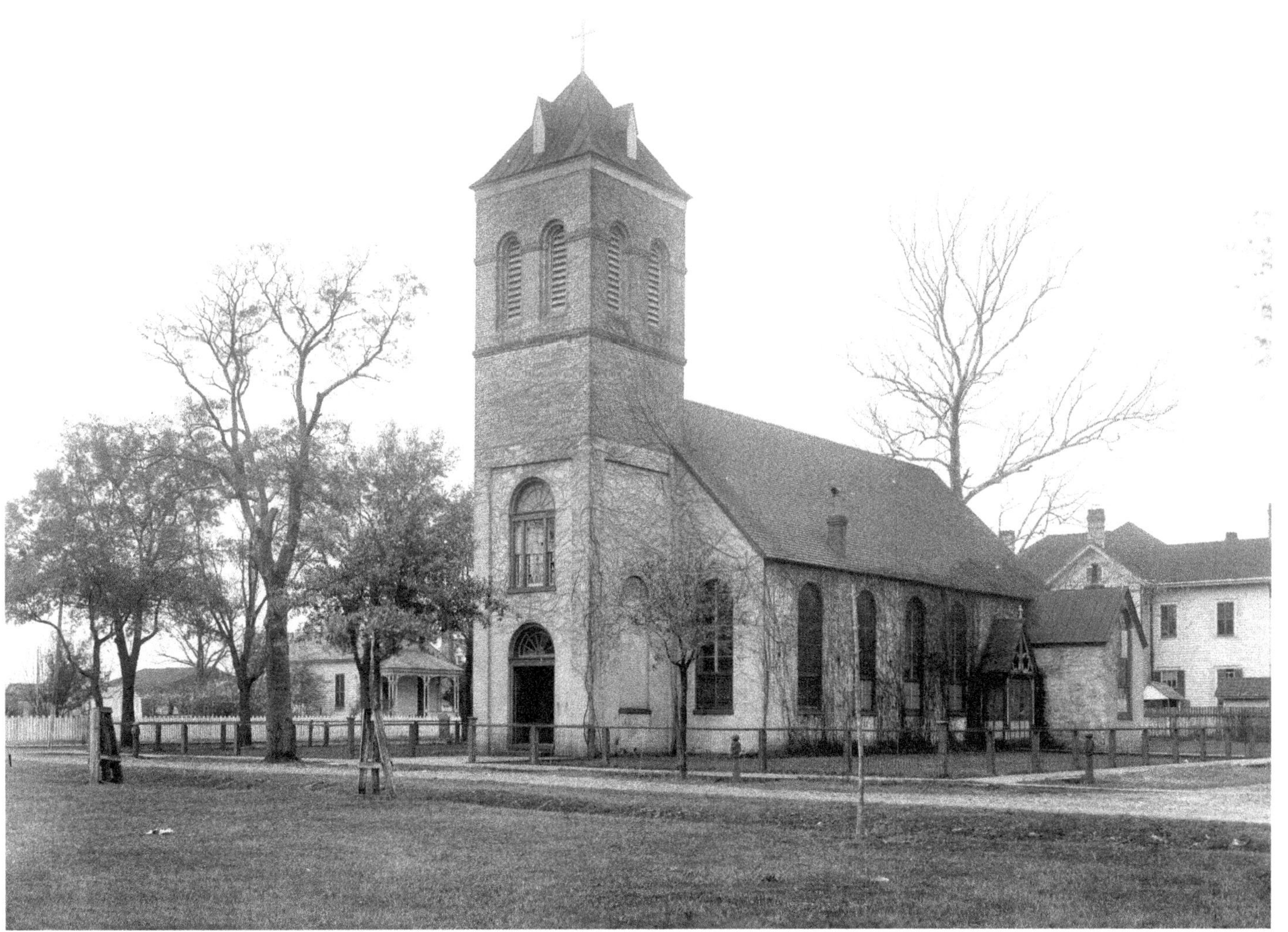

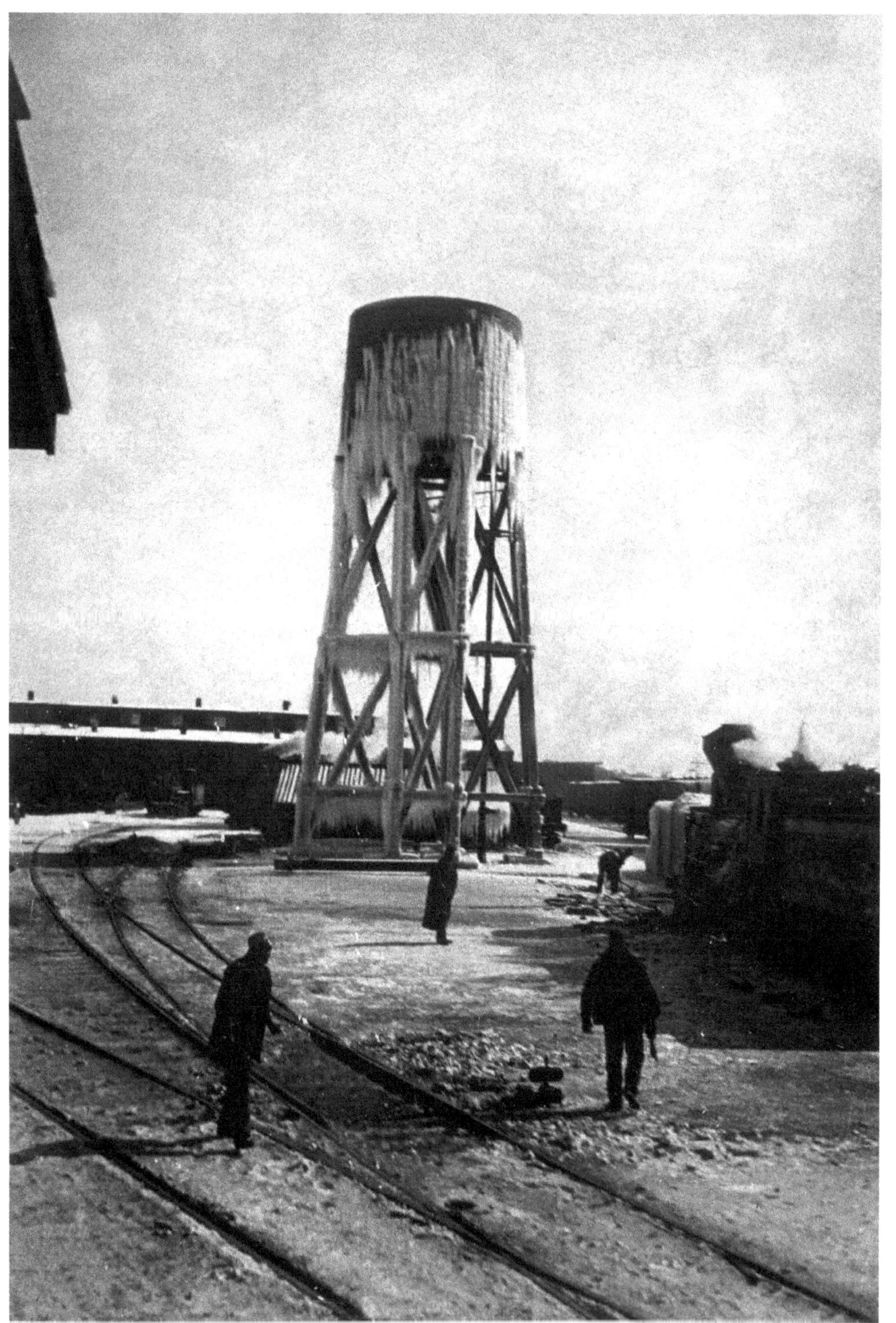

The Great Blizzard of 1899 brought rain, sleet, and snow to Pensacola on February 12 and 13 of that year. Record-breaking low temperatures, at times below 0° Fahrenheit, kept the city covered in snow and ice for several days.

The Garfield Guards, based in Pensacola, was an African-American unit of the Florida State Volunteer Militia.

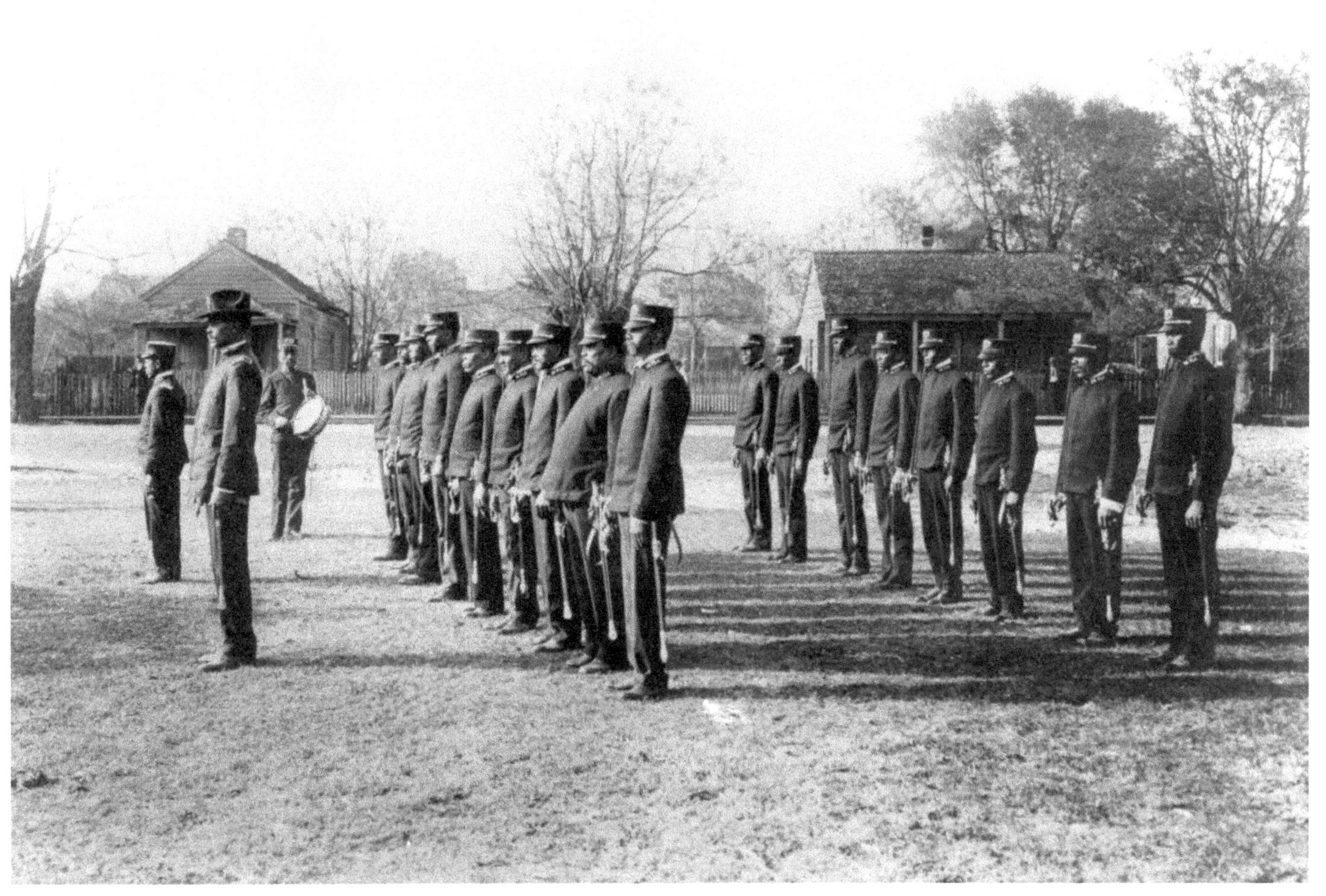

Situated on North Palafox between Gregory and Wright streets, this was the home of General William H. Chase. While serving with the U.S. Army, General Chase oversaw construction of Fort Barrancas. When the South seceded, Chase resigned his commission and joined the Confederacy. By 1898, the home had become the Escambia Hotel.

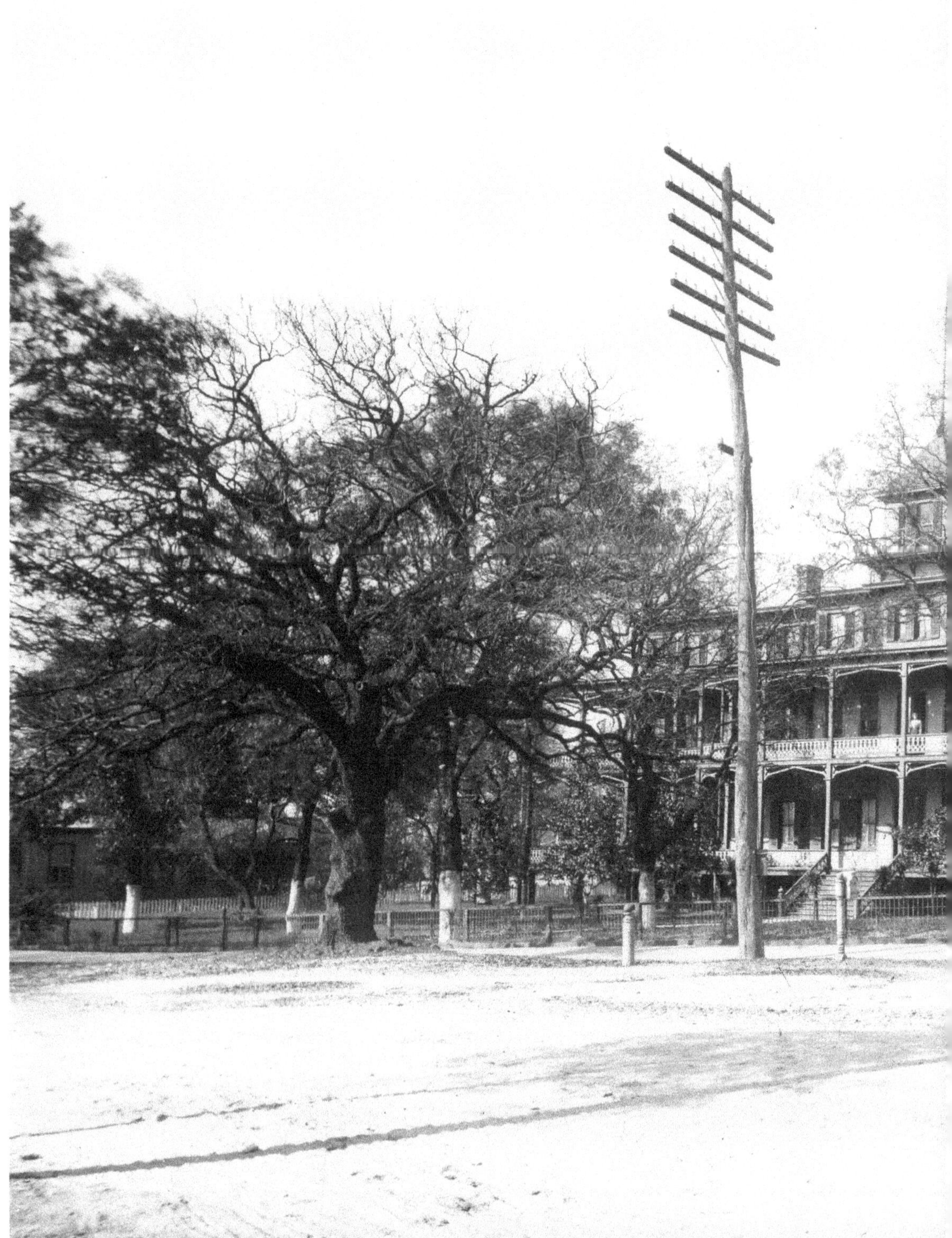

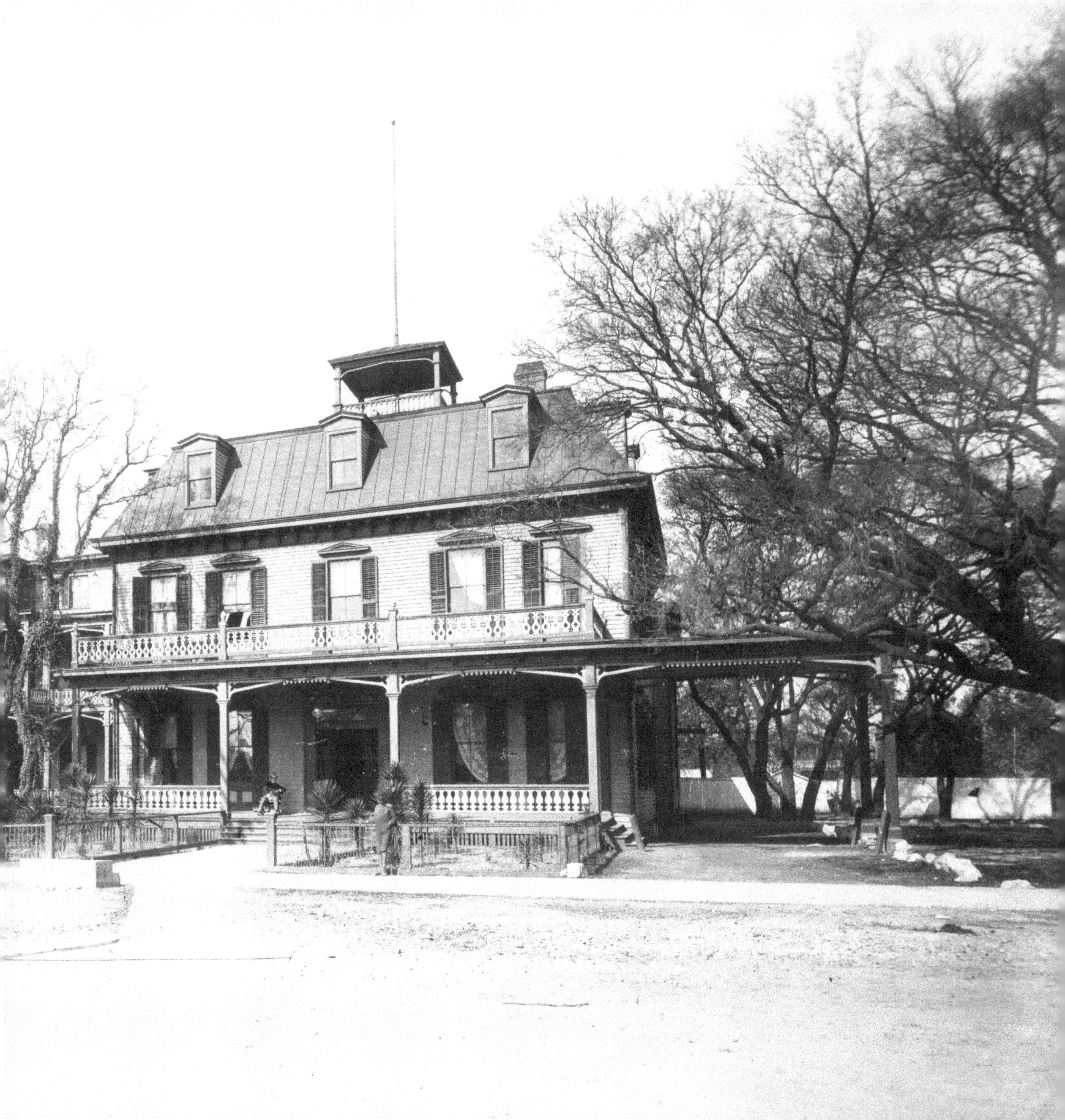

The First National Bank, at 213 South Palafox, was organized in 1880. The building housed the Citizens and Peoples Bank for 80 years and now serves as offices for the Escambia County Tax Collector.

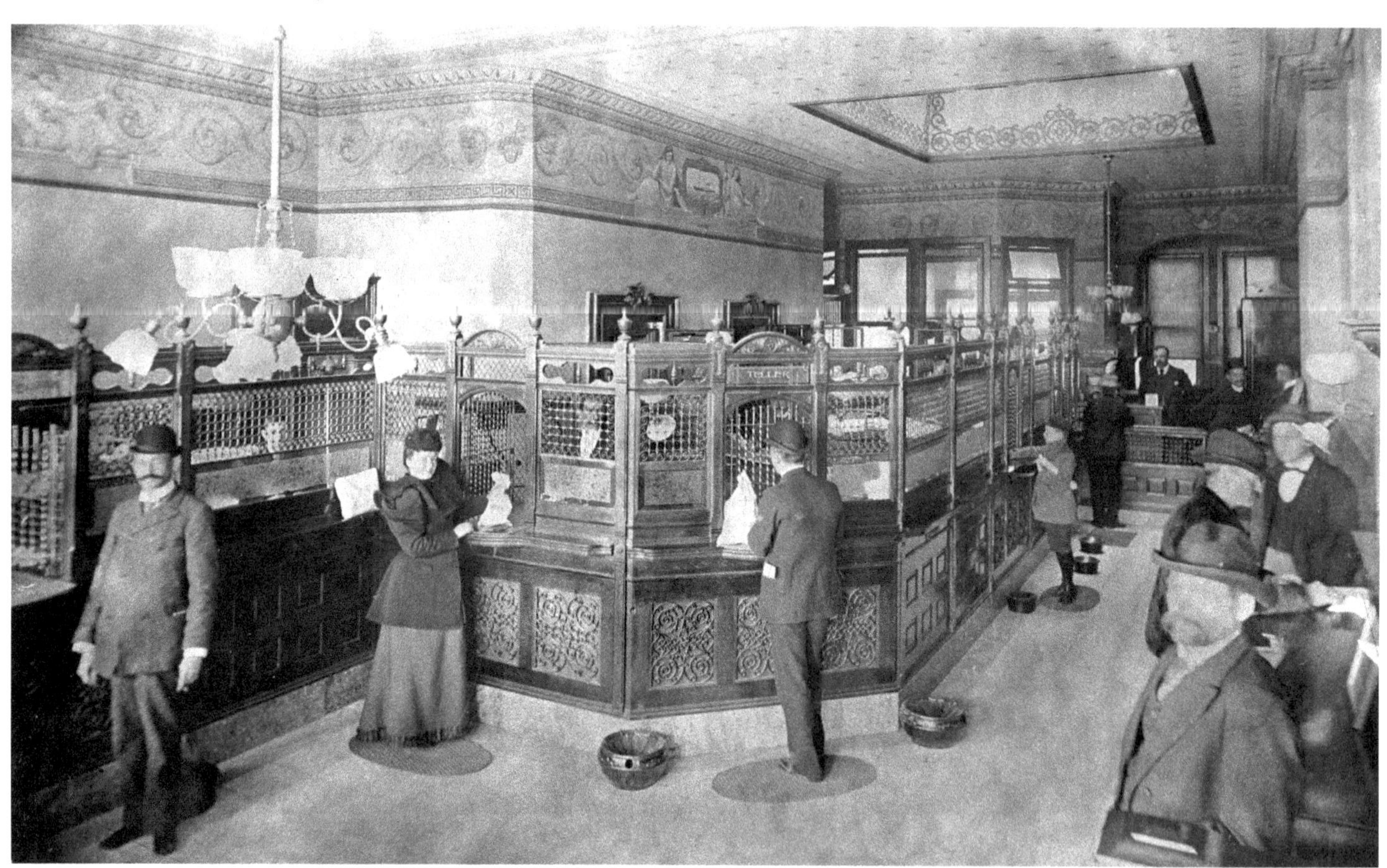

The Pensacola & Atlantic Railroad was the first main east-west rail service to traverse Florida. Groundbreaking took place in Pensacola on August 22, 1881, and the track reached Jacksonville on April 25, 1883. In 1891, the Pensacola & Atlantic became part of the Louisville & Nashville Railroad. Heavy traffic on Pensacola tracks posed a threat if trains ran off schedule.

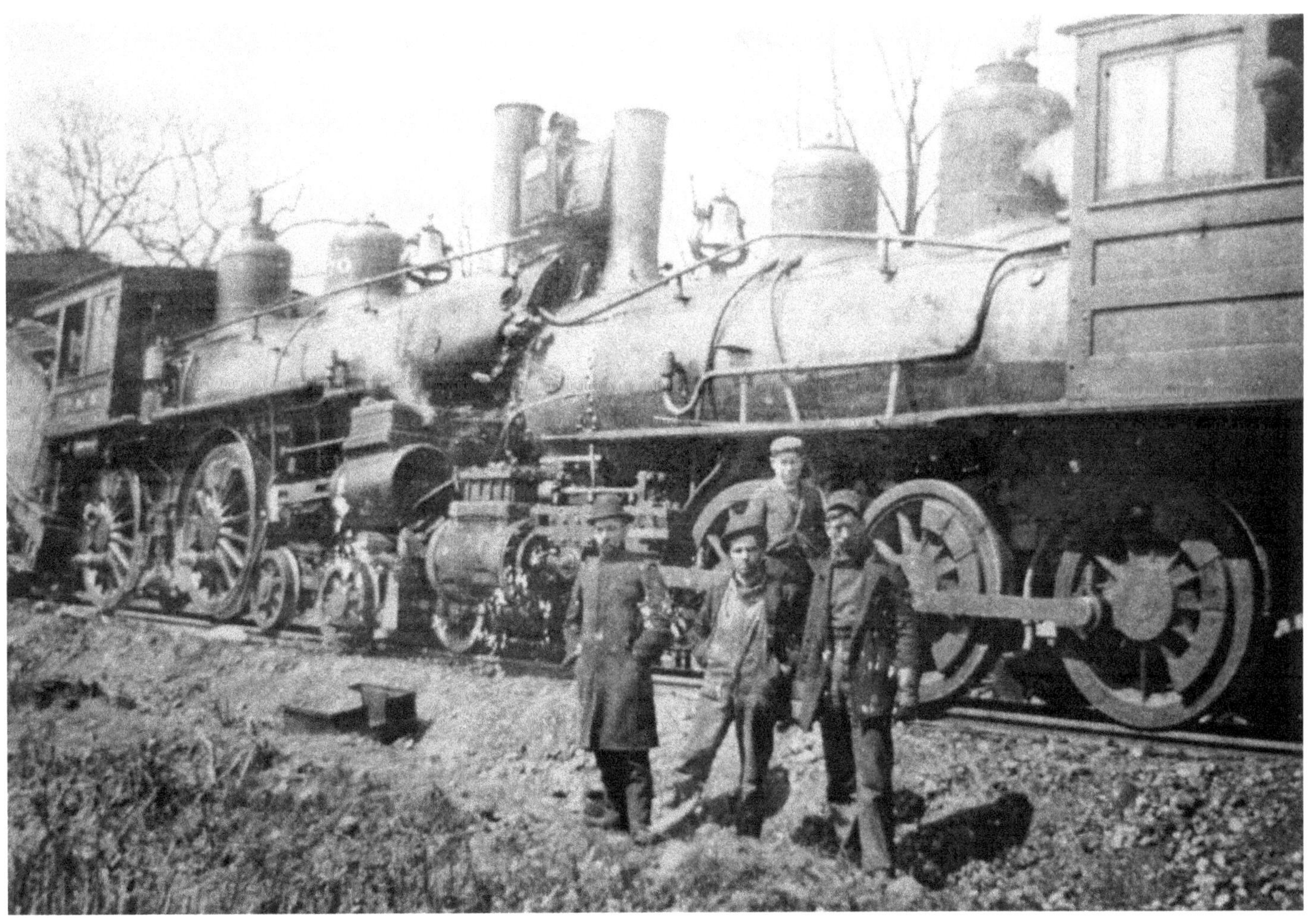

The Southern States Lumber Company owned 340,000 acres of land, four sawmills, a railroad, and a steamship. Pictured in the company office on South Palafox, Mr. Frazier F. Bingham, the assistant manager, sits at his desk third from the left.

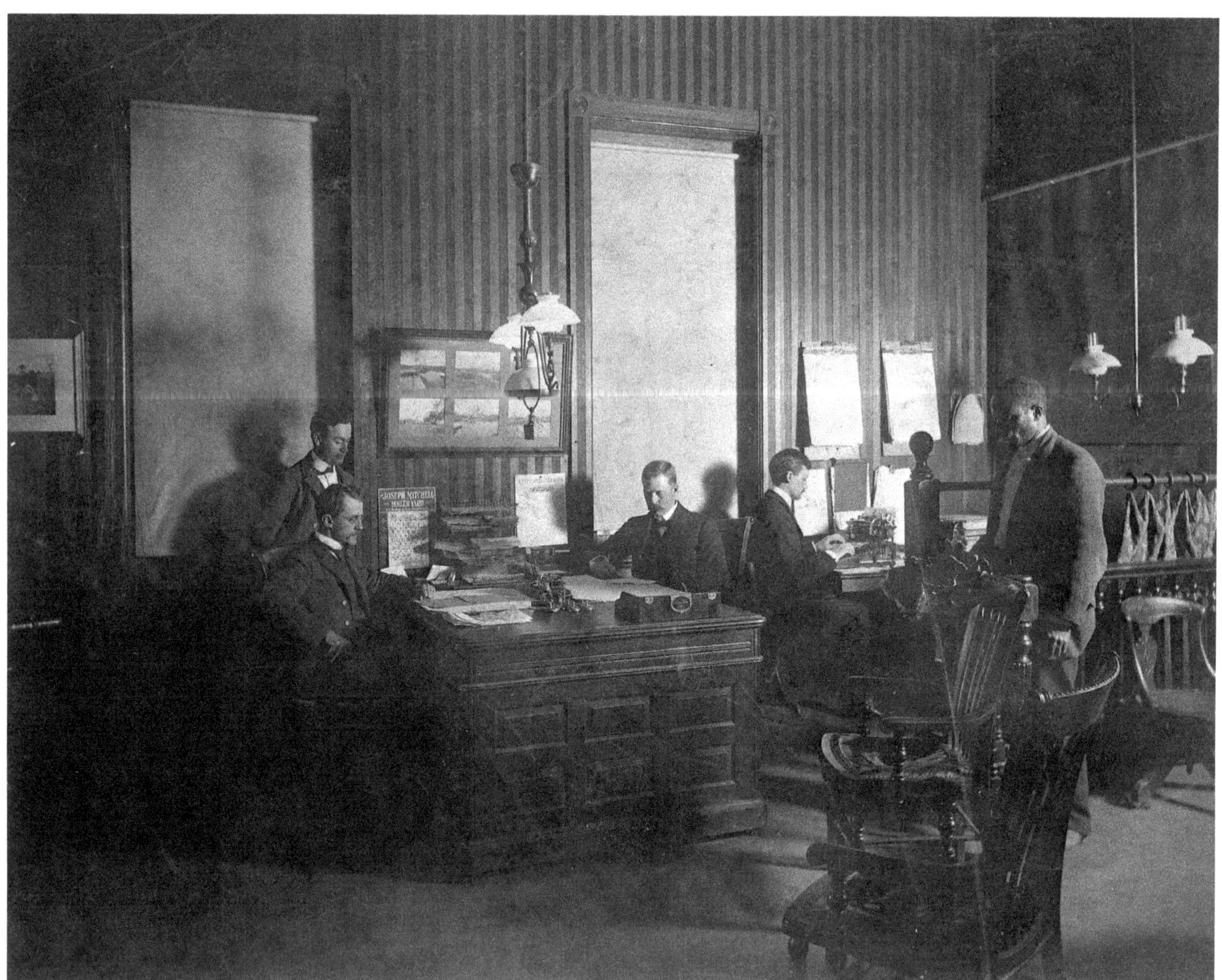

This end station, one of a pair, was part of an Army Ordnance Department experimental target triangulation system established in Pensacola. The pair of stations, outfitted with a telephone, a time interval bell, and an azimuth scope, were used to identify the firing range of distant, moving targets. The firing calculations were phoned to a series of connected buildings that housed the battery commanders and the fire commander. The network became known as the Barrancas System.

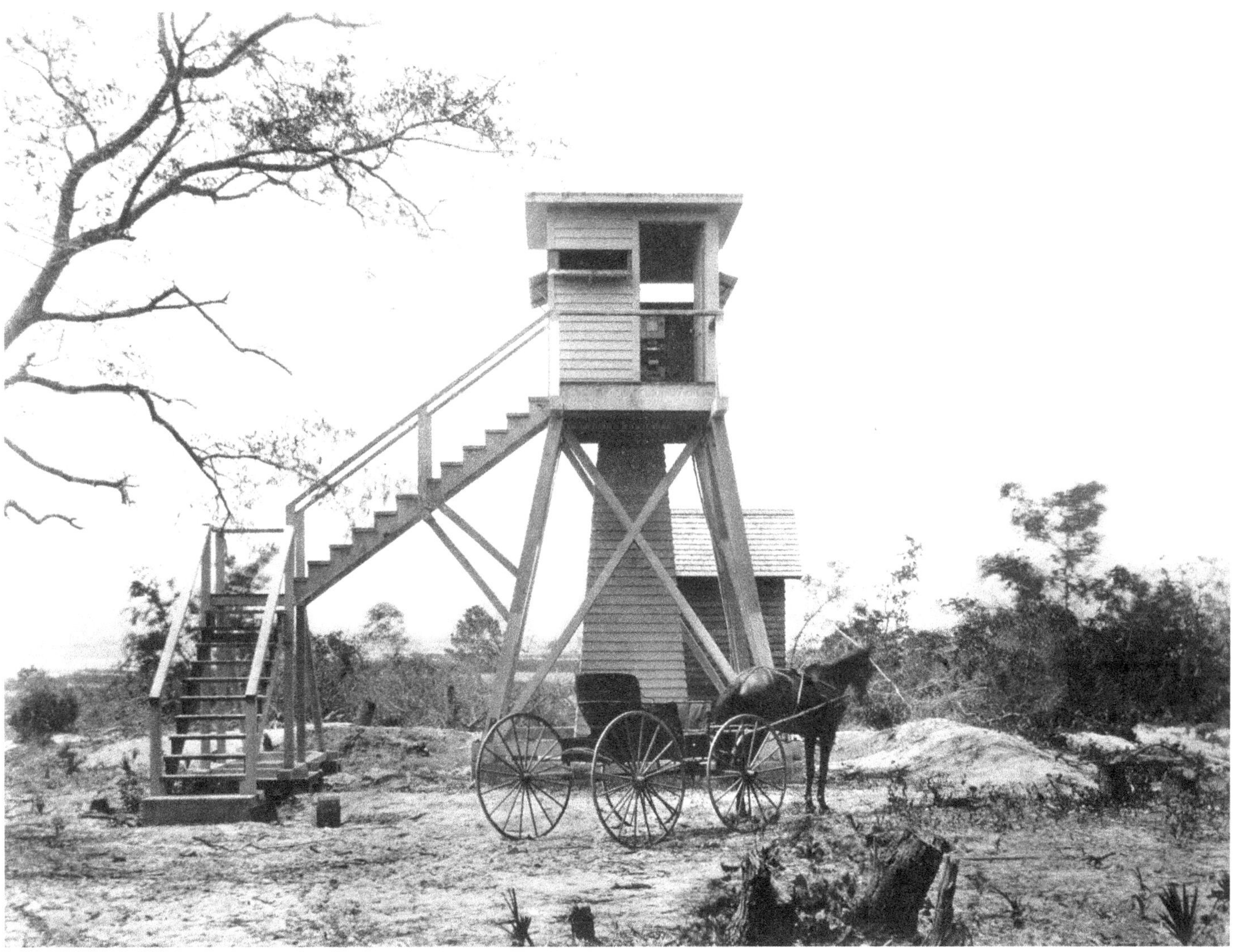

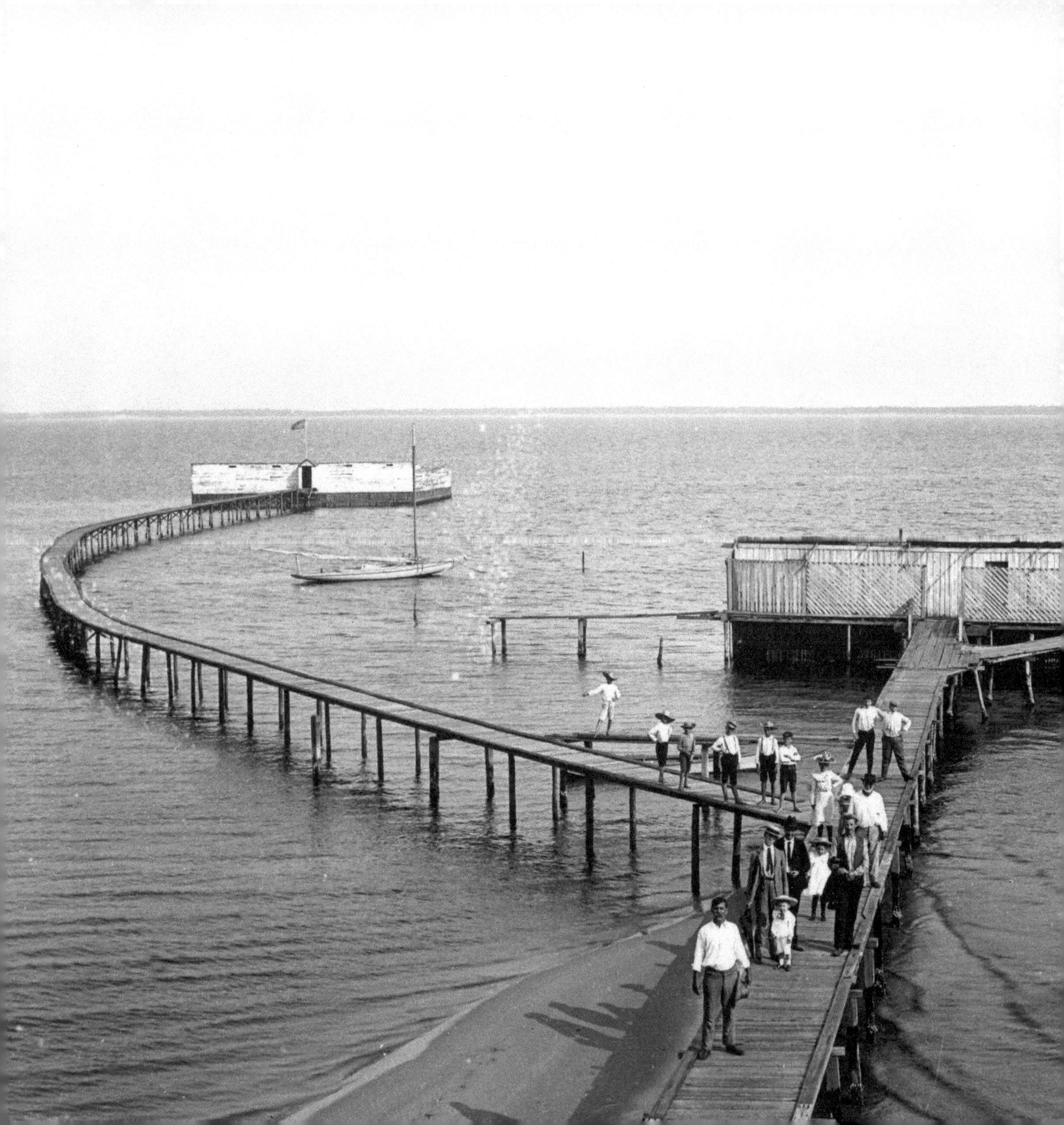

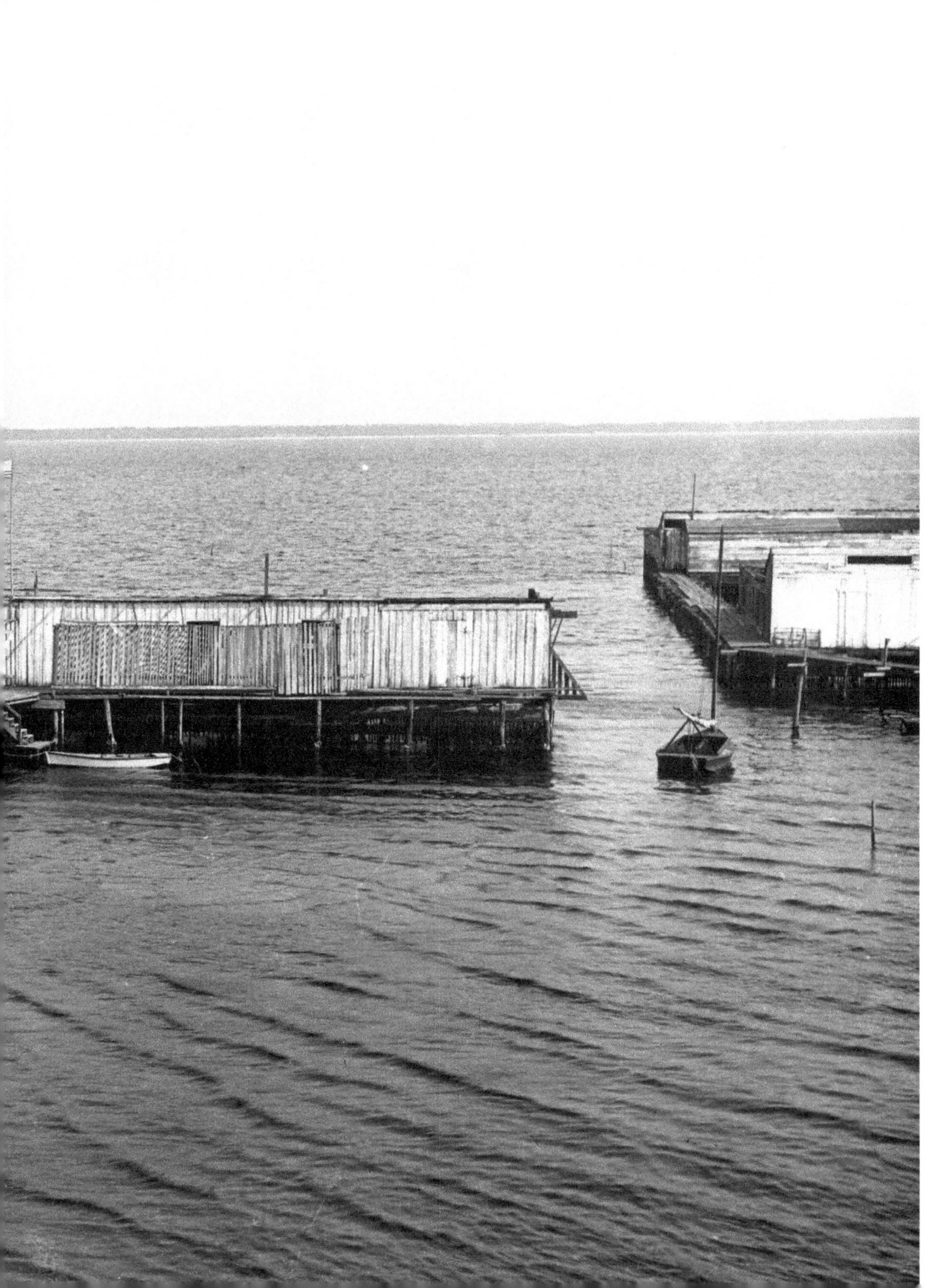

Built at the end of Florida Blanca Street, Saccaro's bathhouses and pier, with separate facilities for women and men, offered Pensacolians a place to frolic on hot summer days. The three teenage boys in a group to the left of the main pier were George Earl Hoffman, Sr., a future U.S. District Attorney, Carl Timothy Hoffman, later an attorney and developer, and Vincent Giblin Hoffman.

Sergeant Butler and engineer William M. Chubb were photographed at the Army's new fire control system. The system consisted of three battery commander's stations and one fire commander's station. Using calculations supplied by the end stations, this network was able to effectively defend Pensacola.

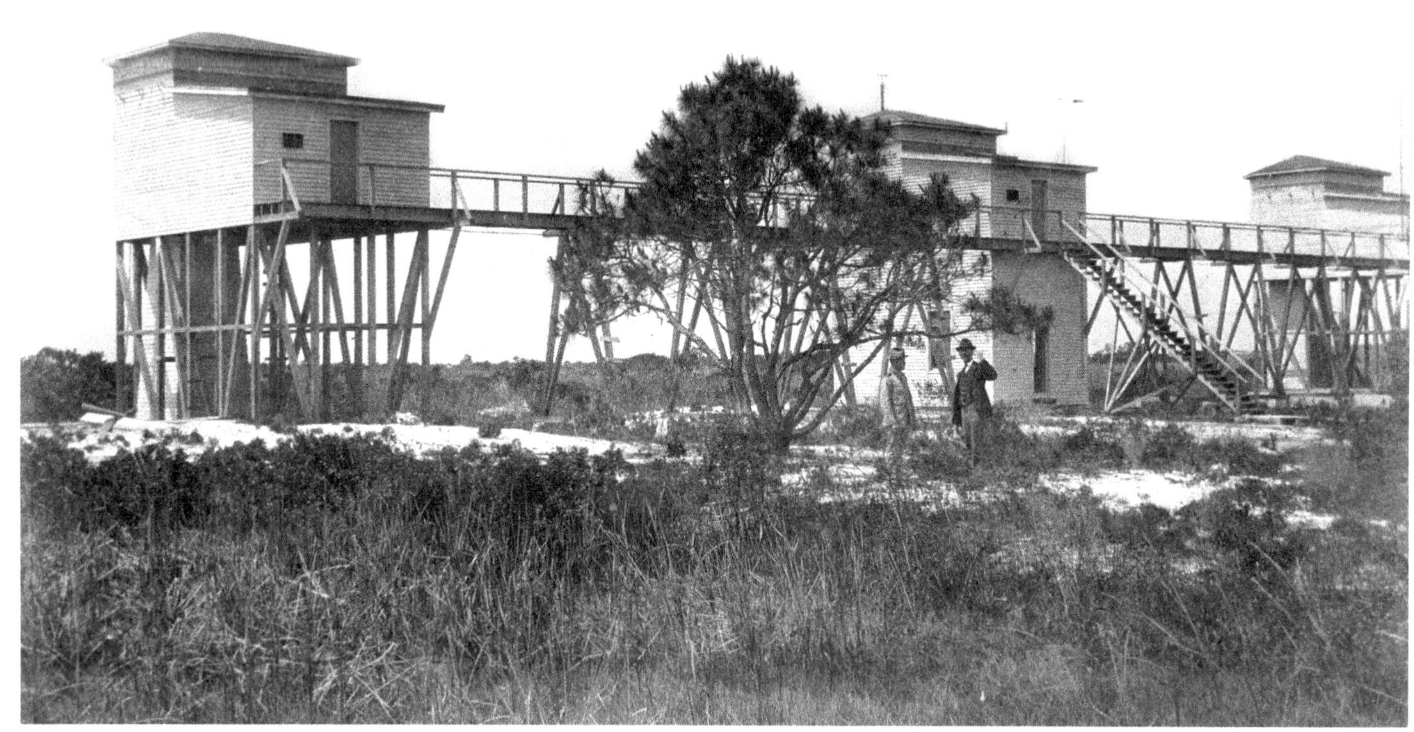

Resilience amid Hardship

(1900–1919)

Pensacola began the twentieth century as the second most populous city in the state—only Jacksonville was larger. The city continued to prosper and grow, paving streets, putting in sidewalks, and adding electric trolley service to replace the horse-drawn system. As the business district expanded and transportation improved, large Victorian houses appeared on North Hill, home to those who could afford to move away from the smell and the bustle of the docks.

The new century brought many hardships. The city was damaged by hurricanes in 1906, 1916, and 1917, which claimed lives and left thousands of dollars of damage in their wakes. The booming red snapper industry, which had shipped $600,000 worth of the popular fish in 1904 and 1905, was unable to recover from the harmful effects of overfishing and damage caused by the 1906 hurricane, and thus faded from importance to the city's economy. Halloween 1905 was a night of devastating tricks. Twenty-five years after fire destroyed buildings from Romana to Zarragossa streets, the Halloween fire destroyed South Palafox Street businesses from Garden to Romano streets. The Opera House was heavily damaged by the 1917 hurricane and was razed. The Navy Yard, established in 1825, was decommissioned in October 1911.

Pensacola nevertheless continued to forge ahead. The 34 ships of the Navy's "Great White Fleet" arrived in March 1905 and continued to return to Pensacola Bay for several years. Yellow fever, a recurrent problem for the city, was finally eradicated from the area in the summer of 1905. A building boom resulted in a new Spanish renaissance–style City Hall. In 1910, Pensacola's first skyscraper, the ten-story American National Bank Building, opened at the corner of South Palafox and Government streets, and Pensacola's premier hotel, the Hotel San Carlos, opened for business. The Daughters of Charity opened the Pensacola Hospital, the city's first modern medical facility, on Twelfth Avenue in 1912. And the Navy's interest in aviation led to reactivation of the old Navy Yard as the United States Aeronautical Station, a seaplane base, in 1914.

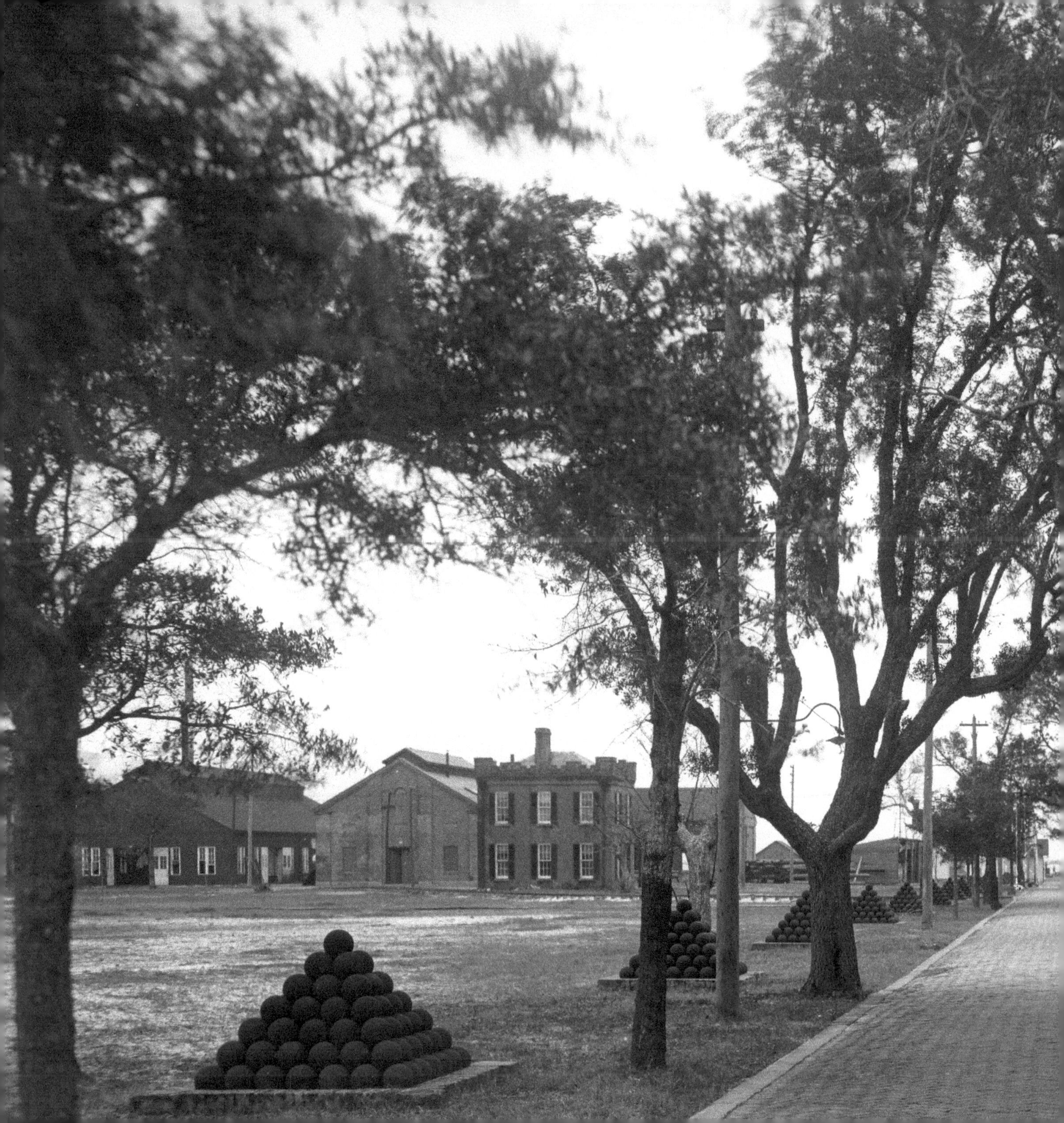

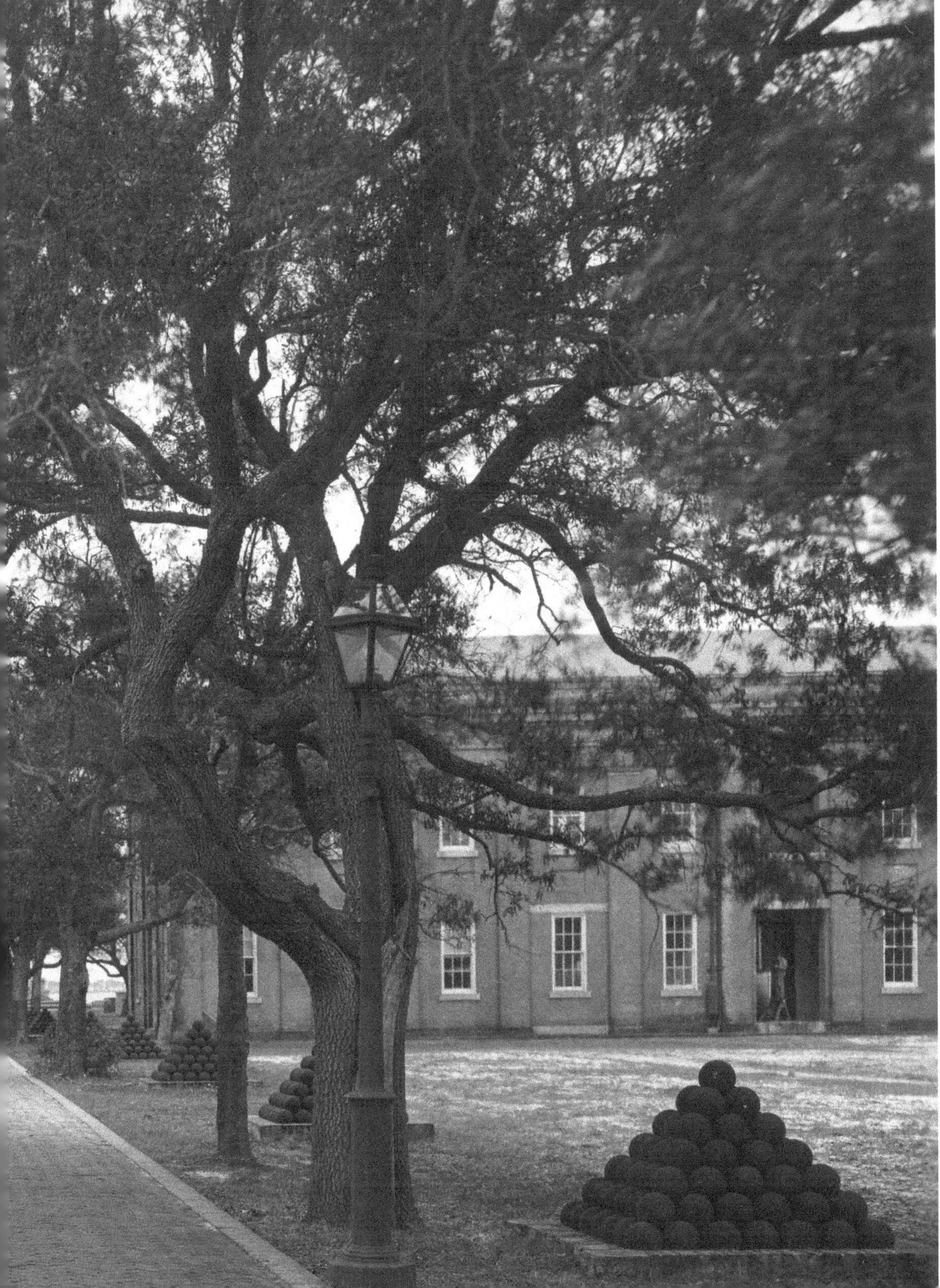

Paved with brick, the Pensacola Navy Yard's Center Avenue leads from the Commandant's Quarters to the Center Wharf. In this 1903 photograph, the administrative building is at right and the chapel is in the building at left.

Pensacola's deep-water port was a mainstay of the city's economy. The port boasted a grain elevator with a 500,000-bushel capacity, and the timber companies exported live oak, yellow pine, and hickory, along with other woods.

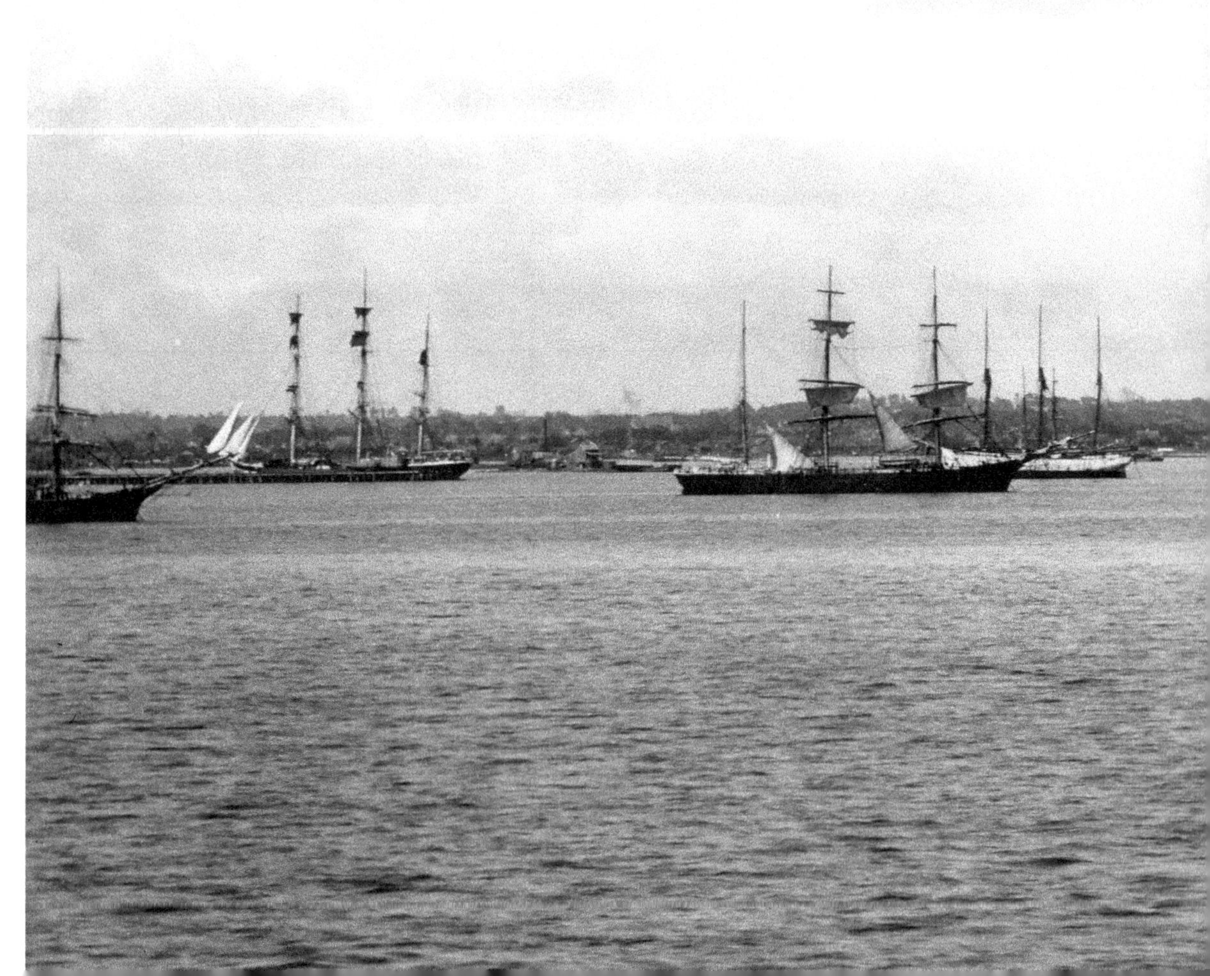

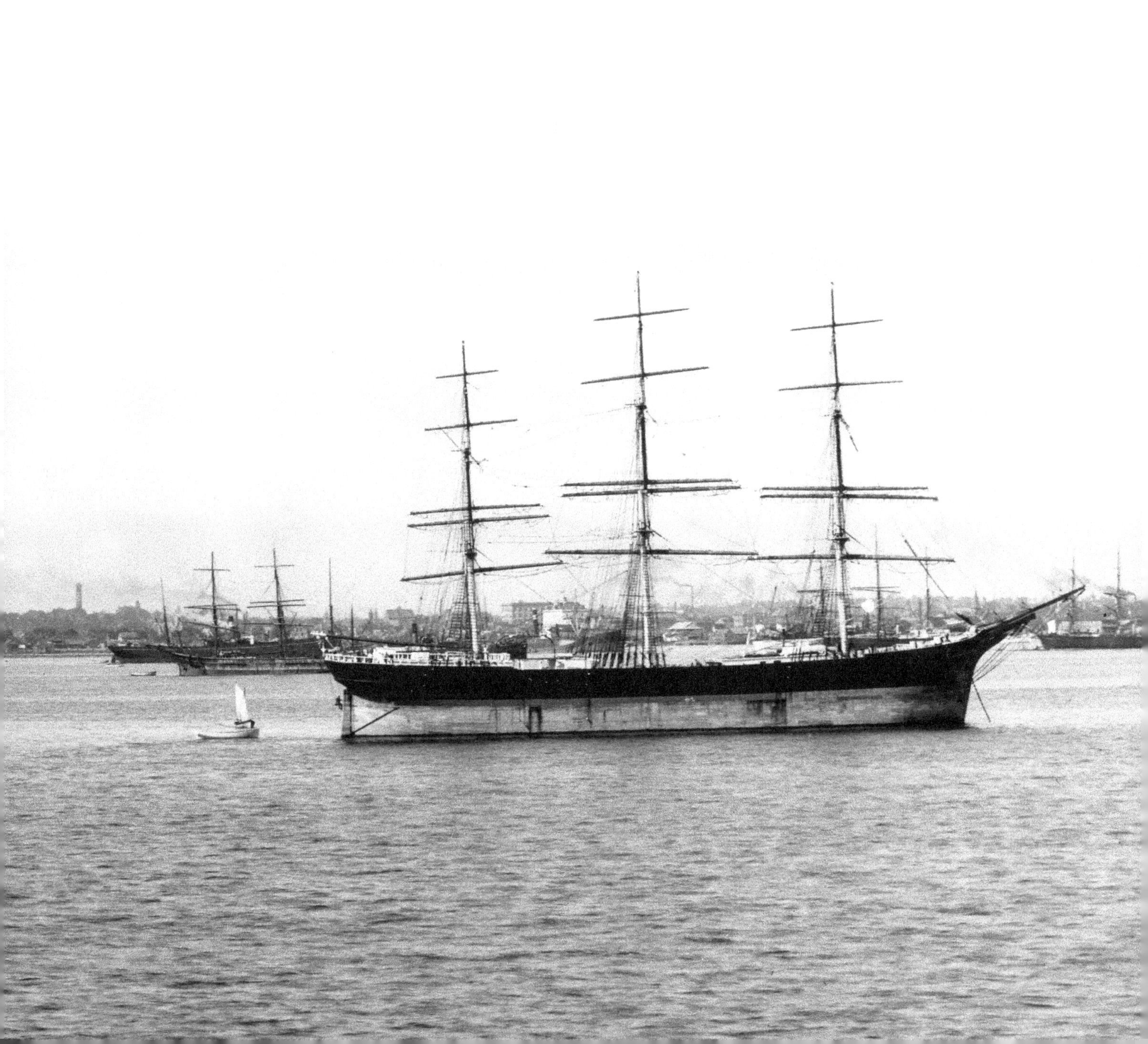

By 1903, Pensacola had professional, paid firemen. This firehouse, located at 109 East Garden Street, housed Company 1, a hook and ladder company, and company 2, a hose reel company.

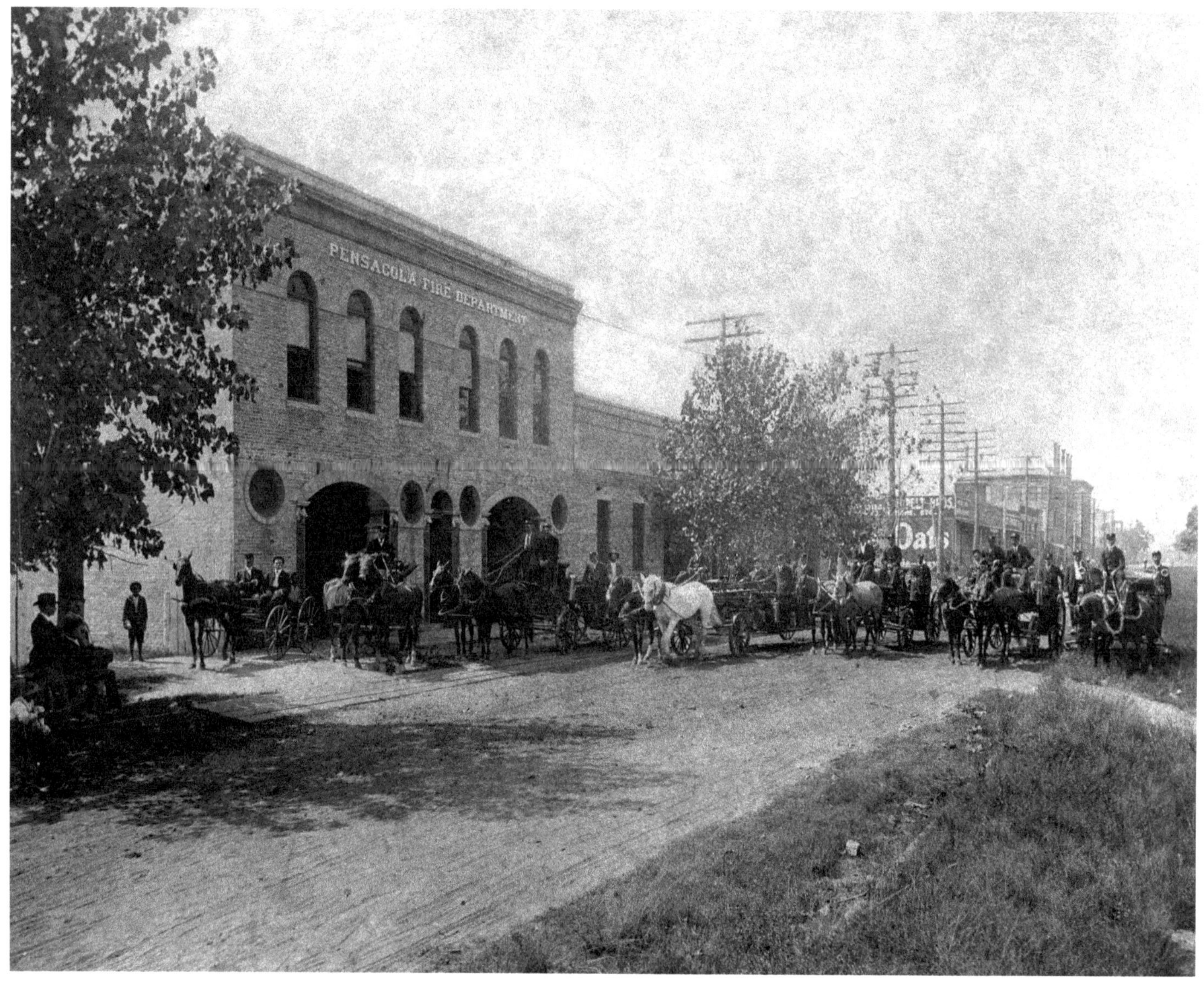

A group of young ladies show off their finery and their ankles as they go wading. Mary Frances Hope Holifield, daughter of William and Minor Dansby Holifield, is third from the left. Miss Holifield later became Mrs. Jerry W. Carter, Sr.

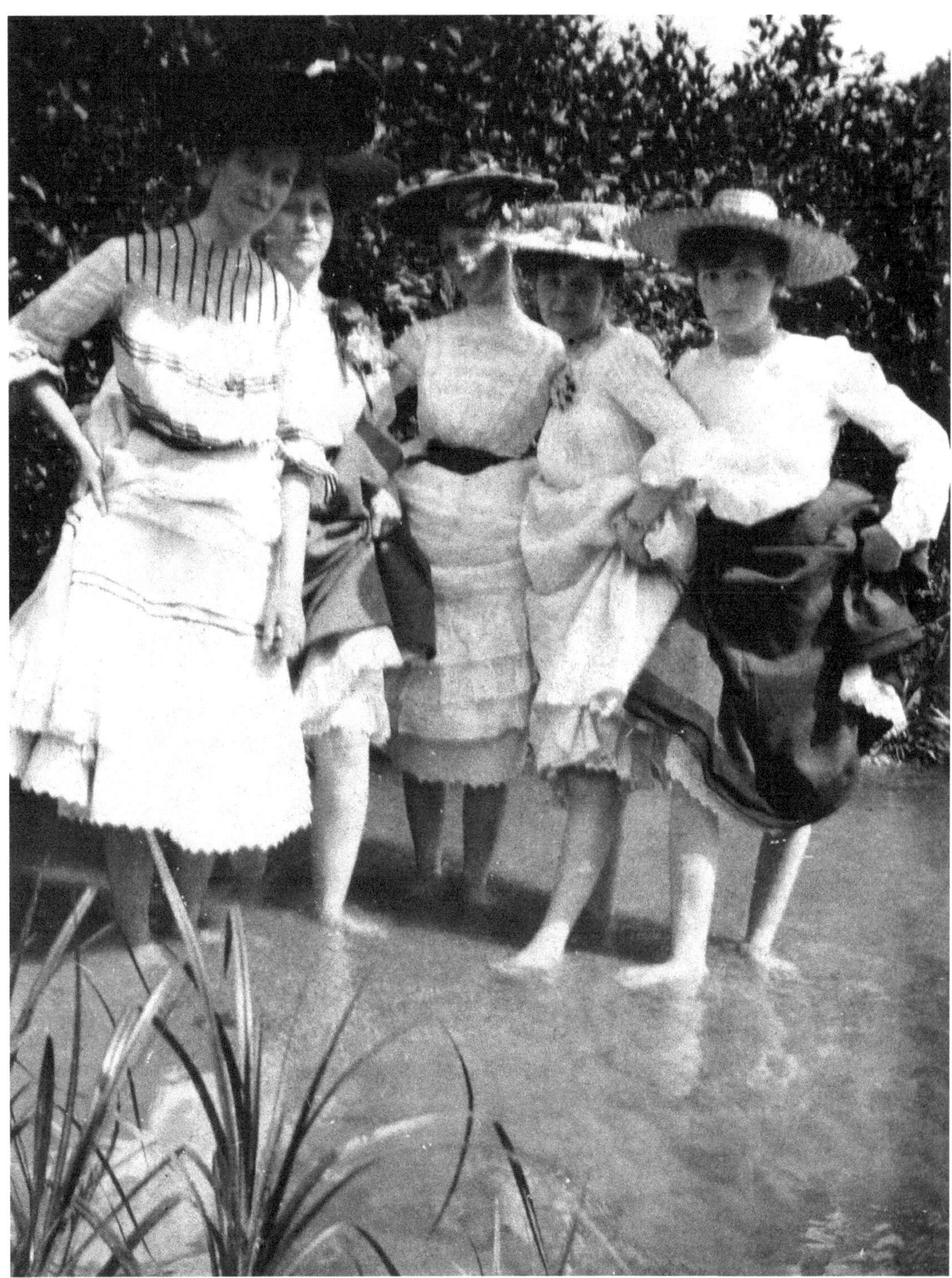

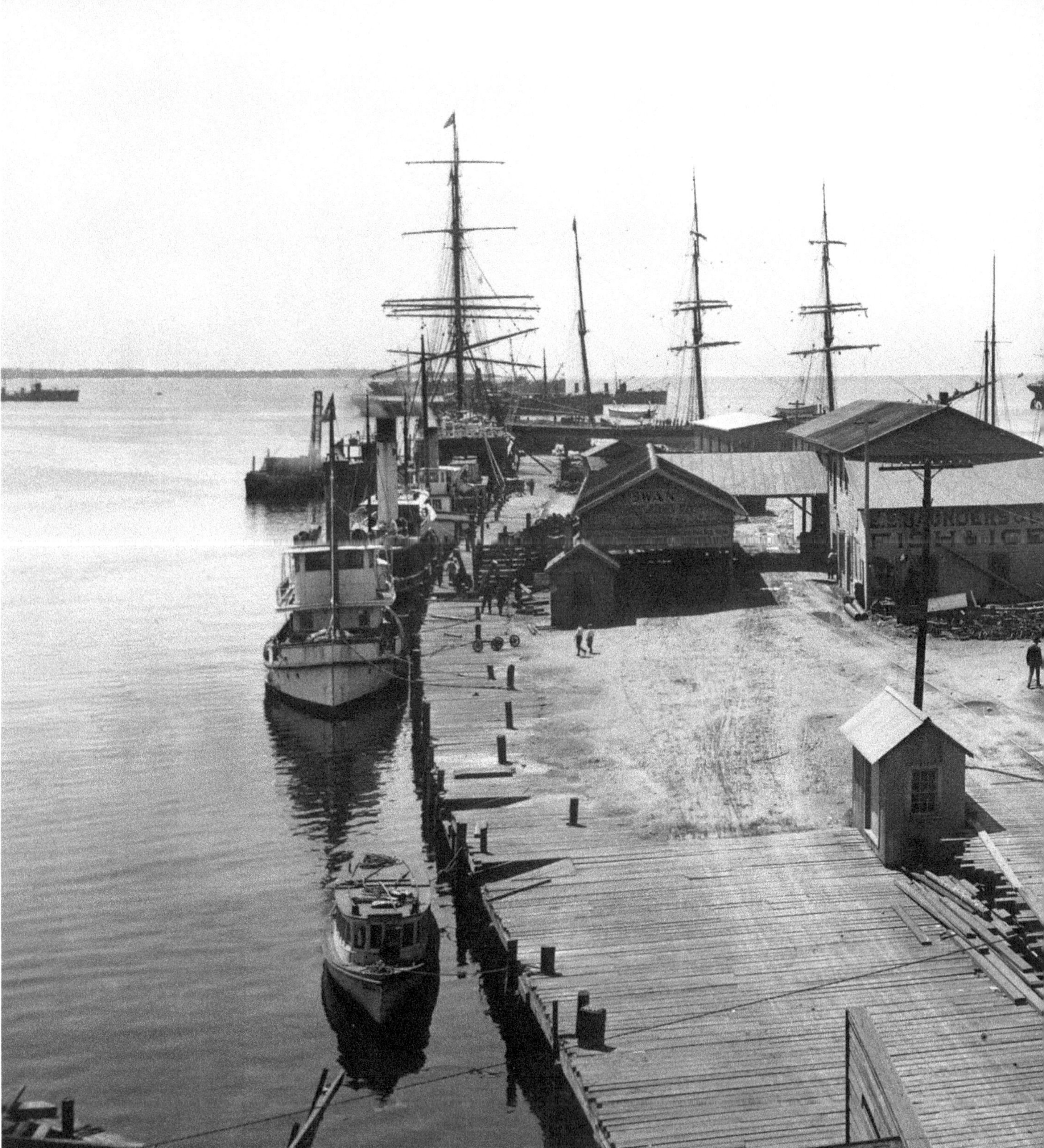

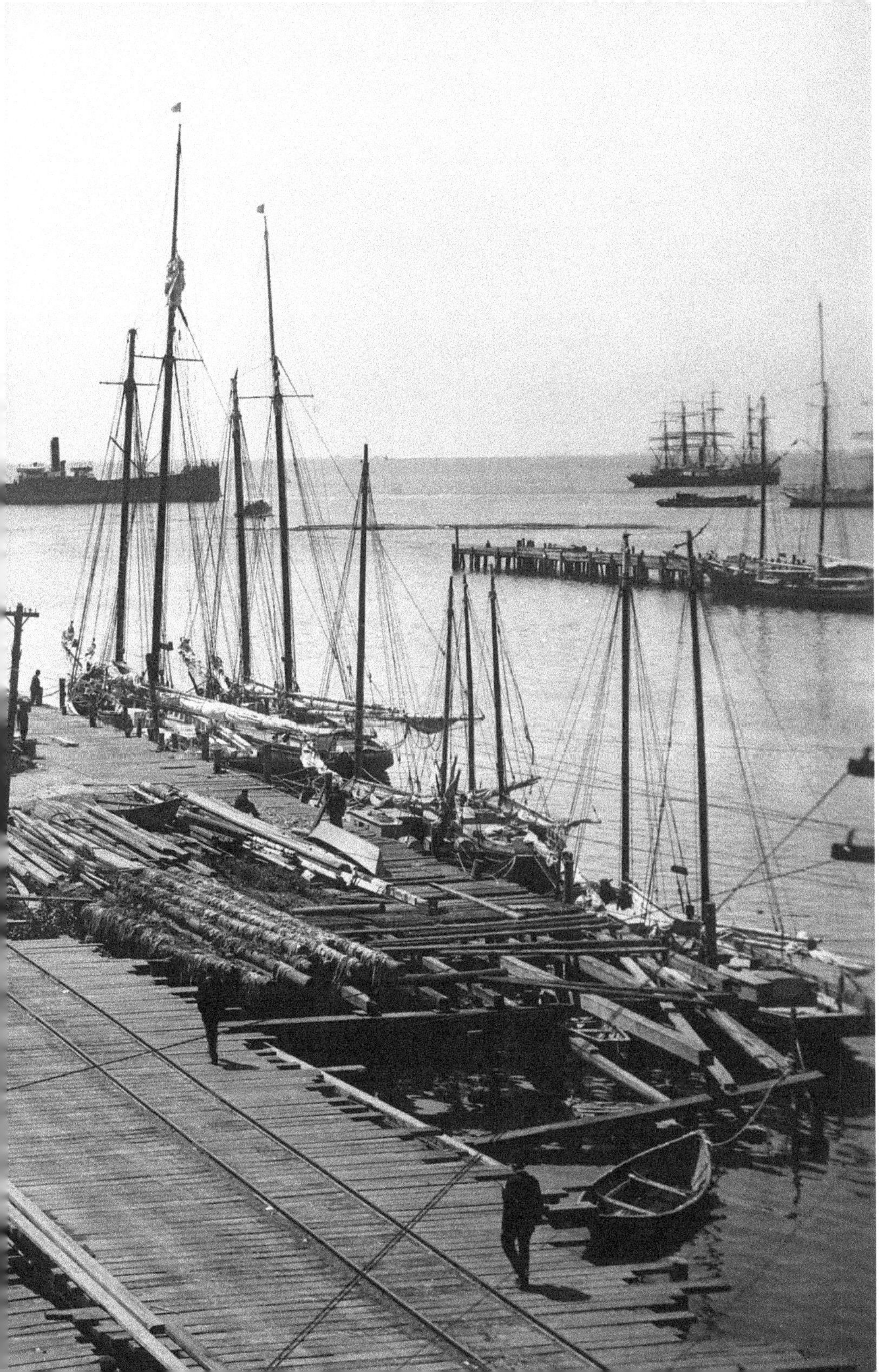

The Palafox Street Wharf was home to a number of businesses, such as E. E. Saunders and Company, in the first building on the right. Other businesses included the Pensacola Fish Company, Gulf Fish Company, U. S. Q. M. Landing, Gulf of Mexico Marine Railroad Company, and the Escambia Fish Company.

This Spanish renaissance building was erected in 1903 to house the growing congregation of Christ's Episcopal Church, replacing the building on Seville Square. Designed in the shape of a cross, the church includes a dome that straddles the intersection of the transept and the nave.

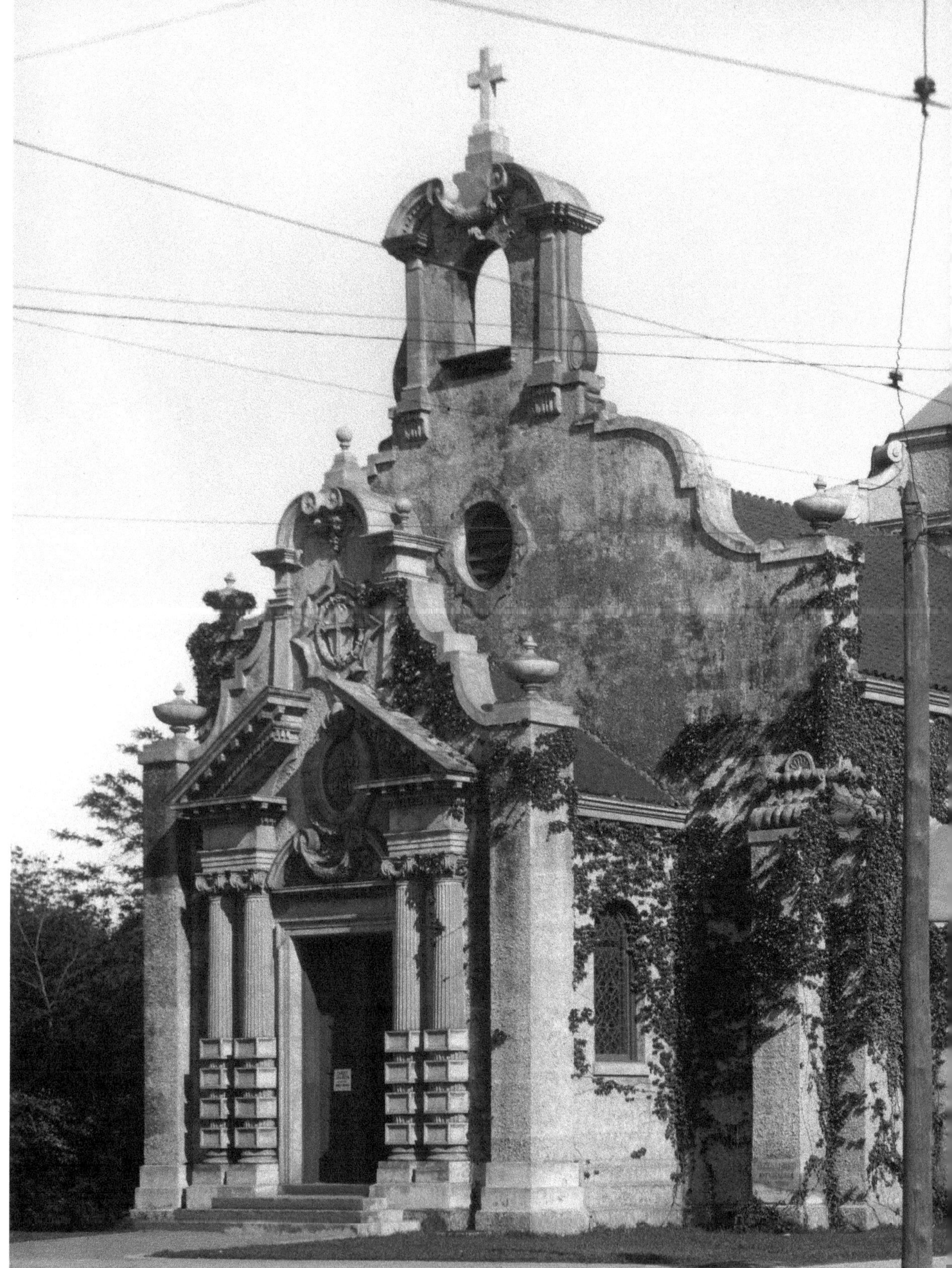

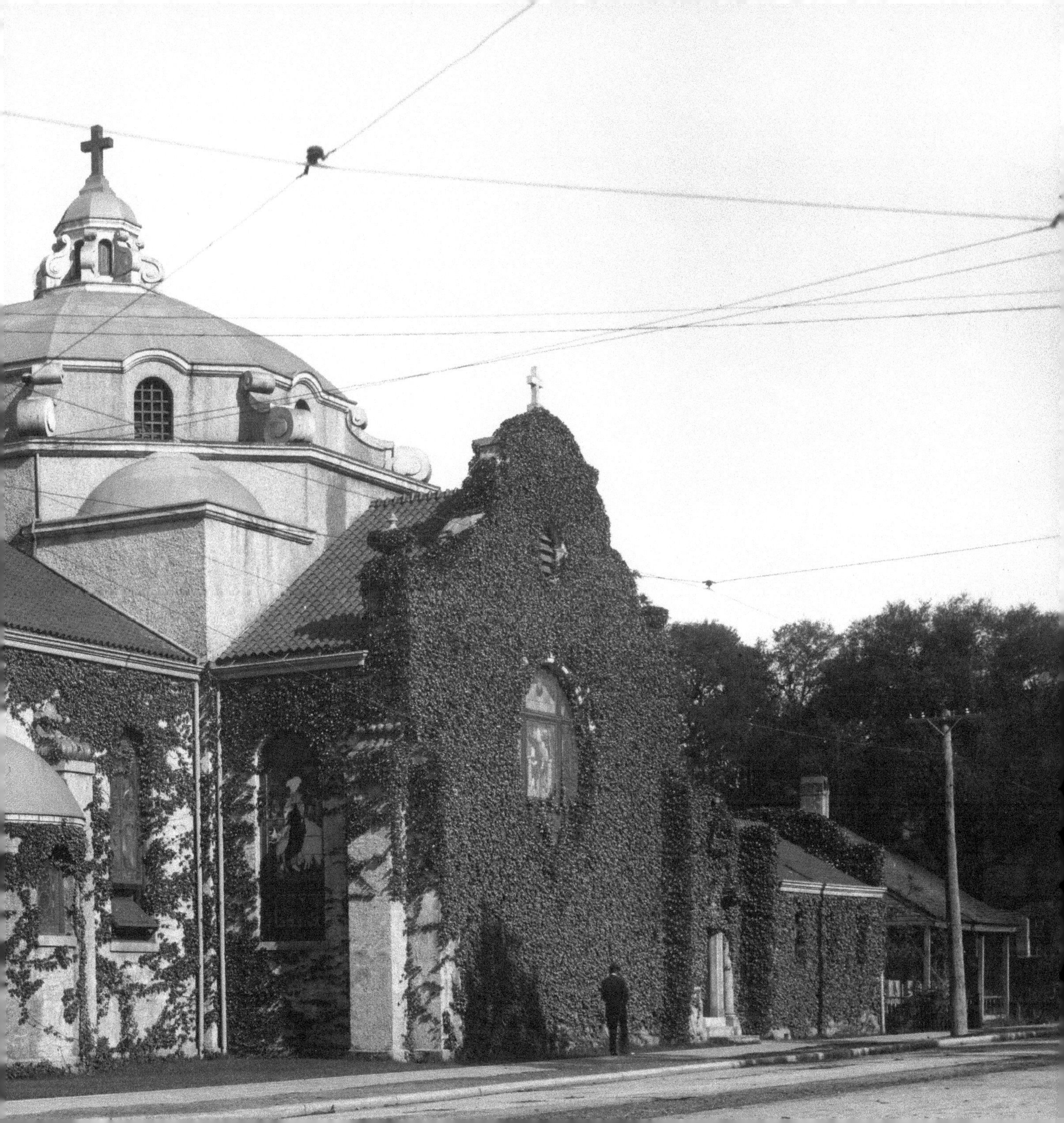

People braved the flooded streets to check for damage after the September 28, 1906, hurricane. The five-story Thiesen Building is on the right and the seven-story Blount Building is visible in the background, at left.

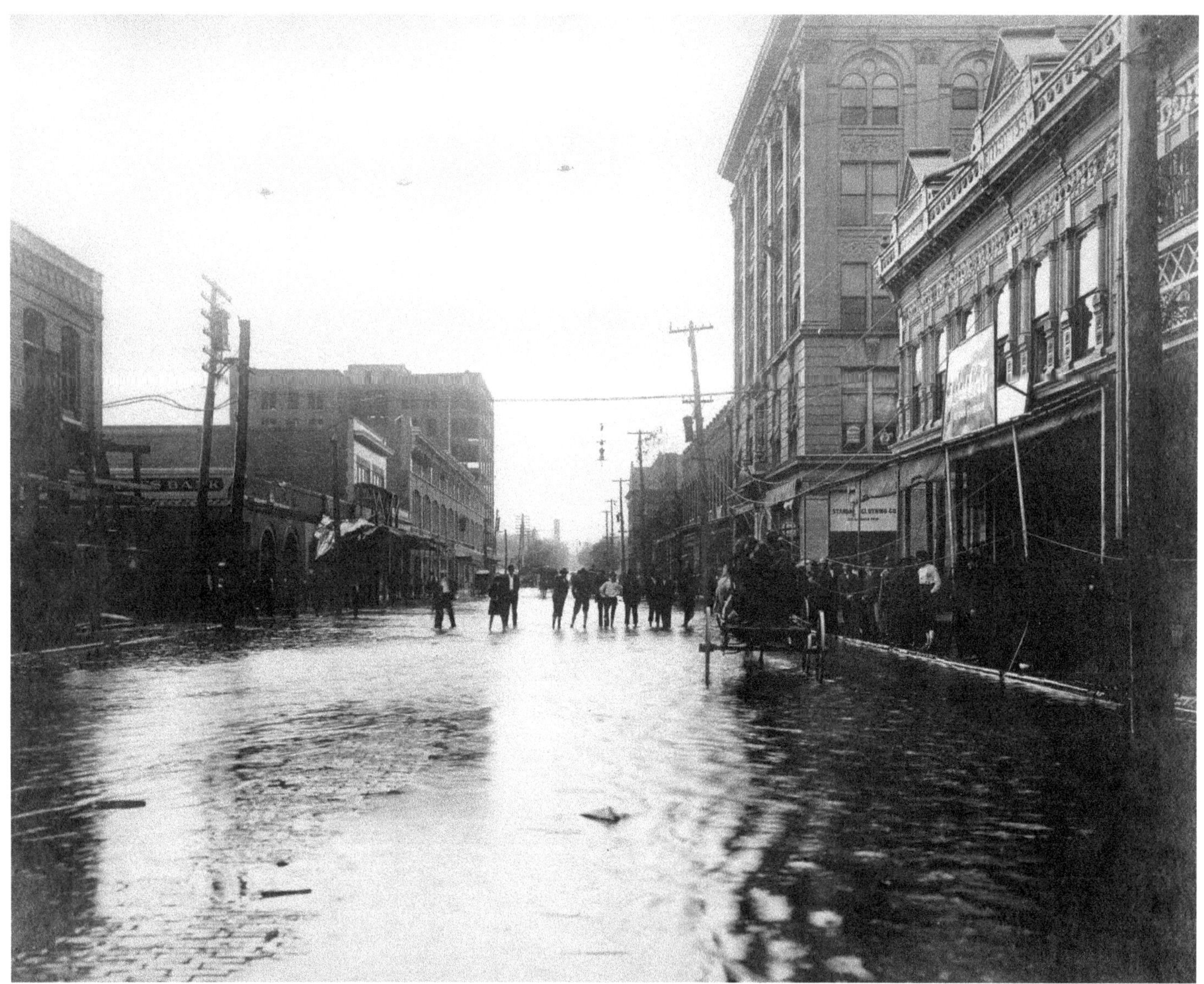

Ten months before the 1906 storm, fire destroyed the businesses in the first block of South Palafox Street, from Garden to Romano streets. Pensacolians endured their last yellow fever epidemic in 1905, just before medical advances eradicated the disease. This view of East Main Street shows the Lewis Bear Company and the Pensacola Electric Company trolleys after the 1906 storm.

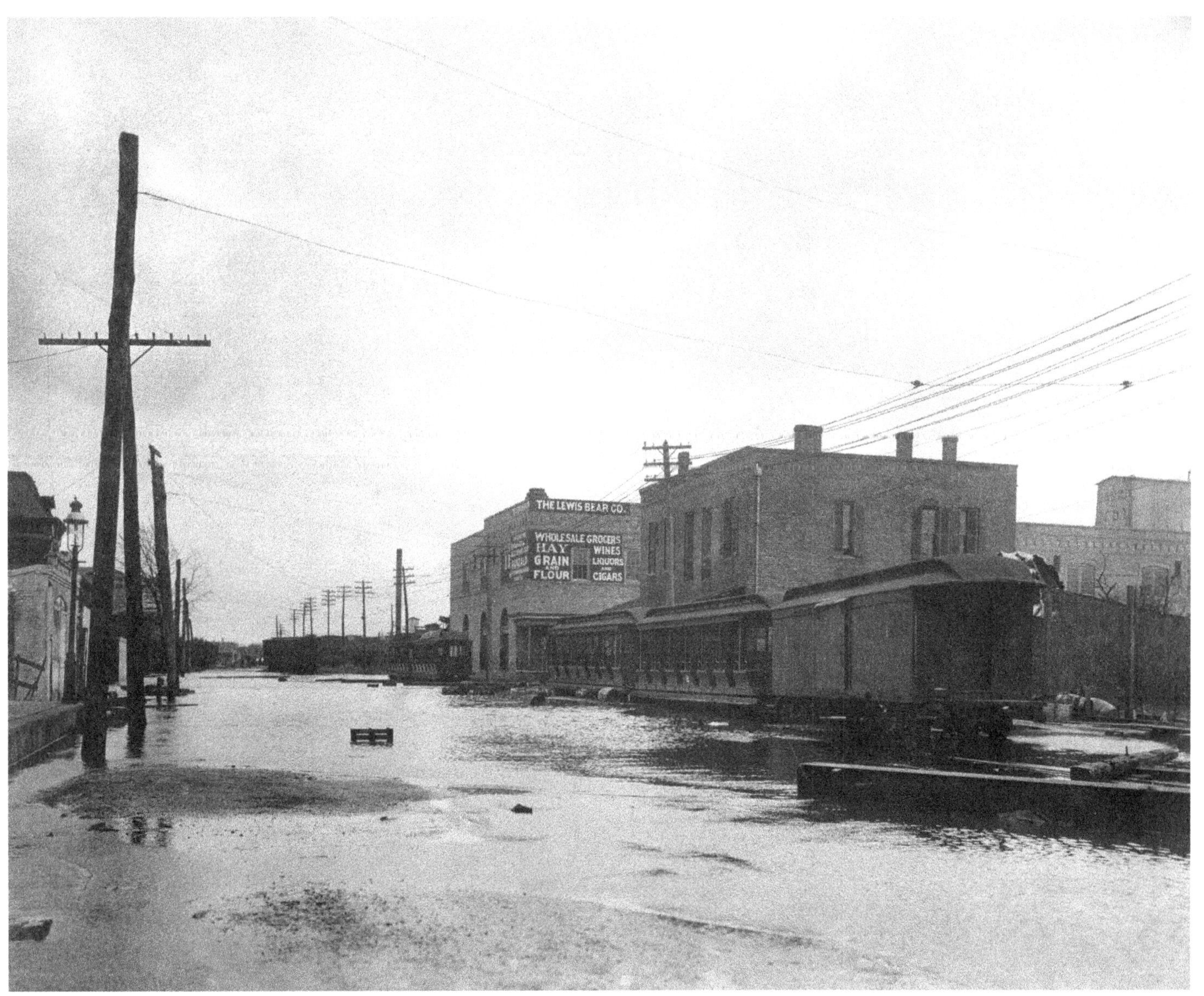

The Great Hurricane of 1906 was deemed to be the most devastating storm to hit Pensacola since the storm of 1559. The hurricane damaged more than 5,000 homes, left more than 3,000 Pensacolians homeless, and killed 134 people.

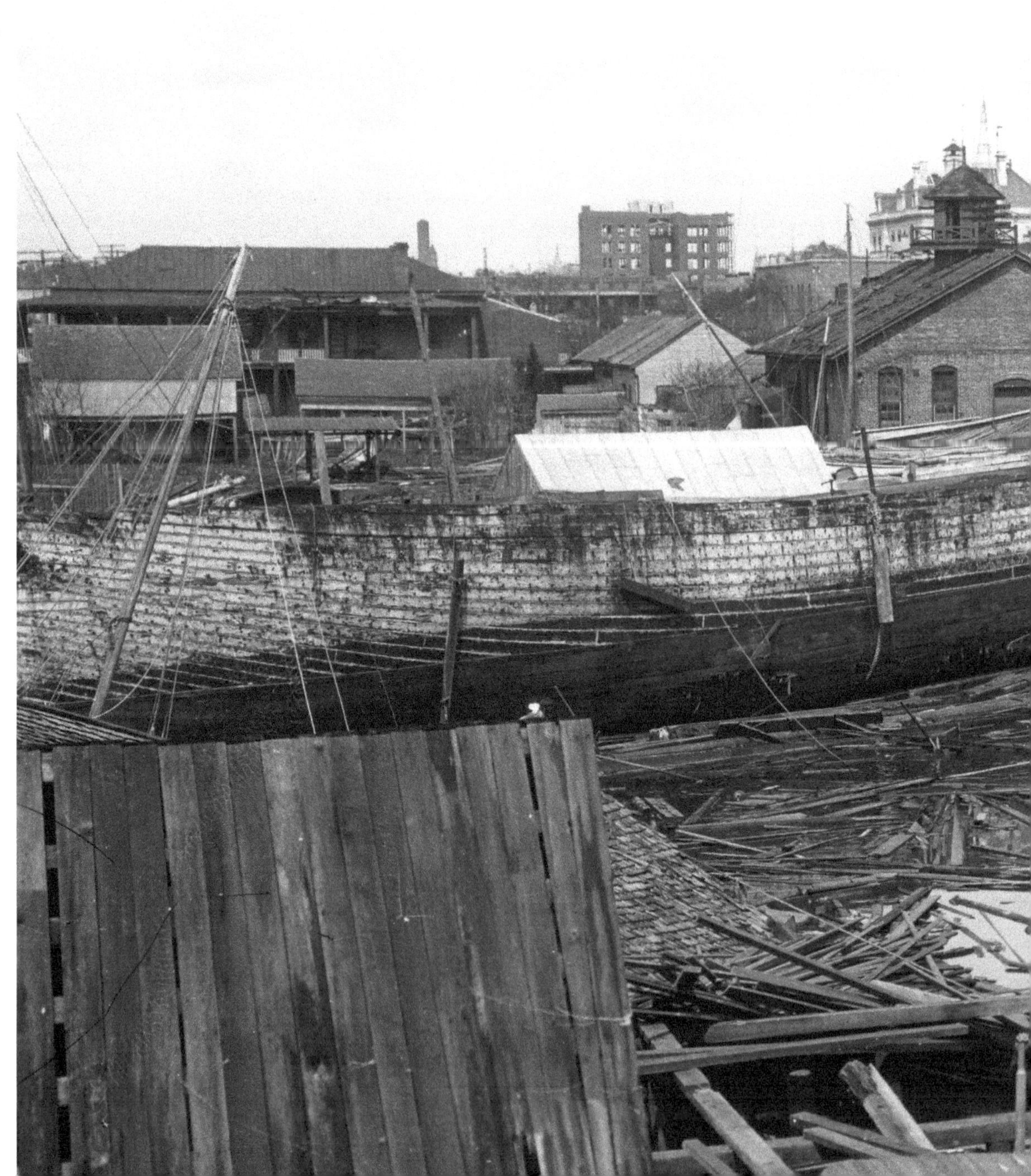

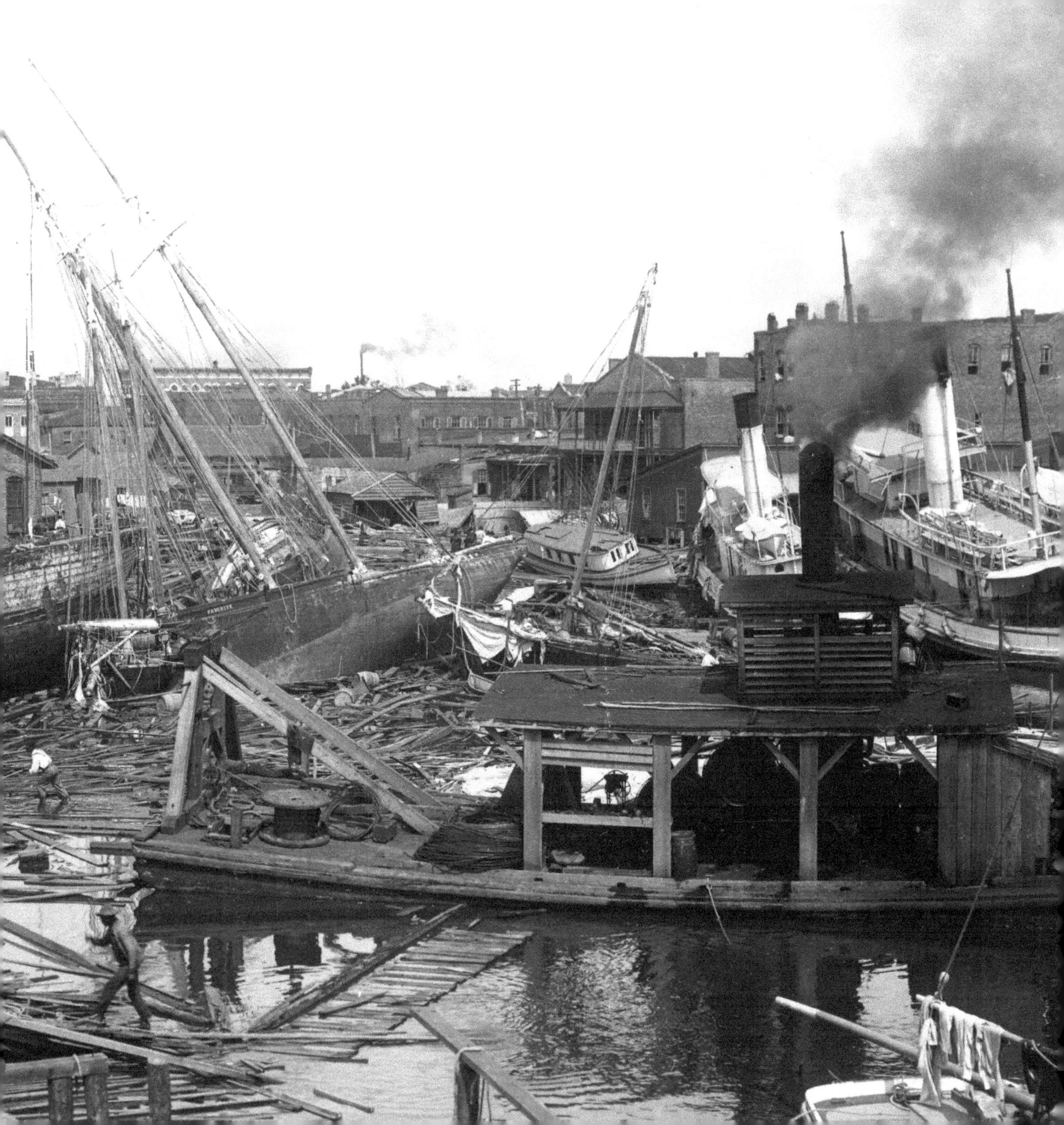

The Category 3 storm of 1906 came ashore in the early morning hours and set a high-tide record at ten feet above normal. The storm serge deposited some boats on ballast rock in the harbor and left others three blocks inland. Winds of 94 miles an hour were recorded before the anemometers at the weather stations were destroyed.

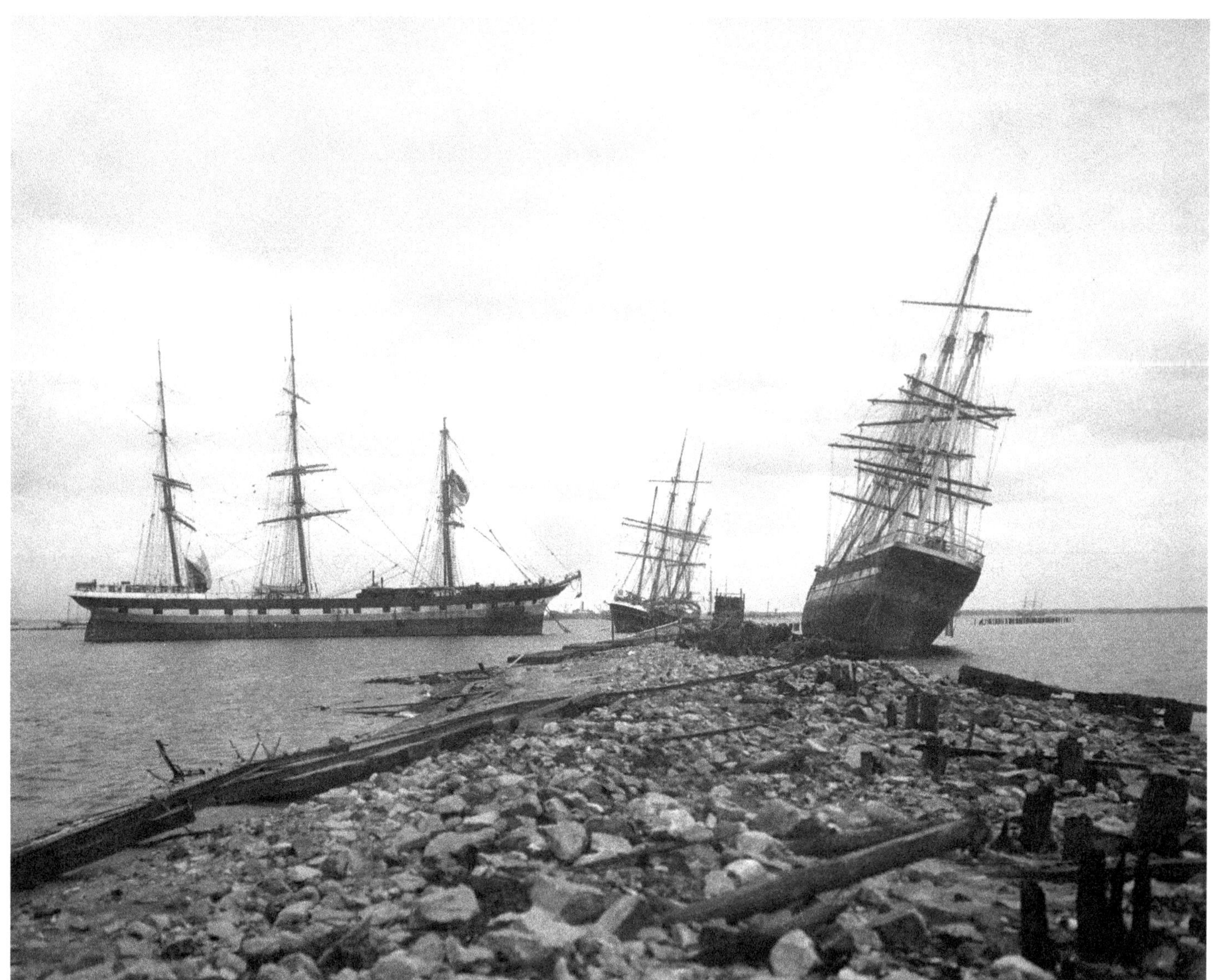

The 150-foot-tall Pensacola Lighthouse, which replaced the one in use from 1825 to 1858, went into service in 1859. It has six revolving lenses, and the 6,200-candlepower light can be seen 22 miles out at sea. The adjoining keeper's quarters was built in 1868. The light was fully automated in 1965, eliminating the need for an onsite keeper. The lighthouse and keeper's quarters have been on the National Registry of Historic Places since 1974.

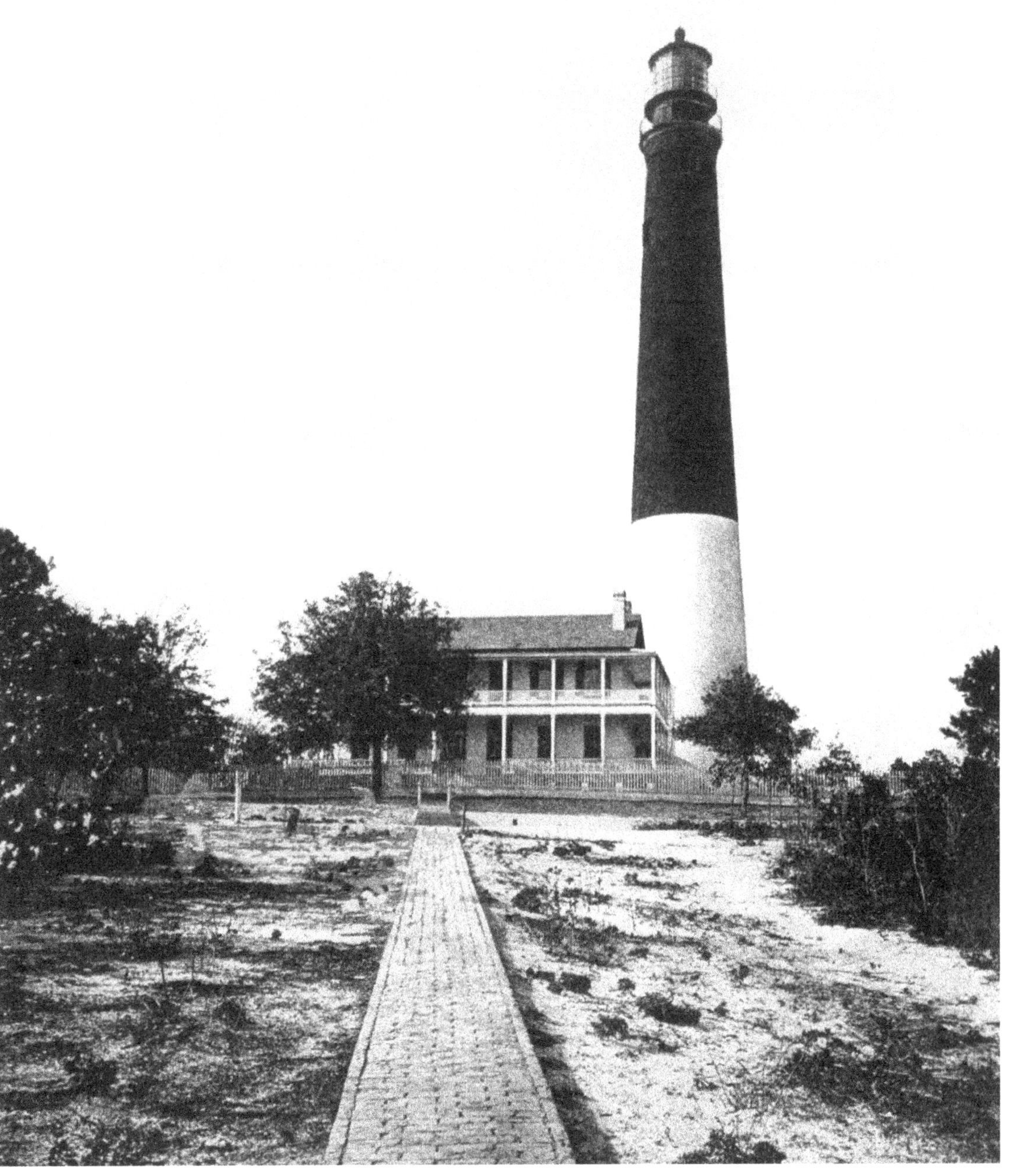

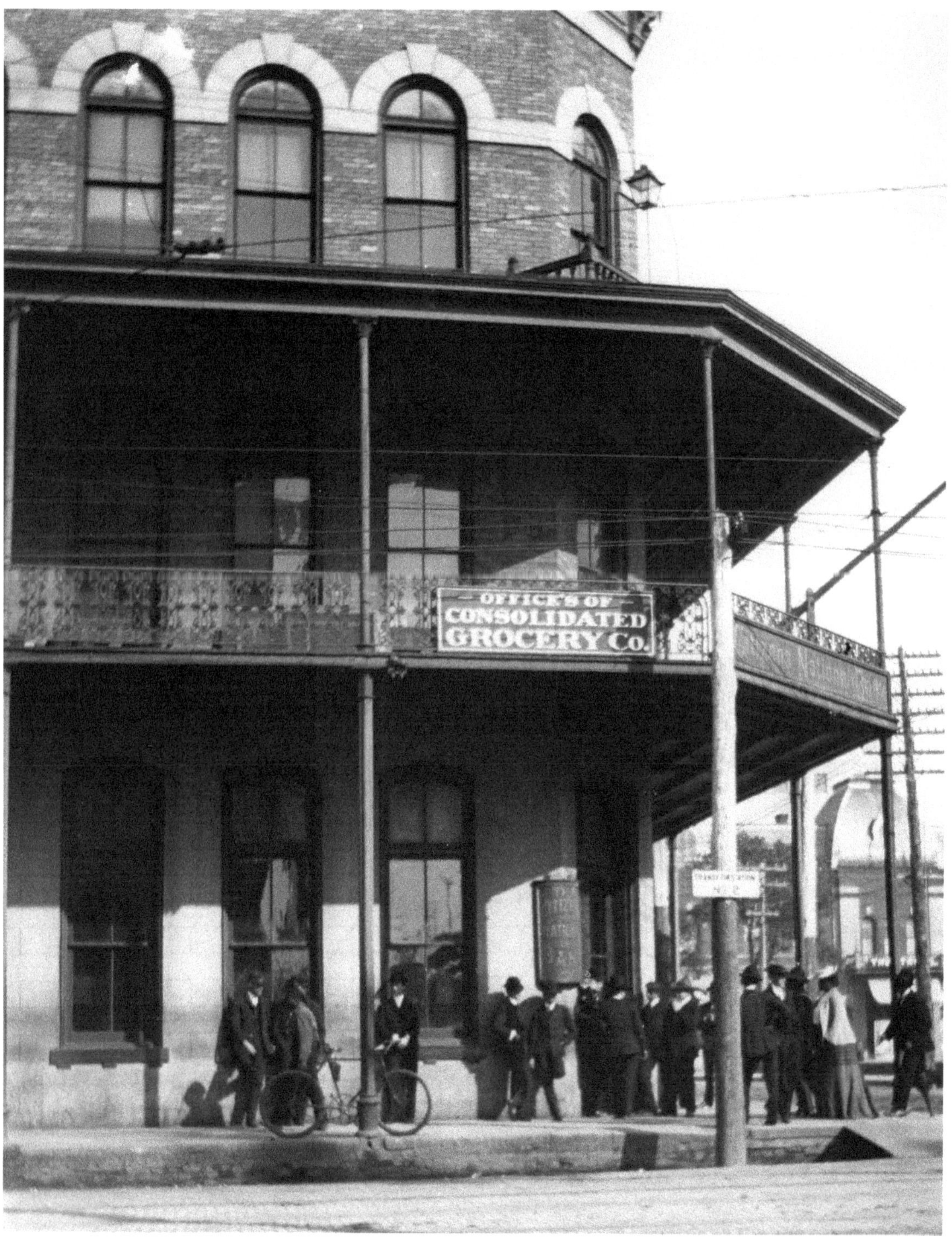

Although the Consolidated Grocery store was at the corner of Chase and Alcaniz streets, the office was located in the Citizens National Bank building at 228 South Palafox. The Pensacola Opera House, at the corner of Jefferson and Government streets, is visible in the background.

Sailing ships lie anchored in the harbor, beyond the rooftops of South Palafox. The L&N silo is visible on the far left. The closer of two trolleys plies the street in front of the Customs House and Post Office building on the west side of Palafox.

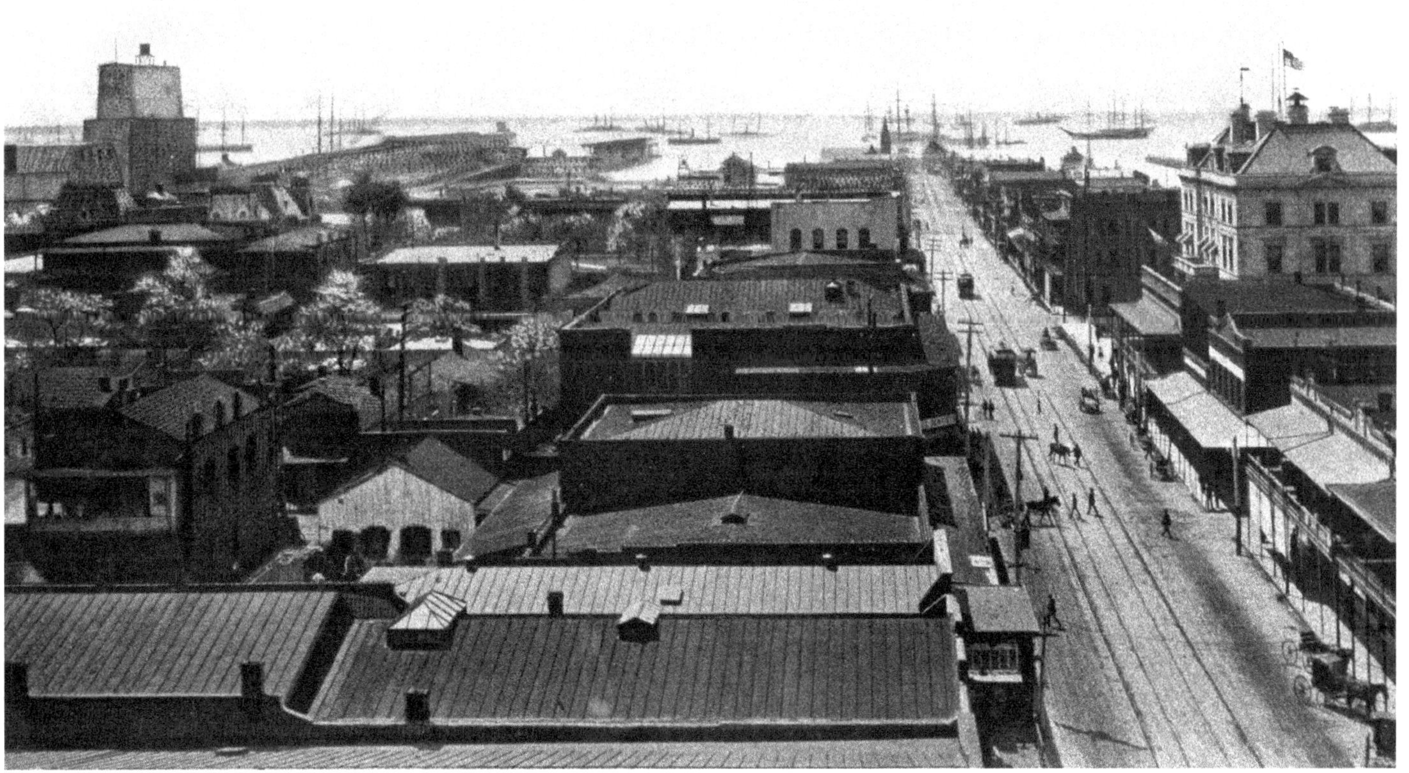

The dense pine forests that were native to the greater Pensacola region attracted lumber companies to the area. These high-wheeled vehicles, pulled by teams of oxen, were used to move timber to the waterways where the logs were floated to the sawmills.

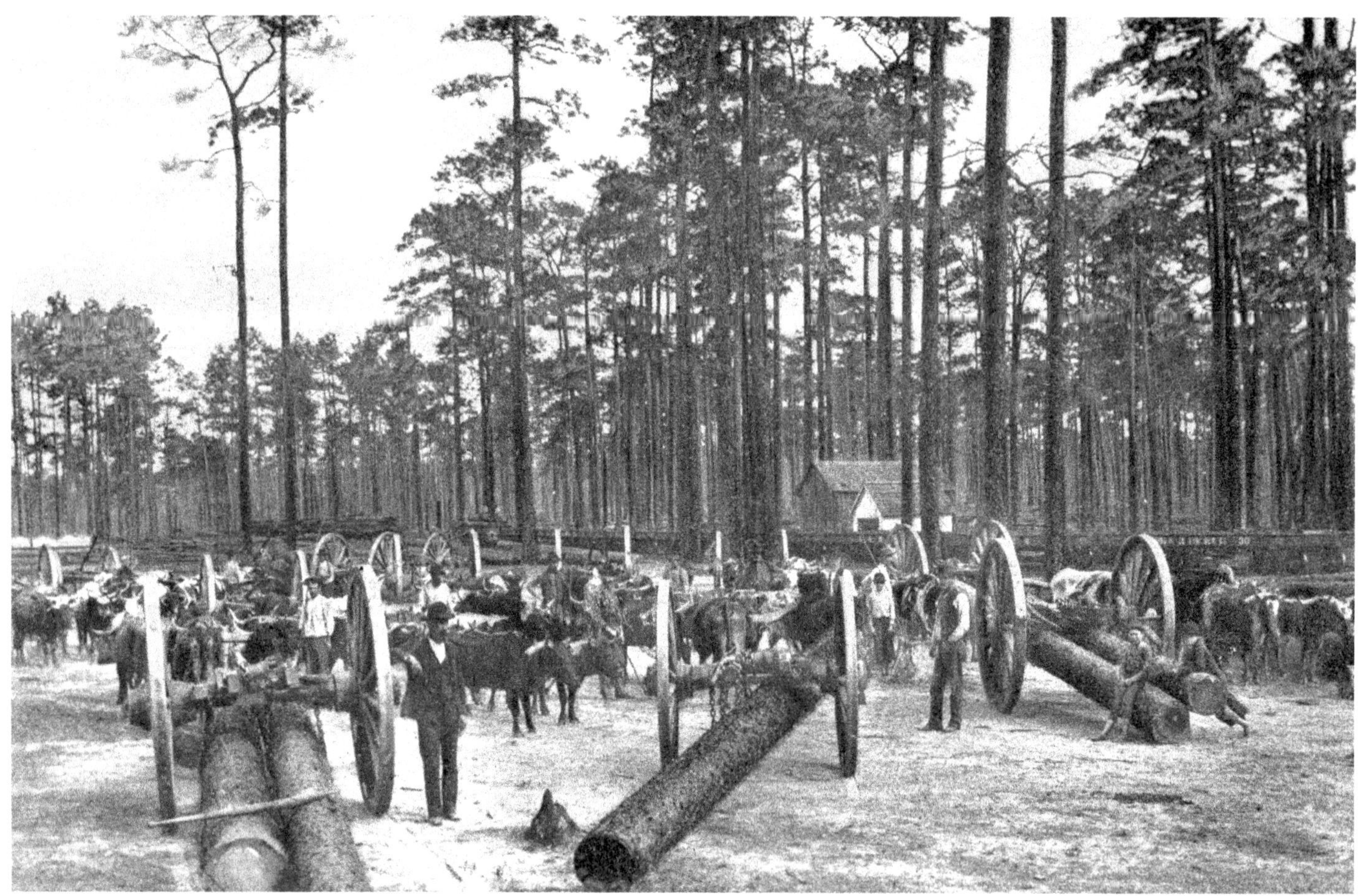

Employees of the Pensacola Electric Company went on strike in April 1908, stopping all trolley service in the city. After the company hired strikebreakers, Governor Napoleon B. Broward ordered the state militia to Pensacola to control unrest and restore order. The mounted patrol of Company L was prepared to maintain peace in the city.

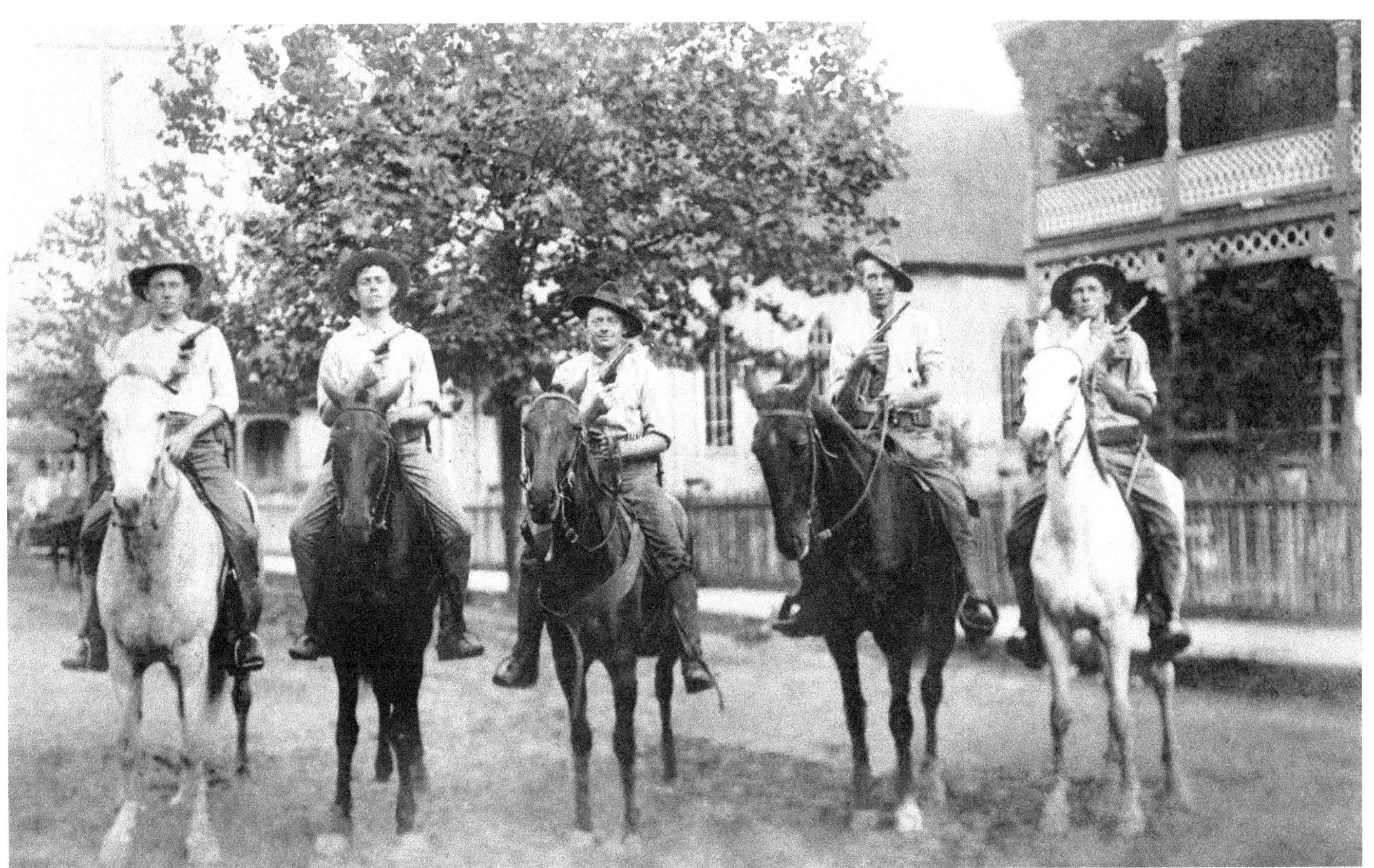

The trolley strike lasted for several weeks. On April 6, 1908, a group of men pose with one of the sidetracked streetcars.

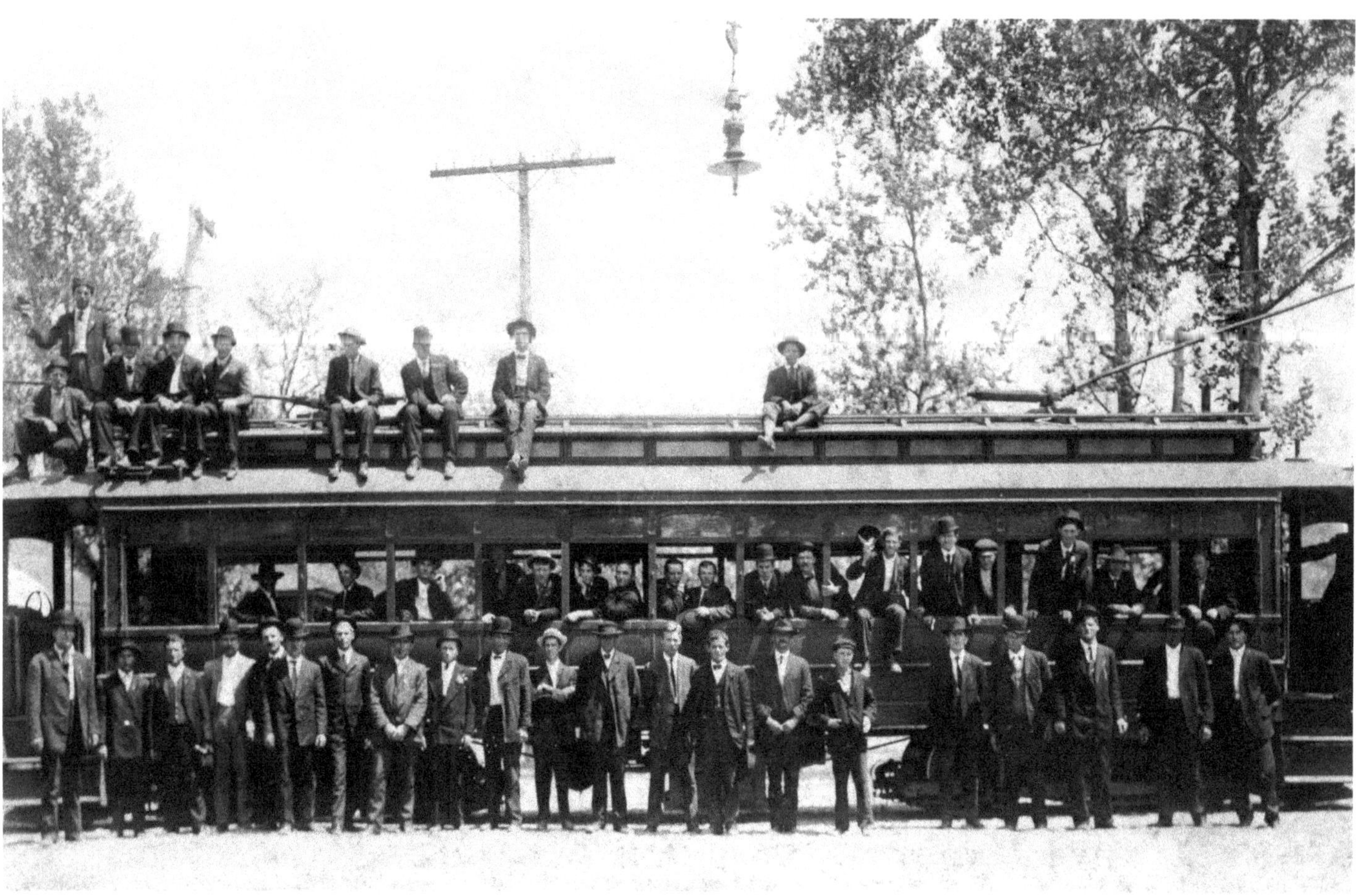

The companies of state militia ordered to Pensacola during the trolley strike set up camps along Palafox Street. These men are guarding the officers quarters established at the Escambia County Court House on North Palafox.

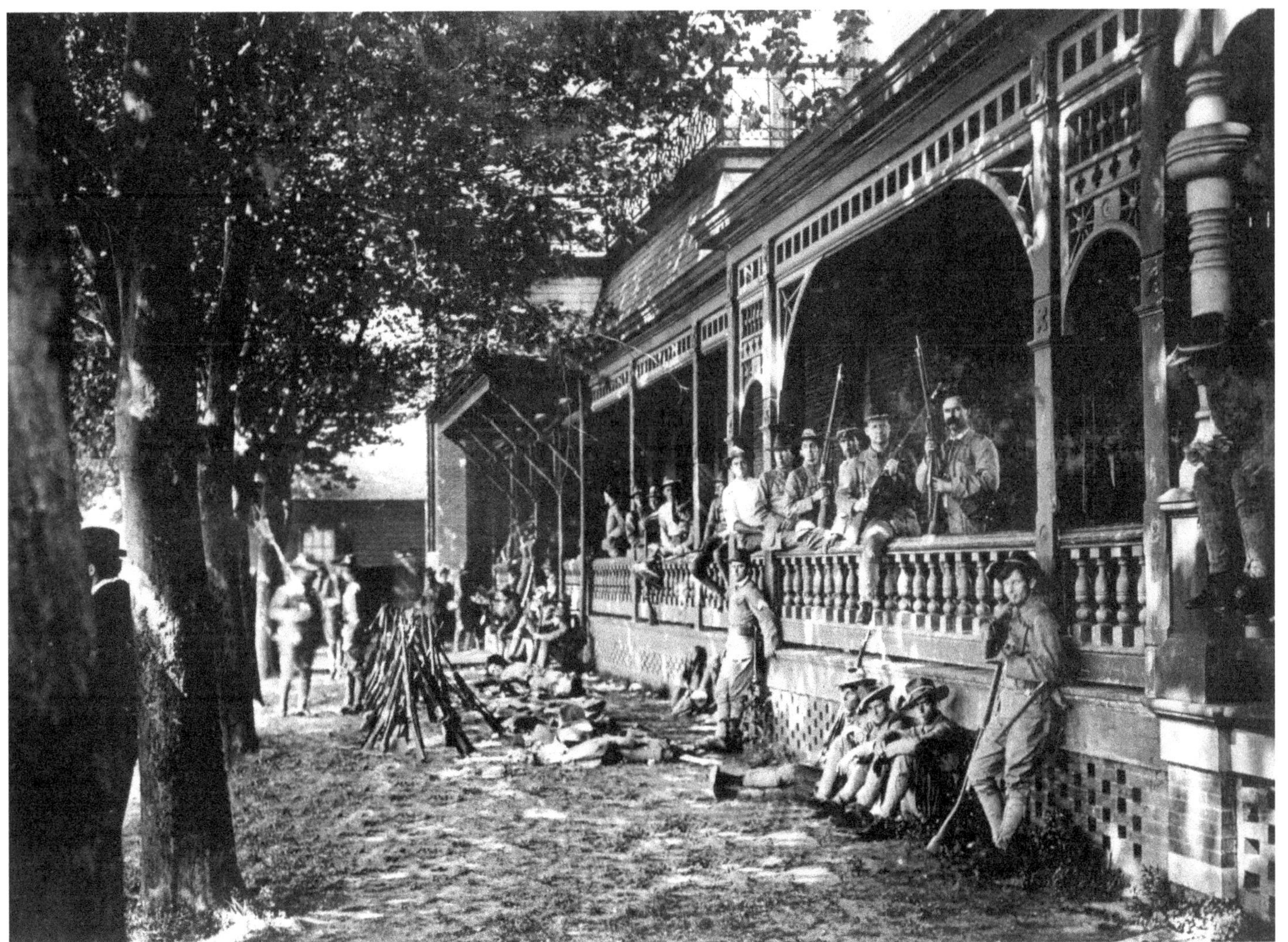

The militia was ordered to report to Pensacola under heavy marching orders, with each man having been issued twenty multiple ball cartridges. Two Gatling guns were also moved into the city. These members of the militia pose on the steps of the Customs House and Post Office on South Palafox.

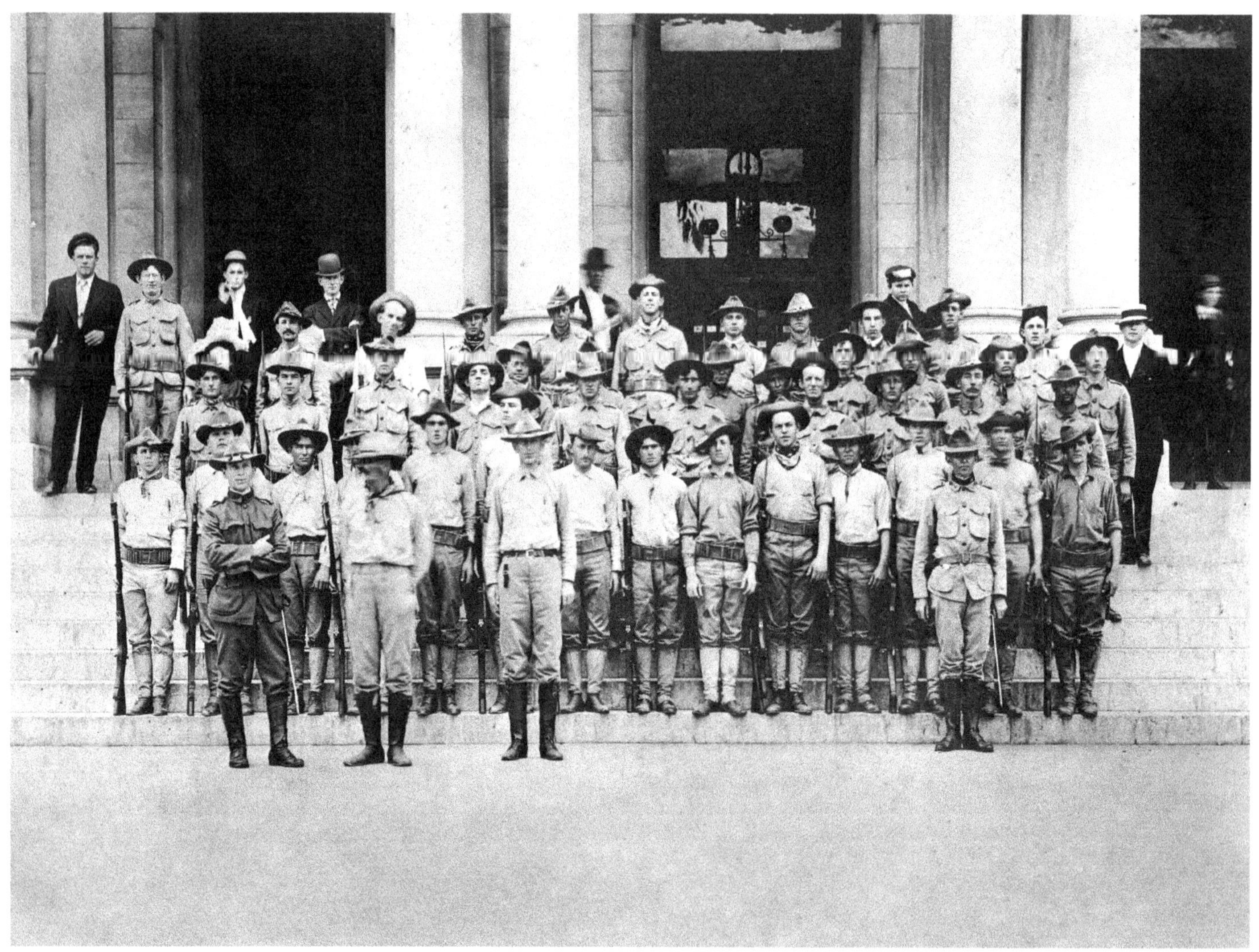

Strikebreakers were hired in New York City and were escorted through the city by the militia after arriving in Pensacola by train. The strikebreakers, with militia protection, reinstated service on April 14, 1908. On April 21, a mob attacked one of the streetcars, killing conductor G. Hoffman.

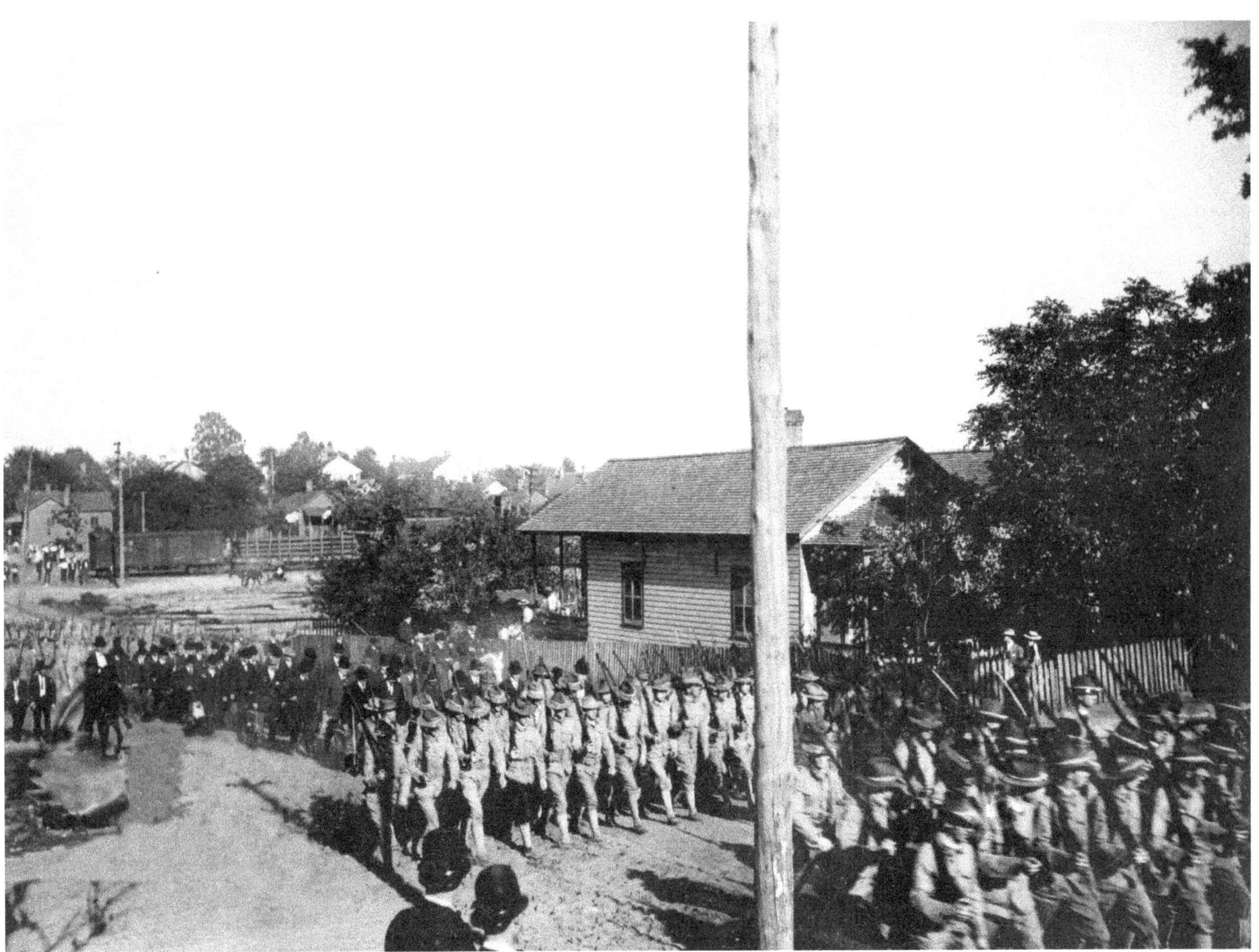

Early in the twentieth century, a handsome brick wall fronted the pedestrian walkway in the median of West Garden Street. The Pensacola Commercial College and the Manhattan Hotel are also visible in this image, at left. The steeple of Immanuel German Lutheran Church appears at right.

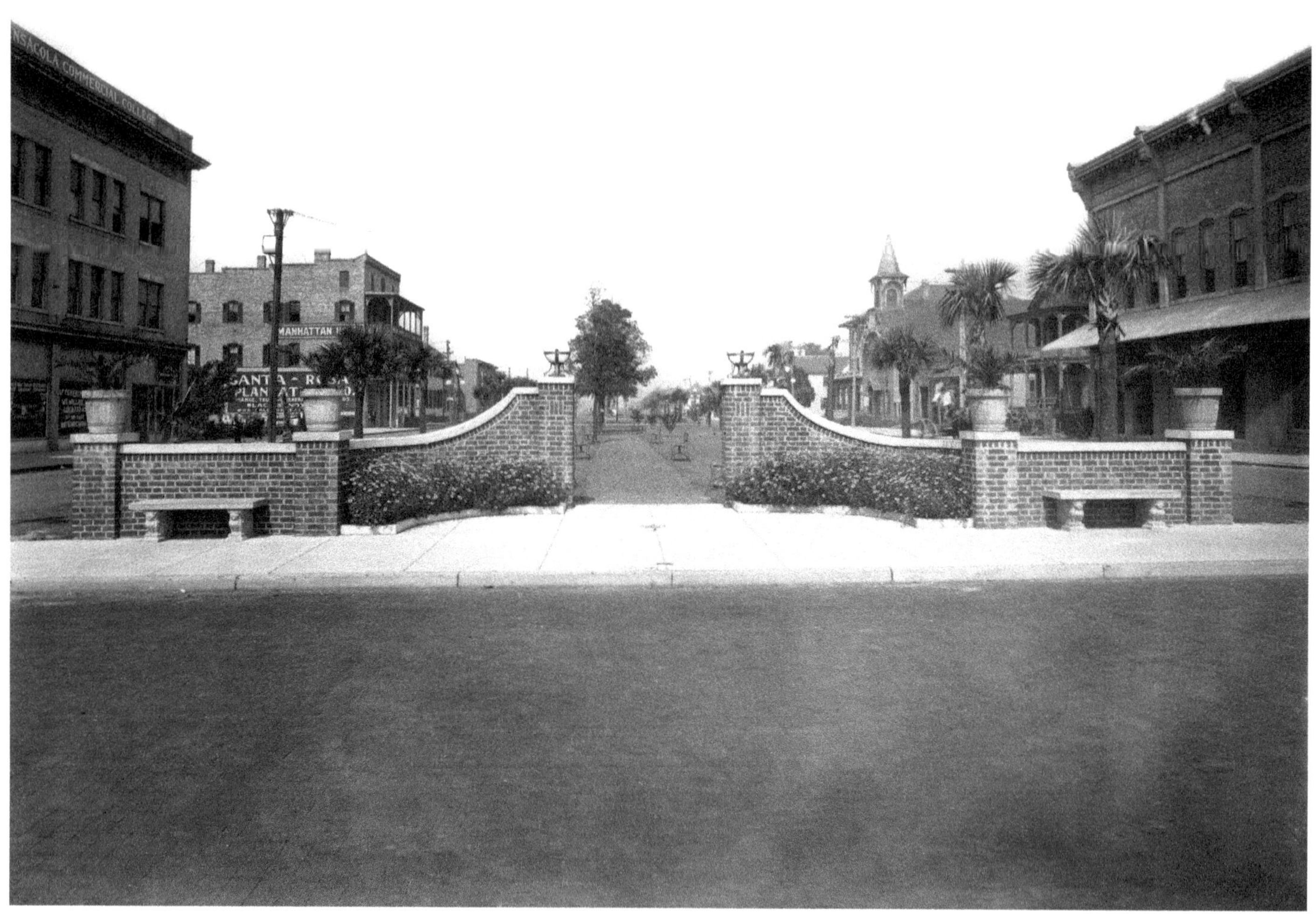

East Hill's A. V. Clubbs High School opened in 1911 at the corner of East Lloyd Street and North Ninth Avenue. By 1950, the school was operating as Clubbs Junior High. Named for local contractor A. V. Clubbs, the school was erected at a cost of $557,812.

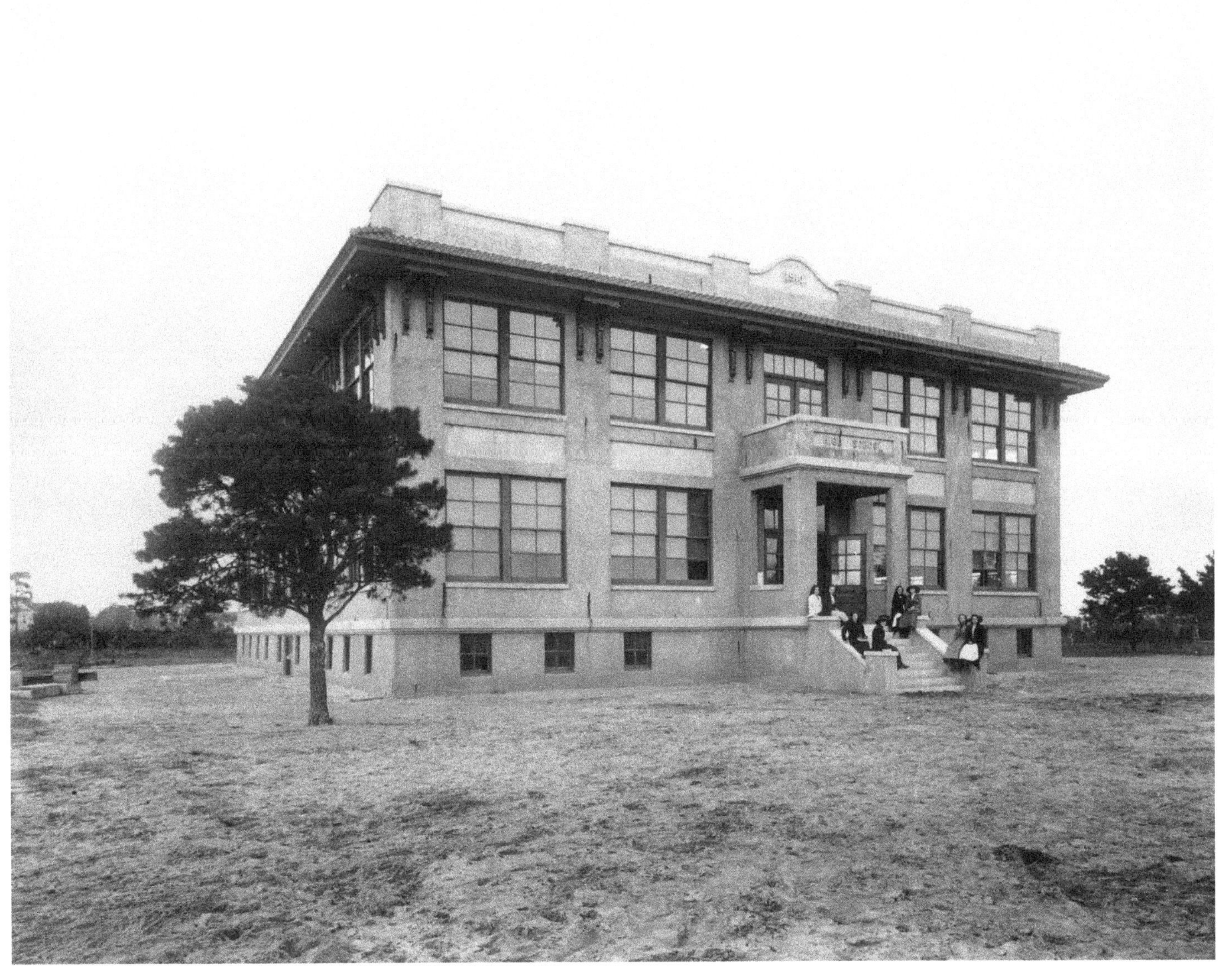

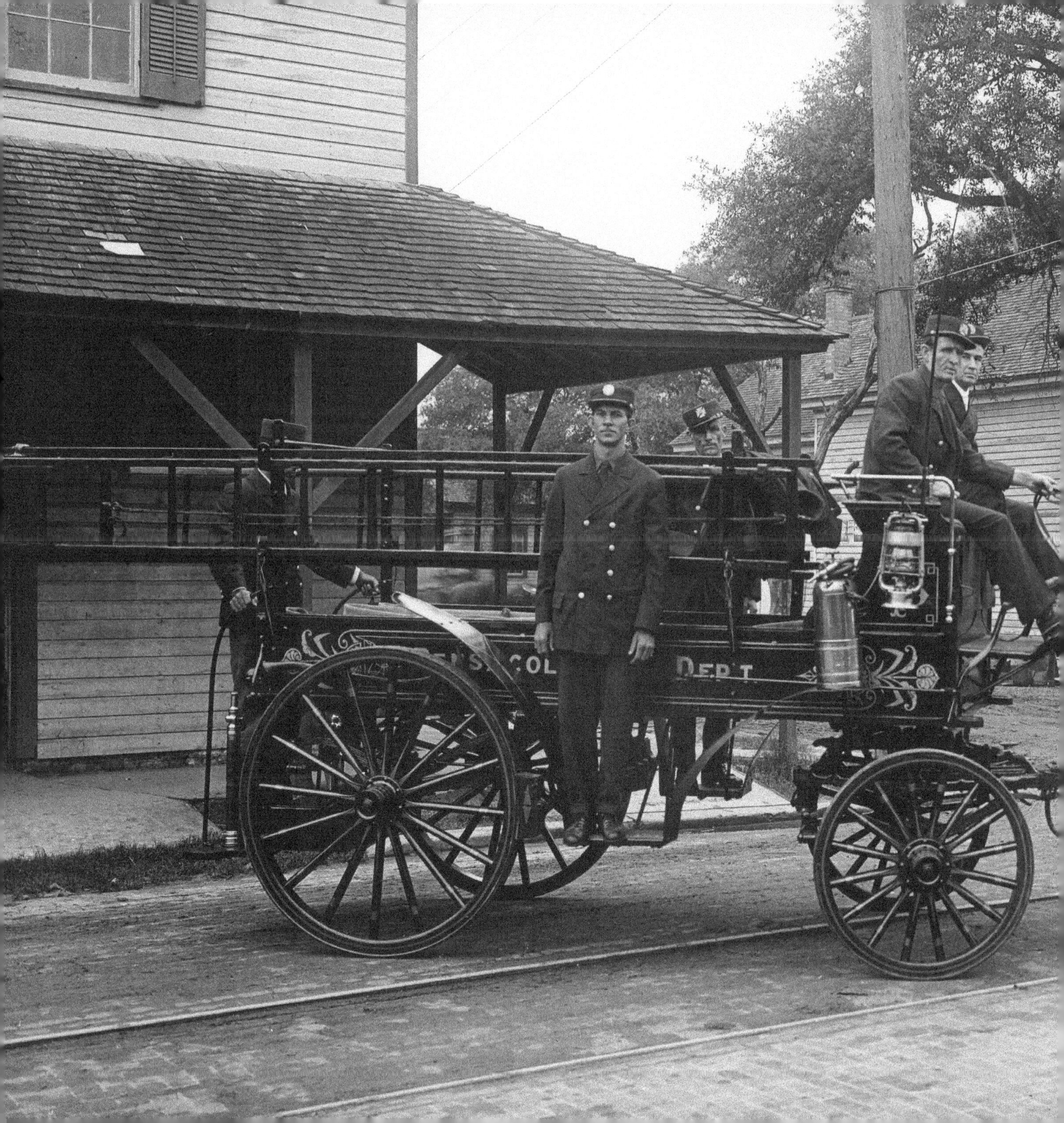
COL
DEPT.

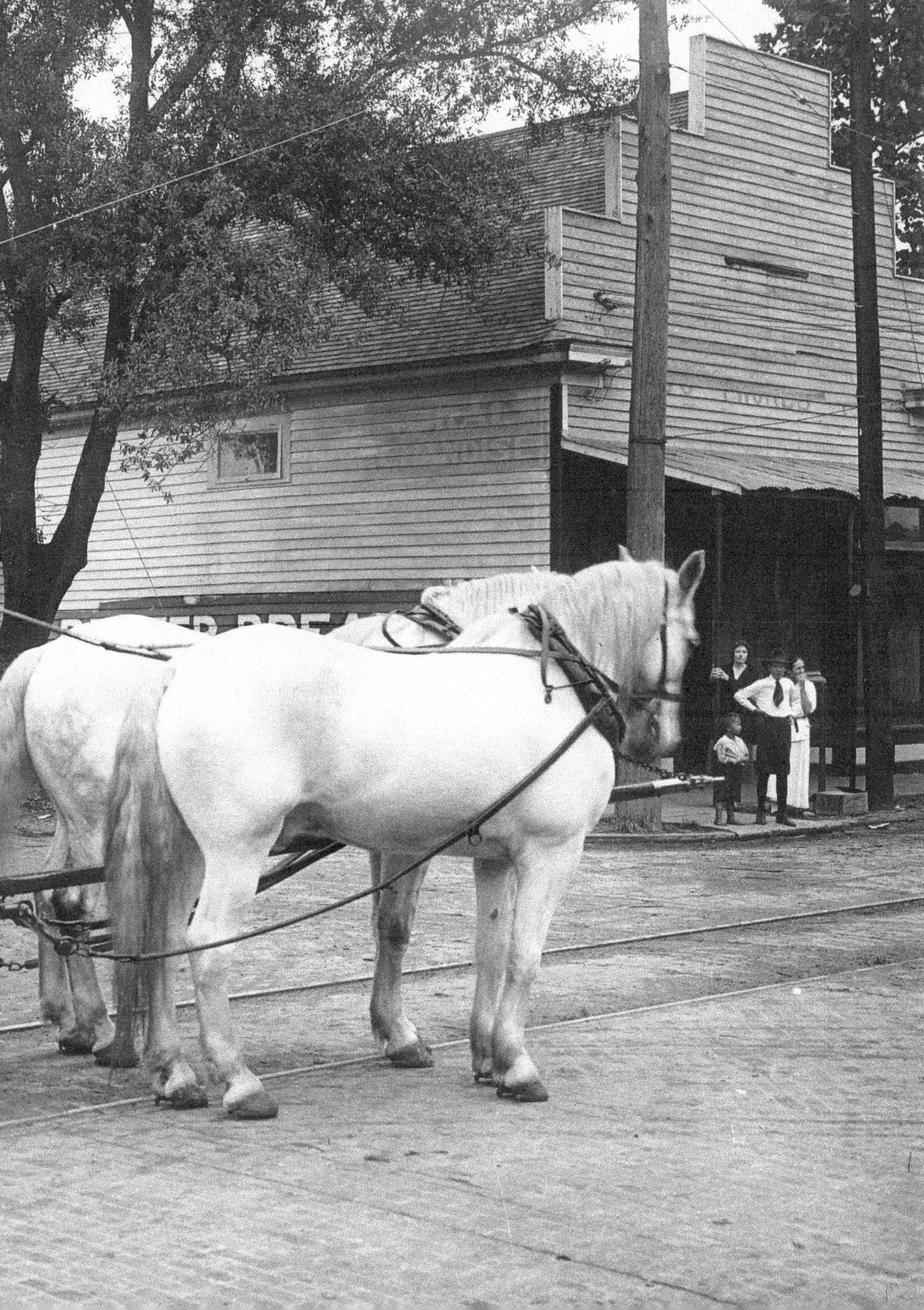

Members of Fire Company Number 4, at 519 North DeVilliers Street, pose with their horse-drawn hose wagon. The store in the background is a grocery owned by James E. Williams, who was also the county treasurer.

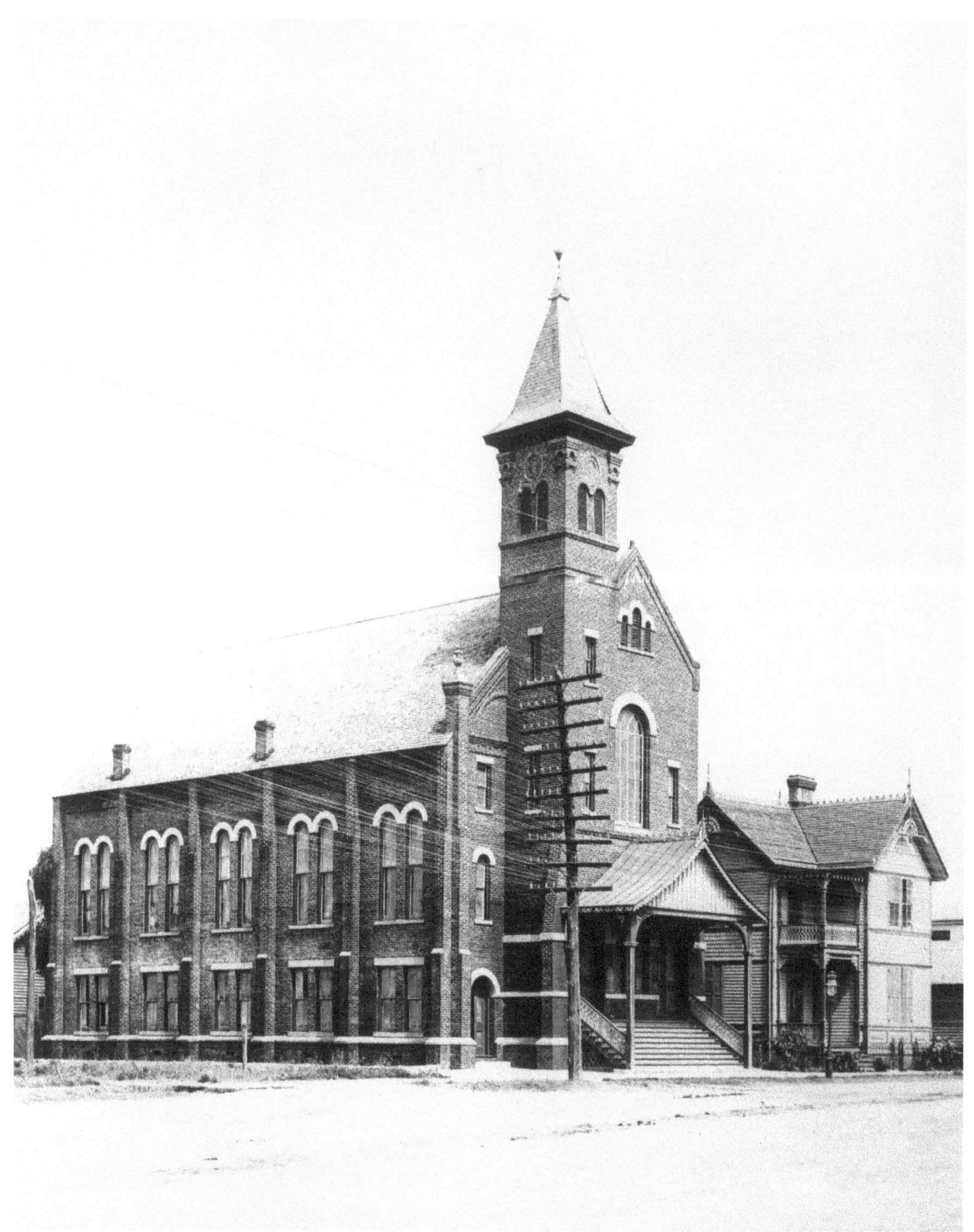

The Methodist Episcopal Church was at the corner of North Palafox and West Garden streets. The church relocated to Wright Street and is now the First United Methodist Church. The North Palafox site became the home of the Hotel San Carlos and now holds the Federal Courthouse.

At ten stories, the American National Bank Building was Pensacola's first skyscraper when it opened in 1910. The U.S. Weather Bureau occupied the top floor. Horse-drawn carriages were still plentiful downtown even after electric trolley service began.

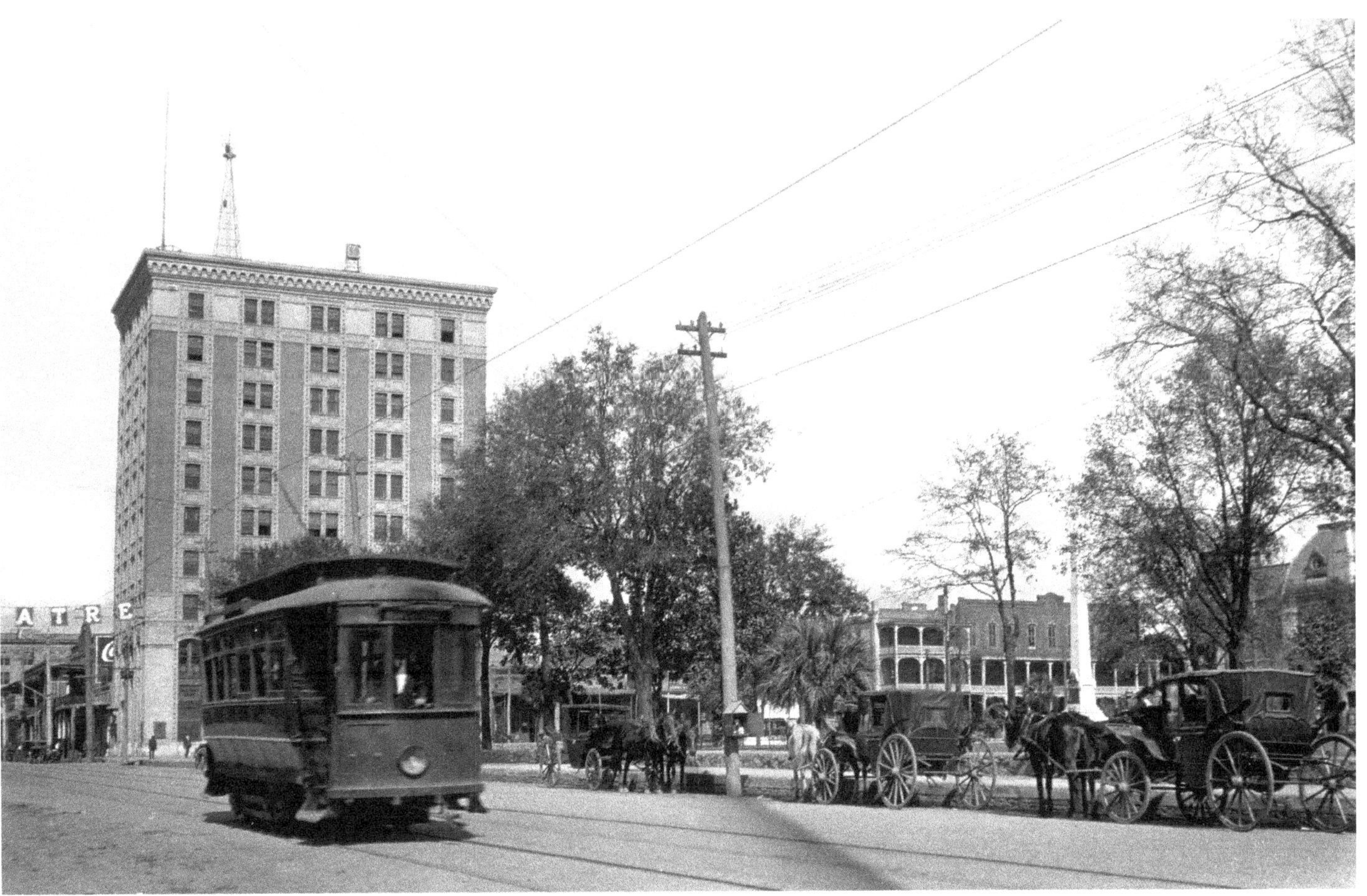

An unidentified man crosses South Palafox in front of the building occupied by Otto Wicke, a tinner specializing in roofing and ship work.

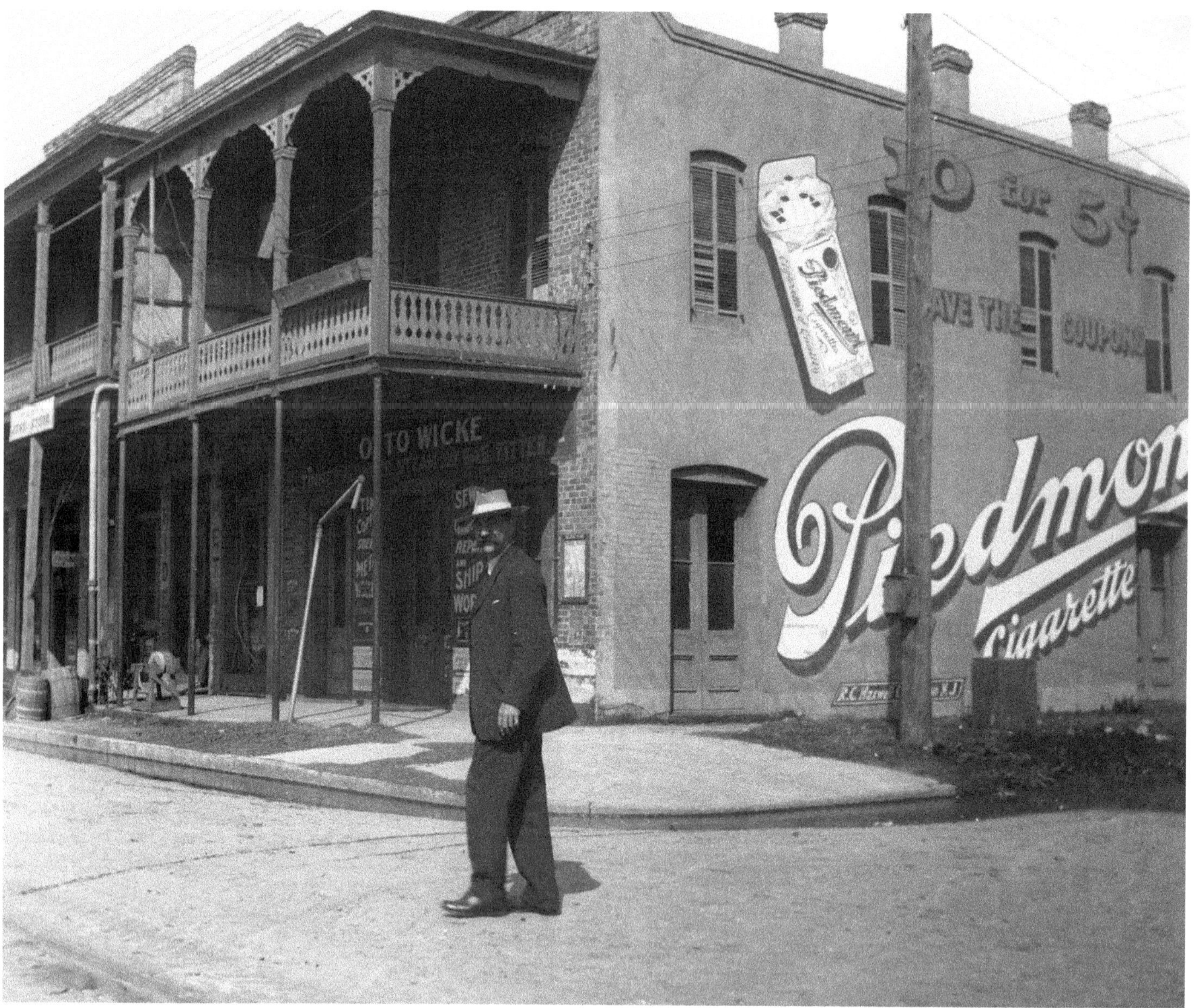

Pensacola threw a big parade for the battle cruiser *Florida* when it came into port in 1911. The Hotel San Carlos dressed for the occasion and Governor Albert W. Gilchrist delivered gifts for the ship, including a silver service from the state and presents from patriotic groups and civic organizations.

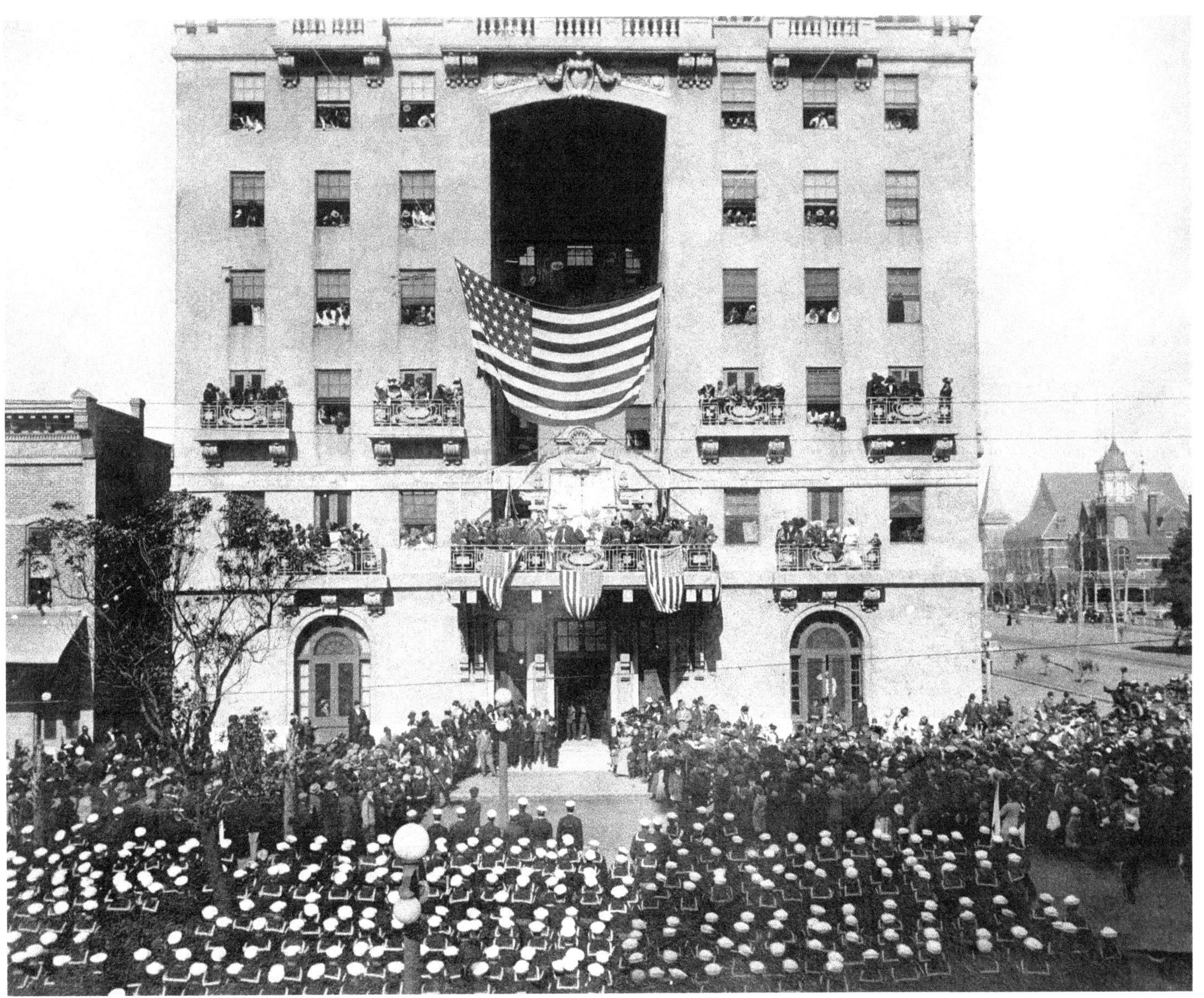

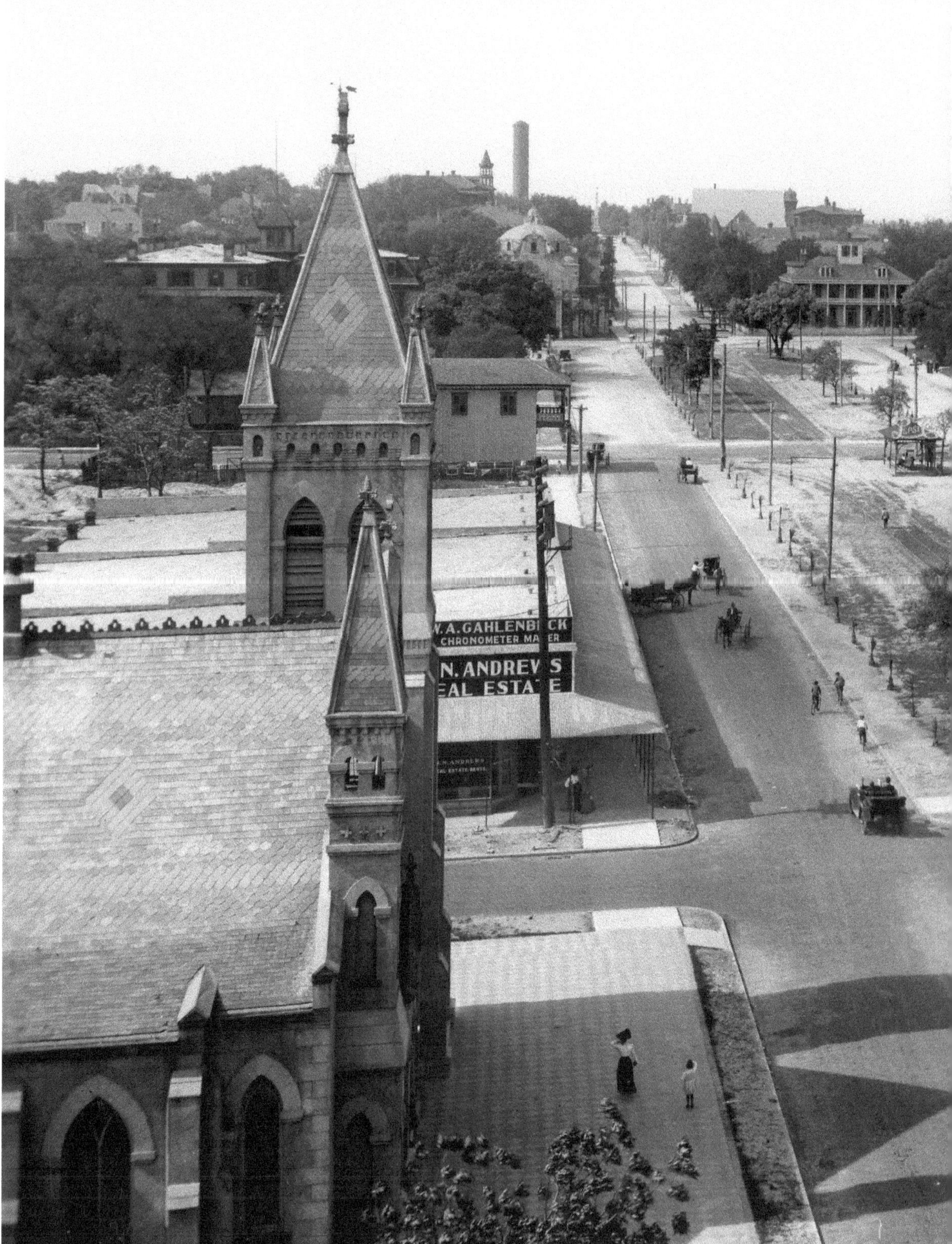

In 1911, Dr. Henry G. Williams, an African American, had an office at the southwest corner of North Palafox and Gregory streets. Mrs. Zarah Mann lived in the building, now known as the Scottish Rite, shown here at center in the background. The water tower still stood on North Hill.

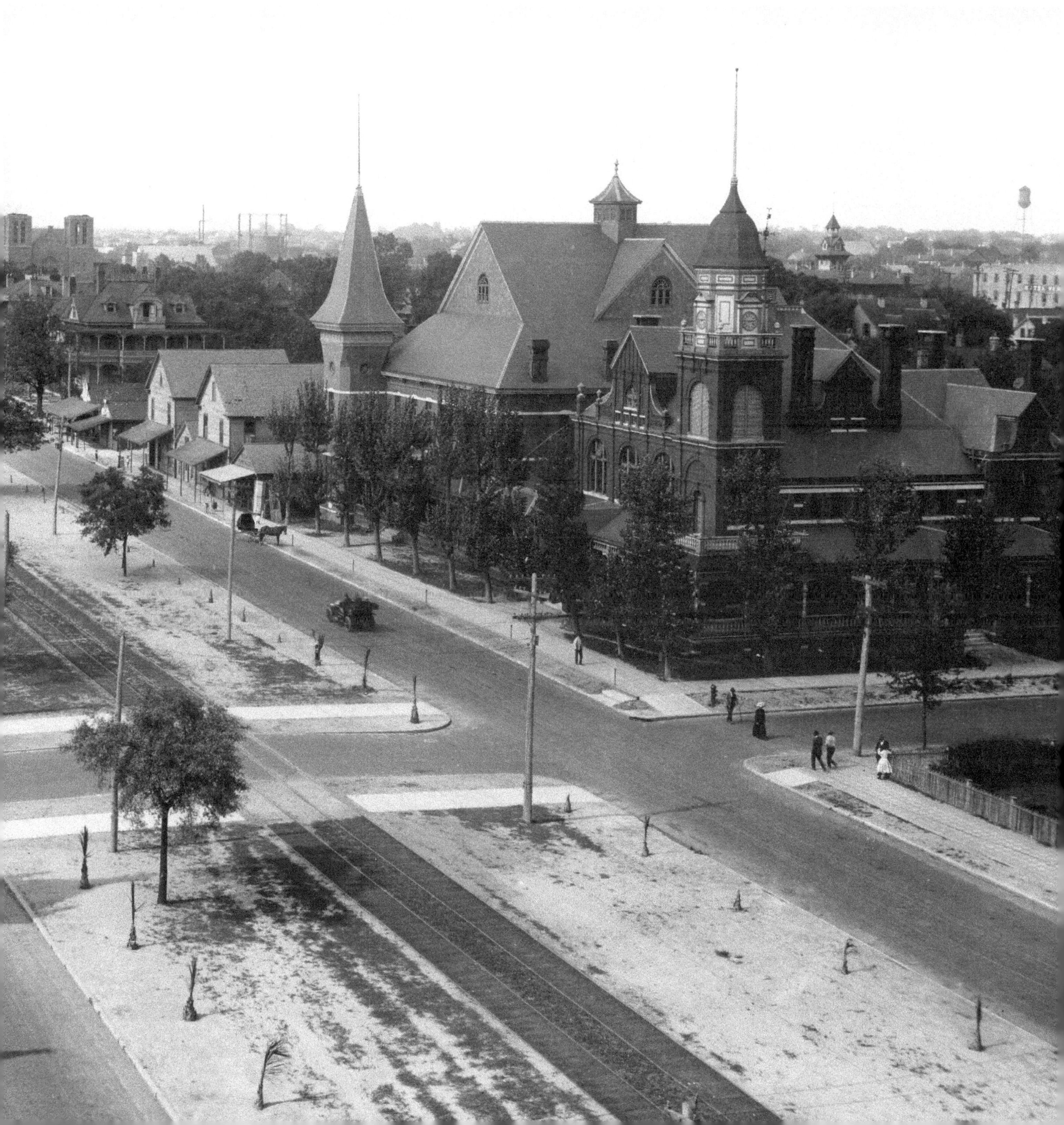

Viewers crowded sidewalks and the median to watch the parade for the battle cruiser *Florida*. The parade stretched for many blocks down North Palafox Street.

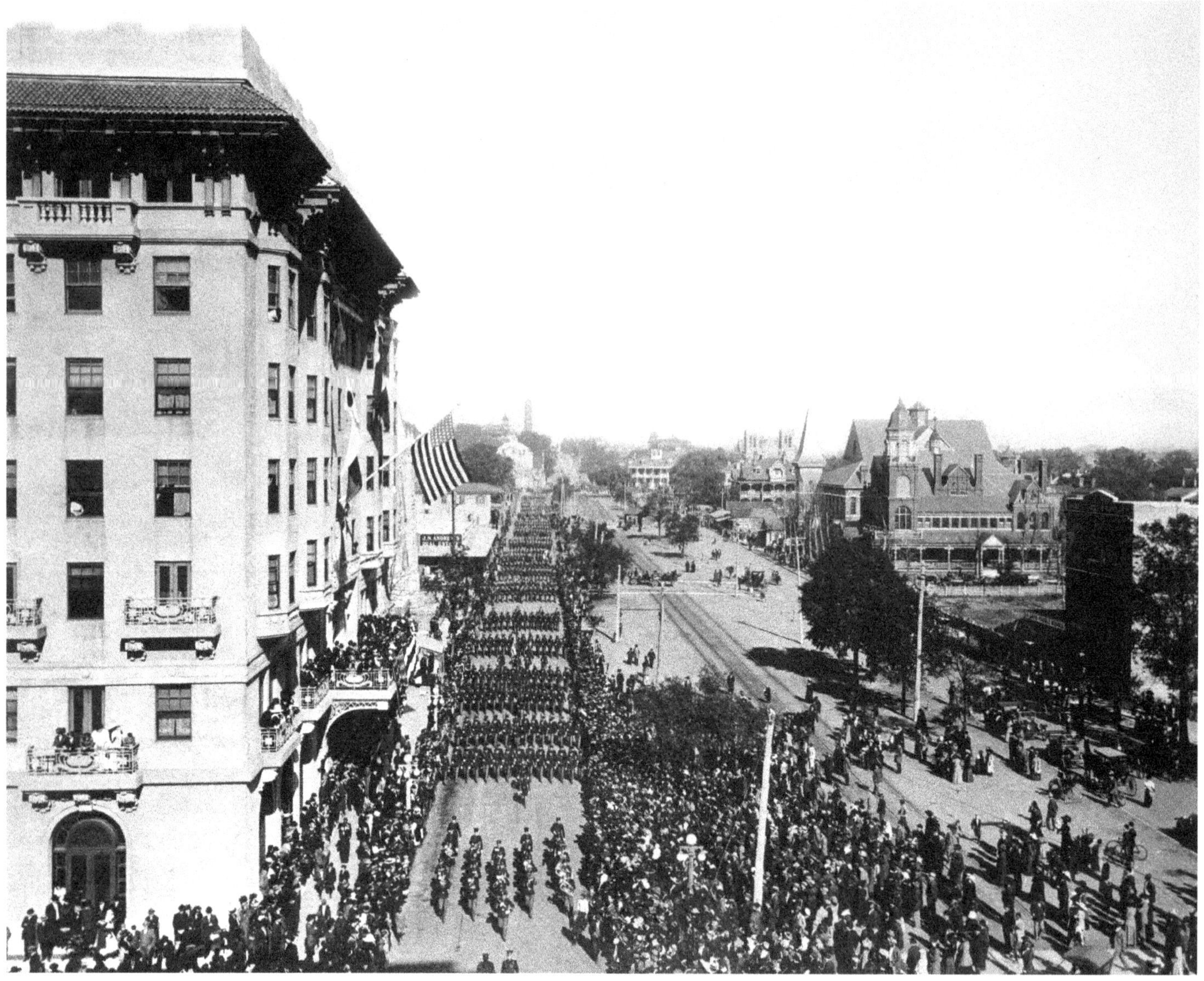

The first airplanes purchased by the Navy were Glenn Curtiss A1 Triads. "Triad" stood for land, air, and water—the planes were amphibian seaplanes.

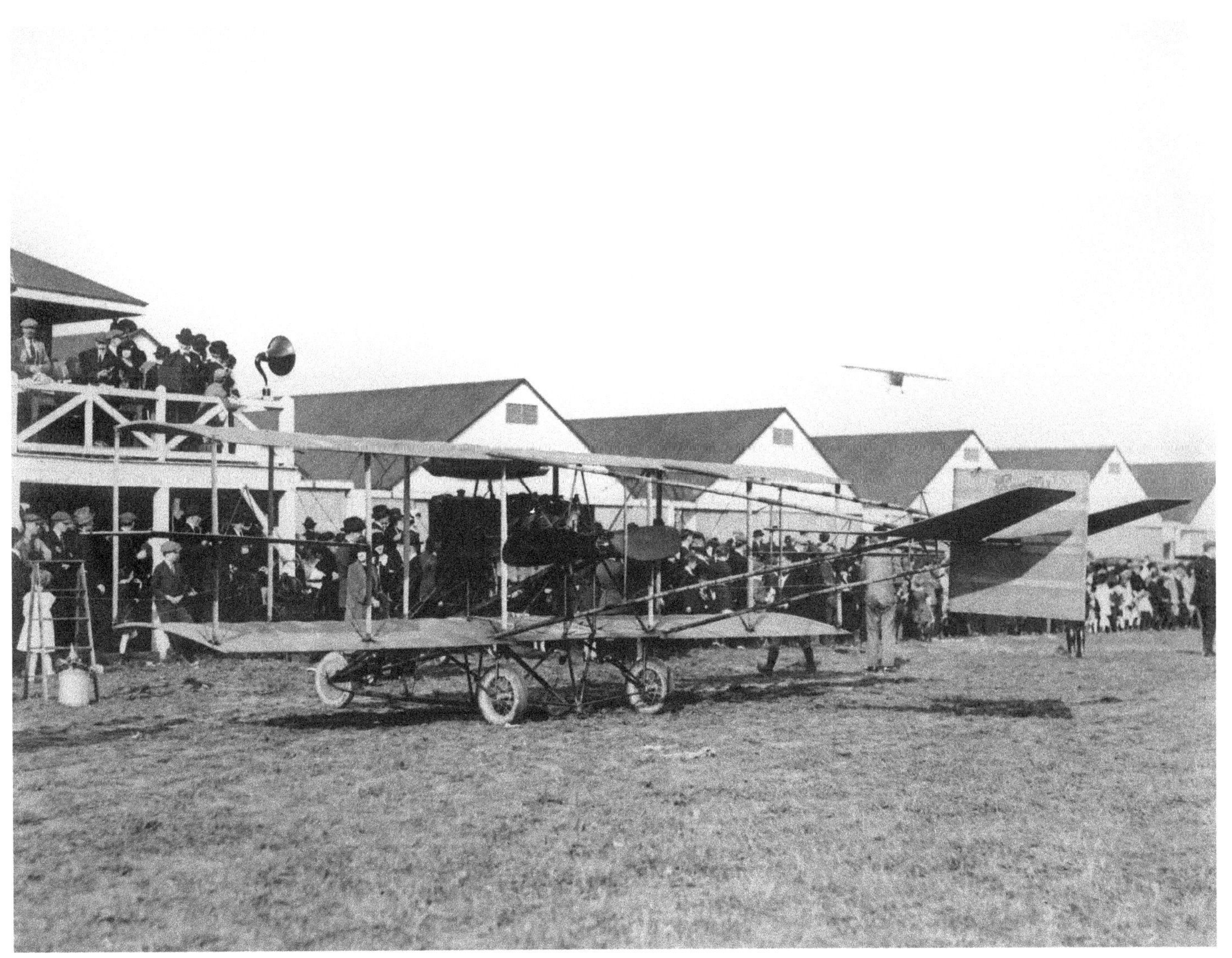

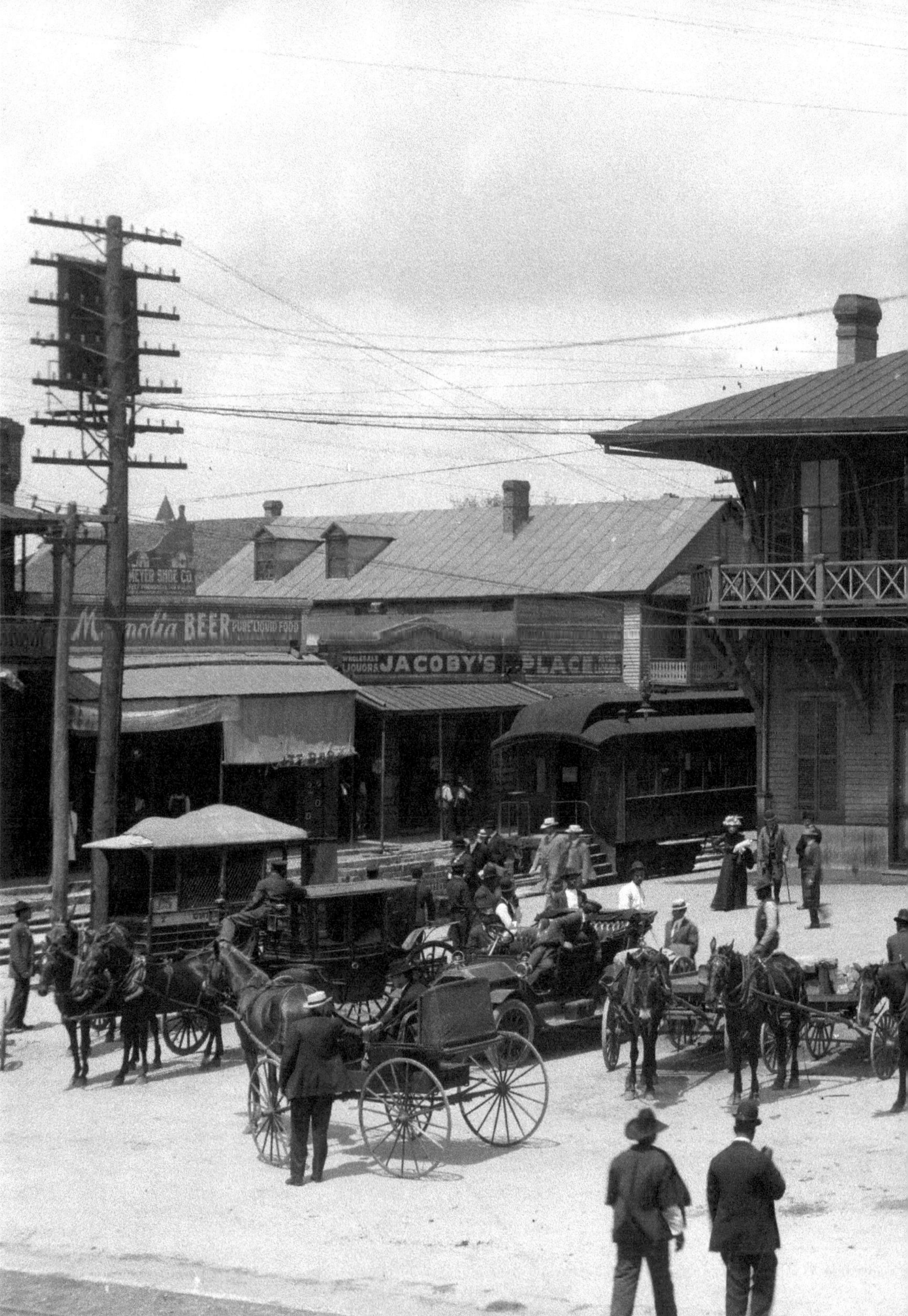

This L&N depot was located at the northeast corner of Wright and Tarragona streets. It was replaced in 1913 with a new depot at the corner of Alcaniz and Wright streets.

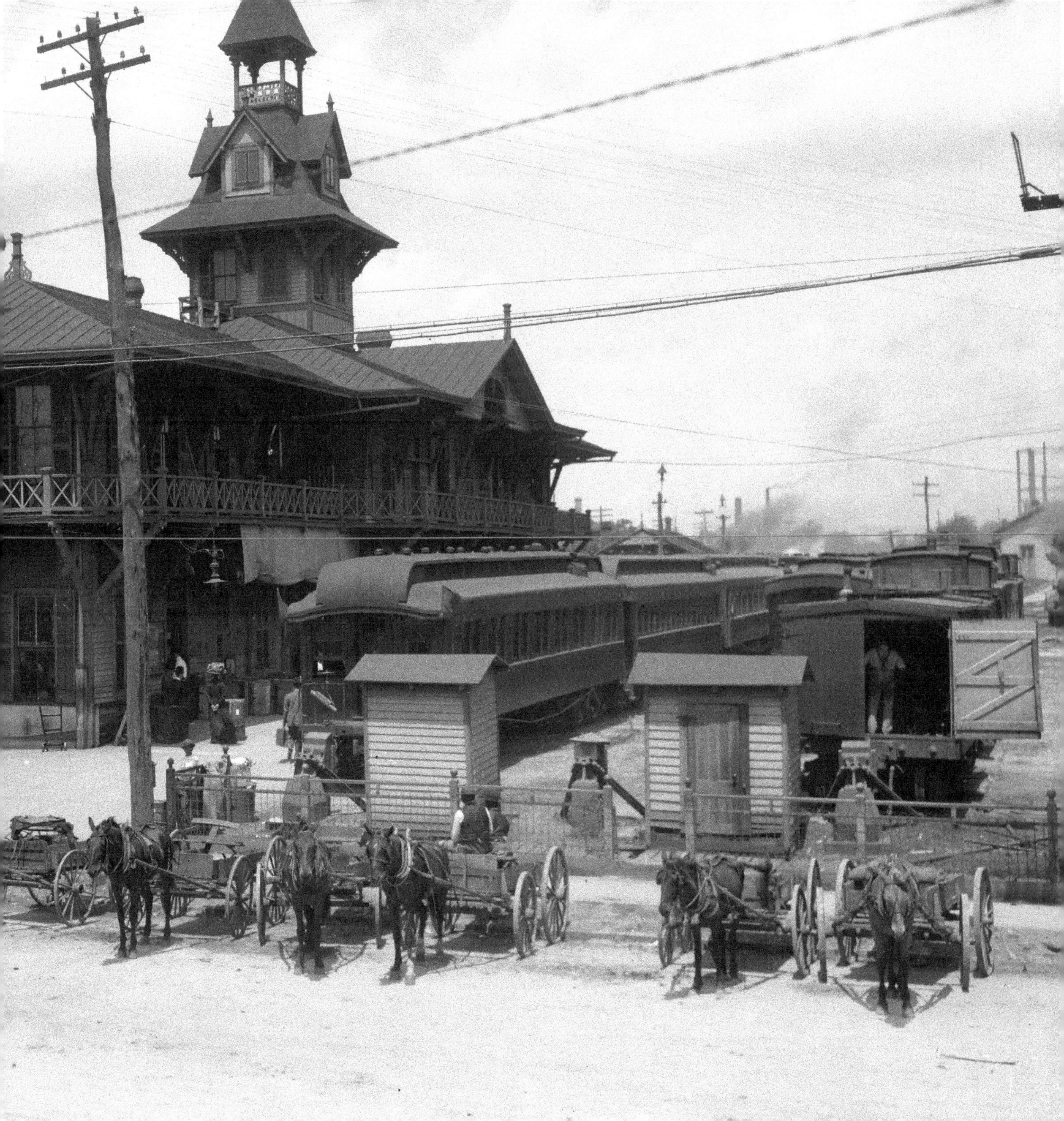

This Escambia County Courthouse, built in 1885 at North Palafox and Chase streets, was in use until the county offices moved to the old Customs House at South Palafox and Government streets in 1939. The old Courthouse was demolished, but the clock in the tower, rescued by the Pensacola Historical Society, is now at the corner of South Palafox and Government streets.

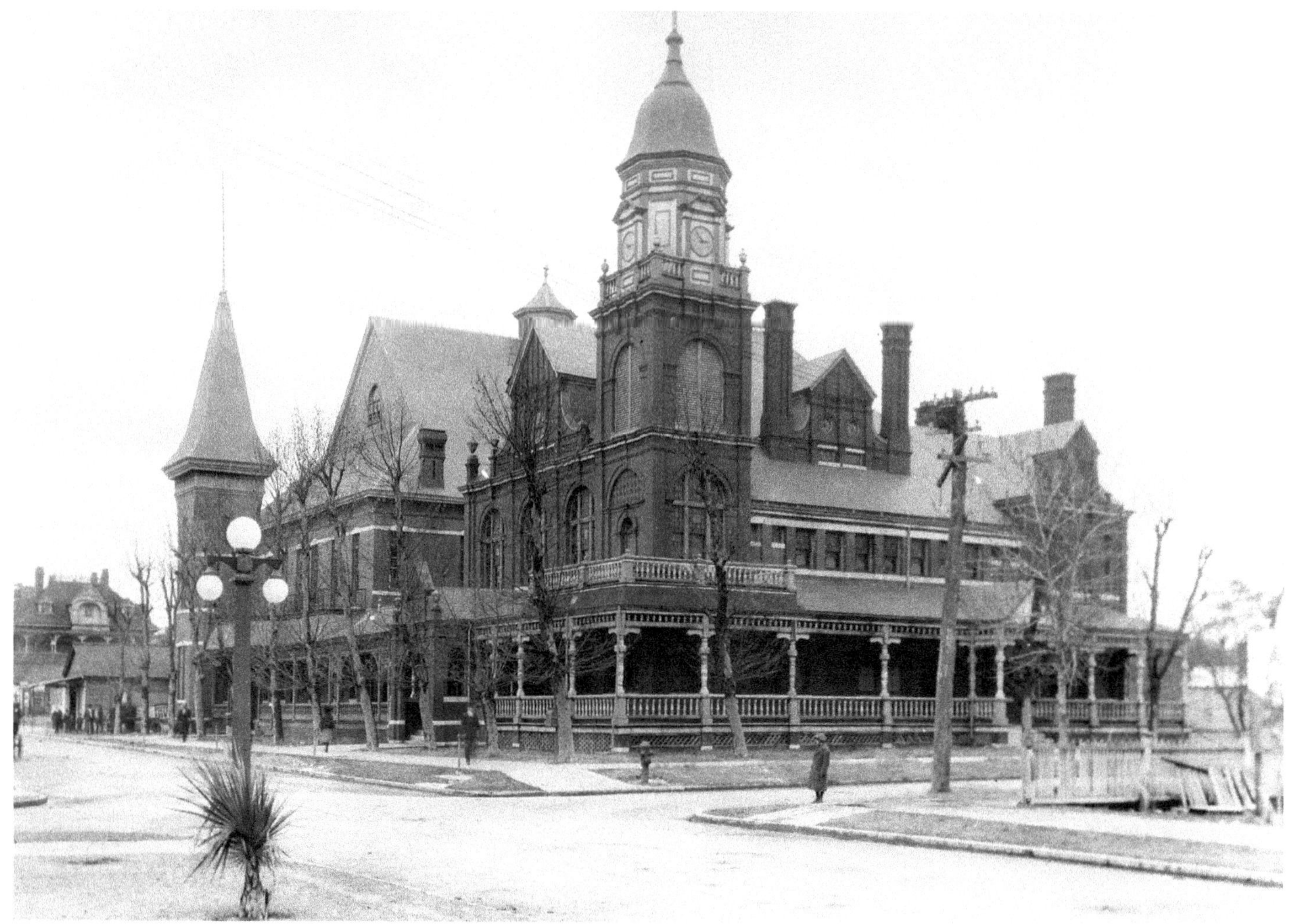

Dr. Louis Blocker donated this fountain, which stood at the intersection of Garden and Palafox streets. The Blount Building and the Hotel San Carlos rise in the background.

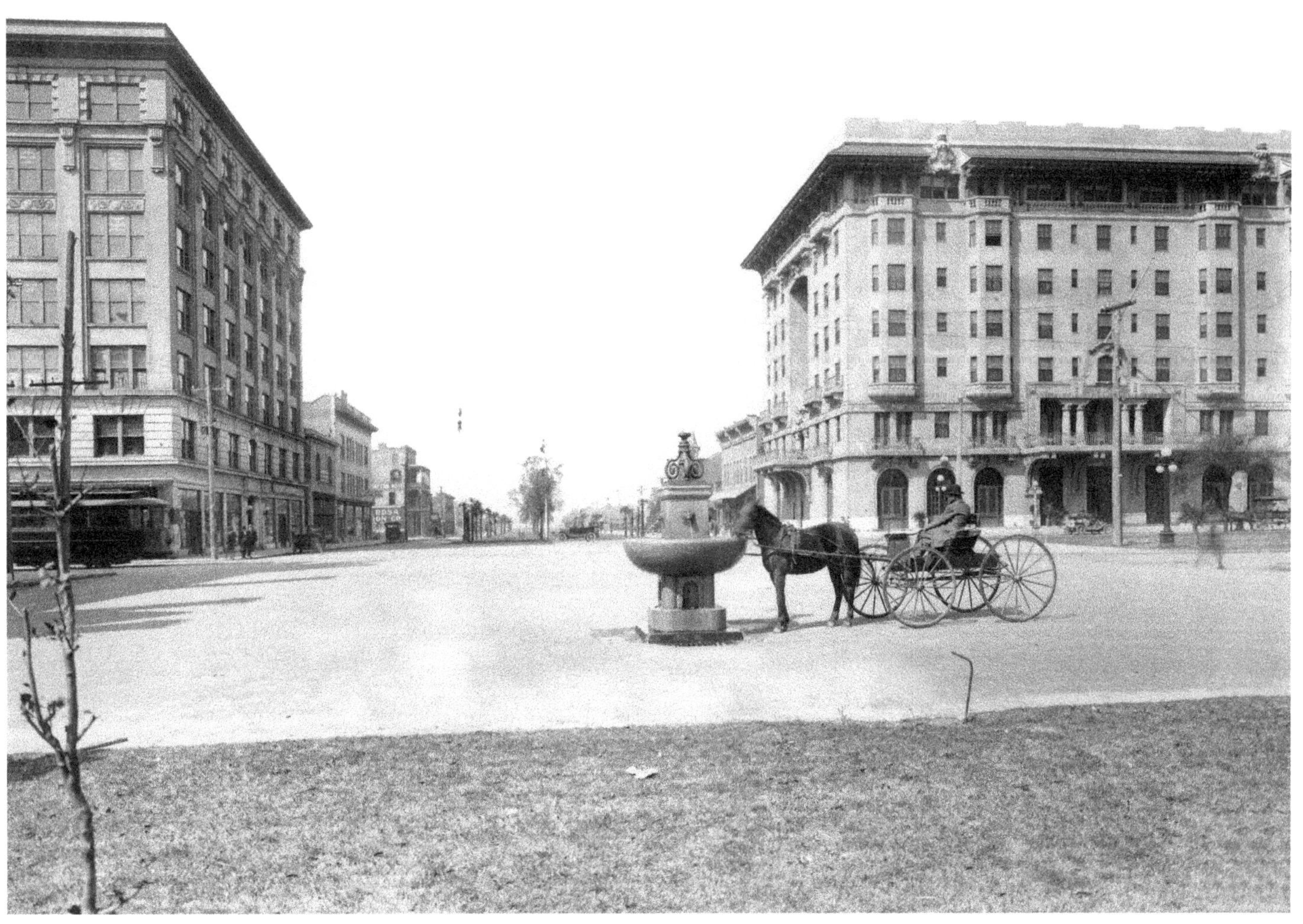

The seven-story Blount Building still stands at the intersection of Palafox and Garden streets. Erected in 1907 by Pensacola attorney William Alexander Blount, the building cost $200,000. This building replaced one that burned on Halloween 1905.

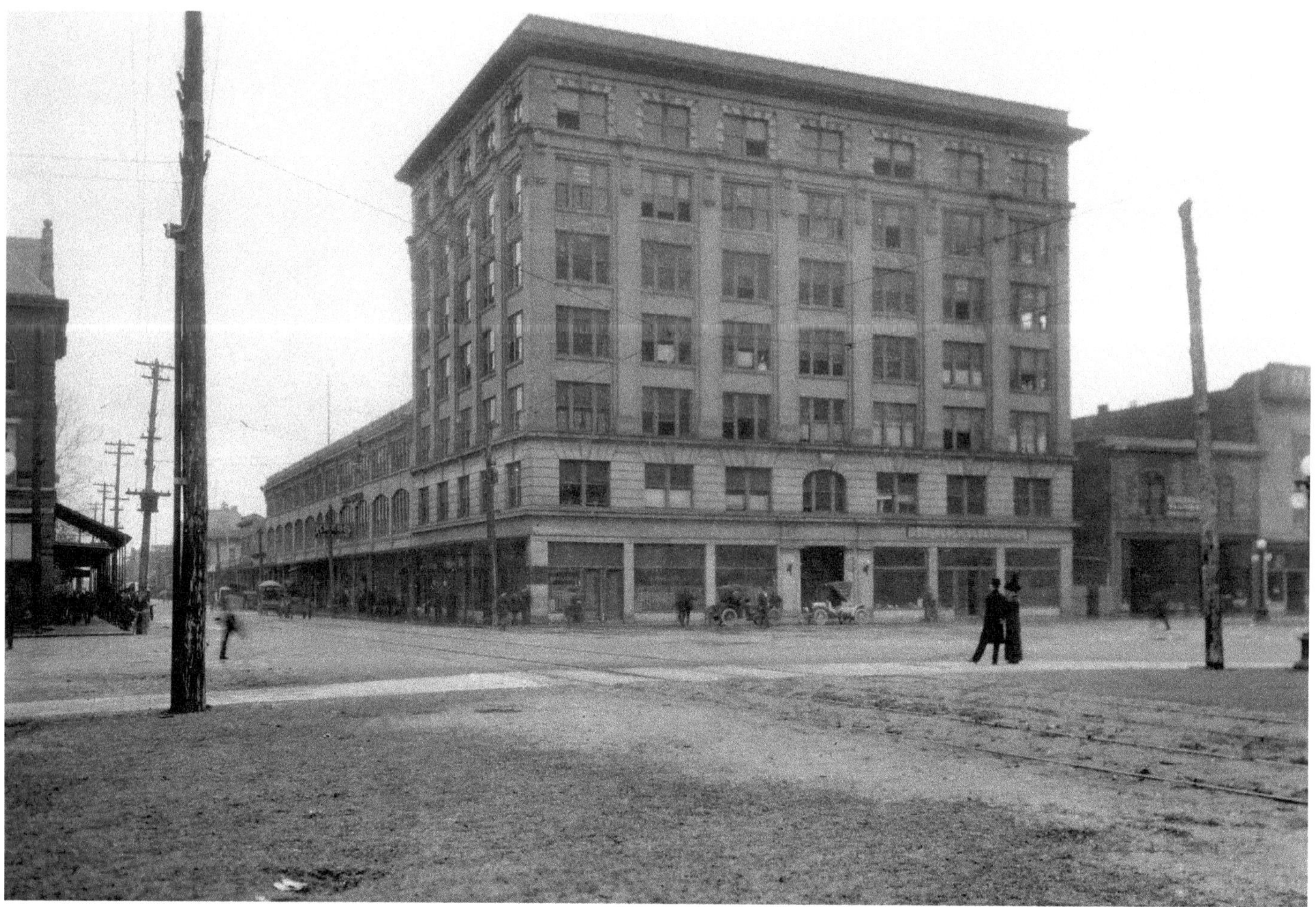

The Pensacola Opera House stood at the corner of Jefferson and Government streets from 1883 until 1917, when it was destroyed by a hurricane. The Opera House hosted some of the most famous artists of the time: Sousa's Band, Sarah Bernhardt, Lillian Russell, Grace George, John Drew, and Billie Burke were a few of the featured performers. The original brick-and-iron balcony rail is now installed in the Saenger Theater.

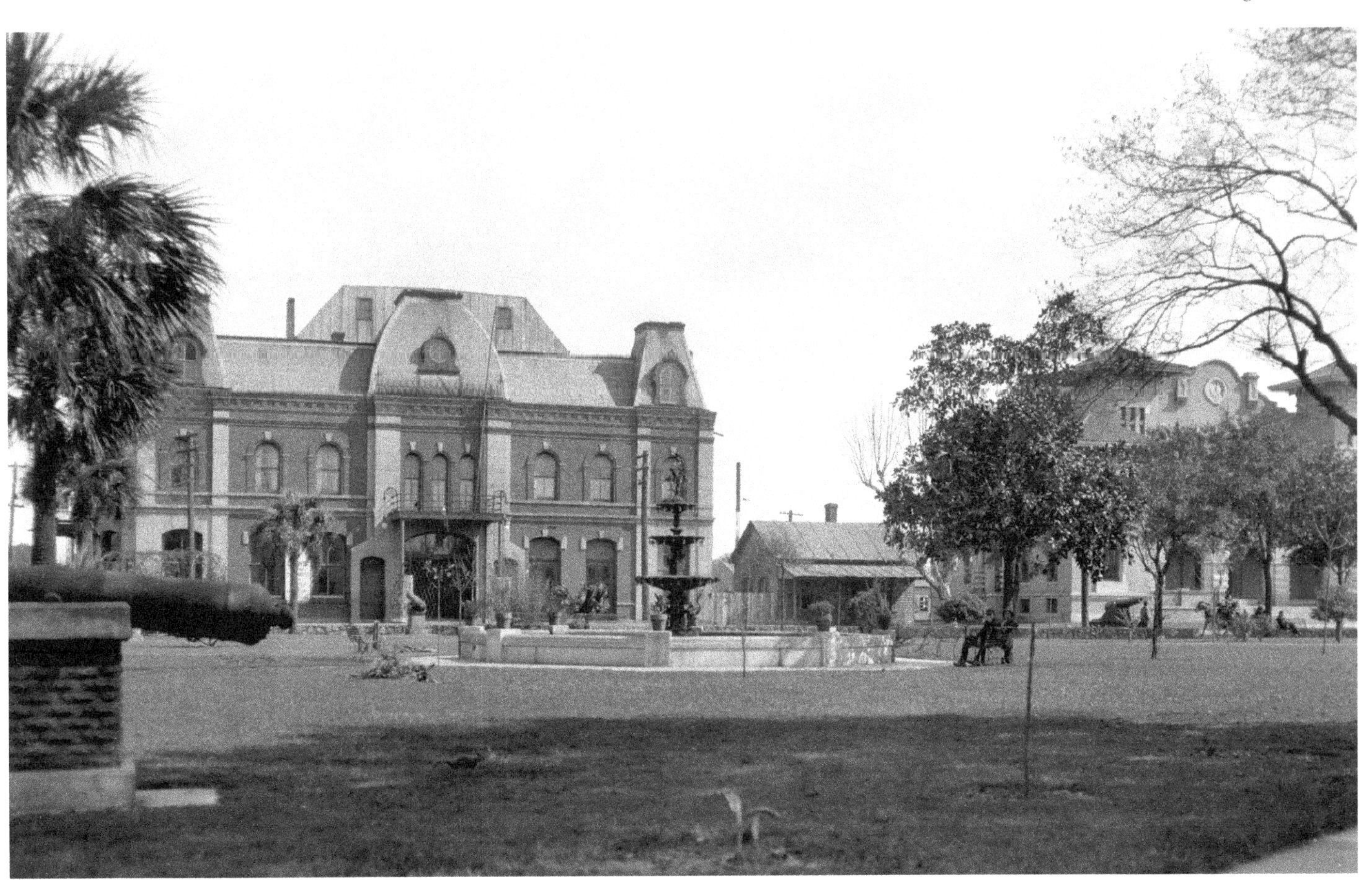

J. P. Sandusky was president of the Star Laundry Company, located at 37 East Garden Street. In 1912, the delivery wagon still had to negotiate many miles of unpaved streets.

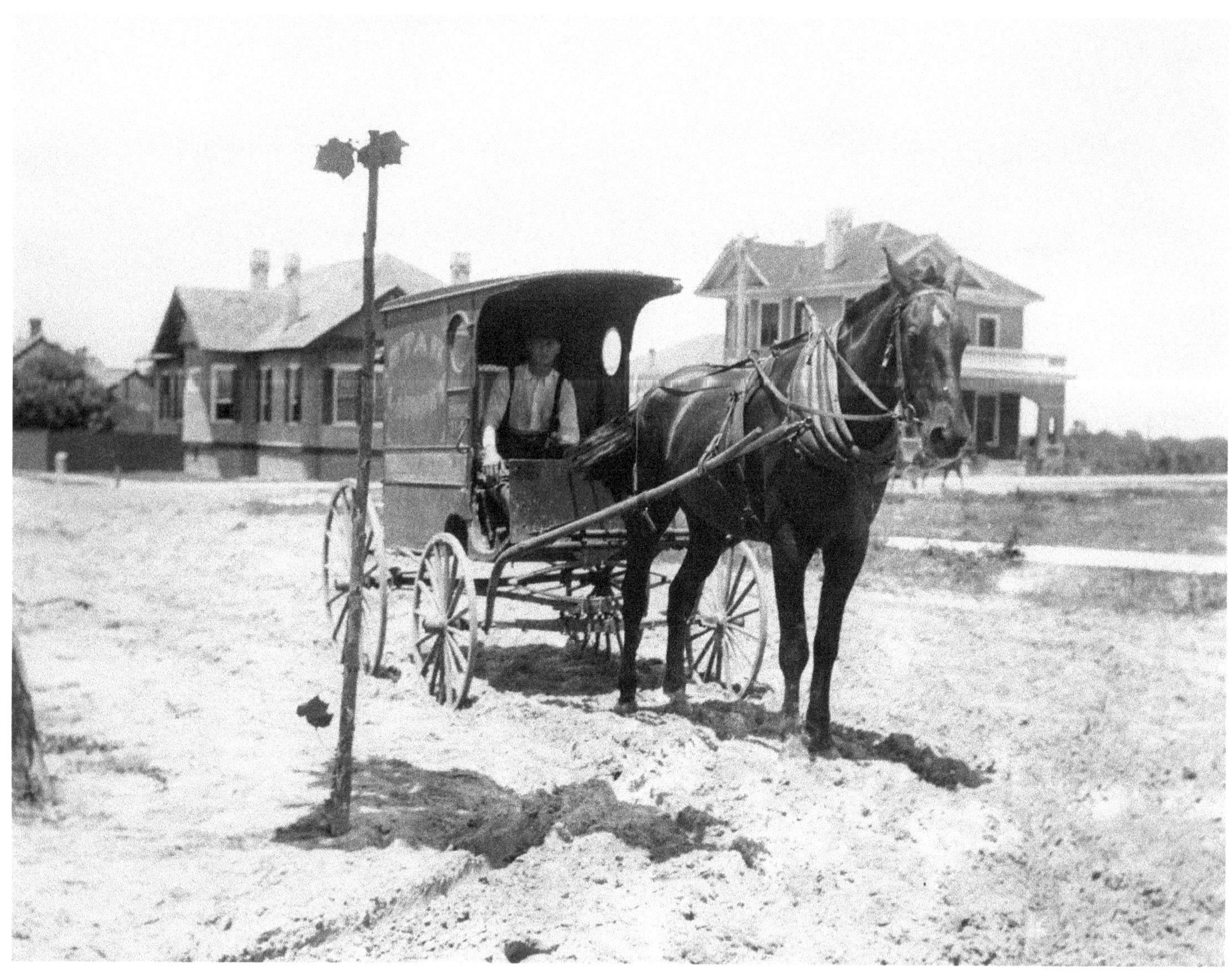

Ten-year-old Richard Bingham (right), son of Frasier F. and Fannie A. Oerting Bingham, travels on public transportation in 1912.

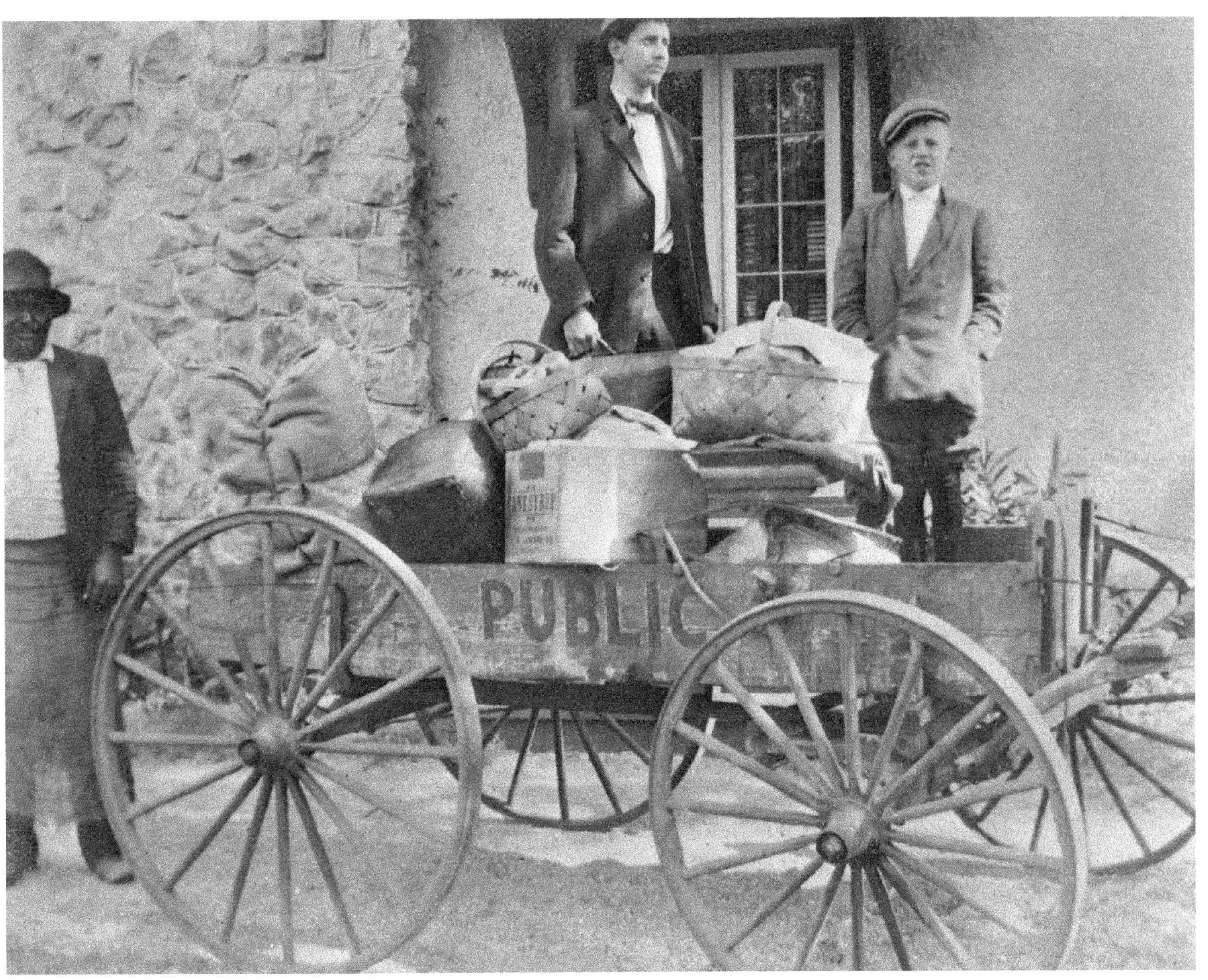

By 1912, Pensacola could boast 25 miles of paved streets and streetcar tracks, and the city had installed electric streetlights. The opening into the interior courtyard of the Hotel San Carlos is visible on the right.

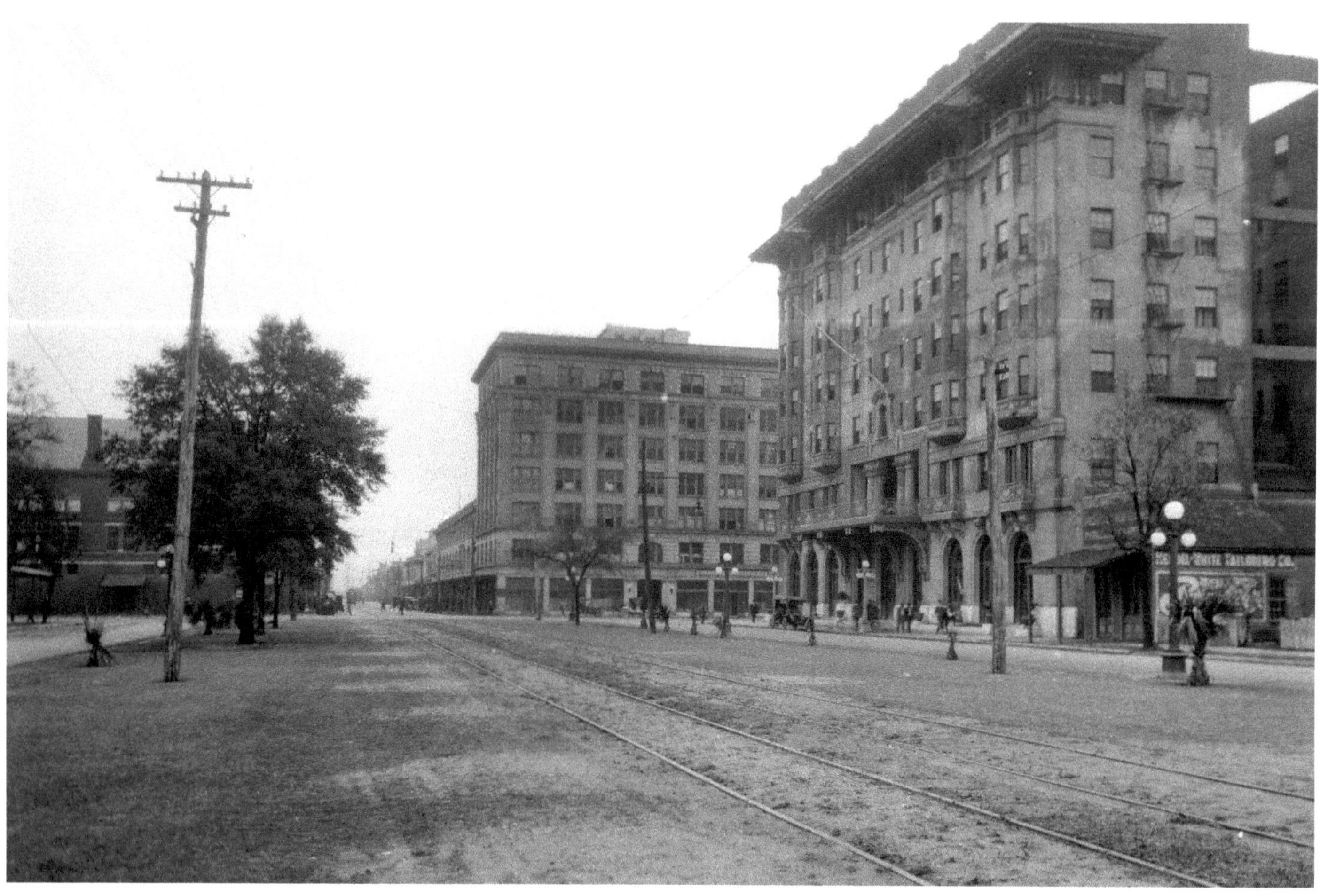

Though still under construction, the new Gulf, Florida, and Alabama Railway pier was put into service on January 1, 1913. The railroad was extended into Pensacola to transport timber harvested in Alabama to the deep-water harbor for shipping.

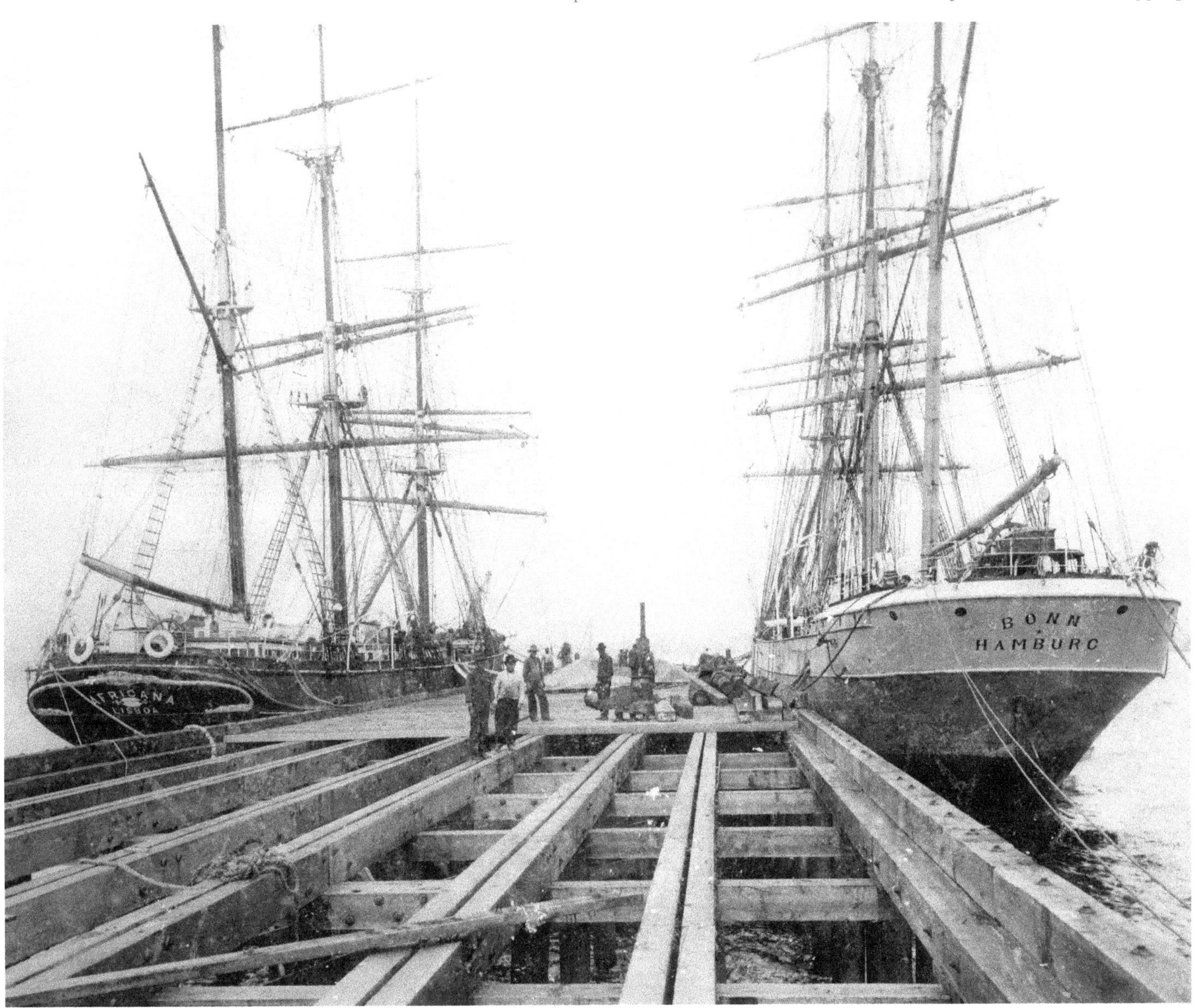

Organized in 1908, the Pensacola Yacht Club had several homes before moving into their permanent location on Cypress Street. In 1913, the club was located on the second floor of the Fisher Building at the corner of Main and Alcaniz streets.

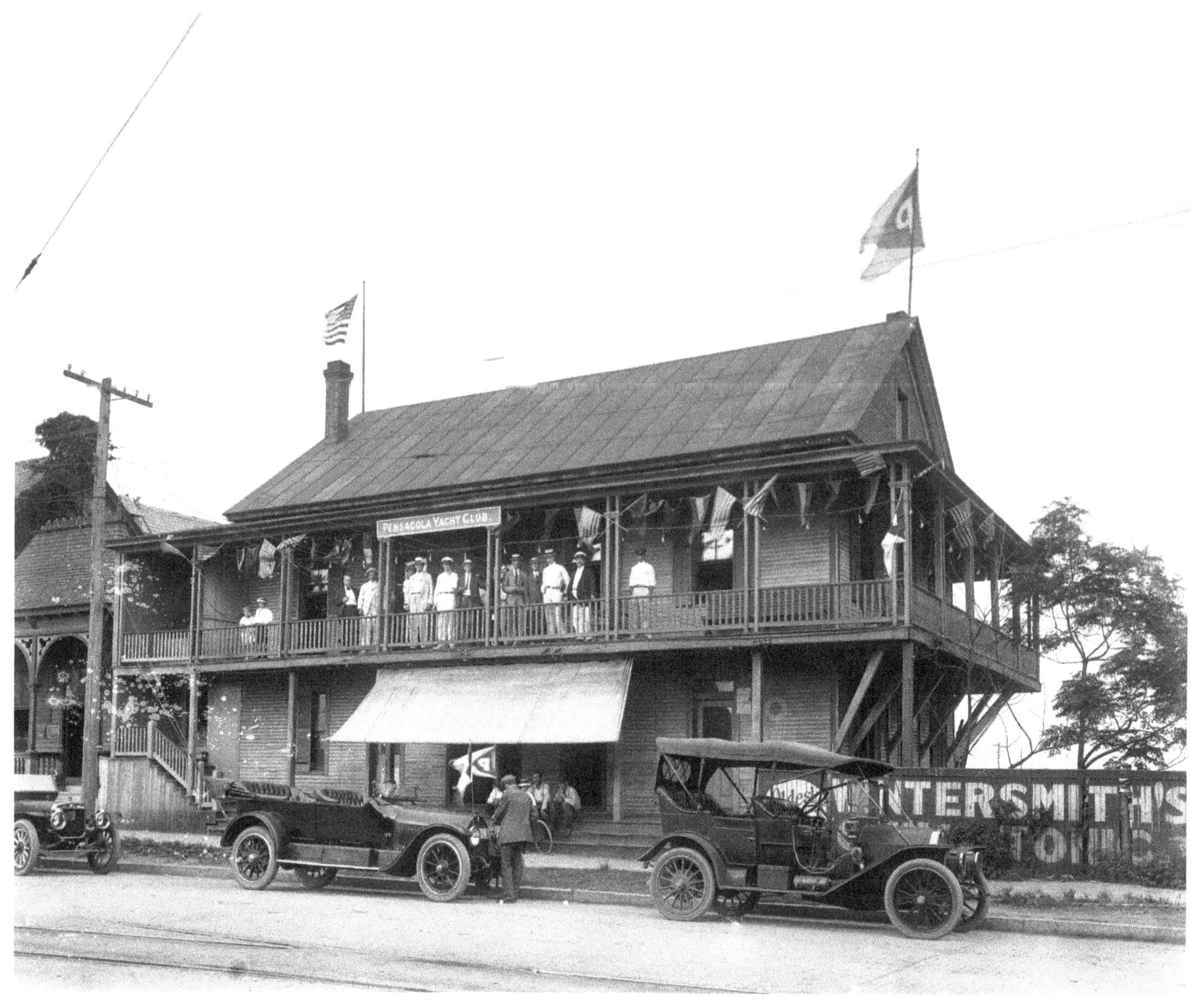

The National Bank of Commerce was located at the northeast corner of South Palafox and East Romana streets in the Thiesen Building.

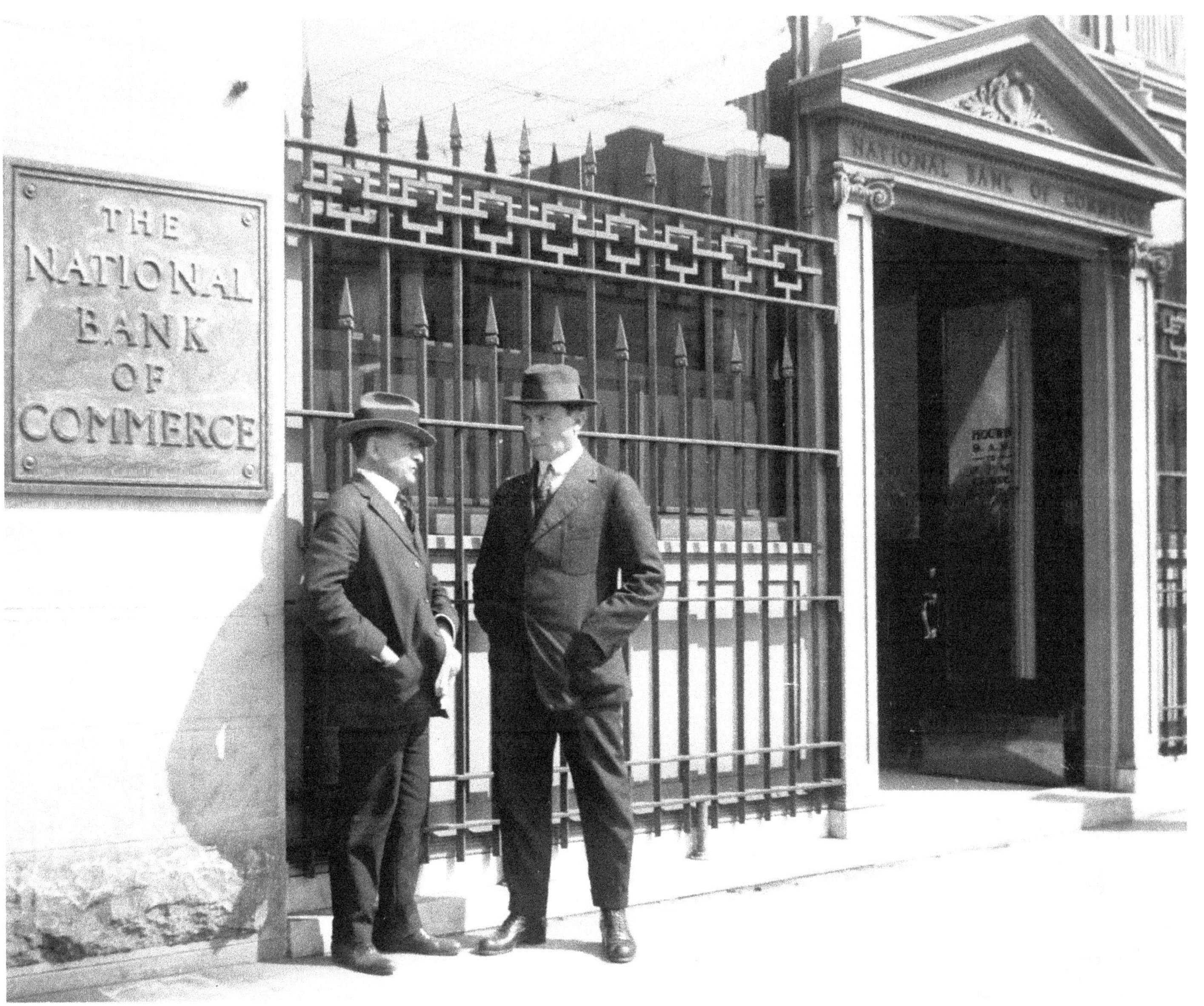

This rail-mounted gun was in Pensacola during World War I.

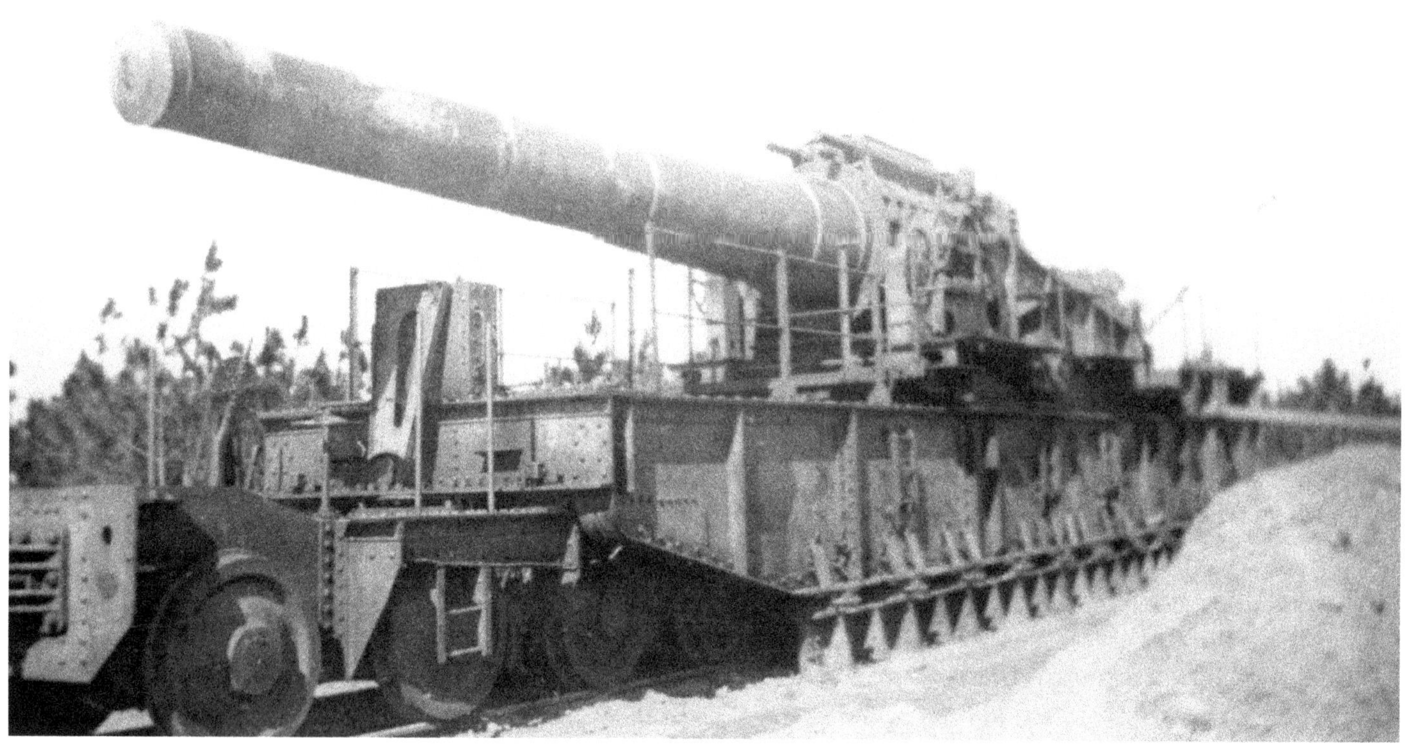

In 1915, the first Catholic hospital in Florida opened as the Pensacola Hospital in this Gothic revival building. Renamed Sacred Heart Hospital in 1948, the hospital relocated to North Ninth Avenue in 1965. The building housed the Pensacola School of Liberal Arts from 1969 to 1978, and now holds restaurants and business offices.

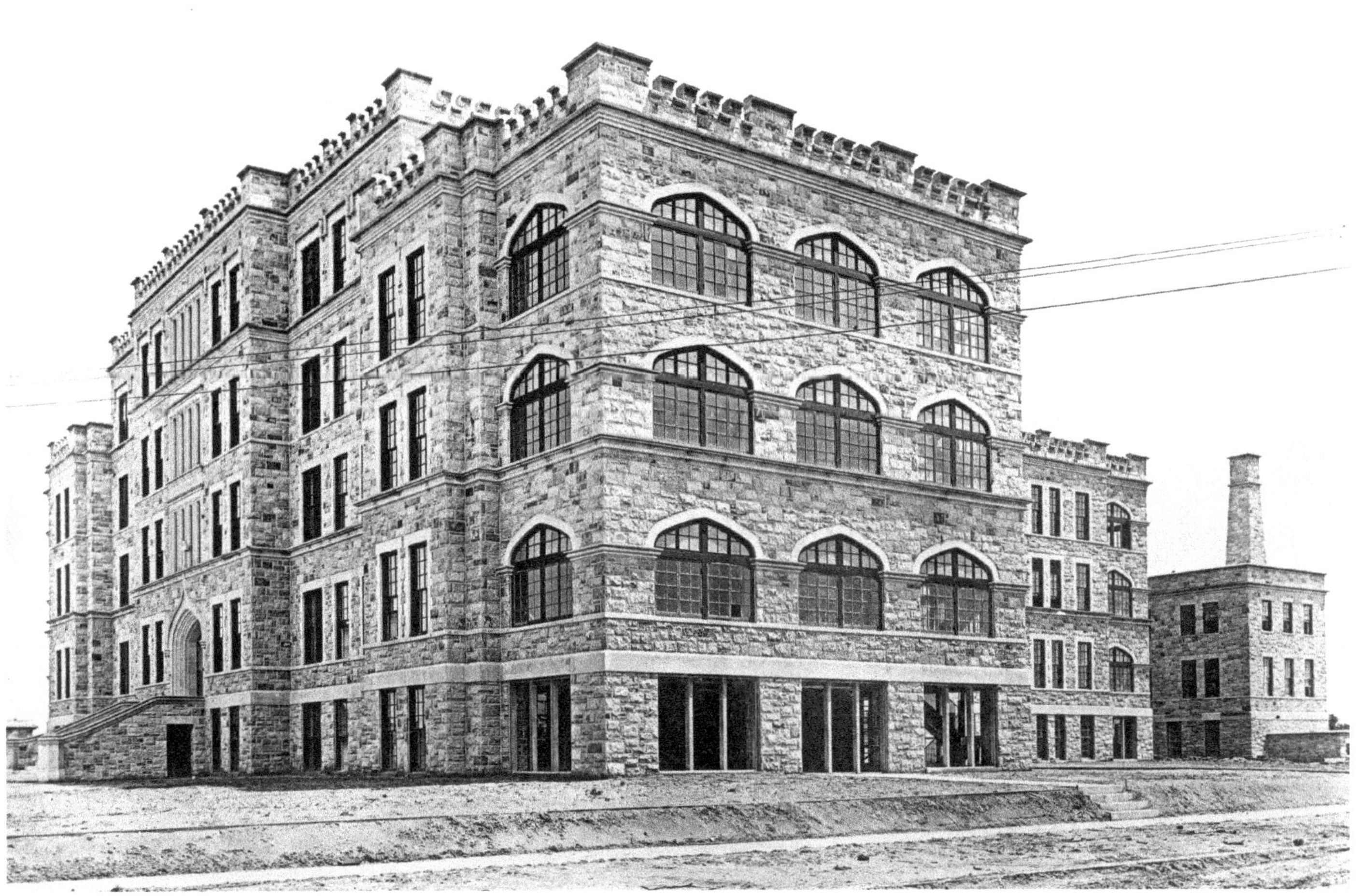

The Navy Yard was closed in 1911 but reopened as the United States Aeronautical Station, a seaplane base, in 1914 under Commander Henry C. Mustin. At that time, the new base was the only naval-pilot training facility in the nation. This Wright experimental seaplane was one of the early planes ordered for the new base.

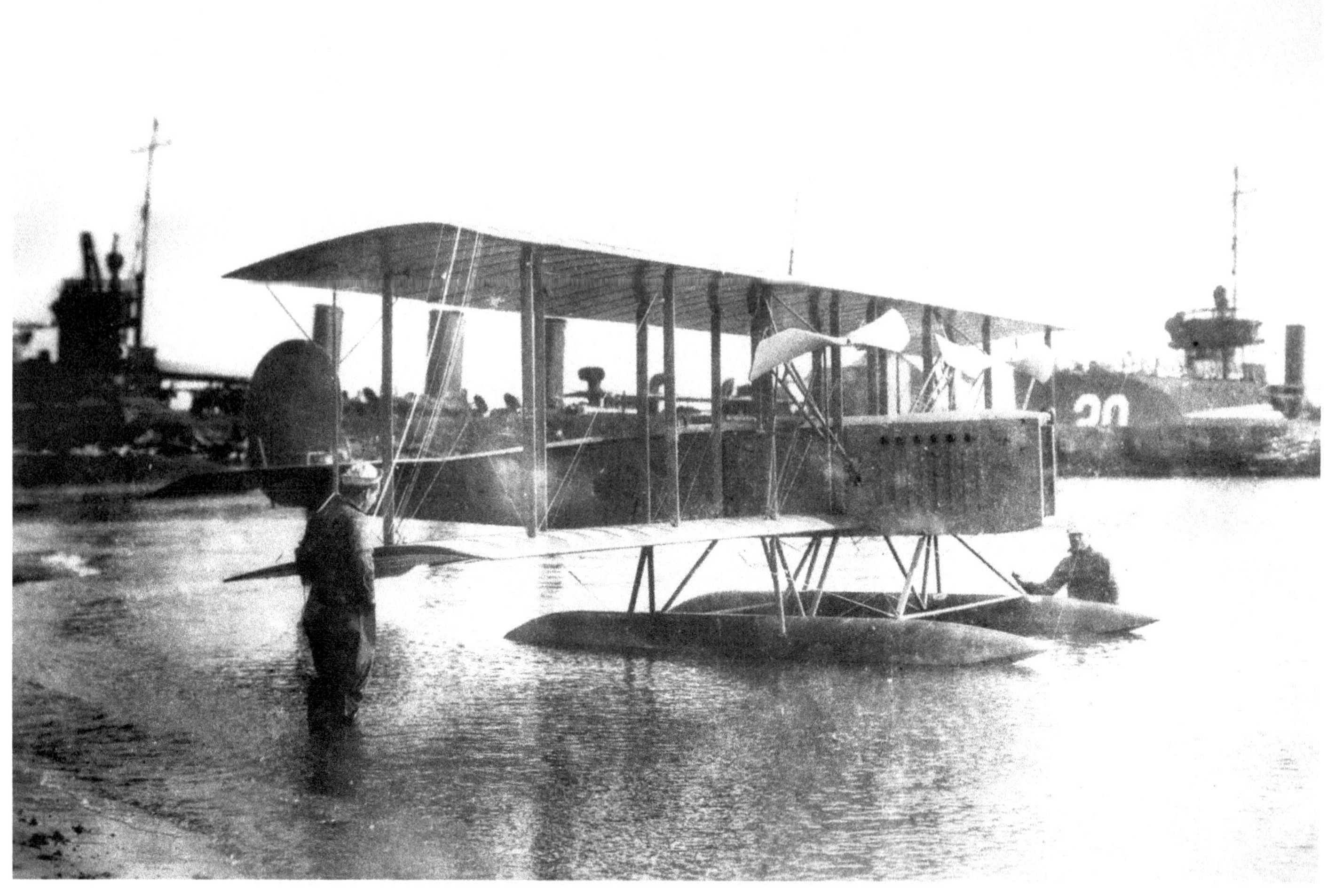

Obid Richards visited with a World War I soldier at his camp in Pensacola.

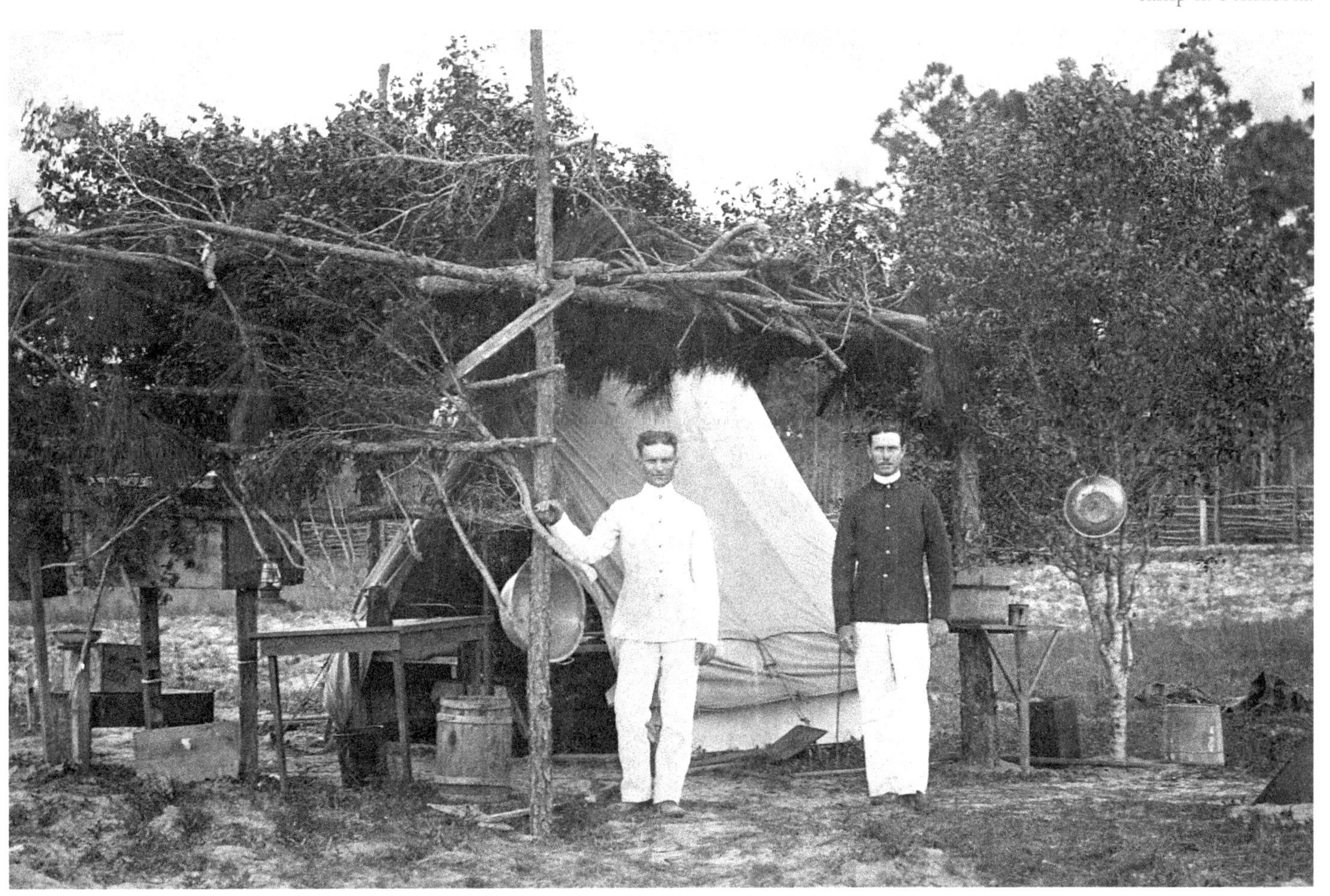

The United States was the first nation to devise a ship-mounted catapult to launch seaplanes from aboard ship. The amphibious planes, equipped with wheels and pontoons, landed on the water and were hoisted back aboard.

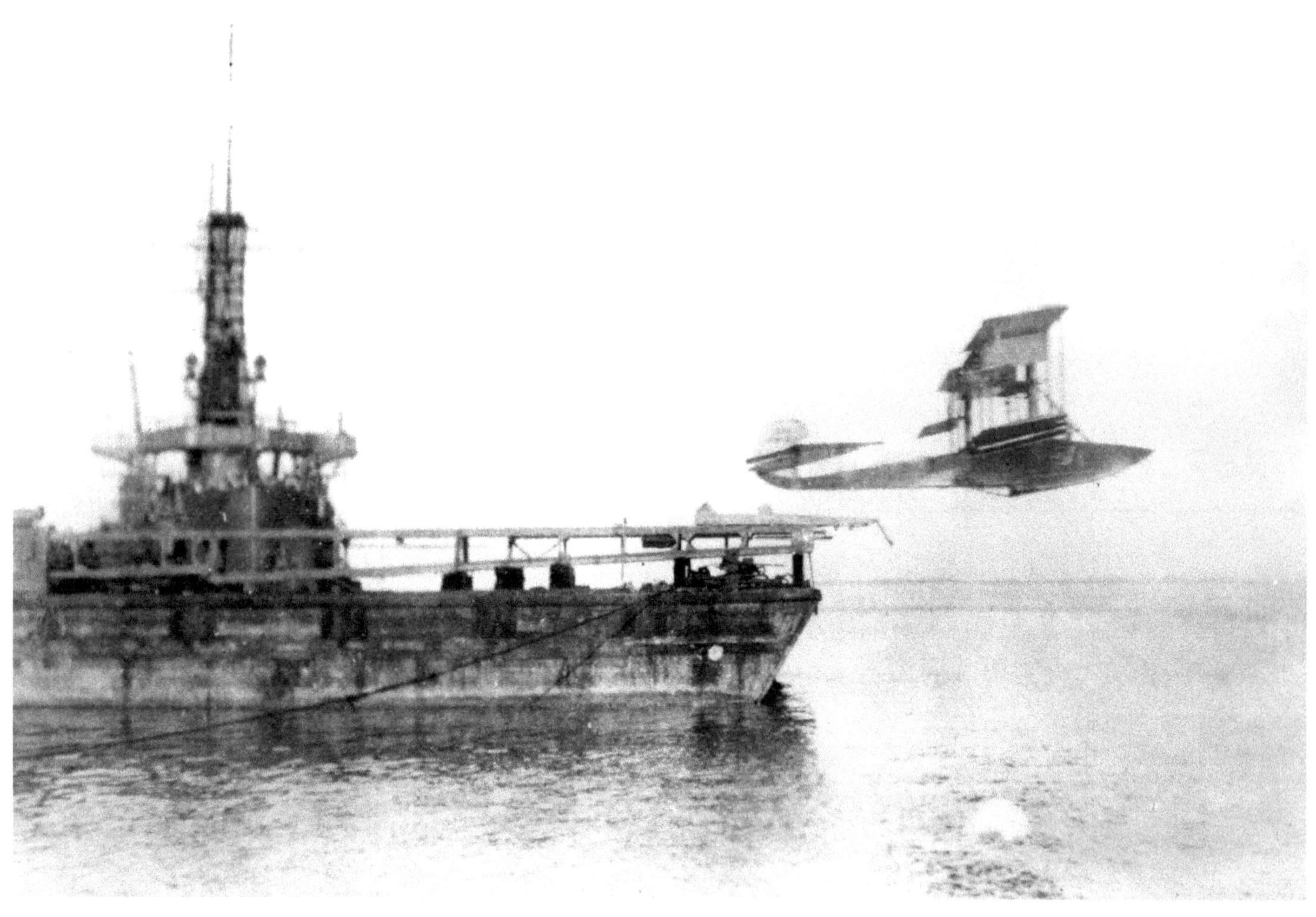

The Pensacola Naval Air Station was the site of the Navy's first naval aviation assembly and repair depot.

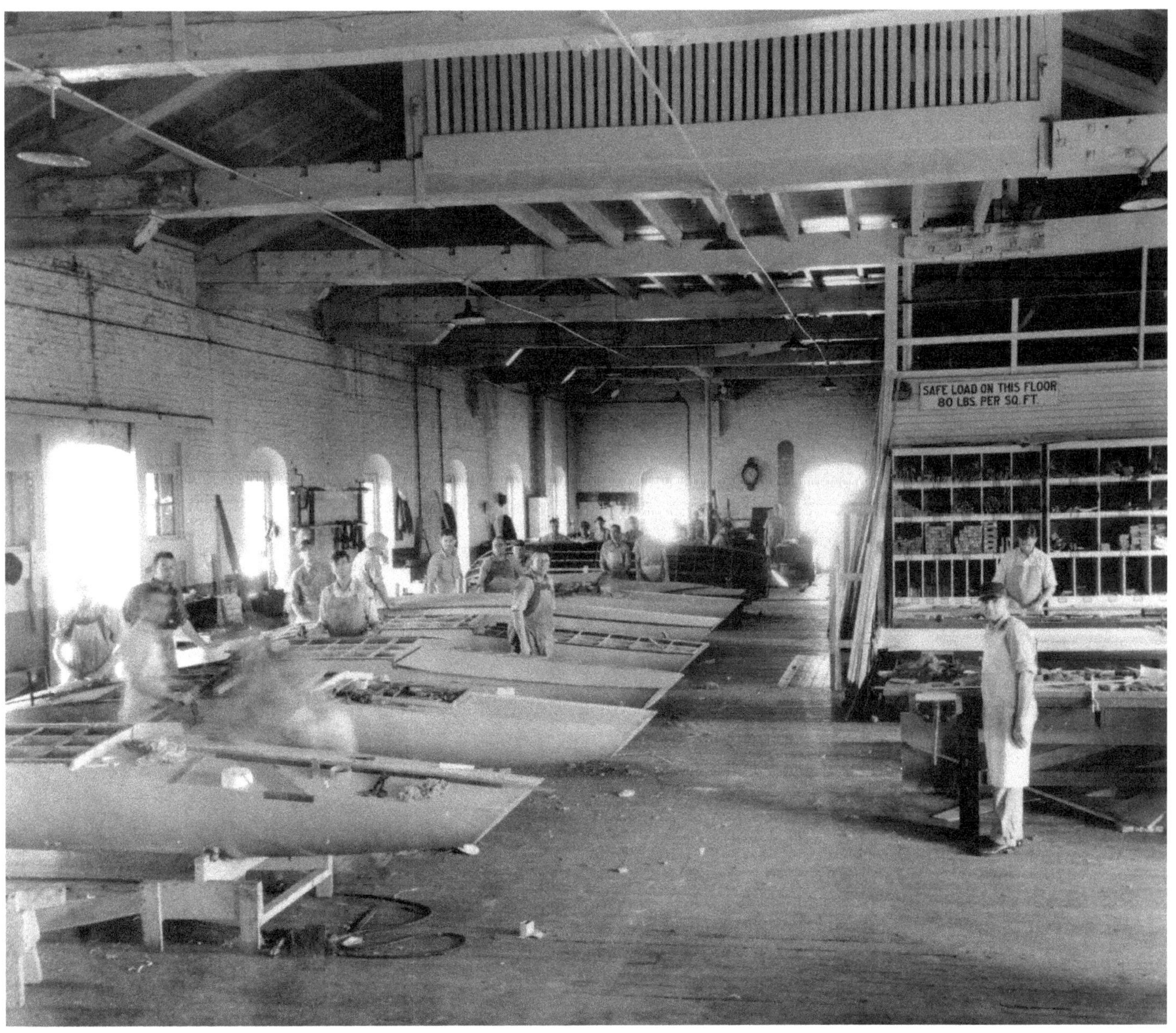

Lieutenant Commander William Corry, Jr., one of the first naval aviators to train at Naval Air Station, Pensacola, was designated Naval Aviator Number 23 in March 1916. Corry died in July 1920 from burns he suffered while attempting to rescue another officer from the burning wreckage of their airplane. Corry Field, opened in 1923 and relocated to its present home in 1928, is named for him.

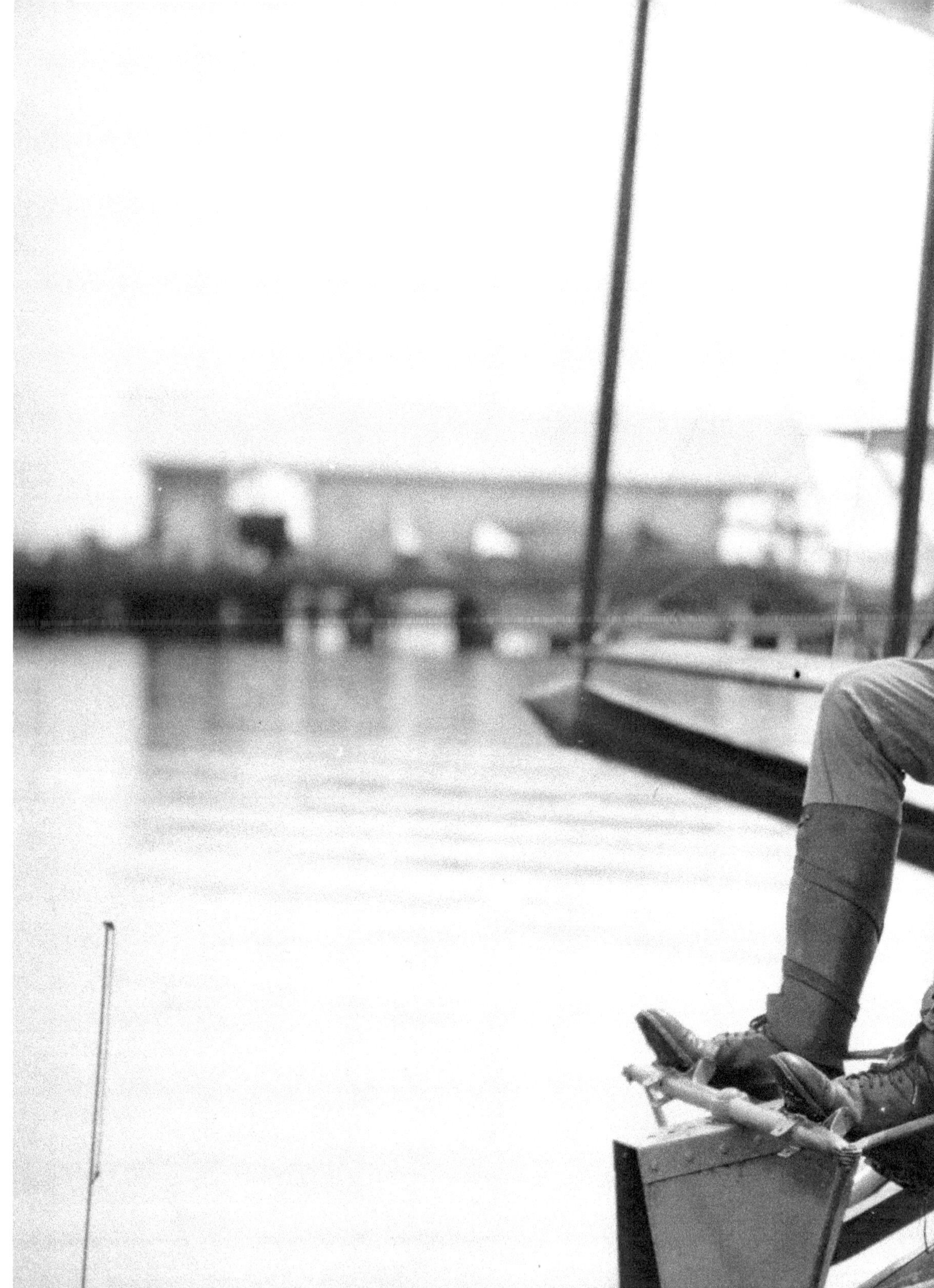

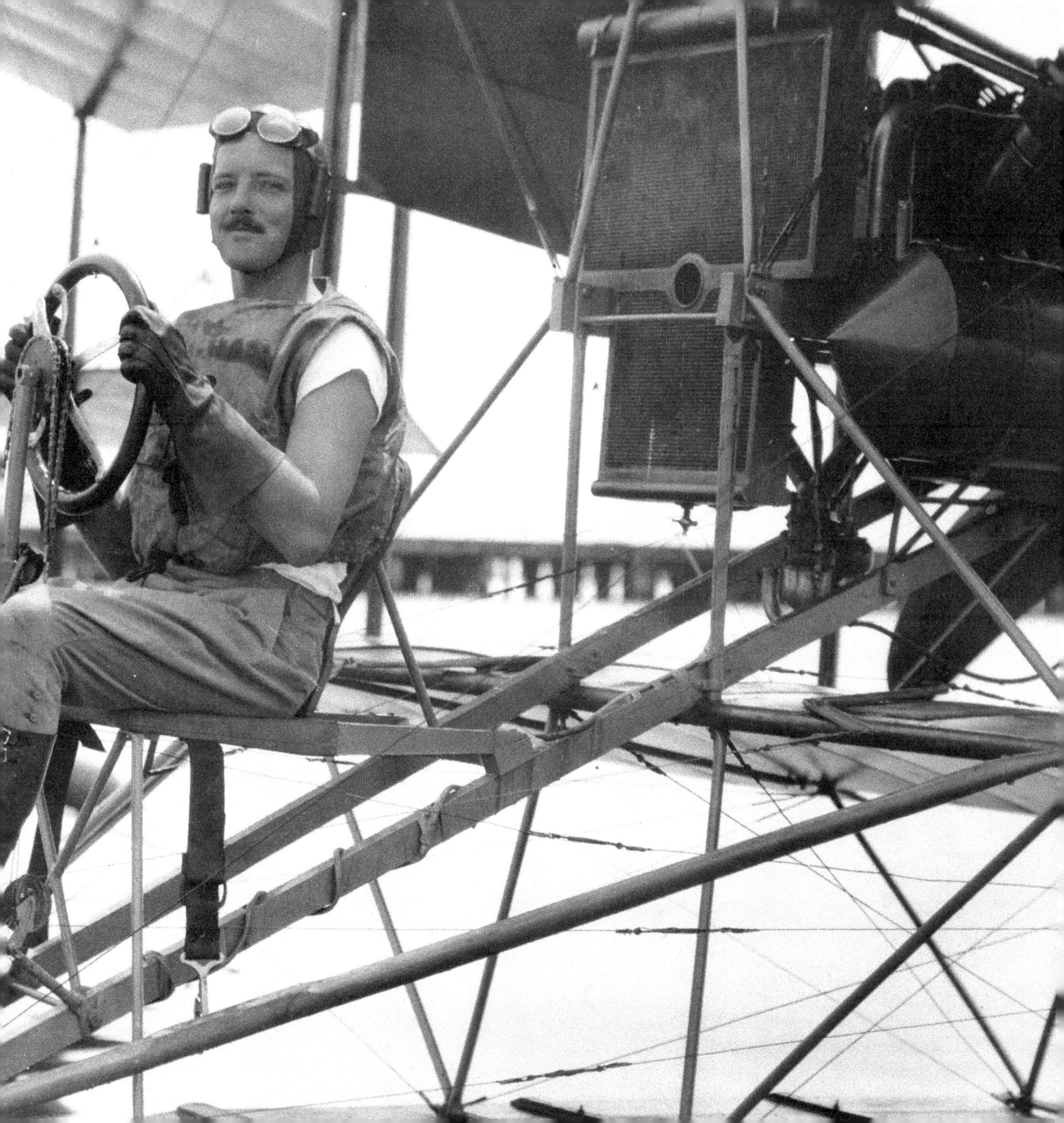

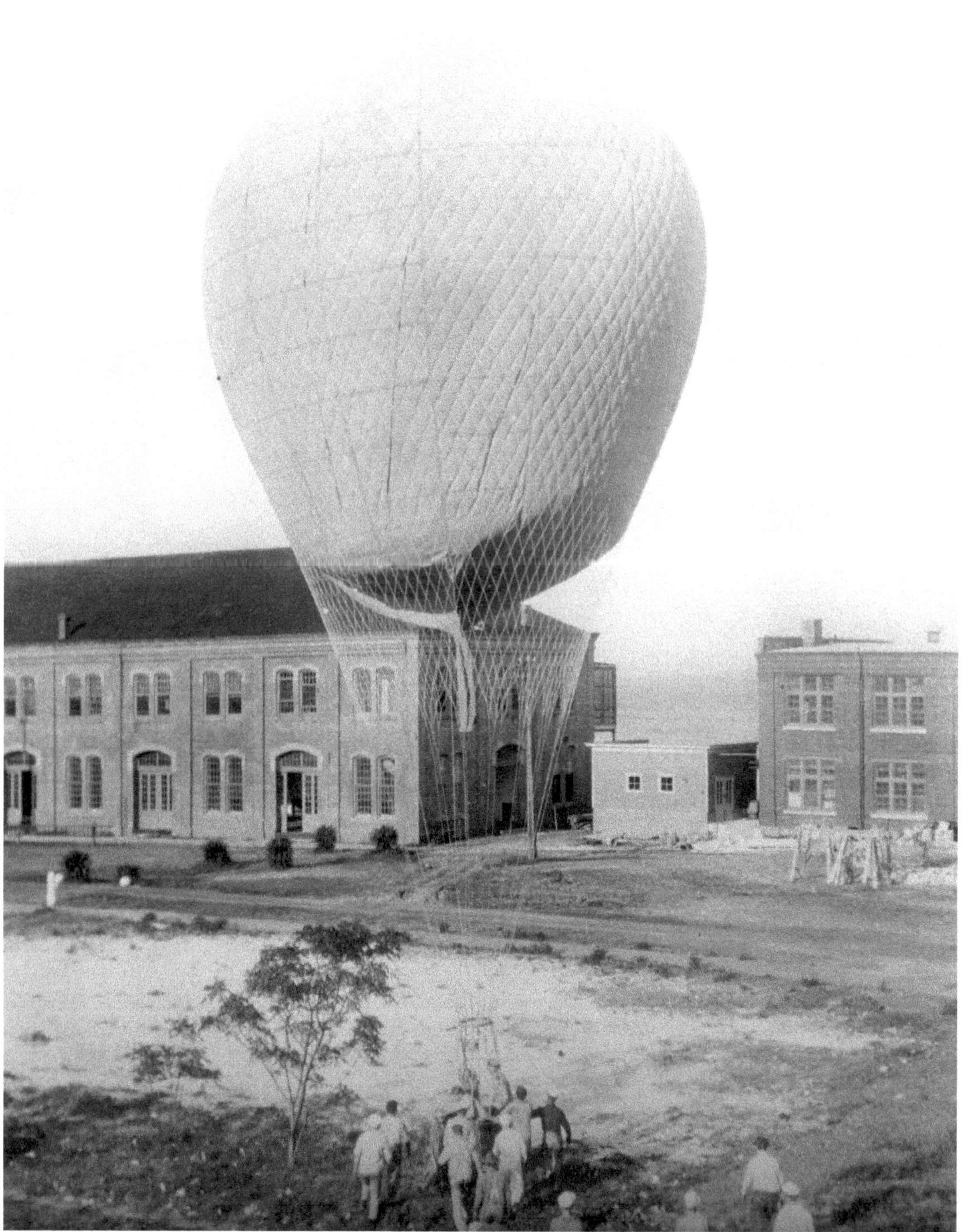

The first free balloon arrived at Naval Air Station Pensacola on April 5, 1916, from the Goodyear plant in Akron, Ohio. On April 7, high winds damaged the balloon, but it was repaired and put into service.

The Navy awarded George Curtiss the first contract to build airplanes for its new aviation branch. The design of the Curtiss HS flying boat placed the engines above the fuselage, away from the water.

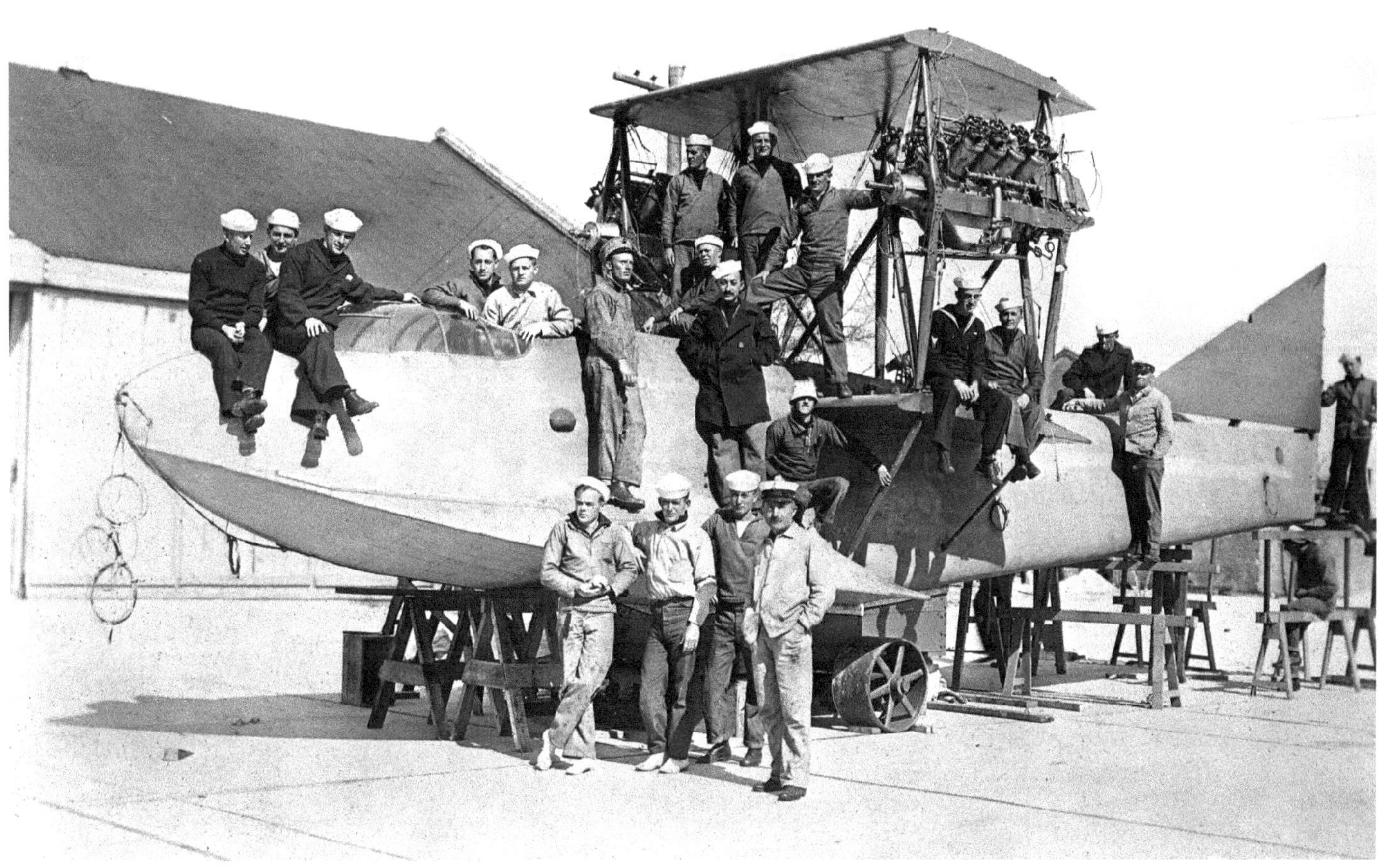

The family of Charles White sits on the steps of their house at 109 Florida Blanca Street waiting for Papa to come home. Pictured left to right are Bessie, Evolyn holding Ruby, Freddie, Louise, and Clara in this 1912 photograph.

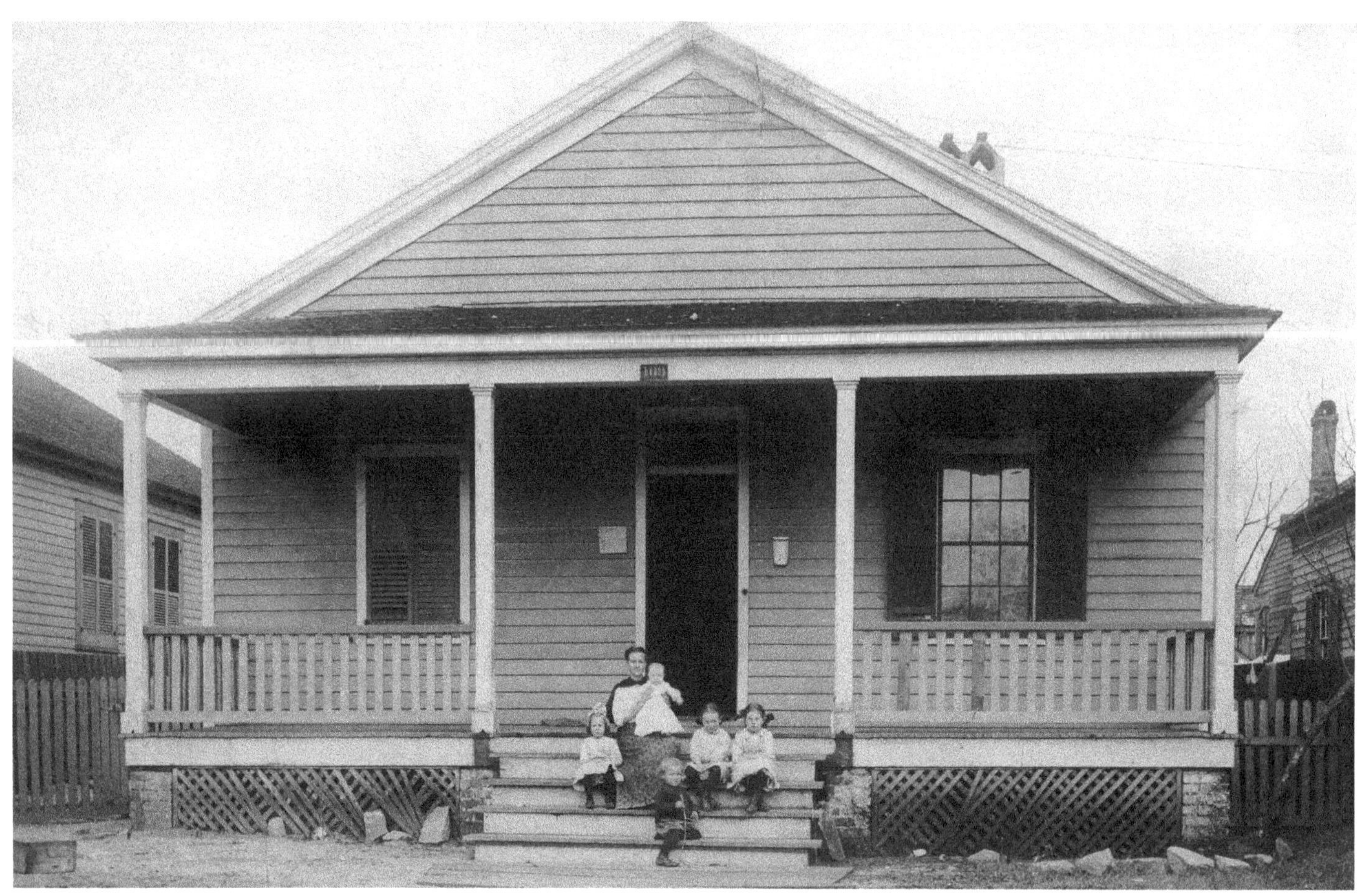

The USS *Huntington* arrived in Pensacola on May 28, 1917, to conduct a series of tests of its new catapult system. The catapult was installed incorrectly, causing the carriage car to be lost over the side of the ship every time it was used. The catapult was later removed.

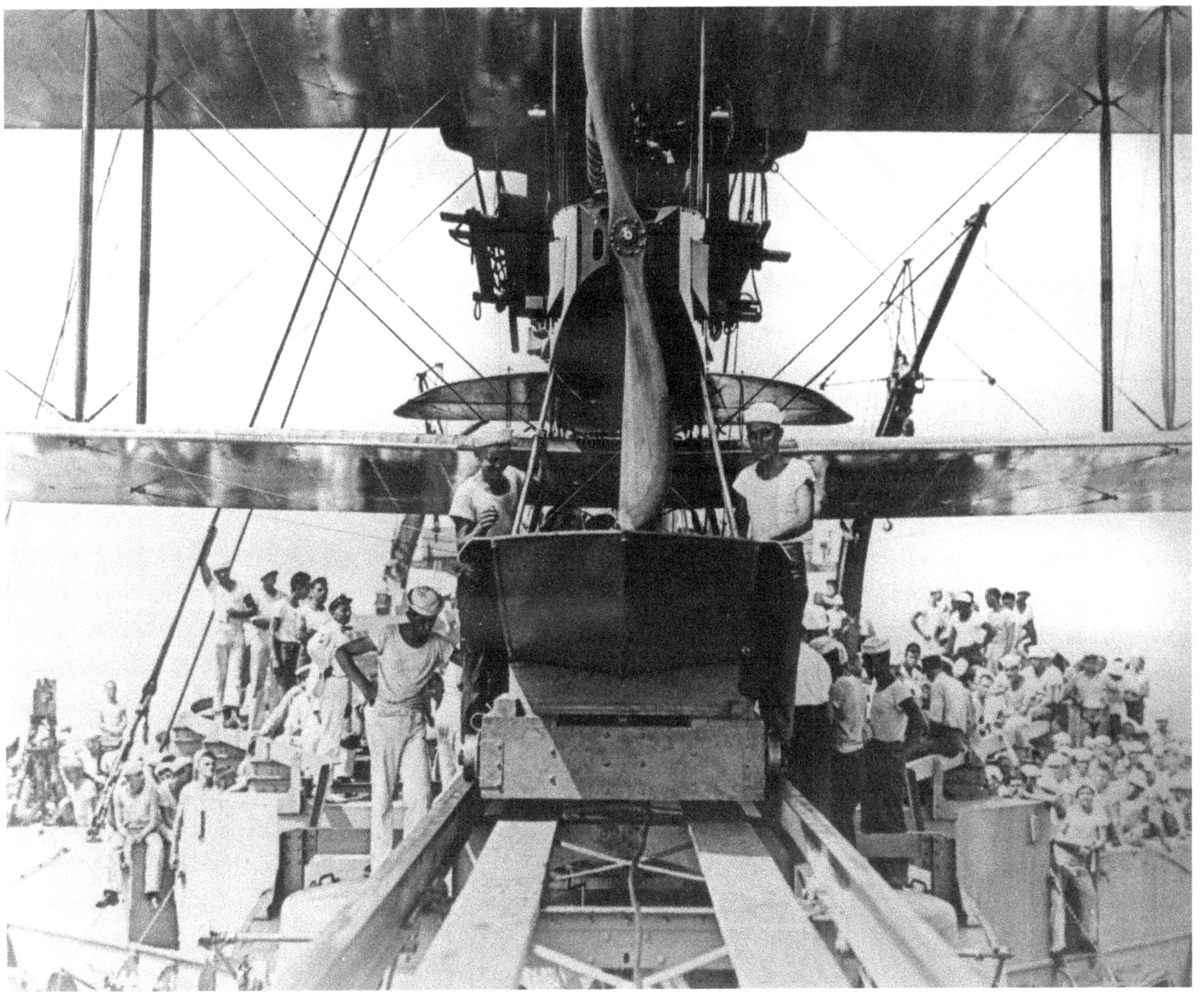

First flown in April 1917, the lighter-than-air DN-1 airship made six flights before it was deemed too flawed to be feasible for use by the Navy. The specially constructed floating hangar, the only floating LTA hangar ever built to house the DN-1, was later used for B-class airships during World War I.

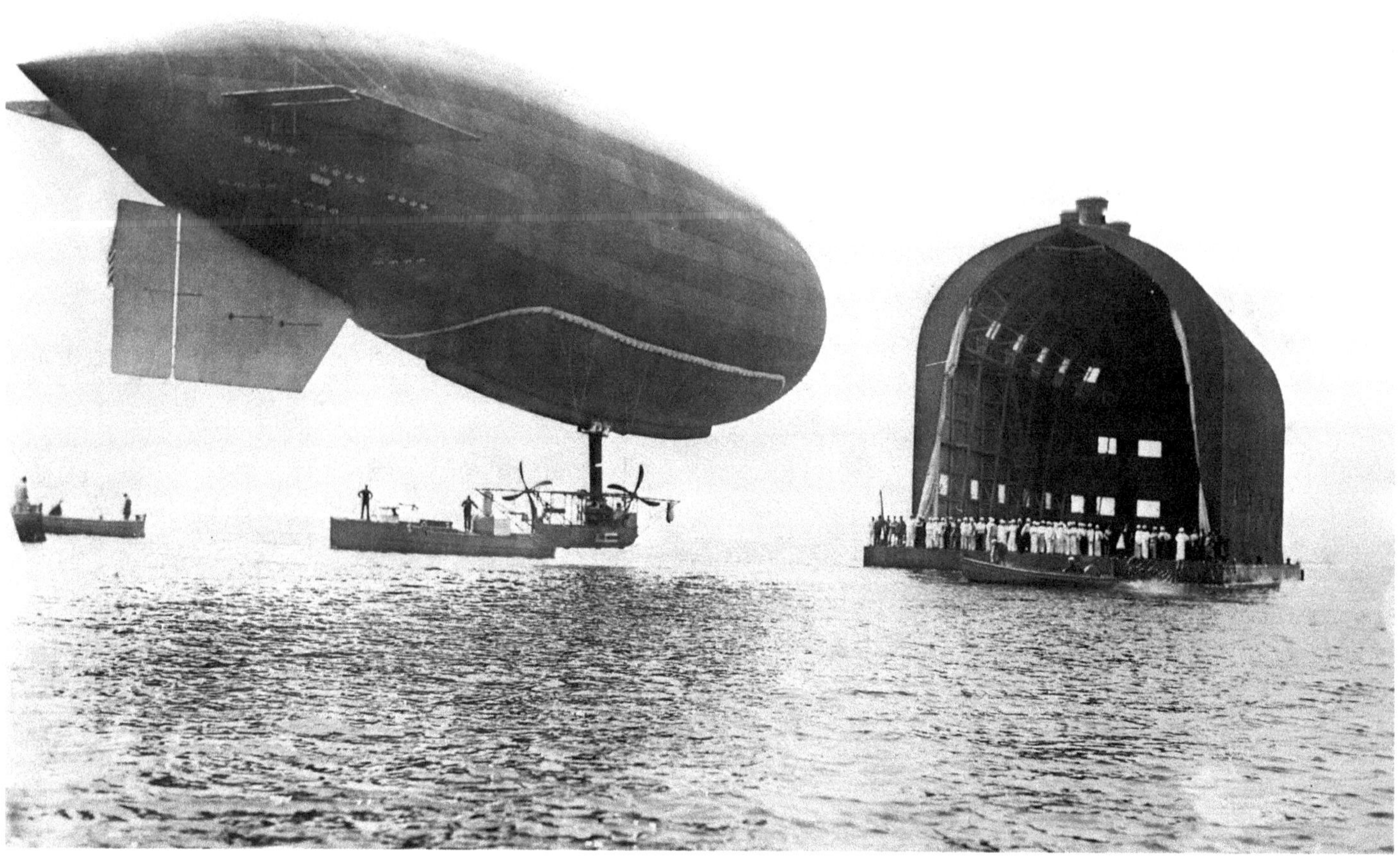

The USS *Pensacola,* a German screw steamer built in Rostock, Germany, in 1901, was originally christened the *Nicaria.* The ship was seized by the U.S. government at Southport, North Carolina, May 8, 1917, was transferred to the U.S. Navy, and was commissioned as the *Pensacola* October 8, 1917. The ship was decommissioned March 14, 1925, and sold.

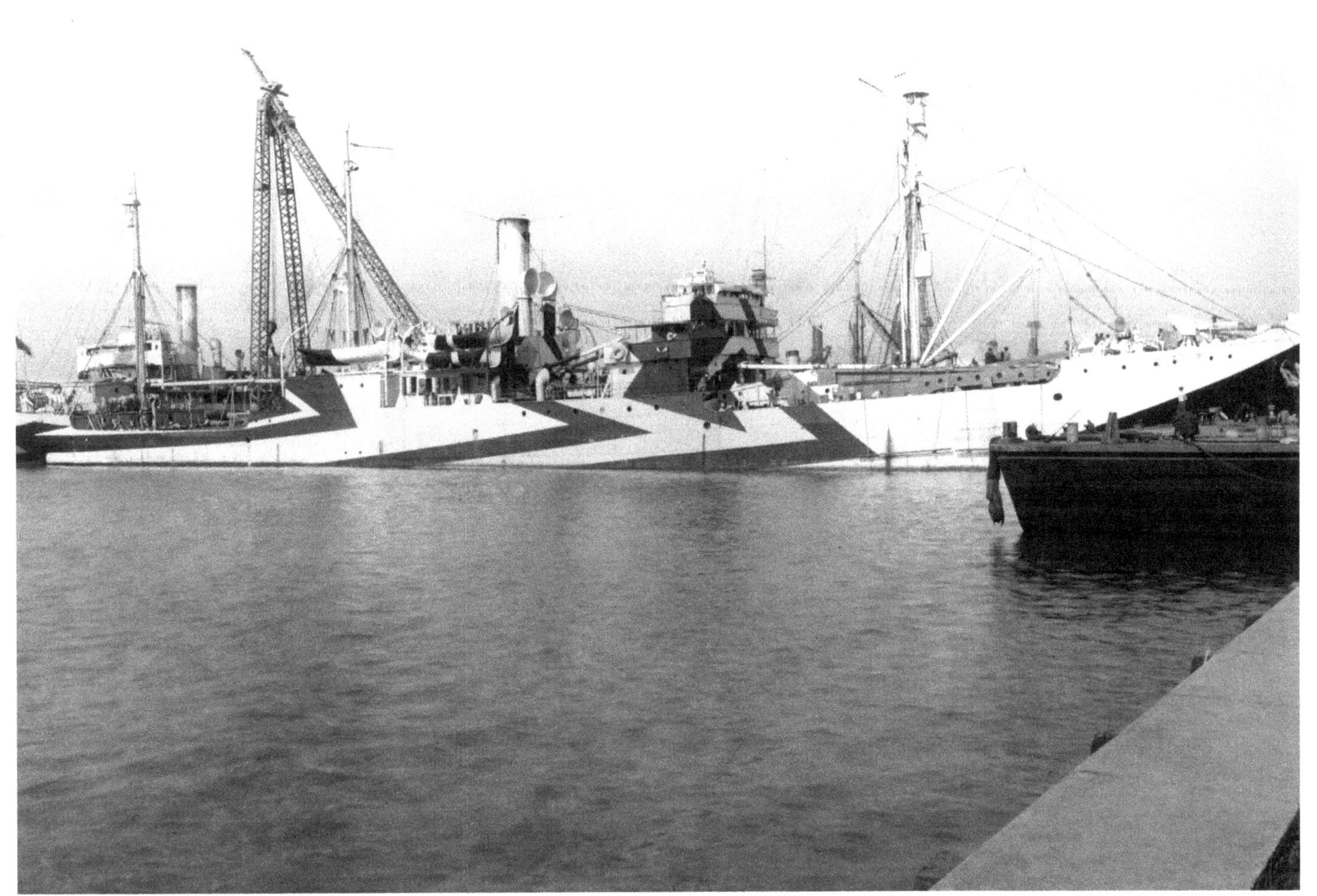

The Patriotic League, known as America's Second Line of Defense, was a women's group organized to perform social services and to support war efforts. The league was very active in Liberty Loan campaigns. This World War I parade was a Liberty Loan Drive to support the war effort.

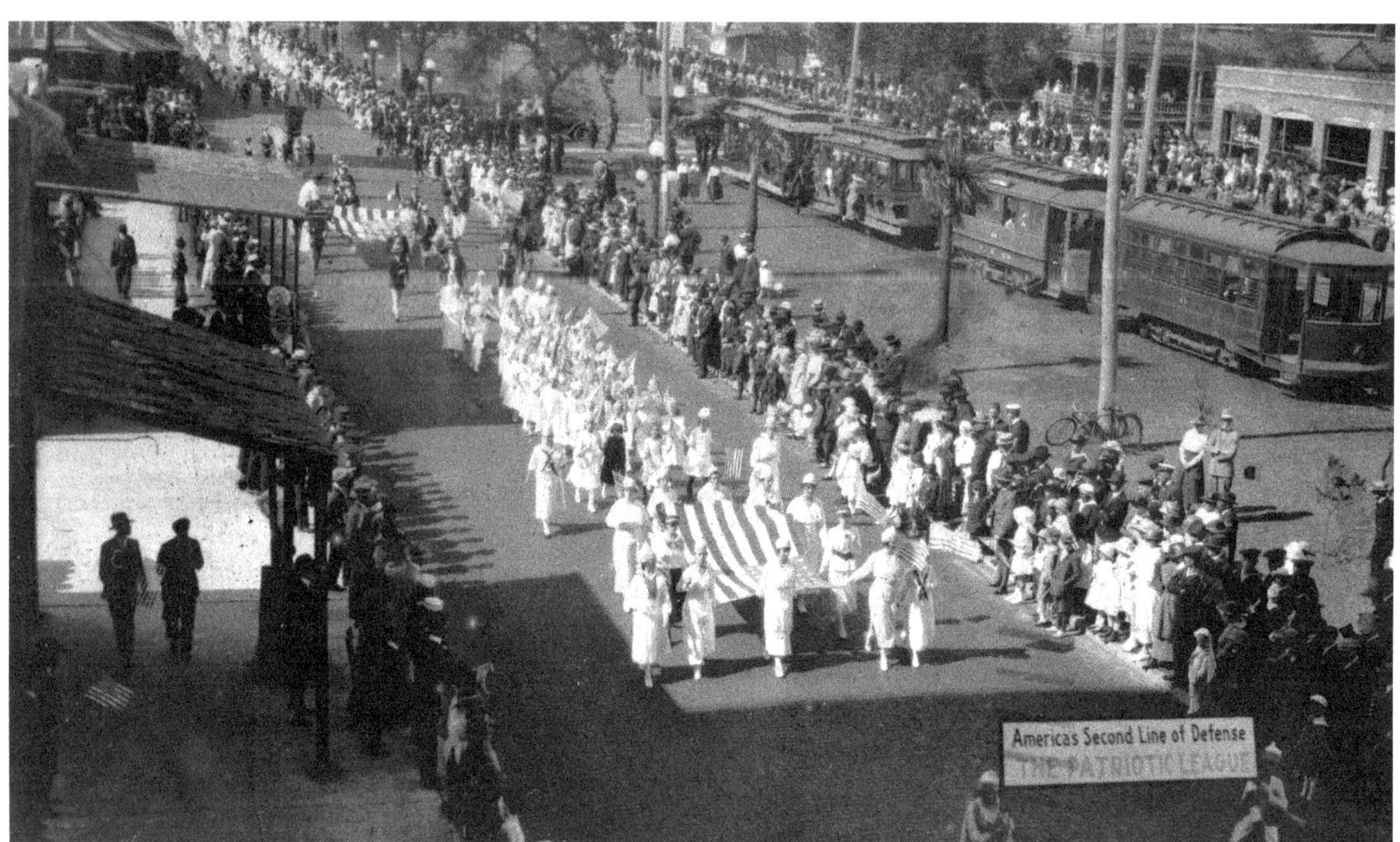

Most buildings at the Naval Air Station, Pensacola, were painted in camouflage colors and patterns during World War I.

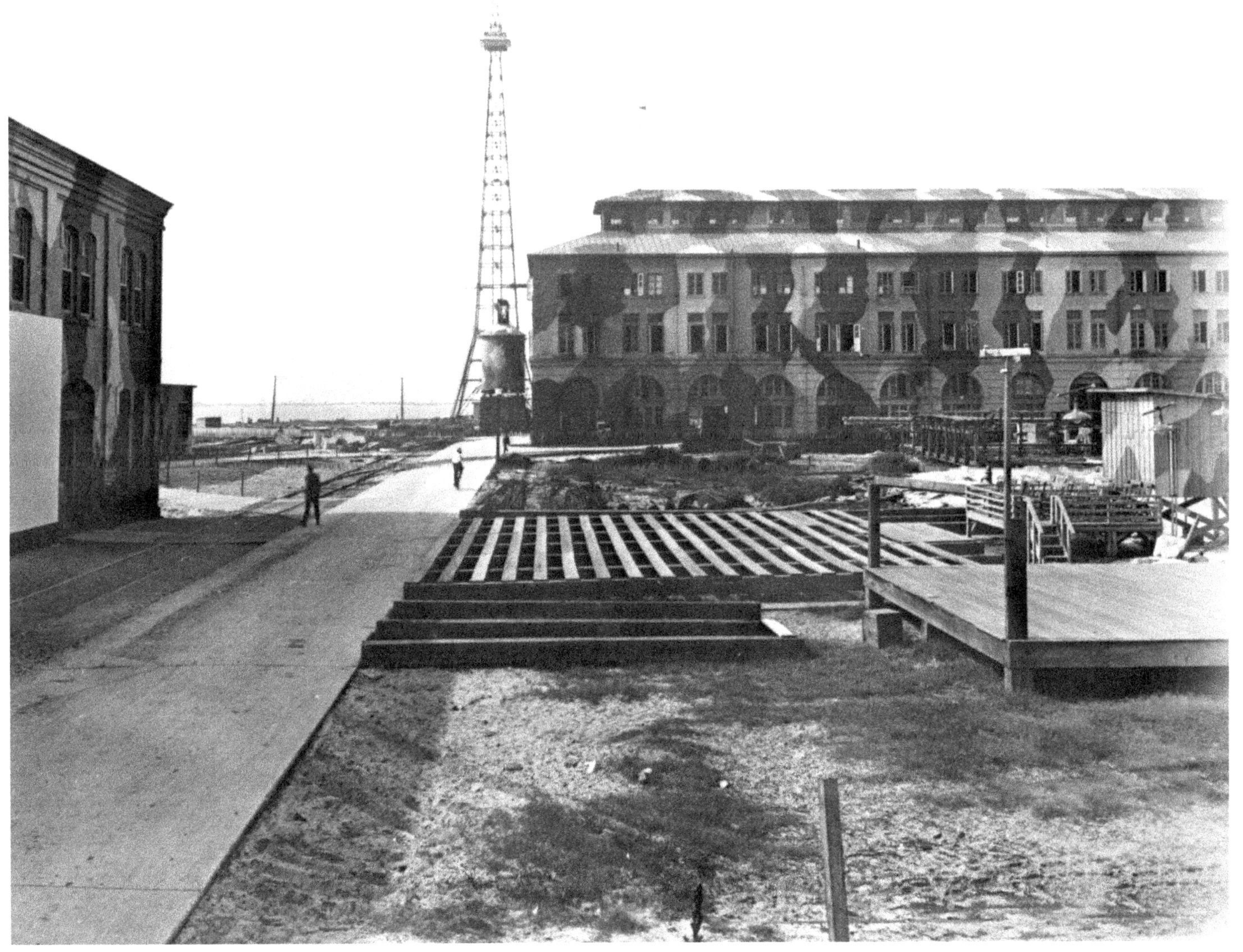

The twin-engine F5L flying boat, with a range of 830 miles, entered naval service near the end of World War I as a patrol plane and was used by the Navy until 1928. This plane could remain airborne for four to six hours.

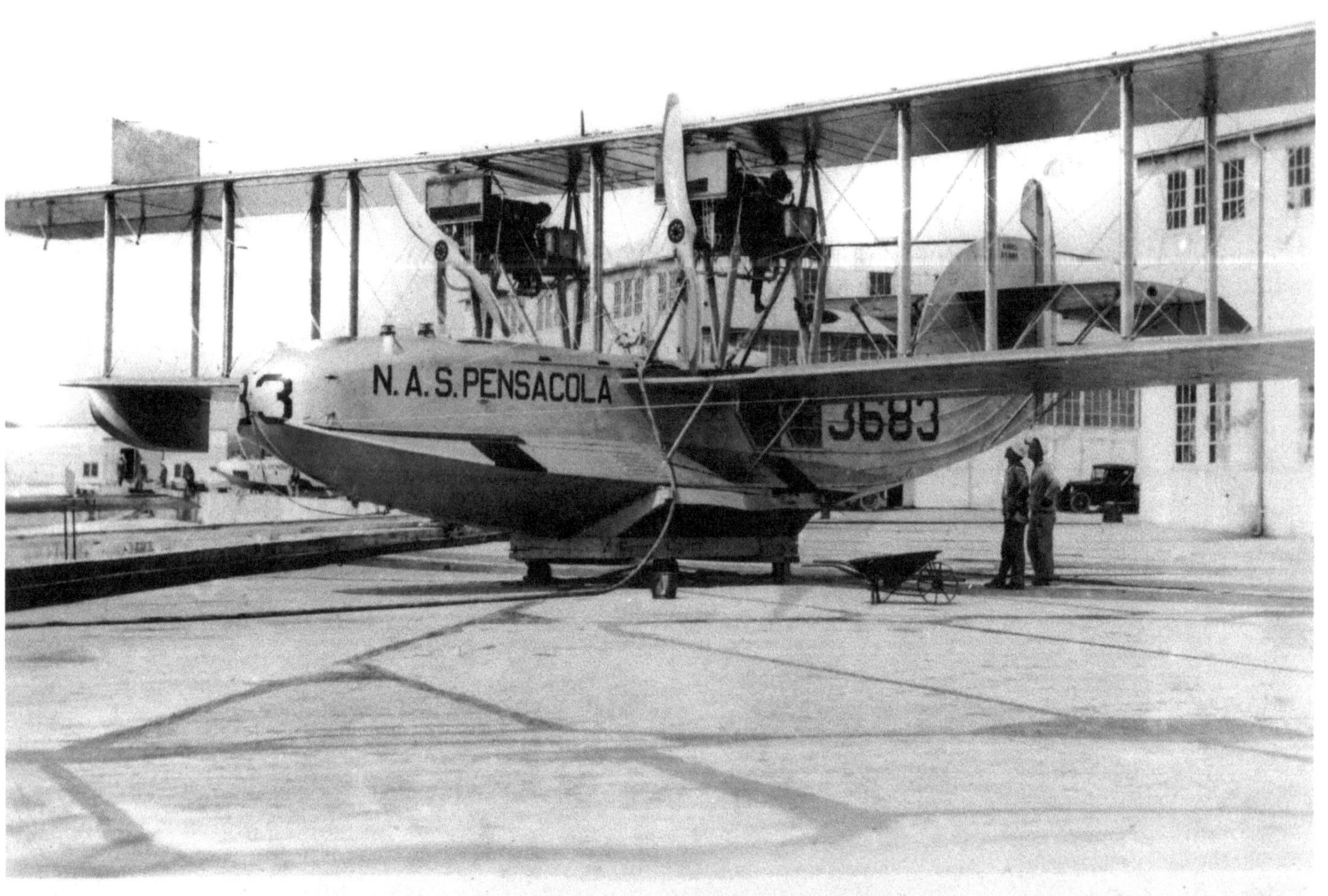

Between the Wars

(1920–1939)

The greater Pensacola area had a population of approximately 37,800 people at the beginning of 1920. By the end of 1939, the population had grown to around 60,000 and there were more than 8,200 telephones in service in the city. Automobiles gave people the freedom to go where they wanted at their own convenience. Trolley service ended in Pensacola in 1931 and horses and buggies disappeared from the city streets. The proud city of Pensacola established a radio station in the new City Hall in 1926. With the call sign WCOA, which stands for Wonderful City of Advantages, the radio station extolled the city's virtues.

Pensacola underwent many changes during the period between World War I and World War II. The new aviation wing of the Navy expanded, bringing many naval aviation personnel to the city and earning Pensacola the title "Birthplace of U.S. Naval Aviation." Defined by water, the city benefited from the construction of many new bridges, which made travel easier and opened new avenues for recreation. Bridges between Pensacola and Gulf Breeze and between Gulf Breeze and Pensacola Beach made the sugar-white sand beaches of Santa Rosa Island easily available to many residents and helped to make sunbathing and water sports popular pastimes in the area. The Casino opened on the beach, offering food and entertainment to beachgoers. With more free time, people demanded recreational activities within easy travel distances. Bayview Park on Bayou Texar helped to fill this need.

The Great Depression did not bypass Pensacola. The Federal Emergency Relief Administration (FERA) established educational and employment opportunities that aided many people in the area. For some, the FERA educational programs were their first opportunity to learn to read and write. FERA projects added bathhouses to Bayview Park and made needed improvements to city docks.

By 1920, automobiles were a common sight in downtown Pensacola. The fountain on the north side of Plaza Ferdinand VII, erected in January 1909, was the first of its kind installed in the city. Replaced in 1963 with a more modern fountain, the original was reinstalled by the city ten years later following public outcry. It is 16 feet tall and features 75 electric lights, a novelty in 1909. The stone wall, made from ballast rock, was erected around the perimeter of the square in 1902.

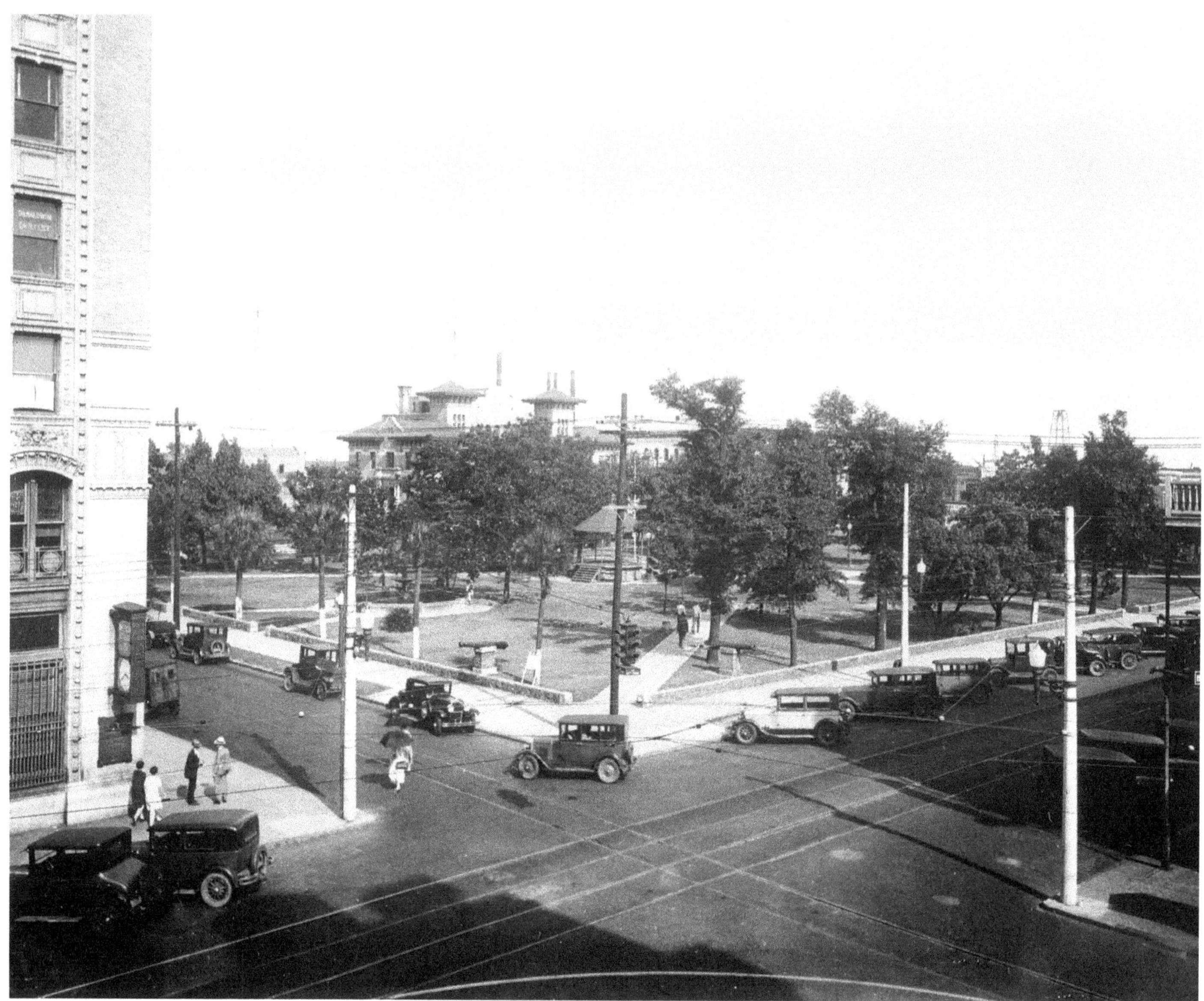

The Barrancas Barracks, the main housing facility for enlisted personnel, was built in 1847 and was in use until the 1930s.

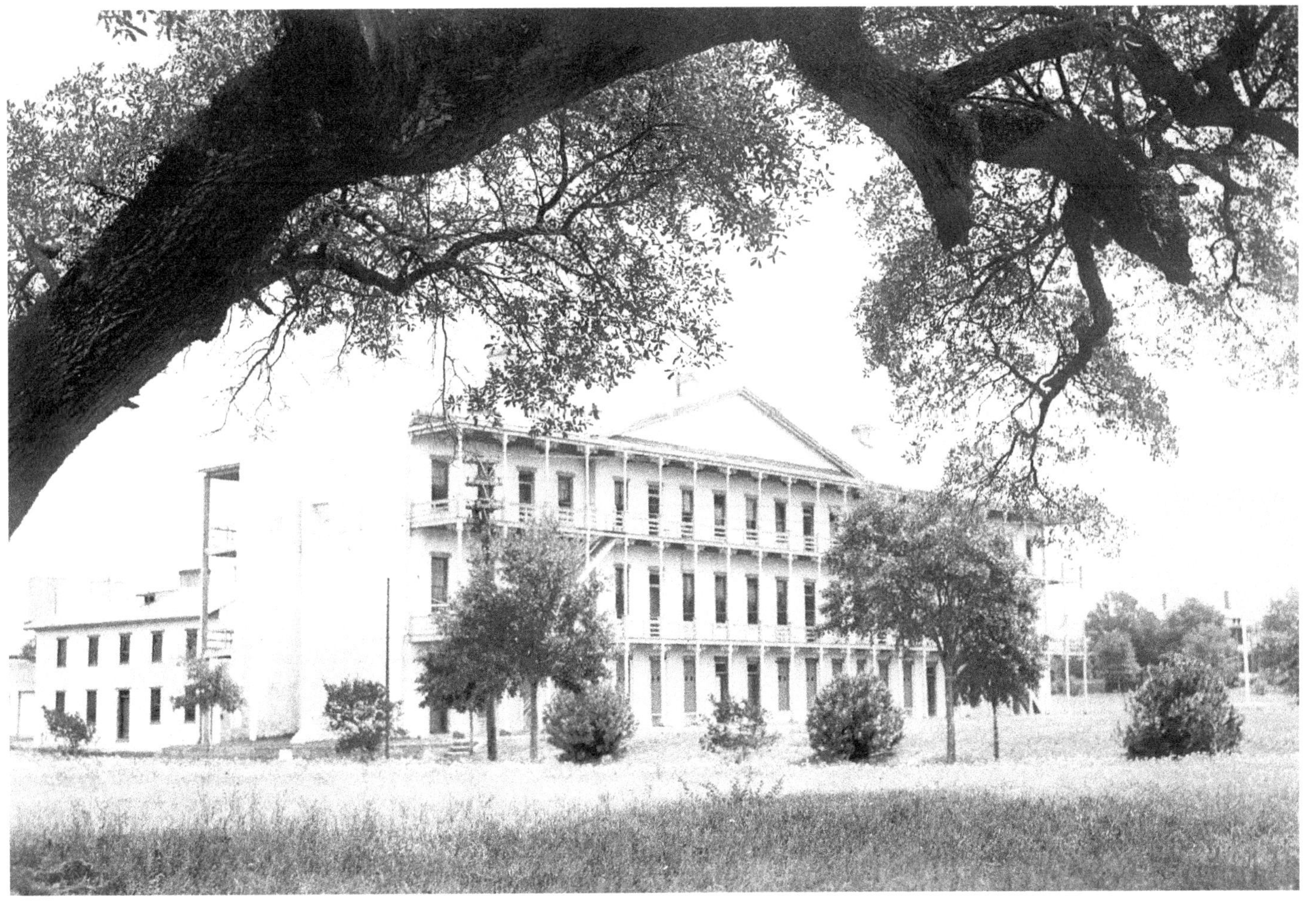

The review ground and surrounding buildings at Fort Barrancas.

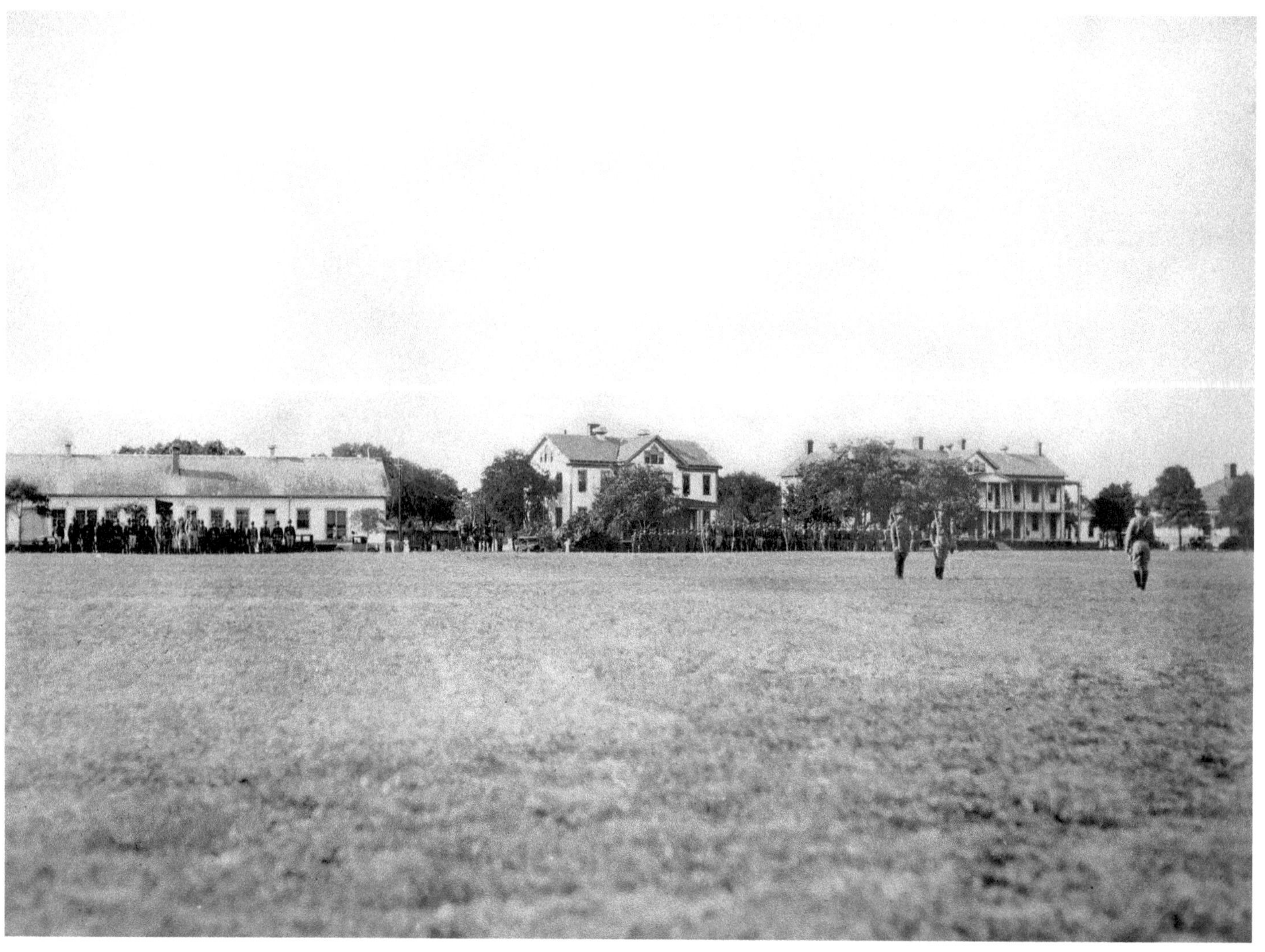

This group of pilots stationed at Naval Air Station, Pensacola, included Luther W. Coleman, Sr., seated third from the left on the wing.

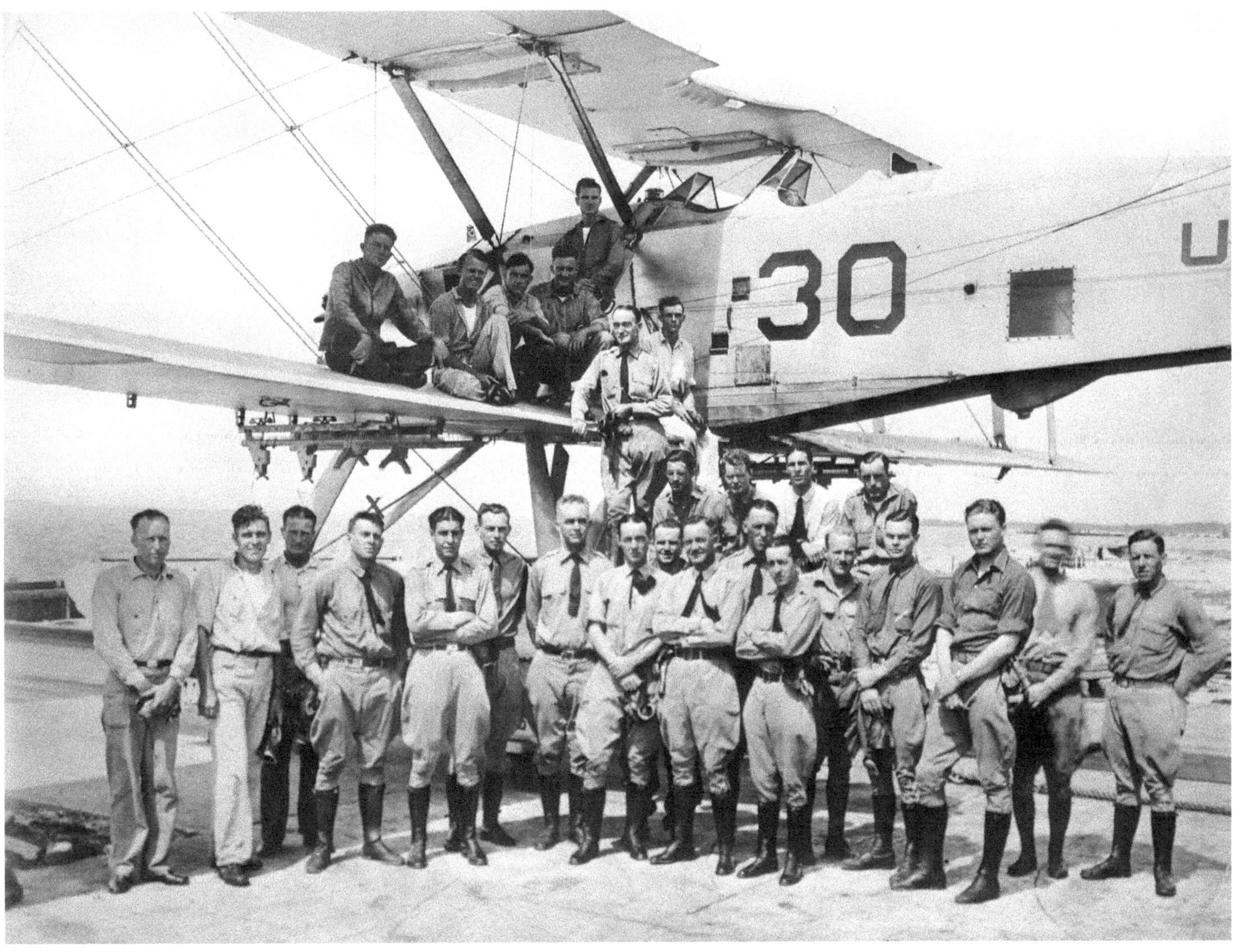

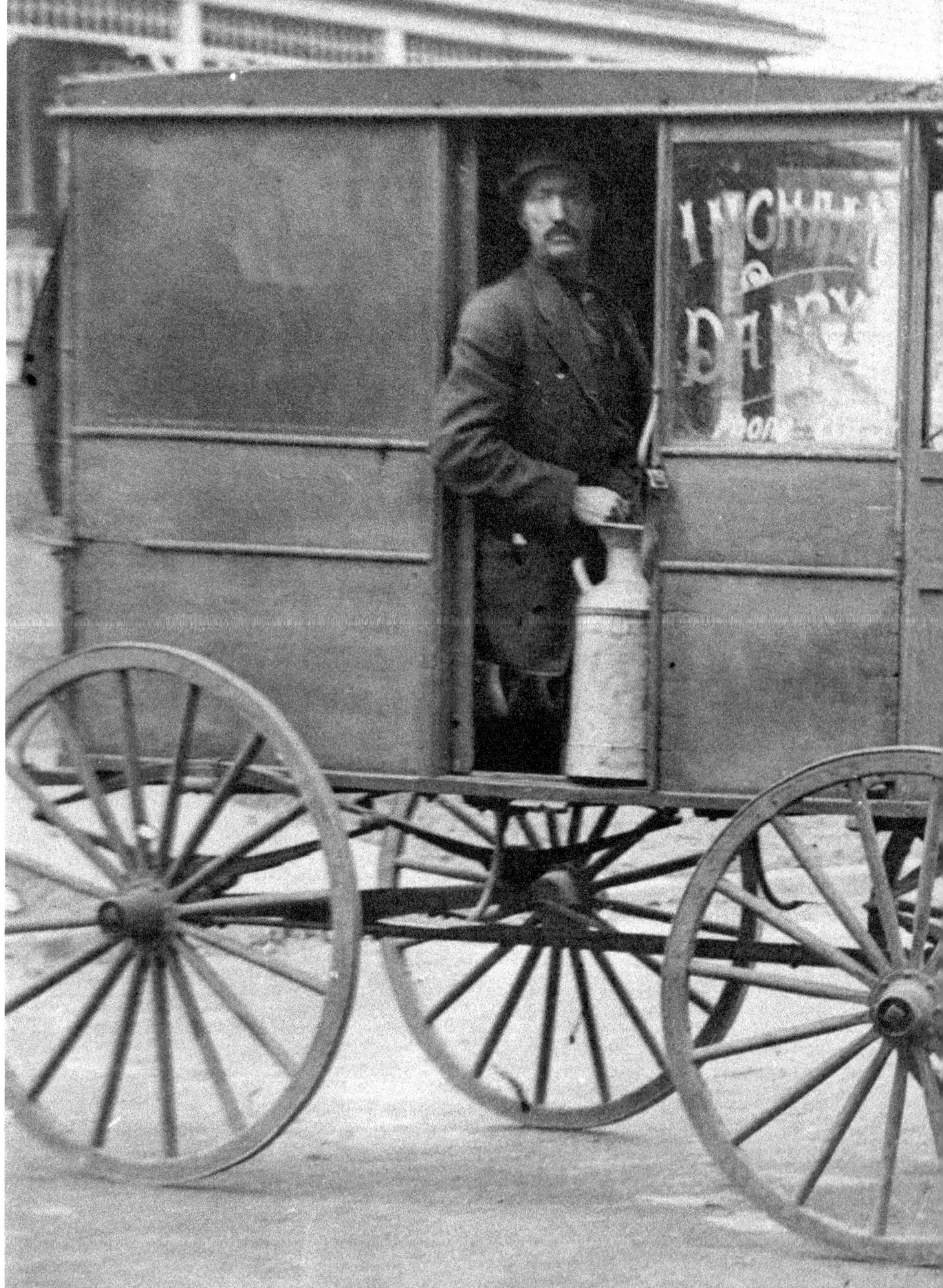

The Ingham Dairy, owned by Stacey E. Ingham, was located at the southeast corner of A and Scott streets.

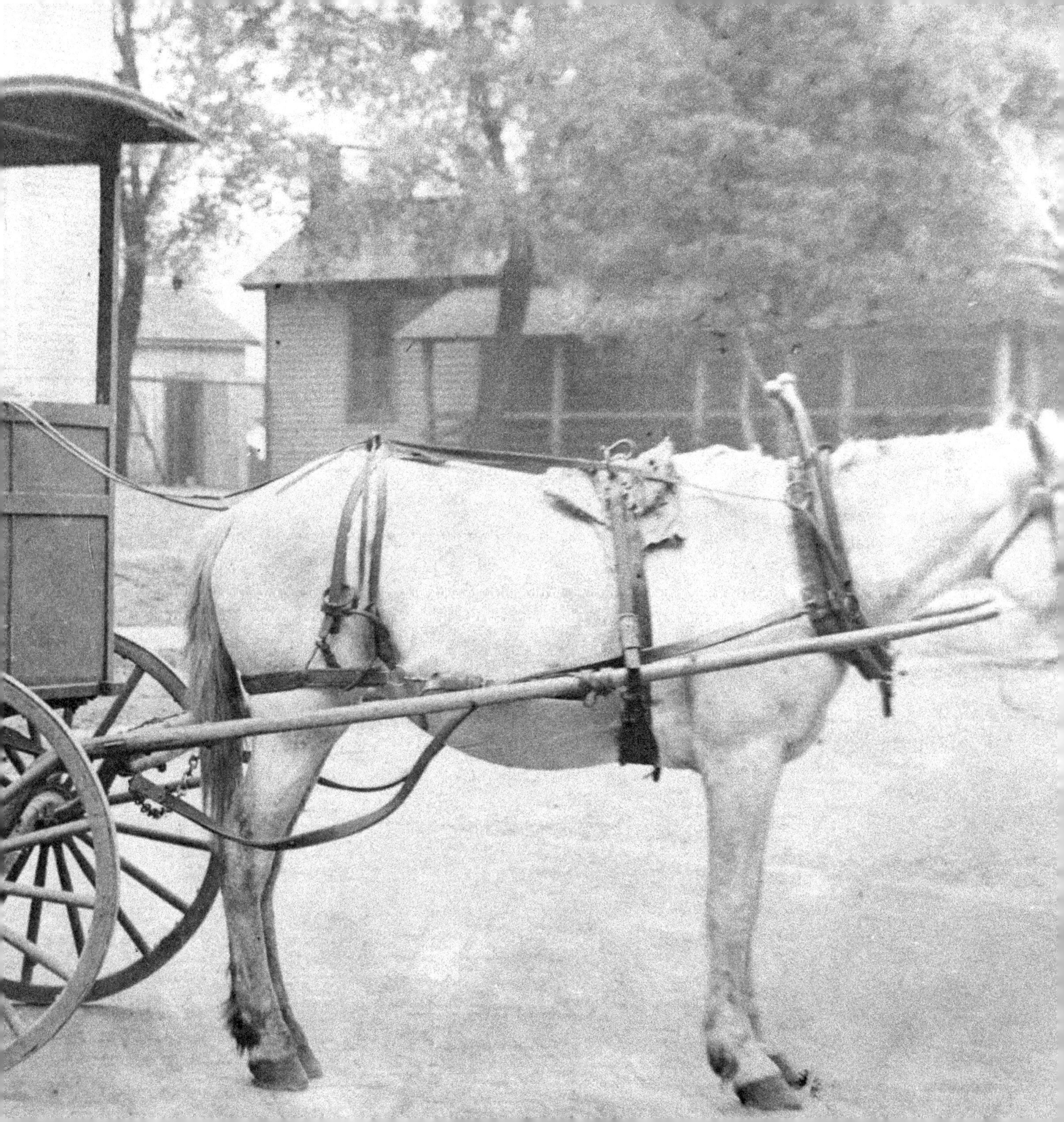

Vincent Joseph Vidal, president and treasurer of the Gulf City Coffee Company, is pictured in his office on East Intendencia Street. The company roasted, blended, and shipped fine coffees for more than 60 years. Mr. Vidal was also Vice-Consul of Guatemala and Uruguay.

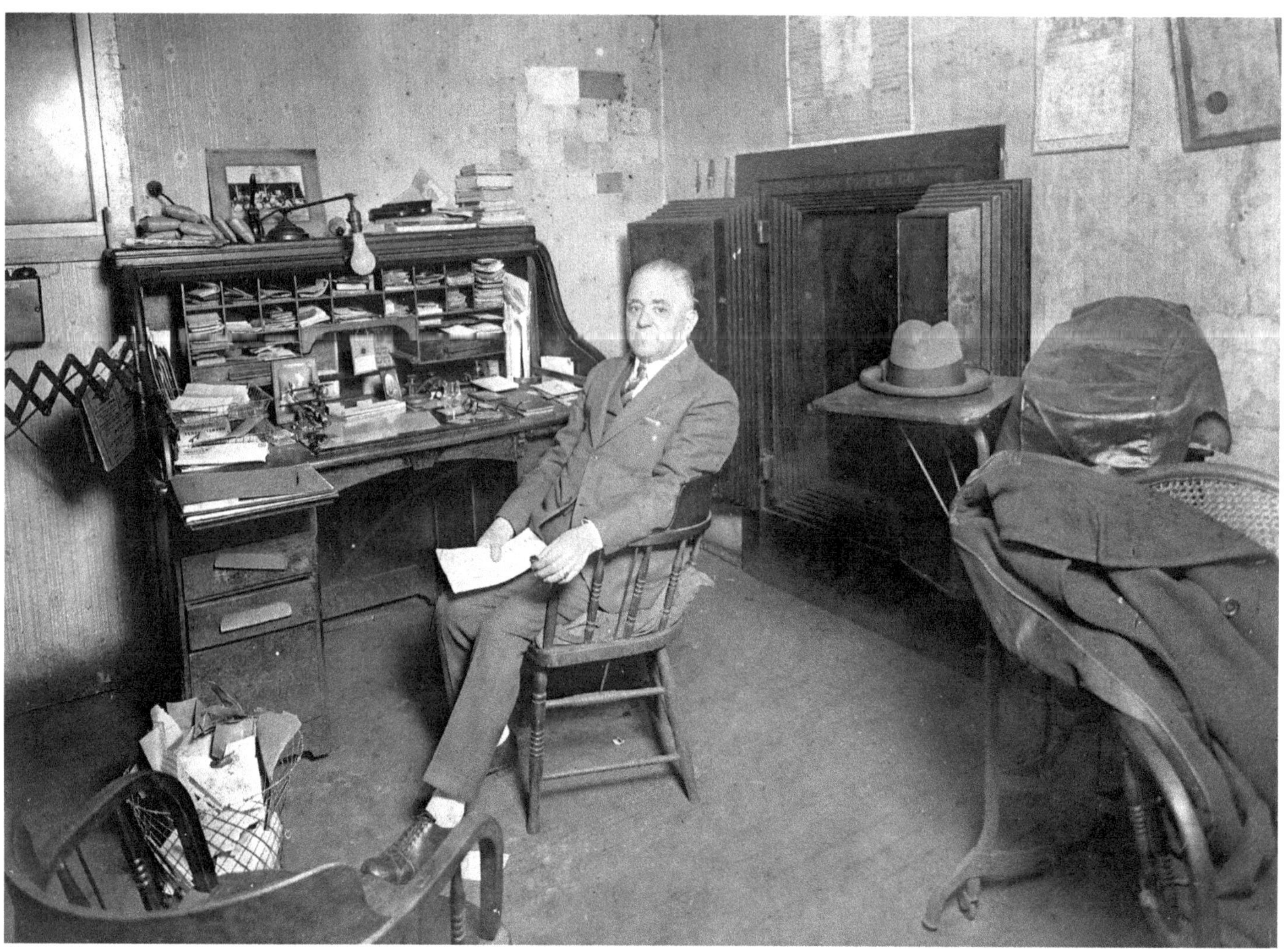

The wide median and deep road frontage enabled a progressive Pensacola to plant shade trees to cool pedestrians and beautify the city.

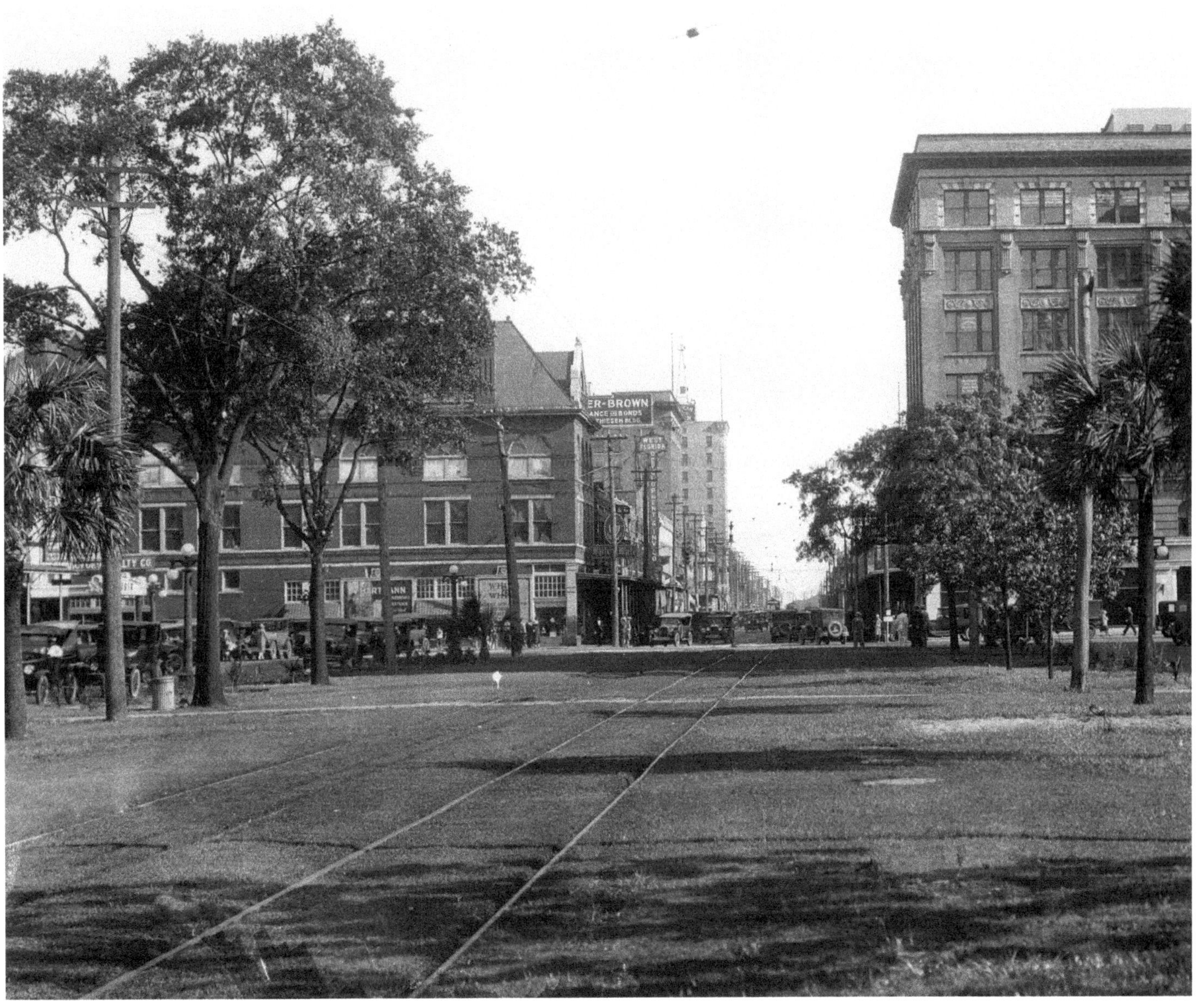

Trains were serviced and rerouted at the L&N roundhouse and turntable at Belmont and 10th Avenue. Early engines were designed only to travel forward. The turntable was used to reverse the engine for the trip out of town.

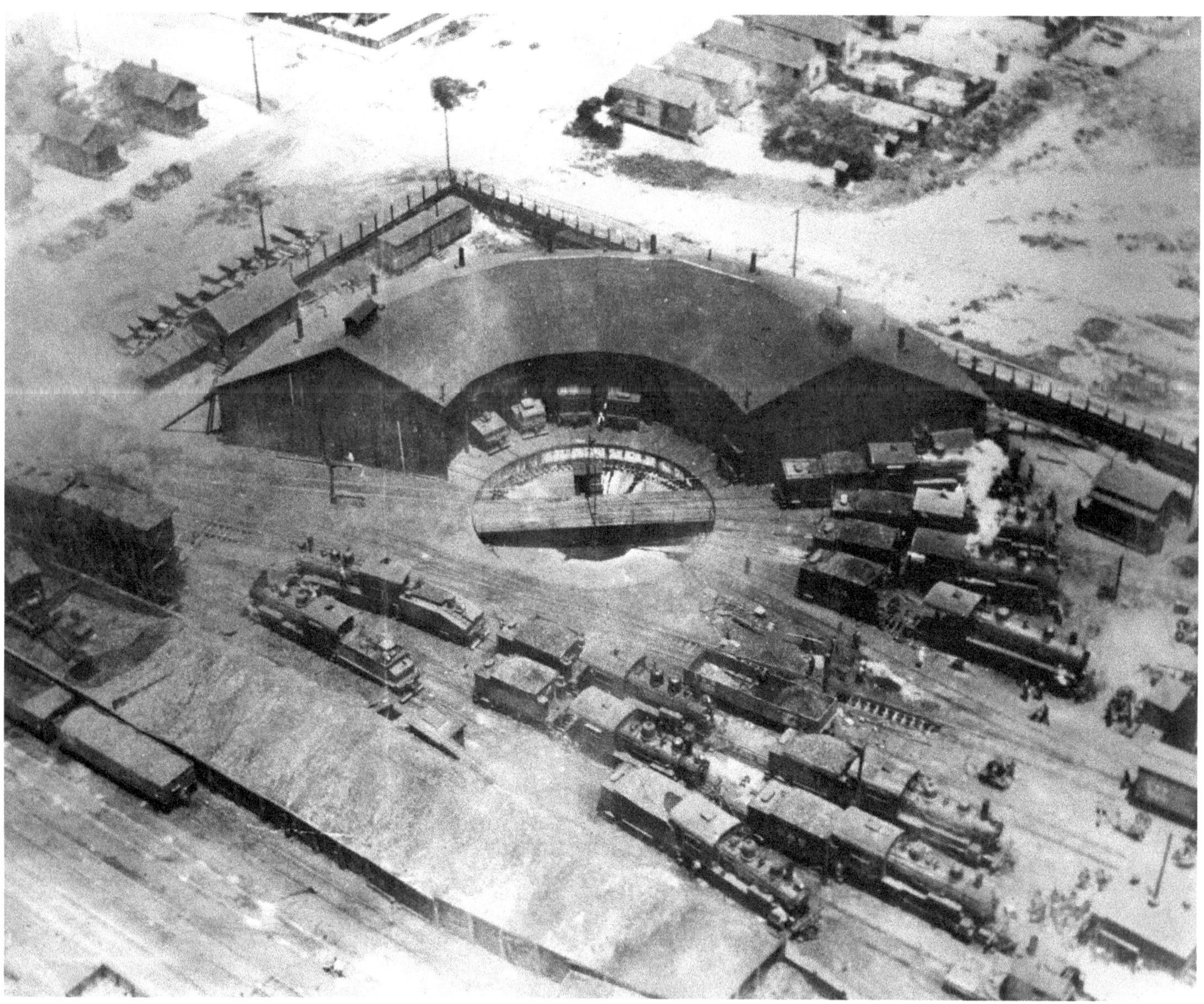

Pensacola is known as the "Mother-in-law of the Navy" because many navy men find wives while stationed at Pensacola. Vergie Cooper and Bessie Cooper became the wives of Navy pilots James Elliott Flynn and William Douglas Faxon.

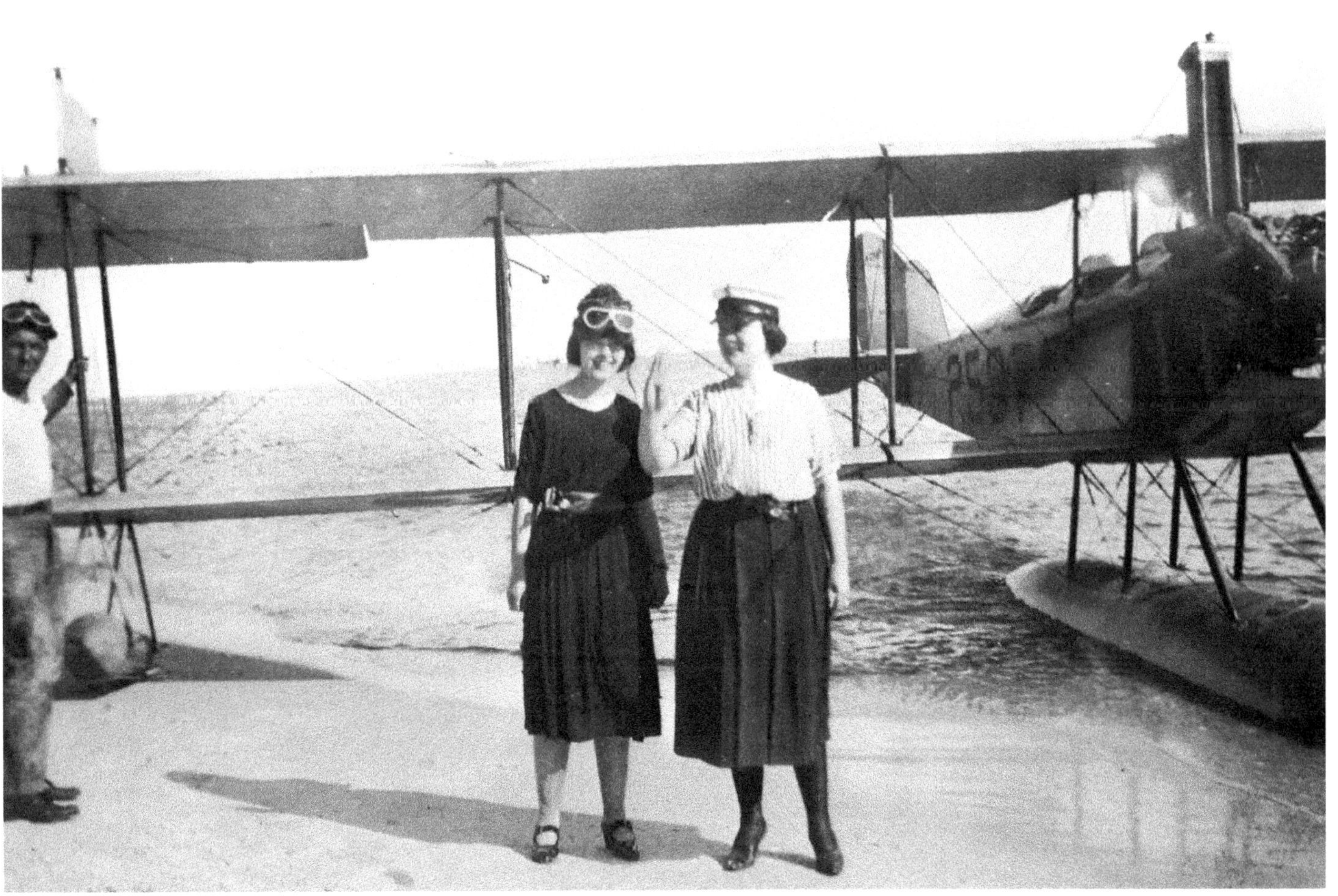

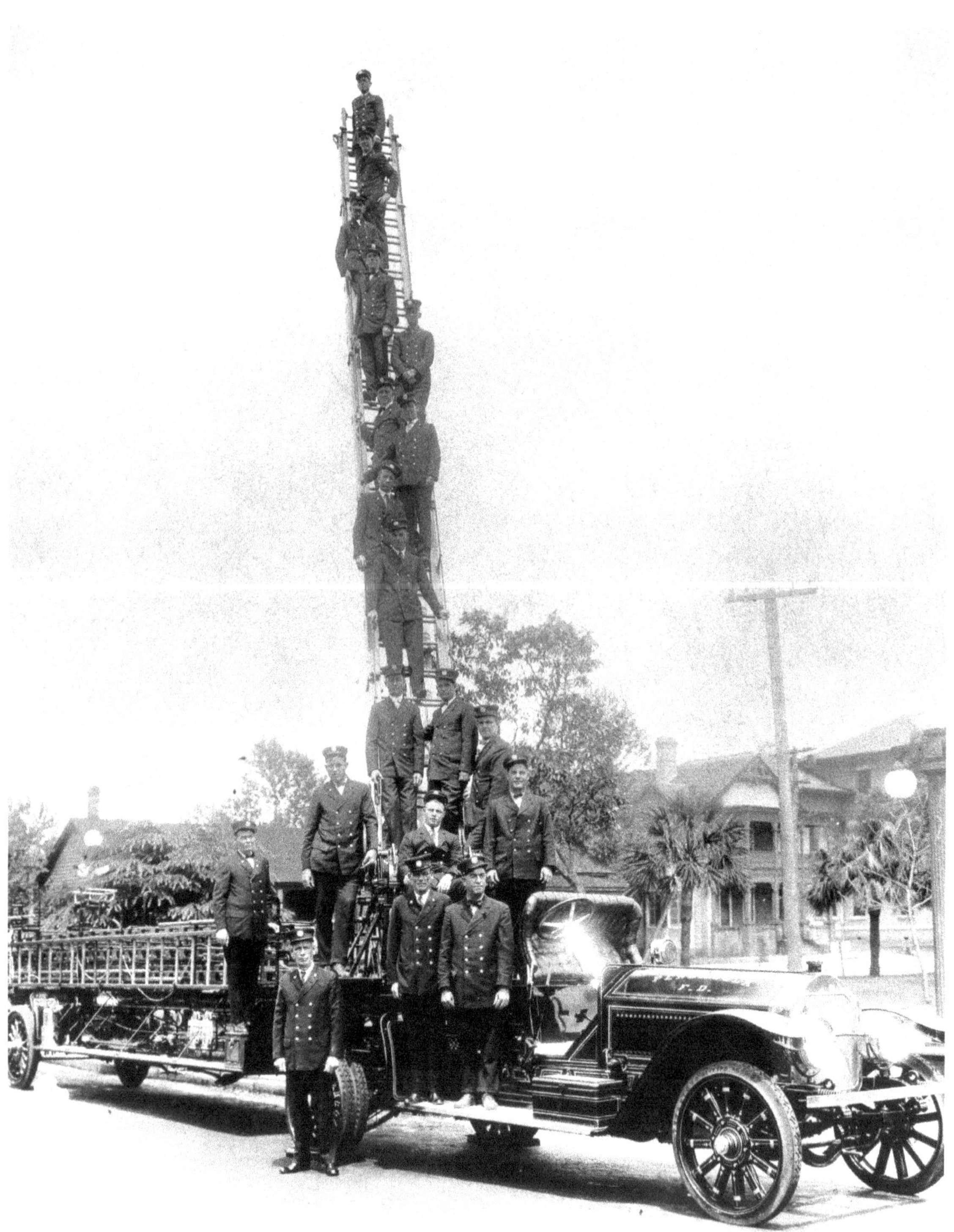

Members of Fire Company Number One demonstrate the new heights they can reach with their new ladder truck.

The City Hall, visible in the background, was also home to WCOA Radio, which touted the charms of Pensacola as the Wonderful City of Advantages. The county building to the right held the jail and the sheriff's office, along with other county offices. The old City Hall now houses the T. T. Wentworth, Jr., Museum, and the renovated county building is today home to the Pensacola Cultural Center.

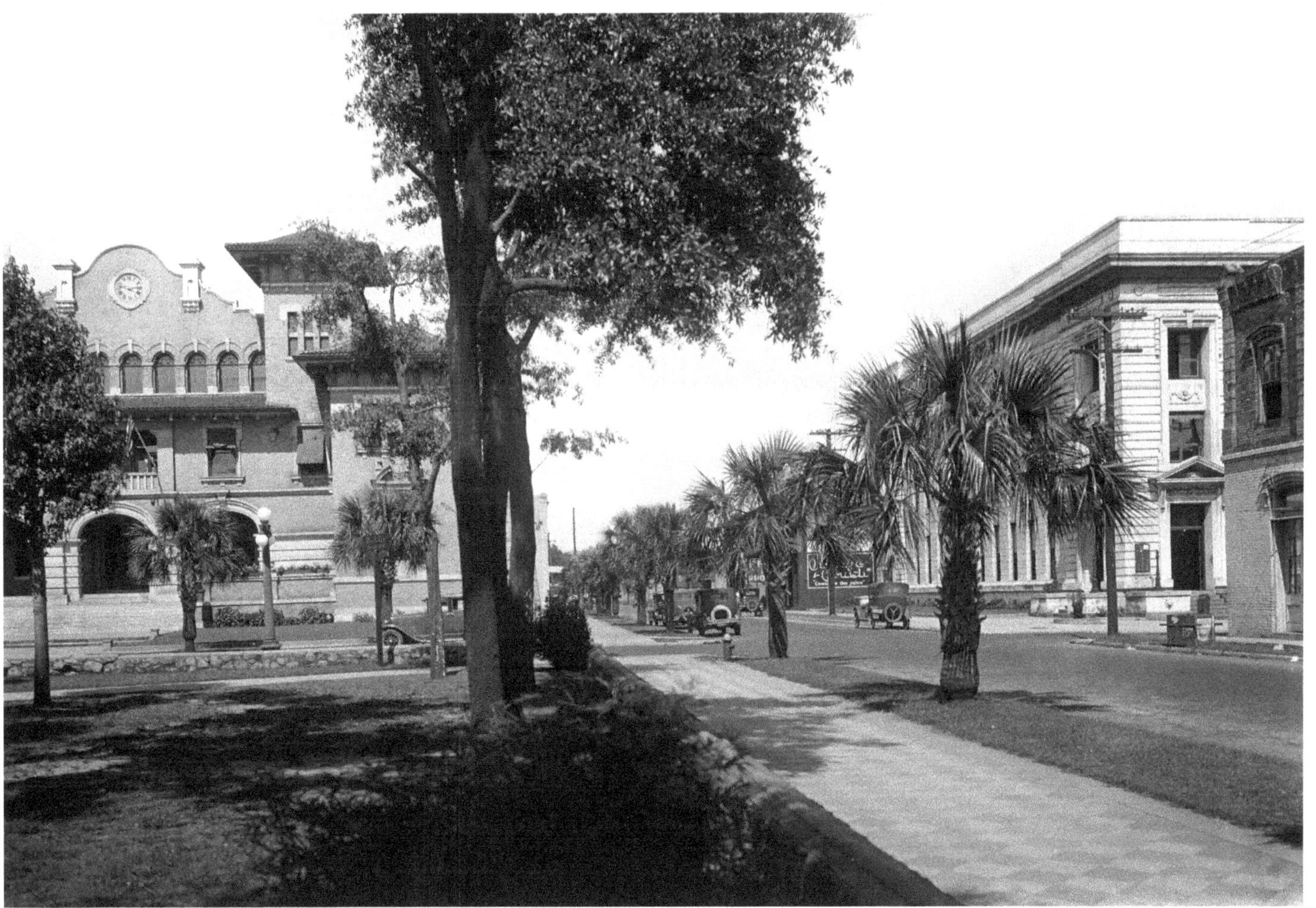

Garcia Beck stands ready to assist customers in the Fit Rite Shoe Store at 124-A South Palafox Street, where a special sale advertises ladies shoes at $1.98. The store was owned by Mr. B. Kaiman.

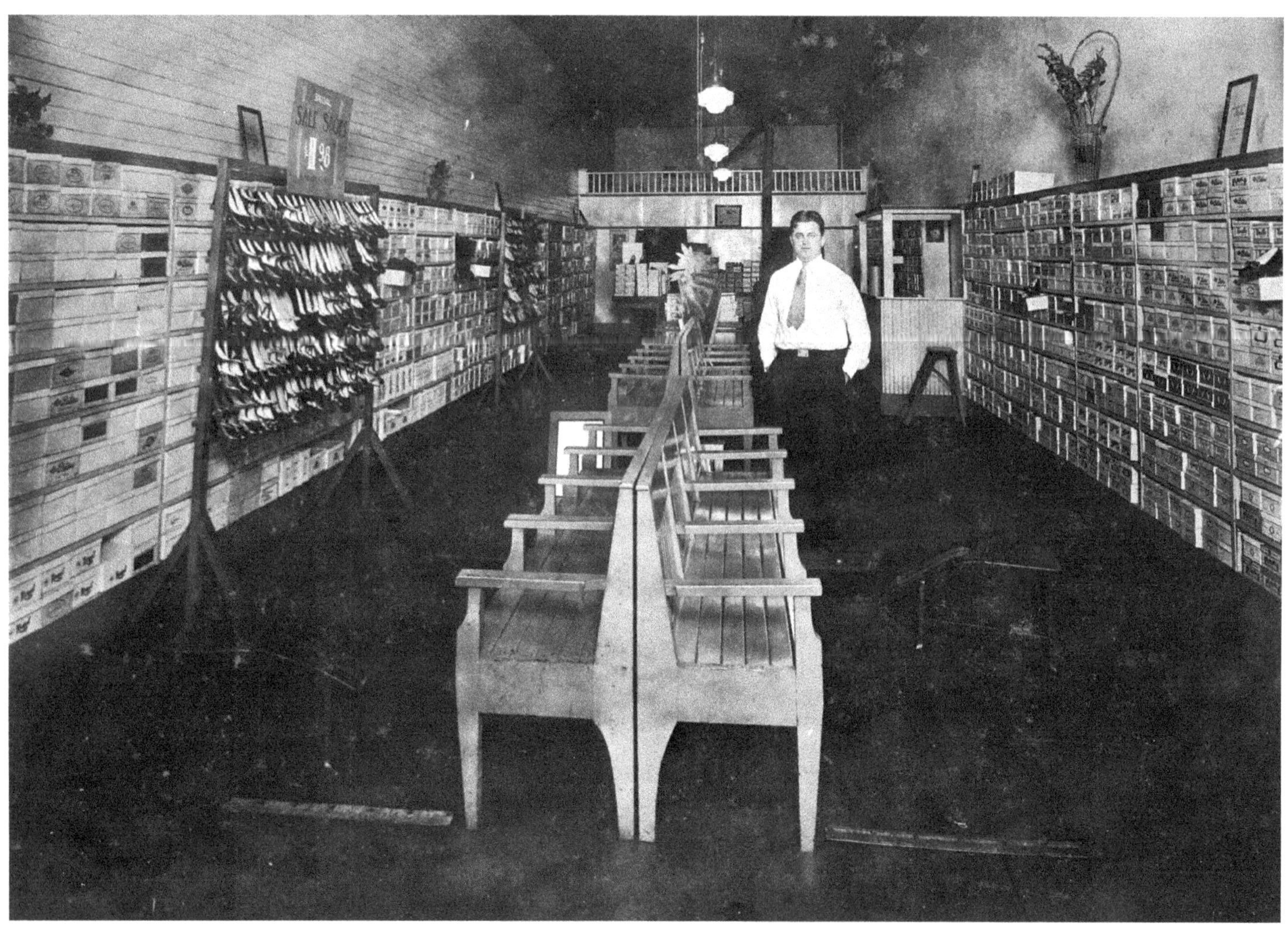

The new designs for hangars and control tower introduced at Corry Field were later used at other area bases. Rear Admiral Ernest King officially dedicated the new buildings December 8, 1934.

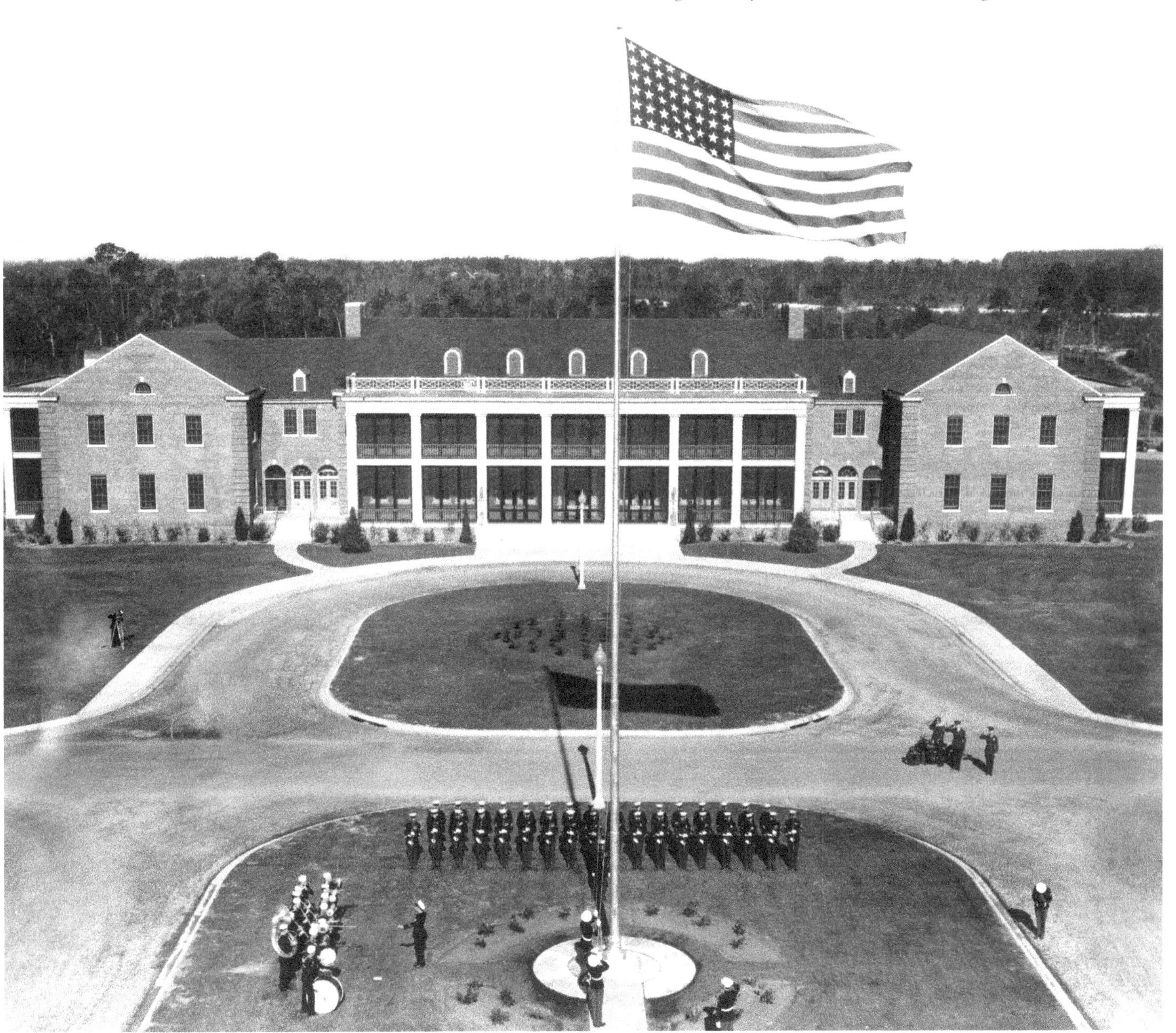

Governor David Sholtz was one of the speakers at the Corry Field dedication ceremony.

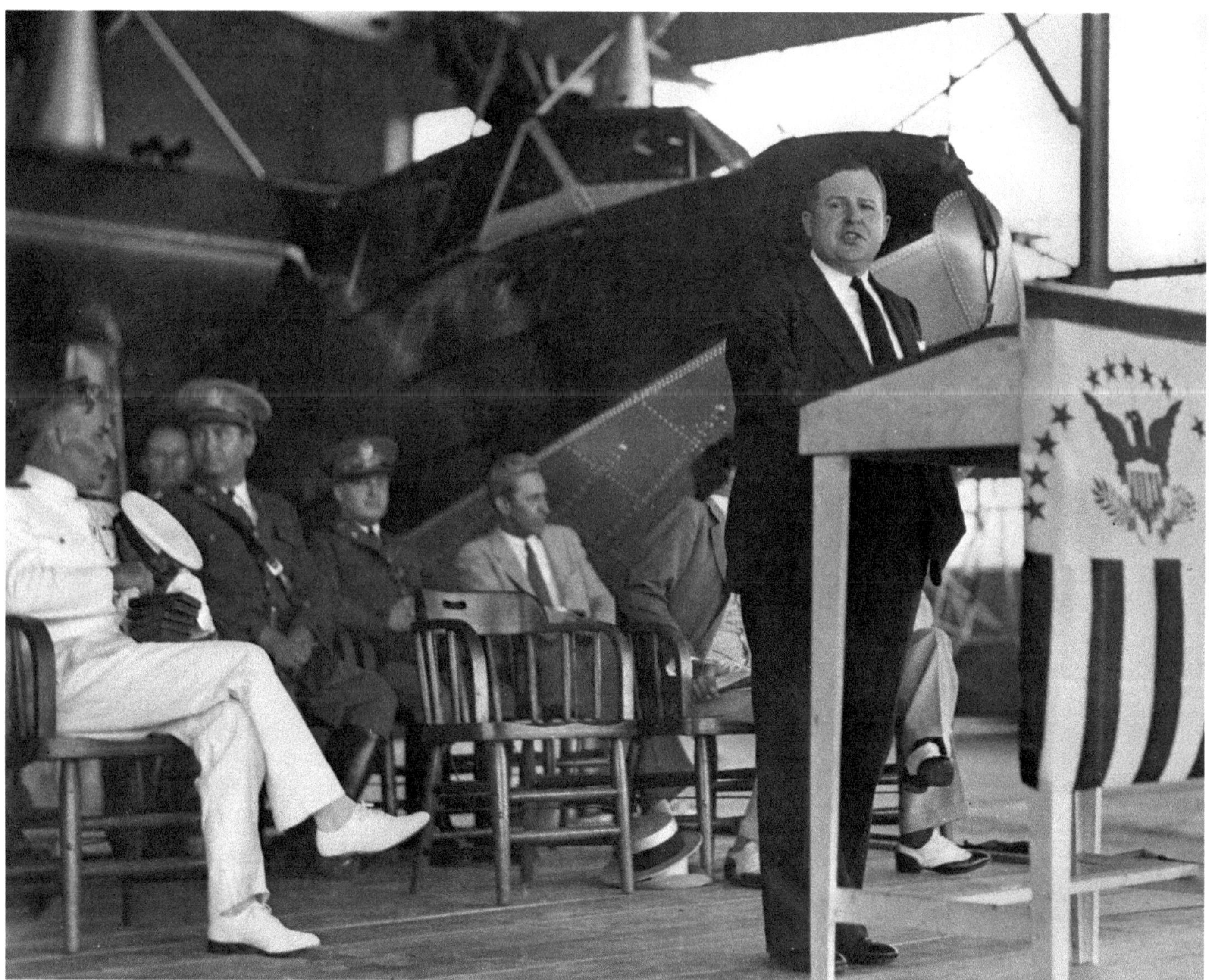

The USS *Pensacola,* a heavy cruiser built at the New York Navy Yard, escorted the USS *Enterprise* and the USS *Yorktown* at the Battle of Midway. The *Pensacola* was torpedoed at the battle of Tassafaronga in 1942 with a loss of more than 120 crewmen. She returned to service in 1943 and participated in battles at Wake Island, Marcus Island, Formosa, and the Battle of Leyte Gulf. The *Pensacola* was decommissioned in 1946.

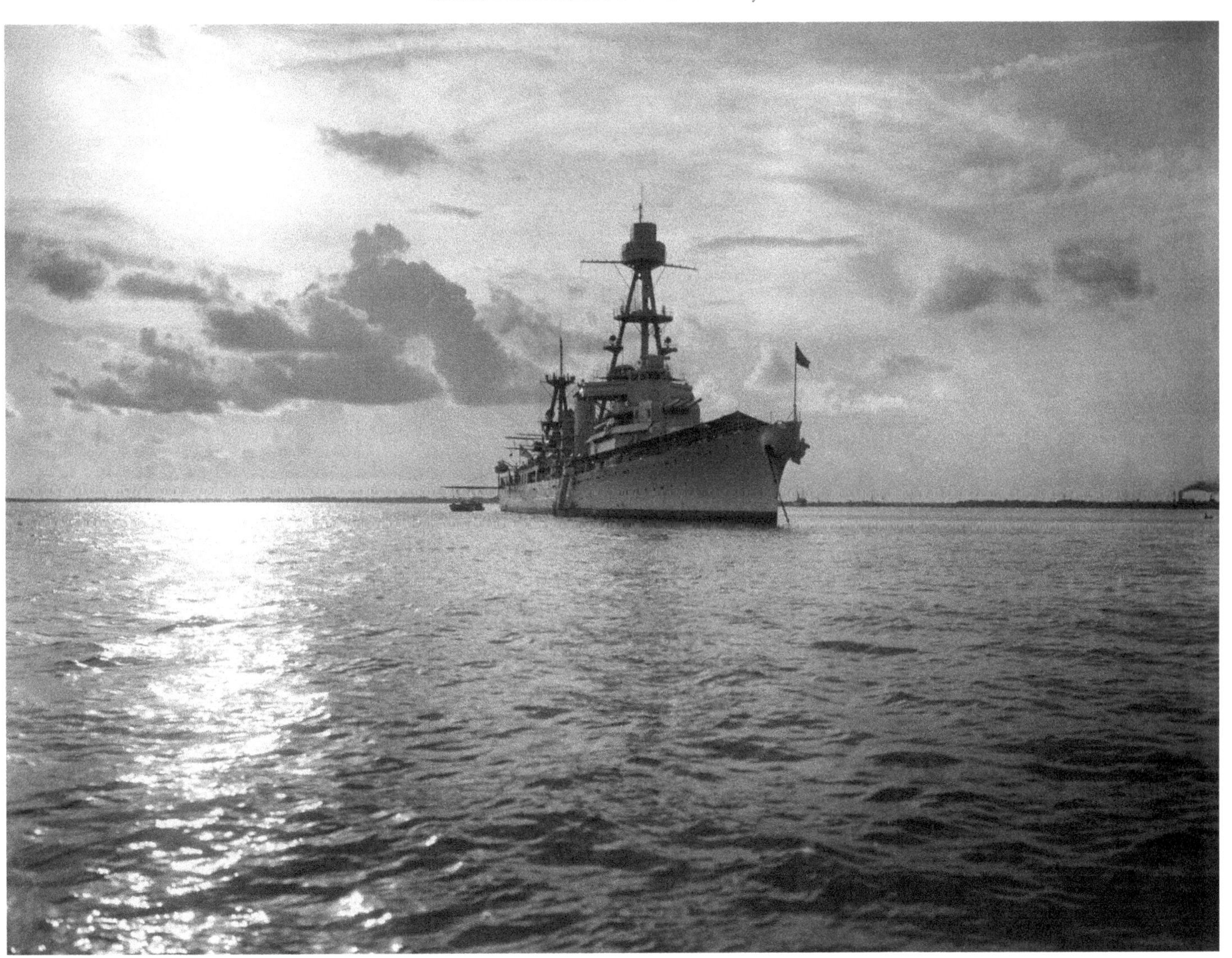

The Federal Emergency Relief Administration, a forerunner of the Work Projects Administration, helped communities during the Great Depression. These students are enrolled in an adult education class taught by the FERA.

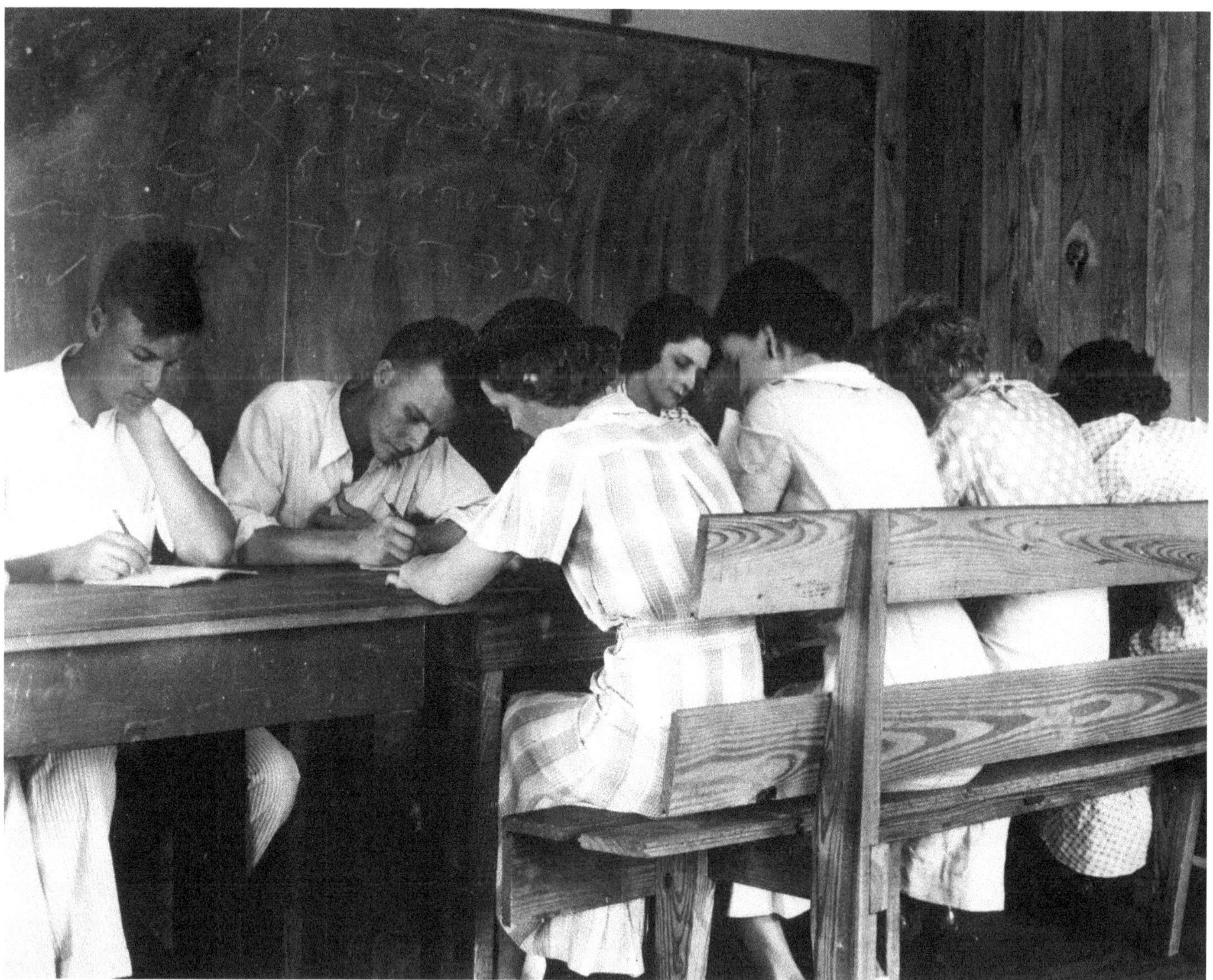

The Federal Emergency Relief Administration also provided jobs. These men are employed at the FERA mobile sawmill transient camp number 2.

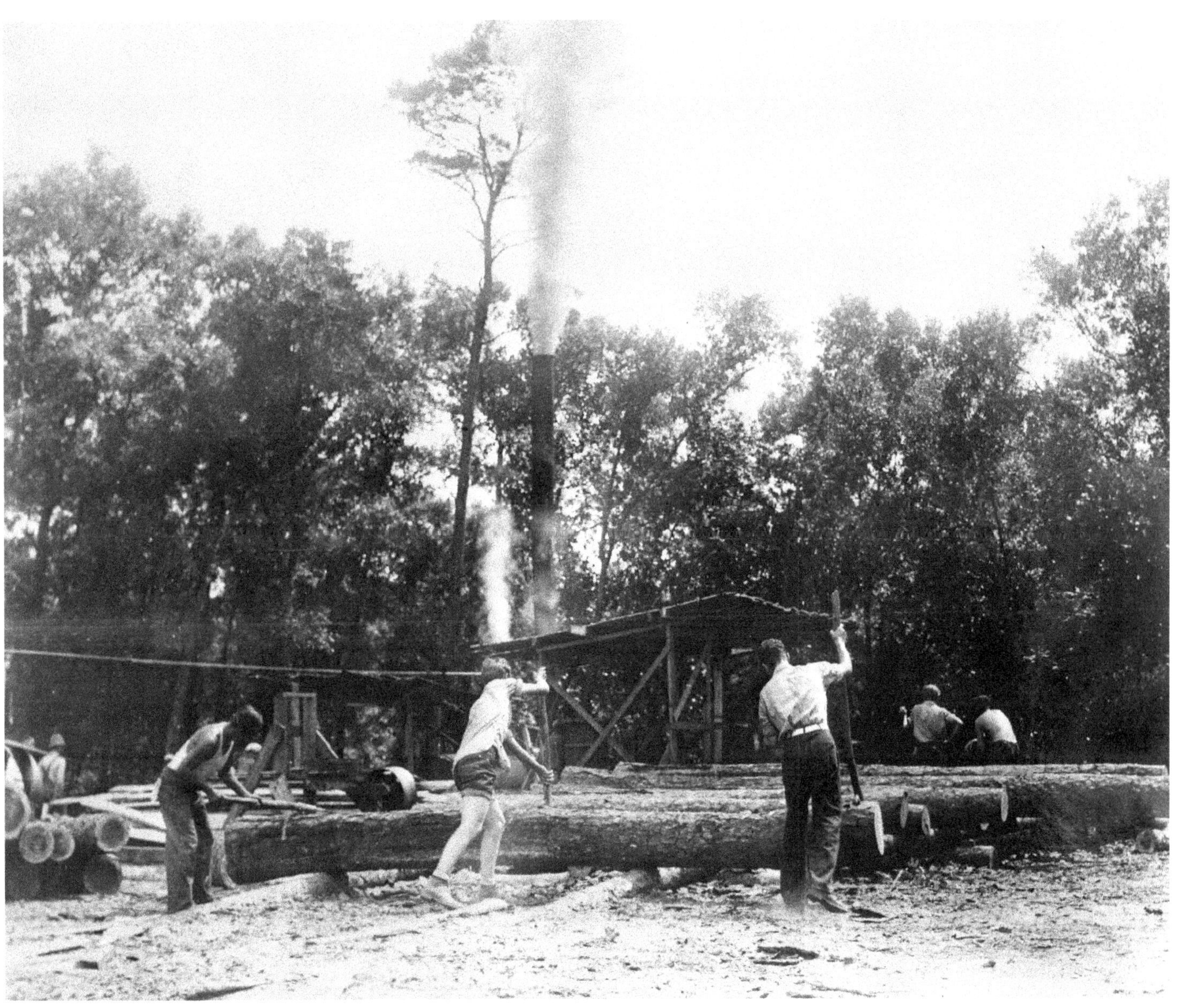

A works project of the Federal Emergency Relief Administration employed men to improve the Pensacola docks.

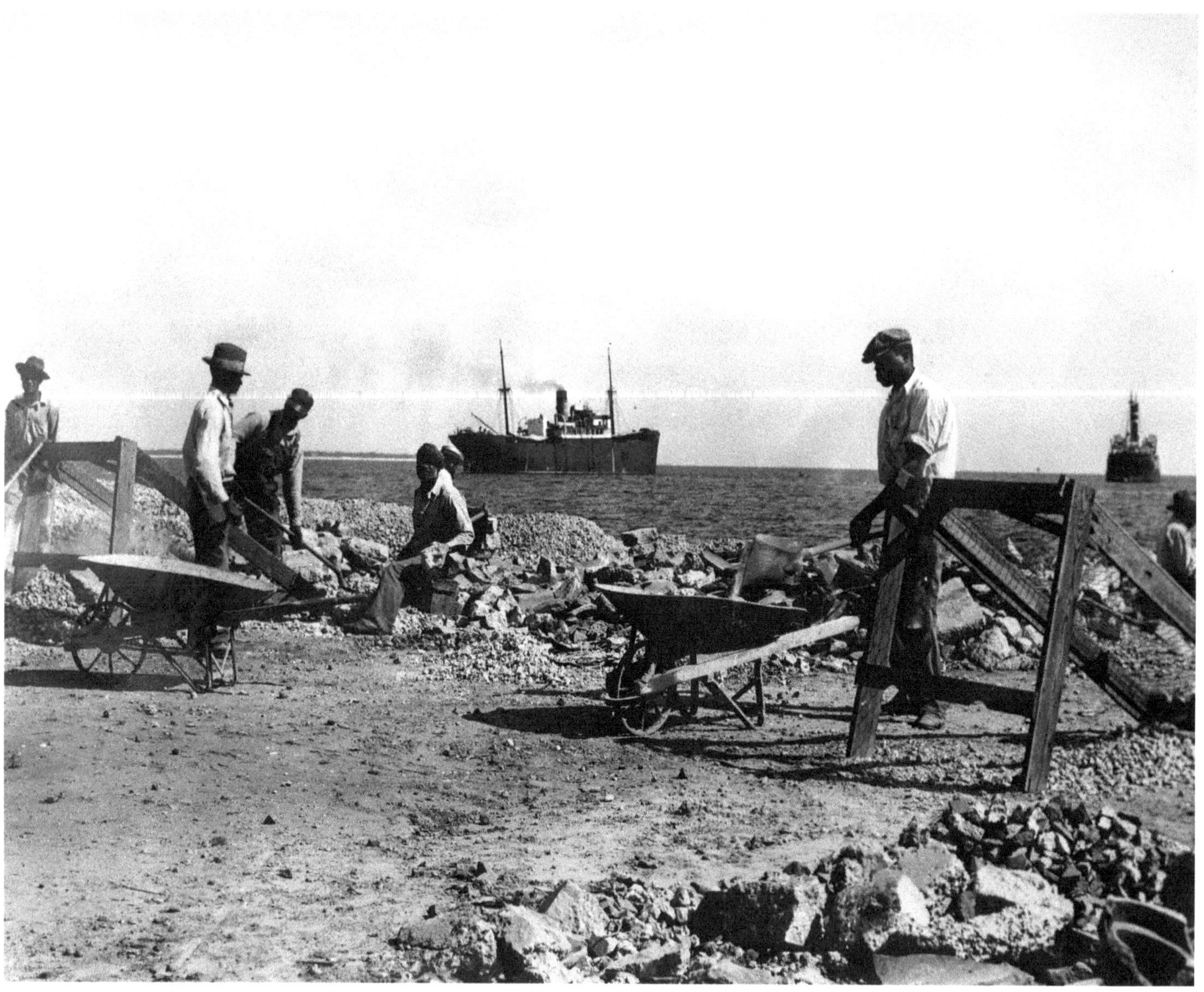

Bayview Park, built on 28 acres of land along Bayou Texar near the turn of the century, offered residents of the expanding city a place to relax and enjoy the water. Today, the park boasts a recreation center, senior center, tennis courts, soccer field, picnic tables, playground, and a dog park. The pier, destroyed by Hurricane Ivan, has been rebuilt.

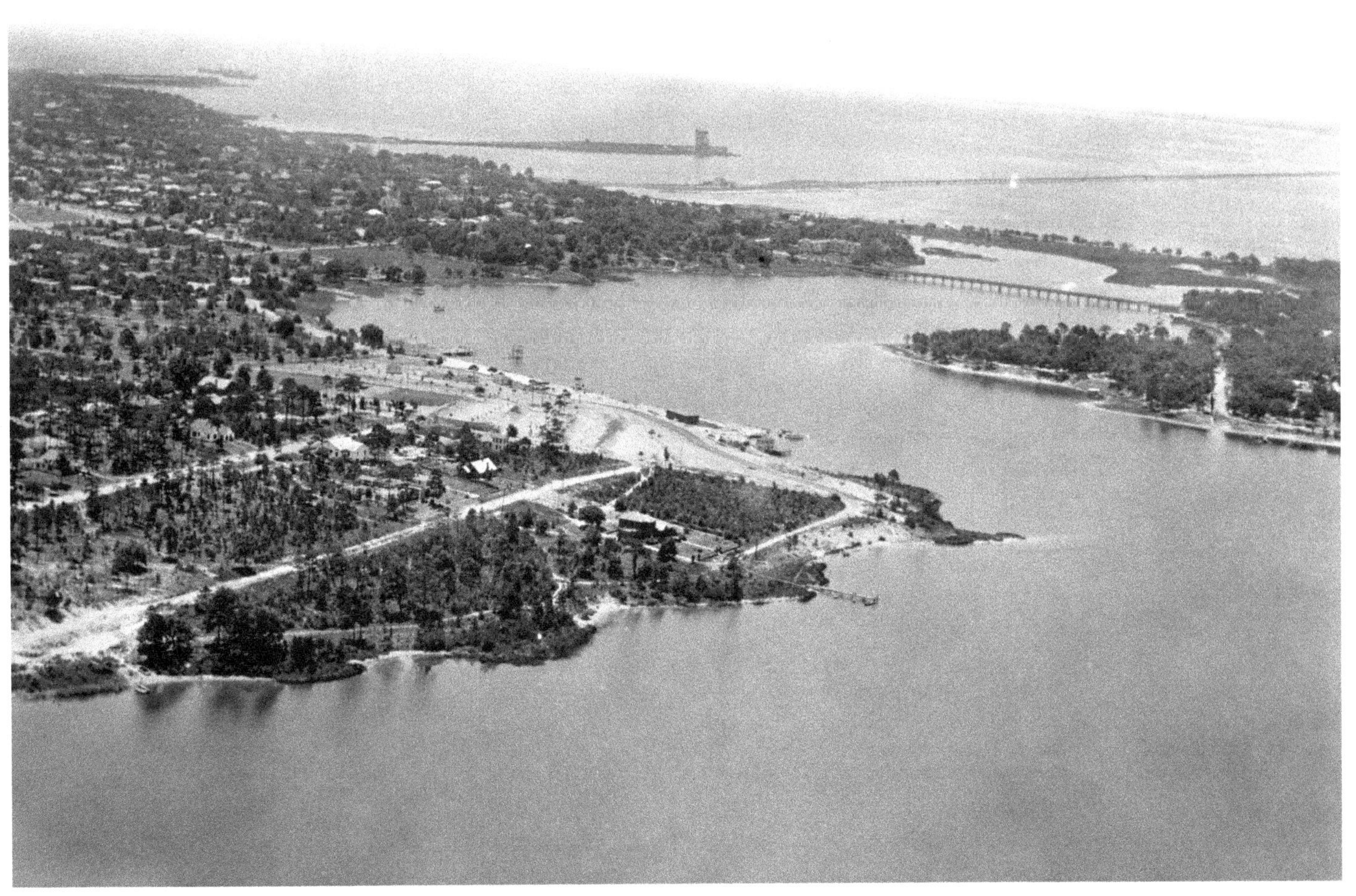

The Federal Emergency Relief Administration also offered opportunities for women. FERA supplied these women with jobs in a local mattress factory.

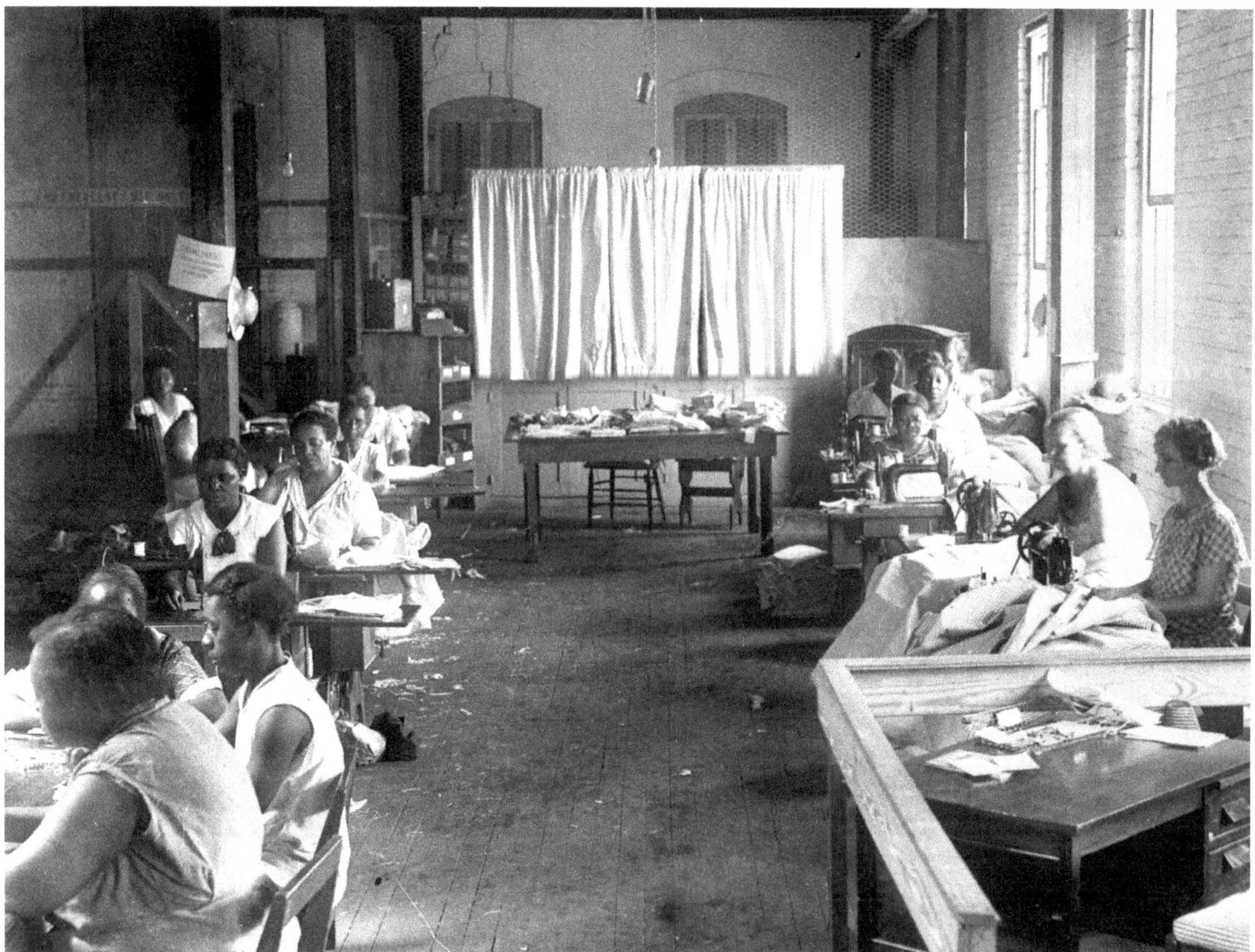

Employees of the Federal Emergency Relief Administration added bathhouses and a pavilion to the grounds of Bayview Park.

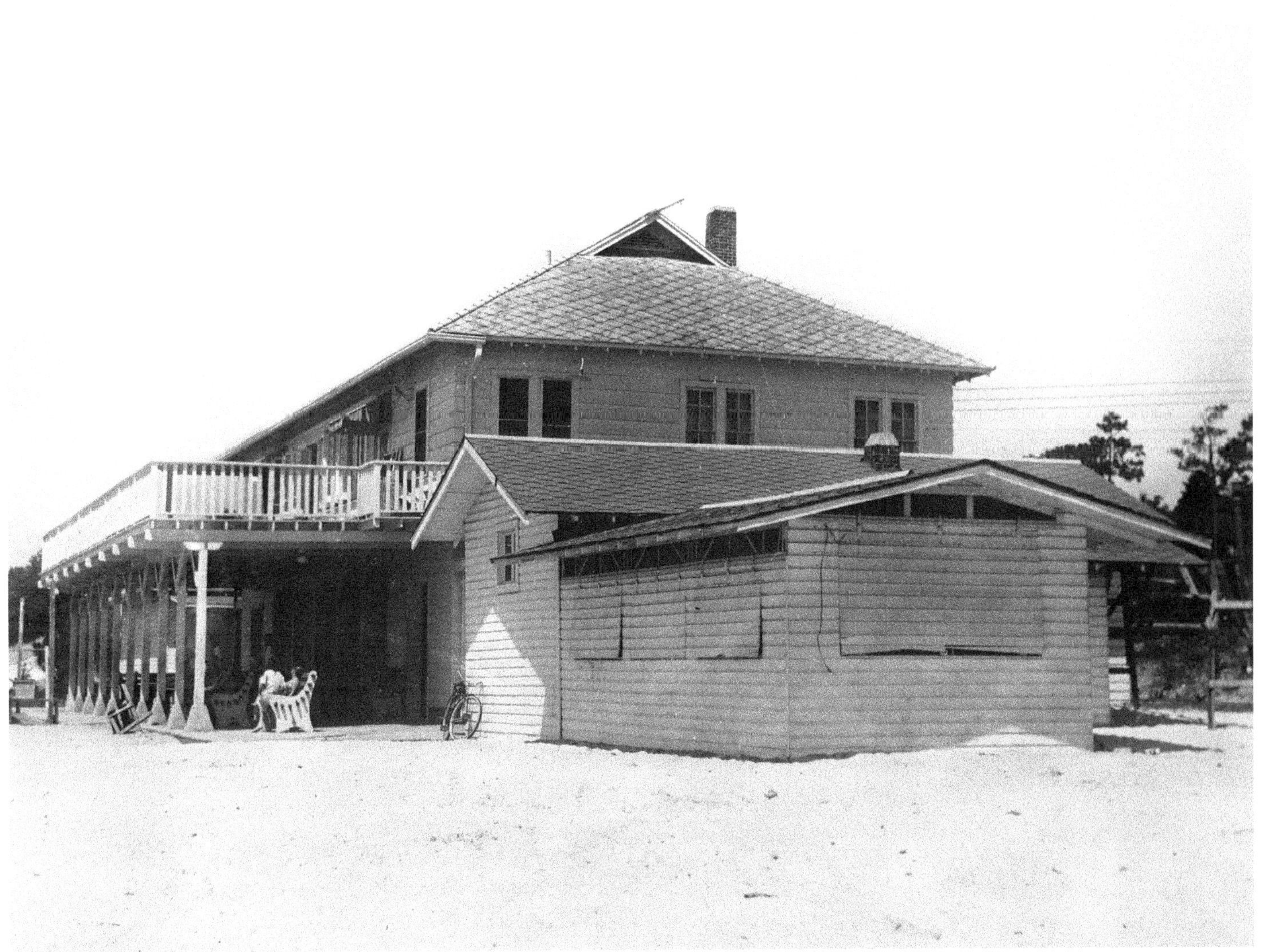

The Federal Emergency Relief Administration offered instruction to adults at Booker T. Washington High School. For some, this was their first opportunity to learn to read and write.

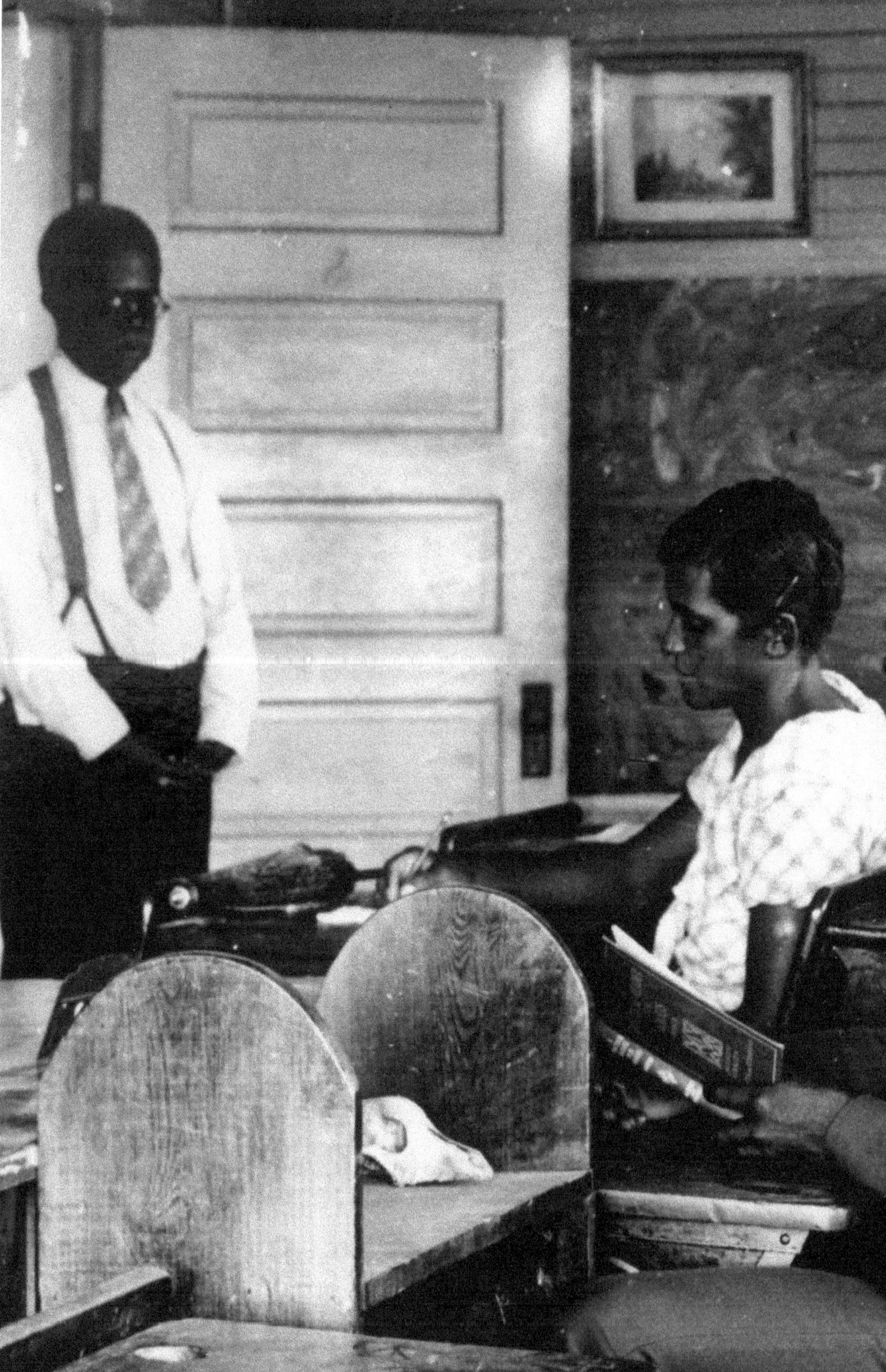

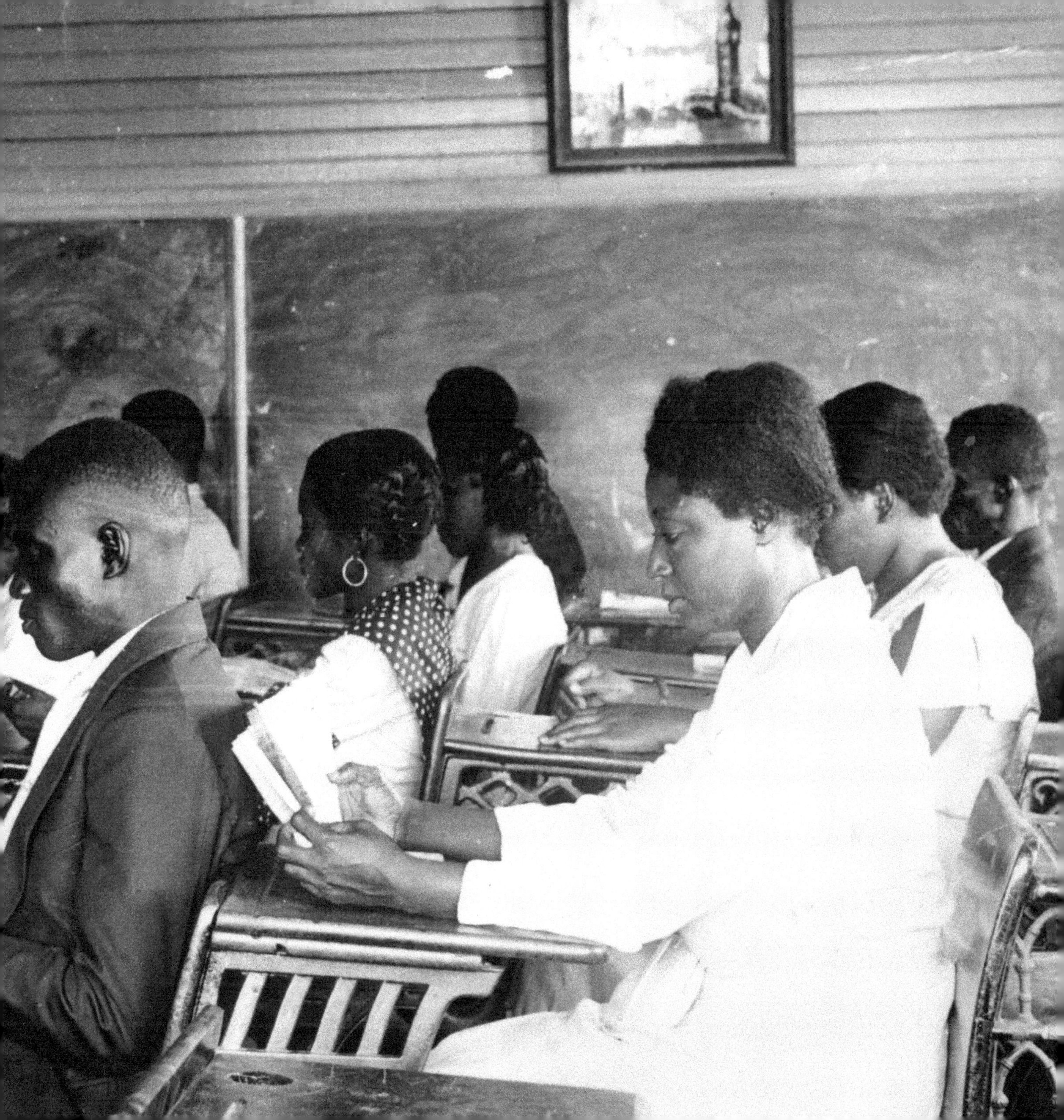

Pensacola Beach was sparsely populated in 1939. The Casino, to the right of the pier, was the retail center of the island. Outdoor concession stands are visible to the left of the pier.

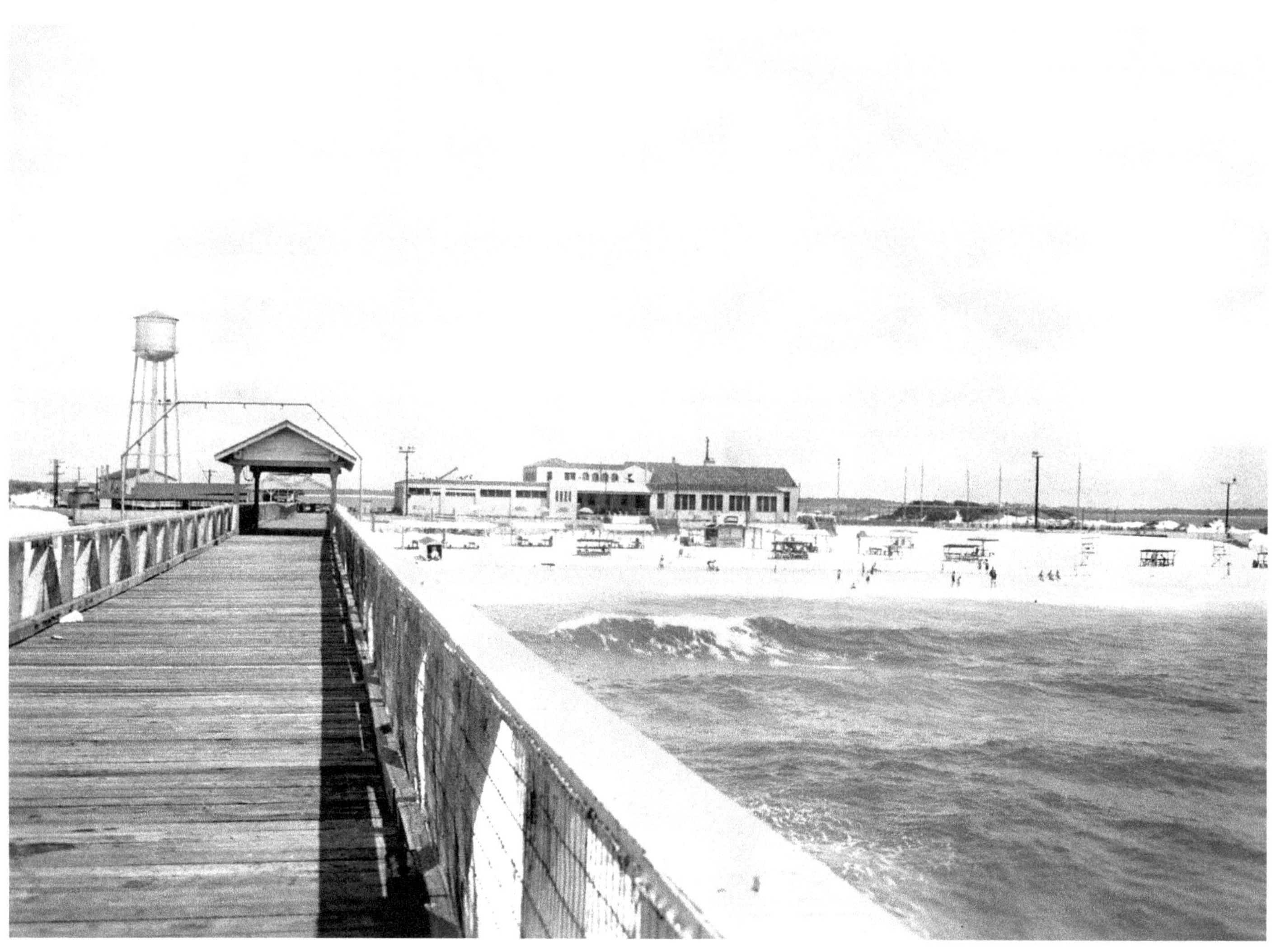

Today, it is rare to see the Seventeenth Avenue Bridge without a generous layer of graffiti. In 1935, the bridge was not viewed as an artist's canvas.

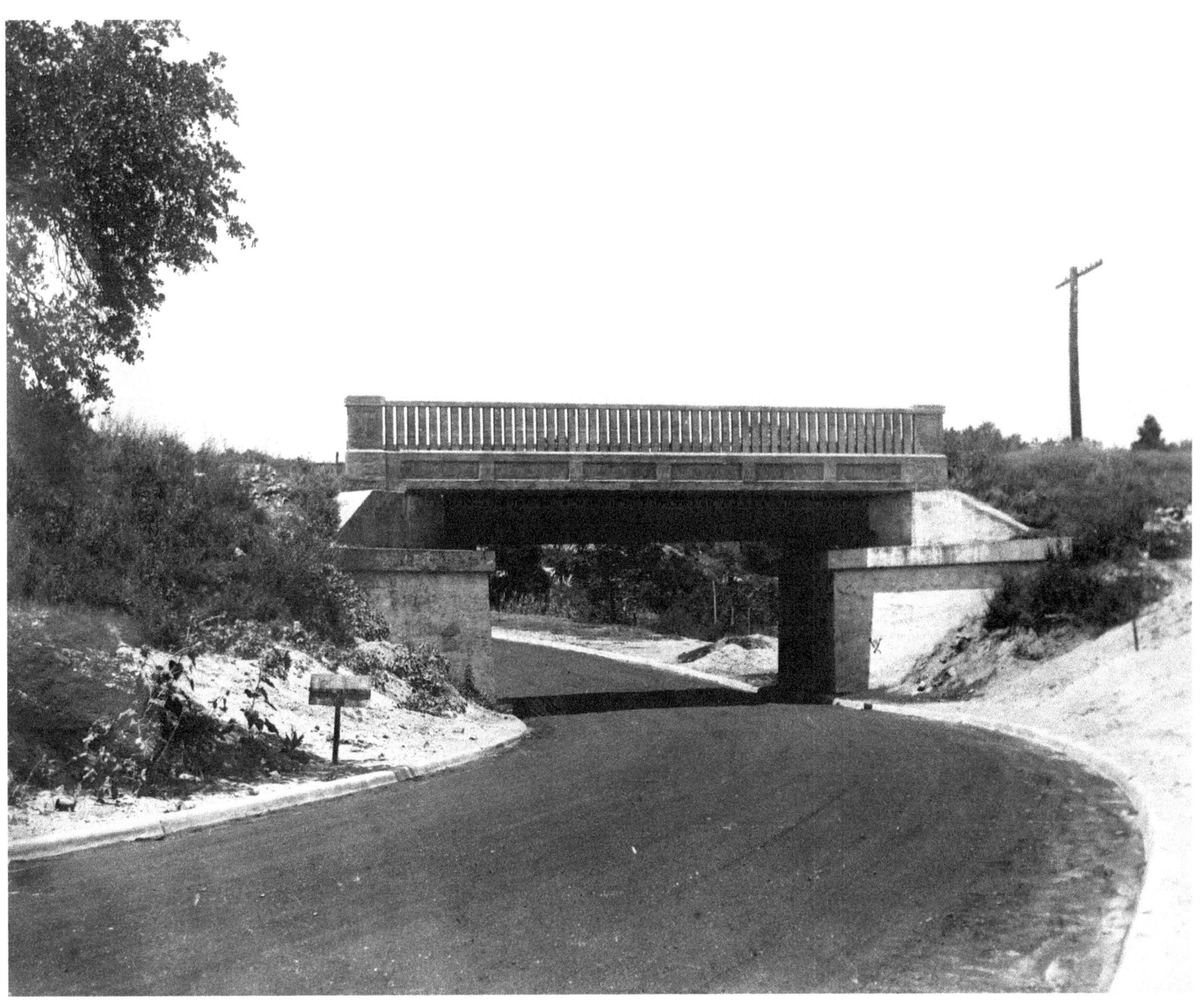

This picture was taken at the Twilight Club on Barrancas Avenue. In the rear, Alphonse Gamblin is partly hidden by the unknown sailor playing the accordion. An unnamed Norwegian tourist is taking a turn on the bass, Charlie Bruton is on the sax, and Cornelius "Ninnie" Bell is on the drums. Ida Goodson is the piano player. Harold Andrews, with his back to the camera, is next to Goodson.

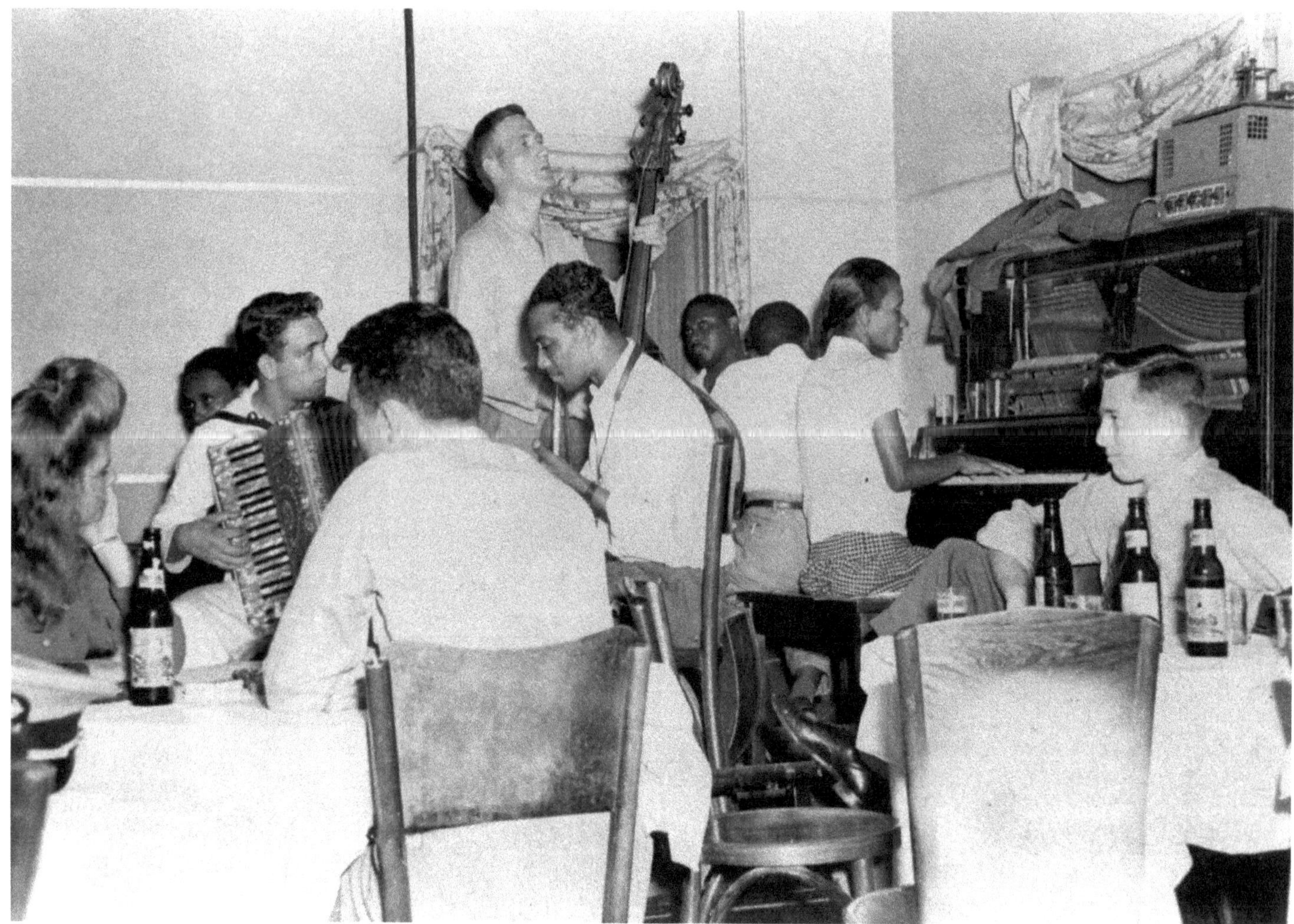

A Changing City

(1940–1960s)

The Navy's presence in Pensacola increased during World War II. Stepped up military efforts brought many new faces to the city. Pensacolians opened their doors to the thousands of young men stationed at the area bases, taking them home for Sunday dinner and offering them a brief detachment from the rigors of the base to relax with a family. The community collected scrap metal, rubber, and other items needed to produce goods for the military. The city's two USOs also offered off-duty service personnel entertainment and a place to make new friends. Patriotism was strong in the city, and the people of Pensacola did what they could to support the war effort.

A postwar housing boom began the movement away from downtown Pensacola. Many young couples welcomed the new suburban subdivisions, moving away from the city proper and into large communities with small, similar houses that boasted modern conveniences. The Navy Point Stores opened near the Naval Air Station in 1946 and the Town and Country Plaza opened at the corner of Pace Boulevard and Fairfield Drive in 1957. These new facilities offered a wide range of shopping in one building and convenient parking, drawing consumers away from downtown.

War-weary Pensacolians were entertained by Mardi Gras activities, which had continued throughout the war. The 1950s saw the beginning of a new tradition, the Fiesta of Five Flags, which celebrates the 1559 landing of Don Tristan de Luna and the first settlement of Pensacola. Festivities include parades, treasure hunts, and dances.

Pensacola has a long history with the Navy. In 1946, the Navy founded their precision-flight team, the Blue Angels, and Pensacola has been the proud home of the Blues since 1955. Even though some bases have closed and some commands have moved, the Navy has retained a strong presence in the area.

Pensacola continues to grow and to change, but Pensacolians are very proud of their past and work to preserve their history. These photographs are an important part of that history.

Pensacola sponsored a United Service Organization (USO) at 313 North DeVilliers Street for African-American servicemen.

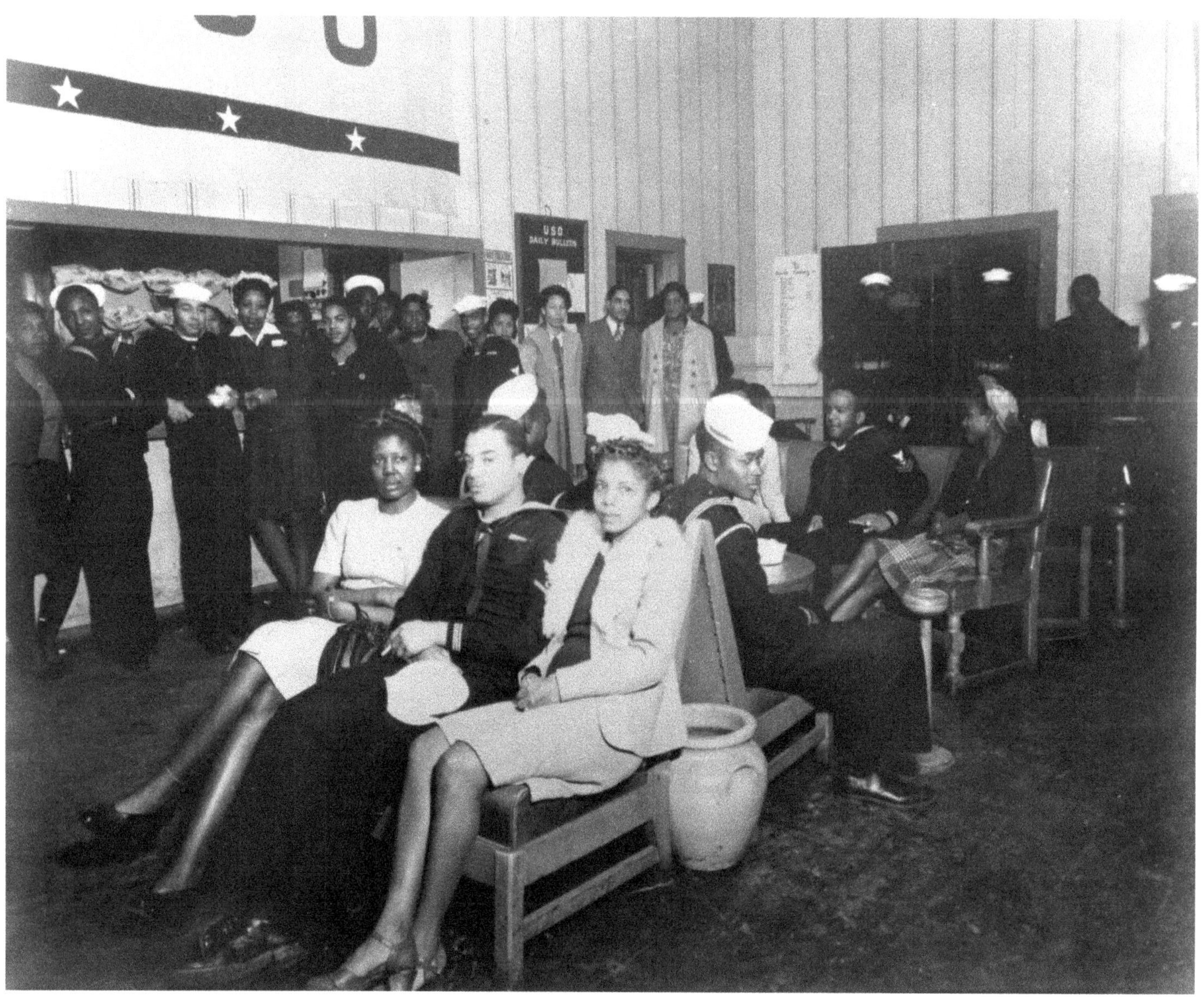

This first group of 130 British Royal Navy aviation students reported to Naval Air Station, Pensacola, for training in July 1941. A total of 800 British pilots trained at NAS Pensacola during World War II.

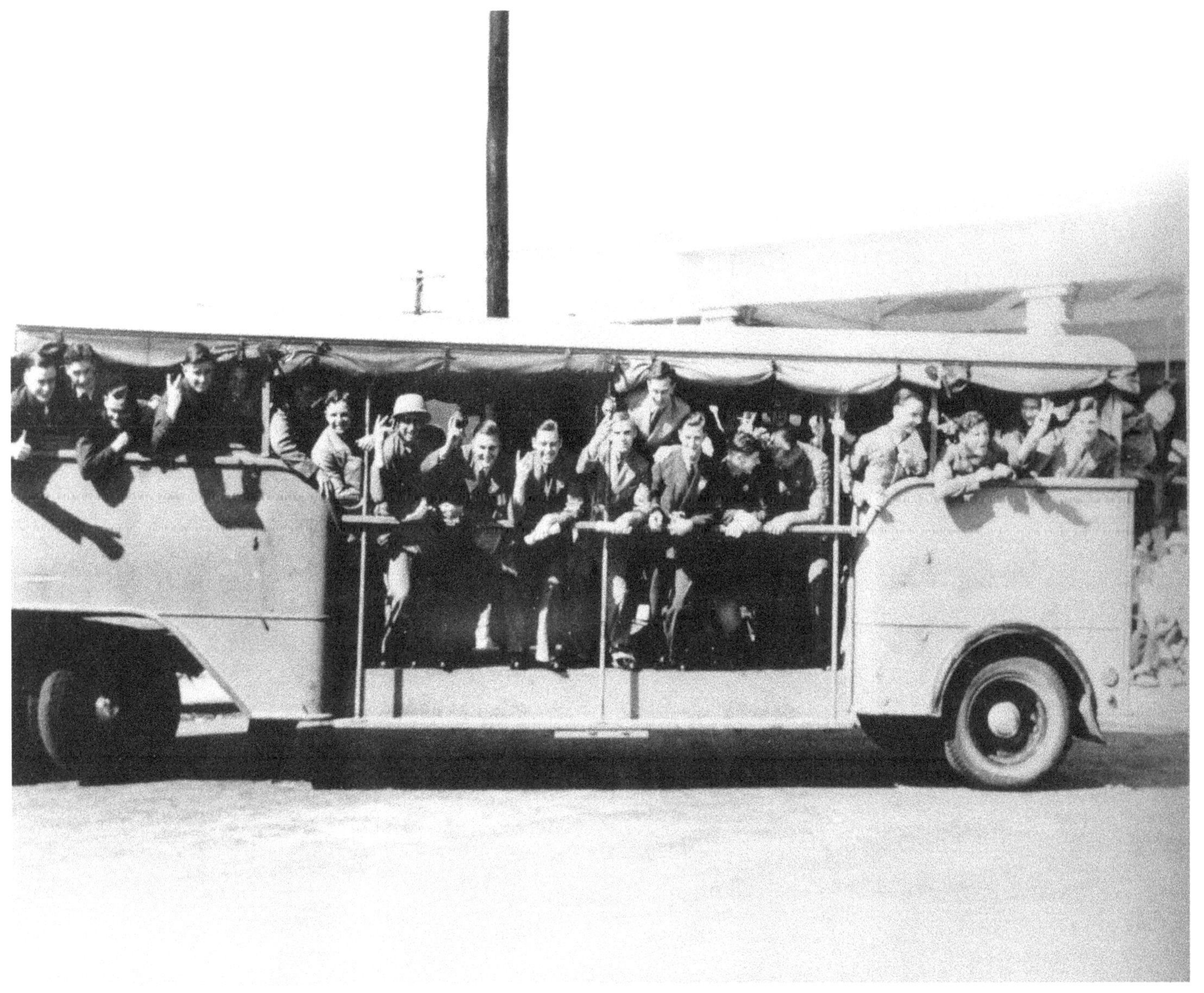

Patriotic Pensacolians were eager to contribute to the war effort during World War II. This pile of rubber and scrap metal, collected in a local drive, was to be recycled into war matériel.

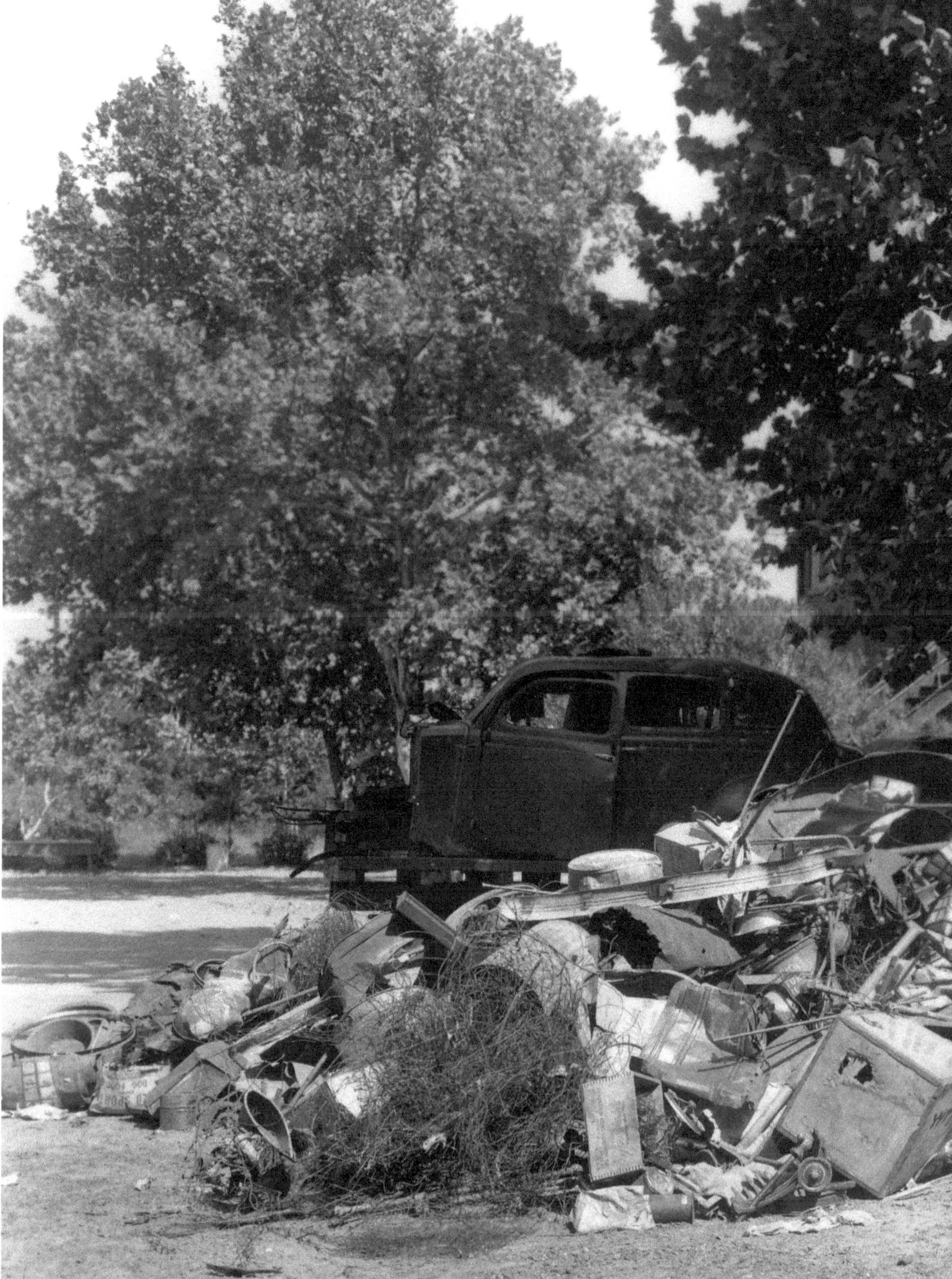

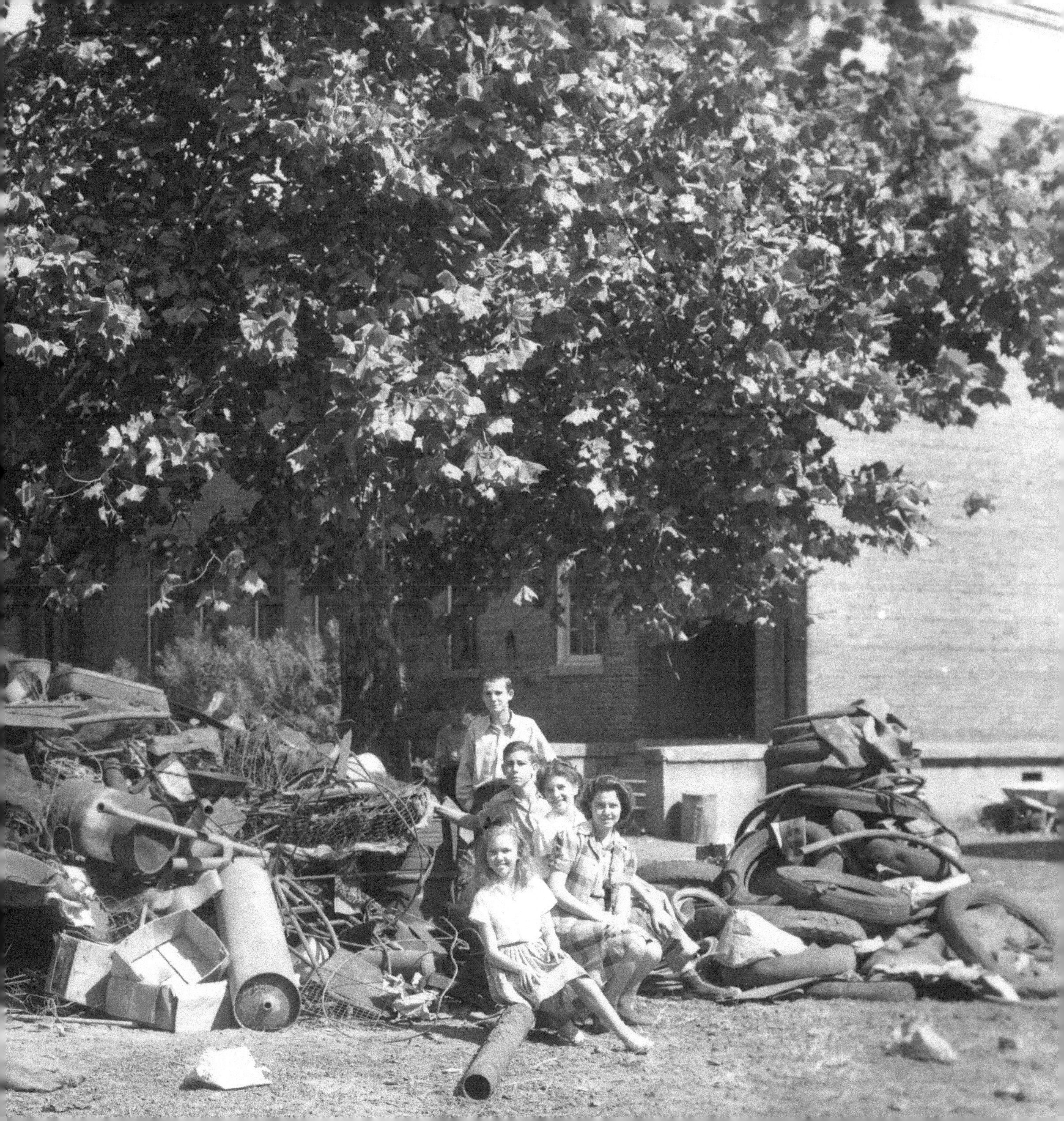

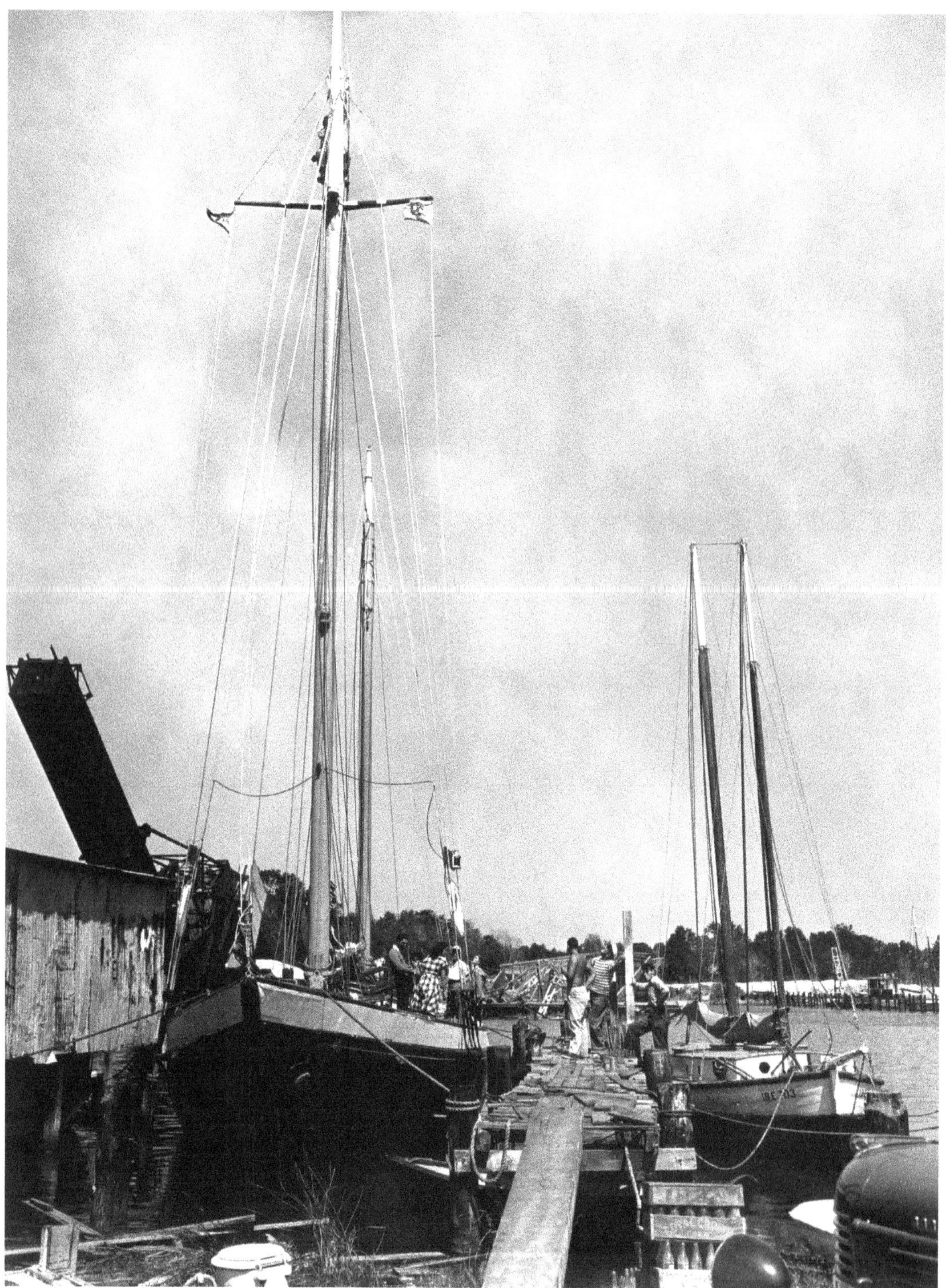

L. M. Harvey, owner of Harvey Supply Company, readies the *Esperanza* for a cruise in September 1947. Damage from tropical force winds that hit Pensacola on September 17, 1947, is also visible in the photograph.

The sugar-white sands of Pensacola Beach have been a favorite escape for local residents and visitors since the bridges connecting Pensacola to Gulf Breeze and Santa Rosa Island were opened in 1931.

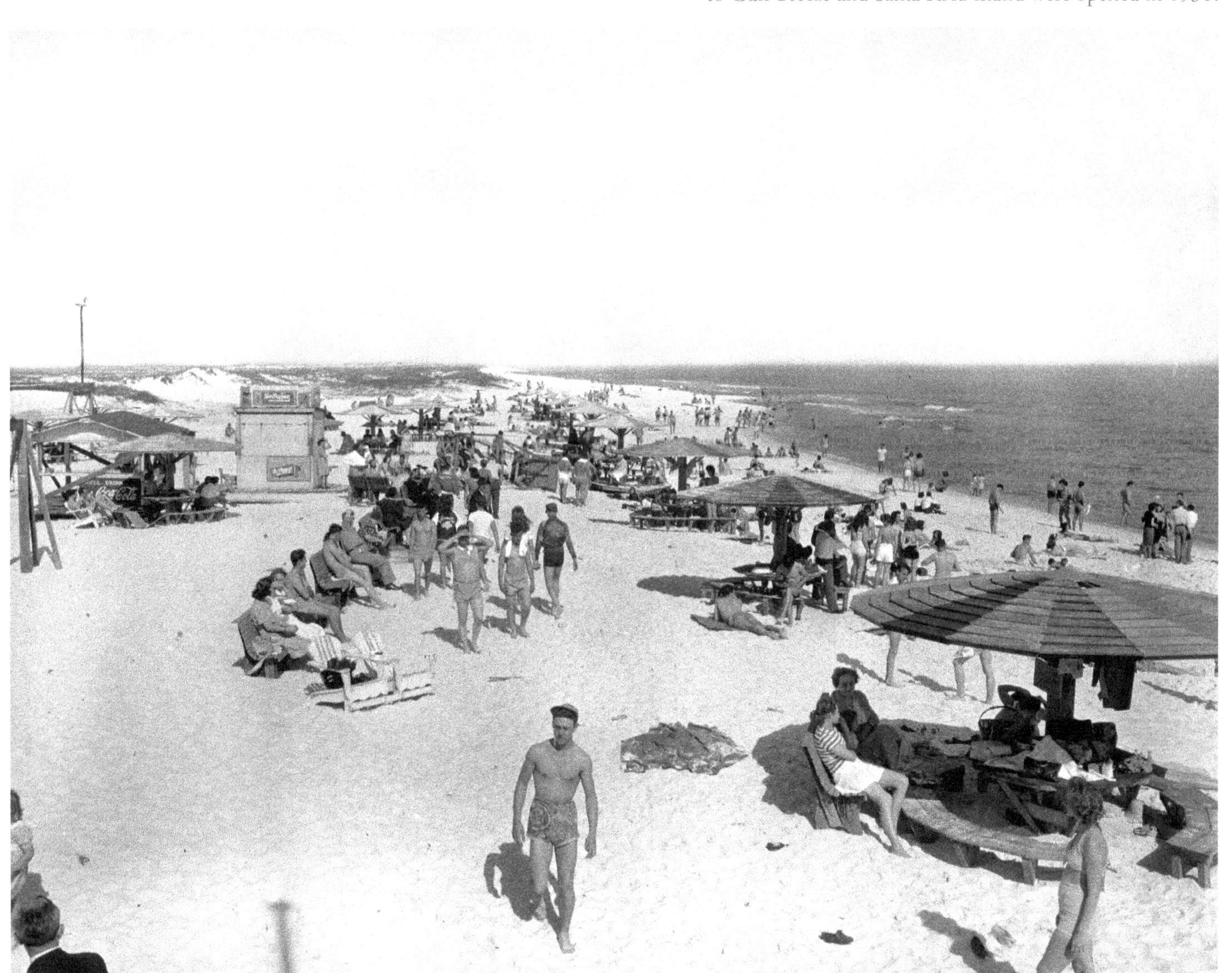

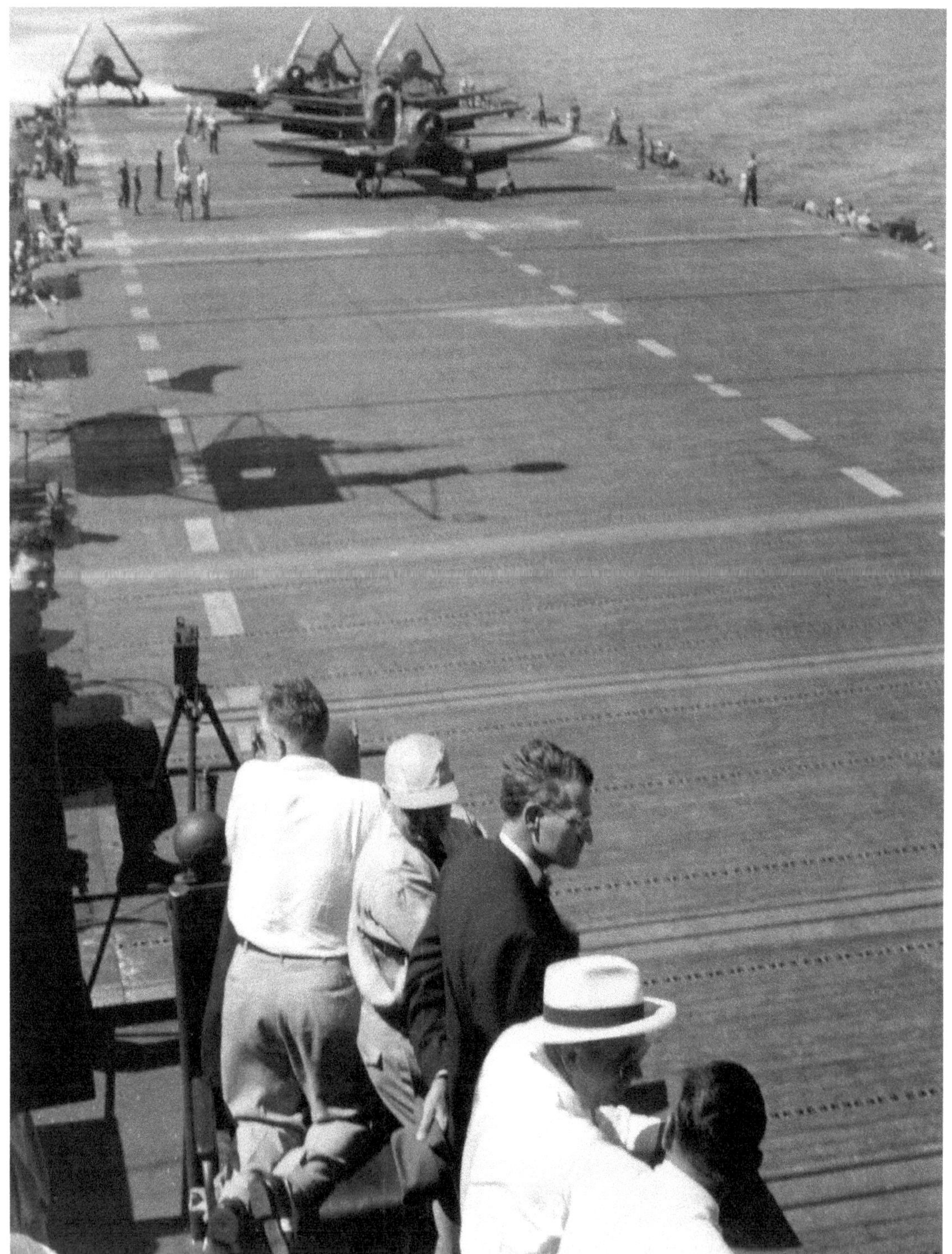

The USS *Saipan,* a small aircraft carrier, was commissioned in July 1946 and stationed at Naval Air Station, Pensacola, from 1954 through 1957. Governor Millard Caldwell, wearing a dark suit, stands amid the group of men in the foreground.

The Frisco Railroad's Spanish mission–style passenger depot, built in 1932, was located at the corner of West Garden and Coyle streets, near where the Frisco engine sits in the median today. The Frisco ended passenger service to Pensacola in 1956 and the building was demolished in 1966.

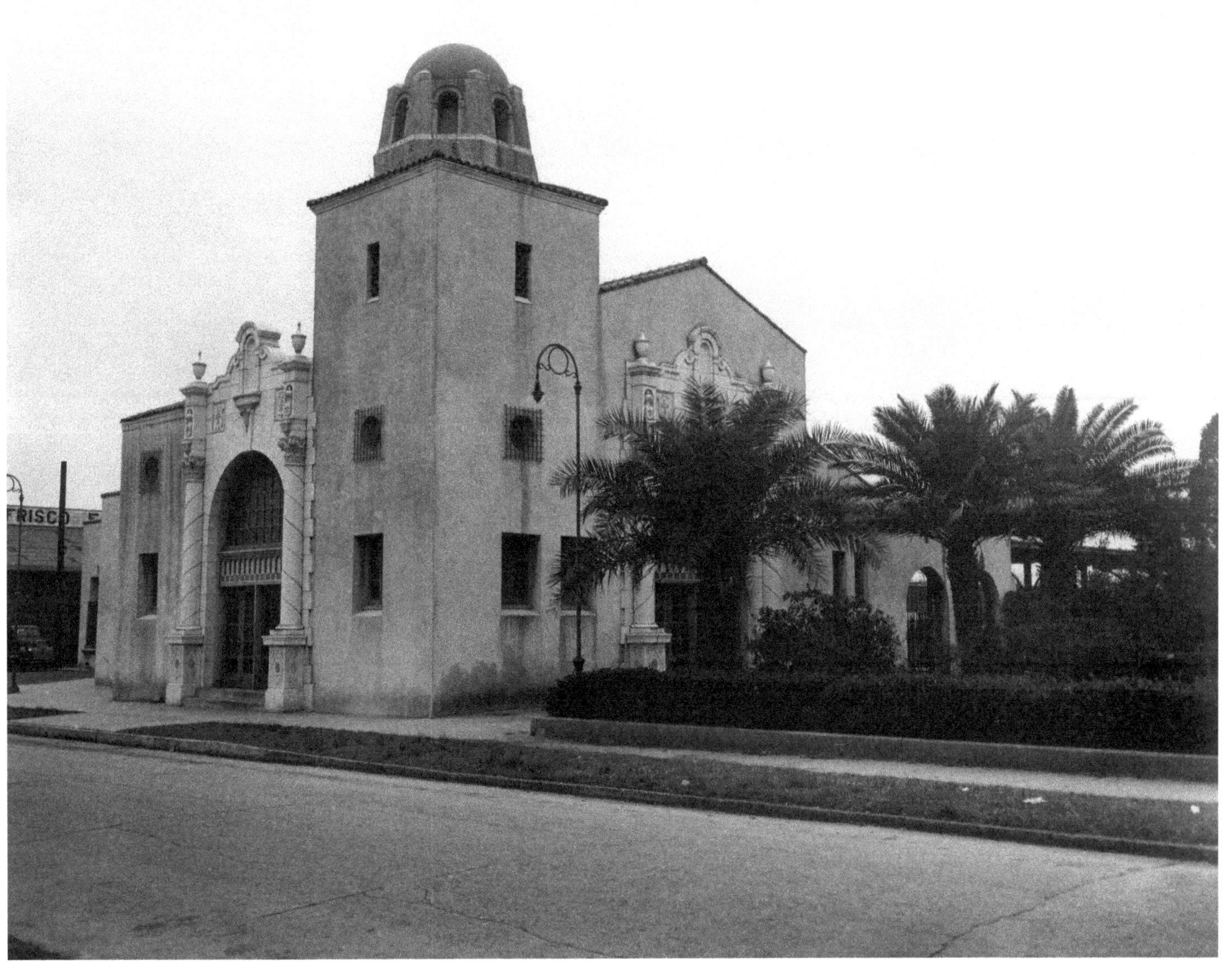

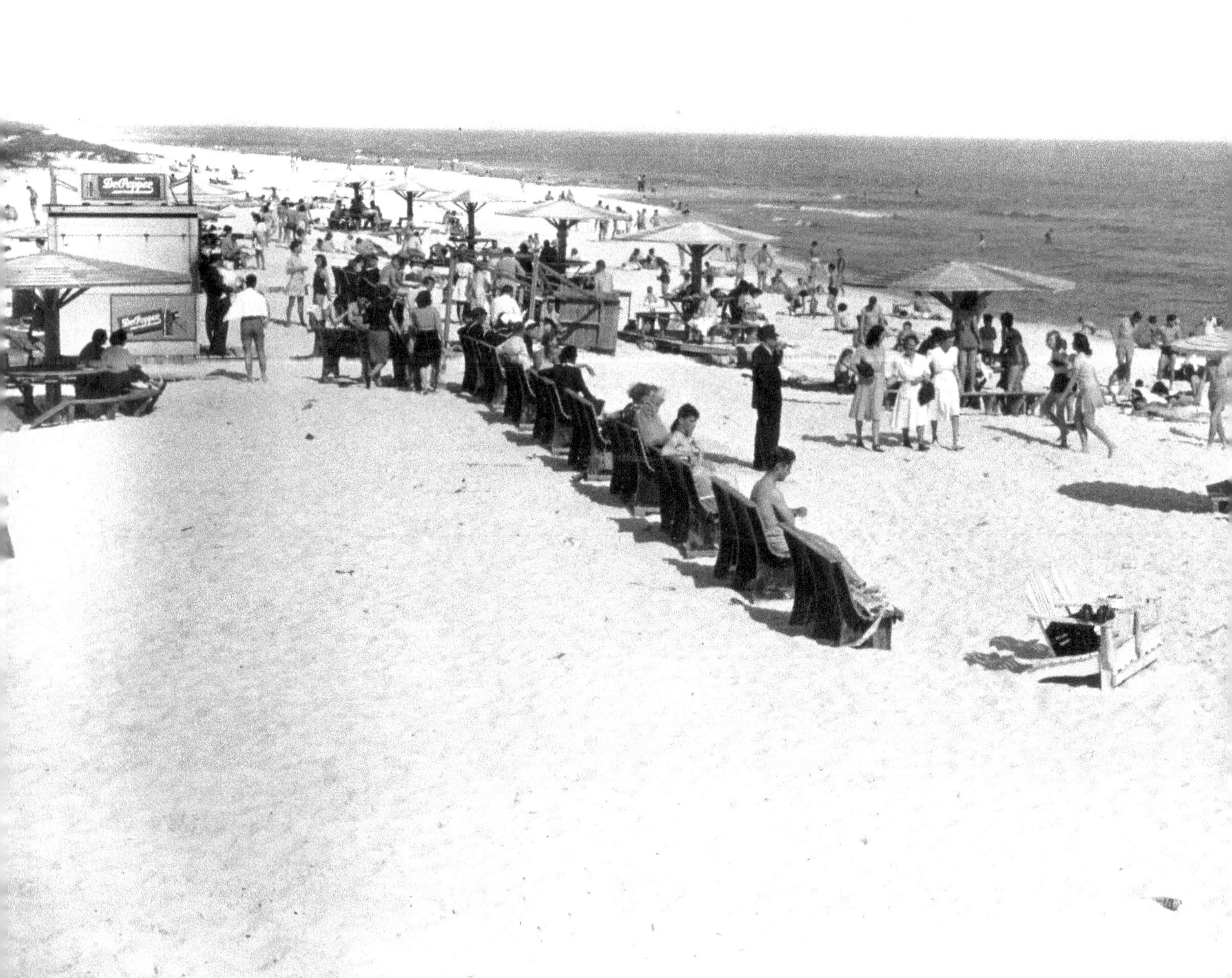
DrPepper
DrPepper

Casino Beach, with its easy access to refreshments and bathhouses, has always been a popular place for seaside diversions.

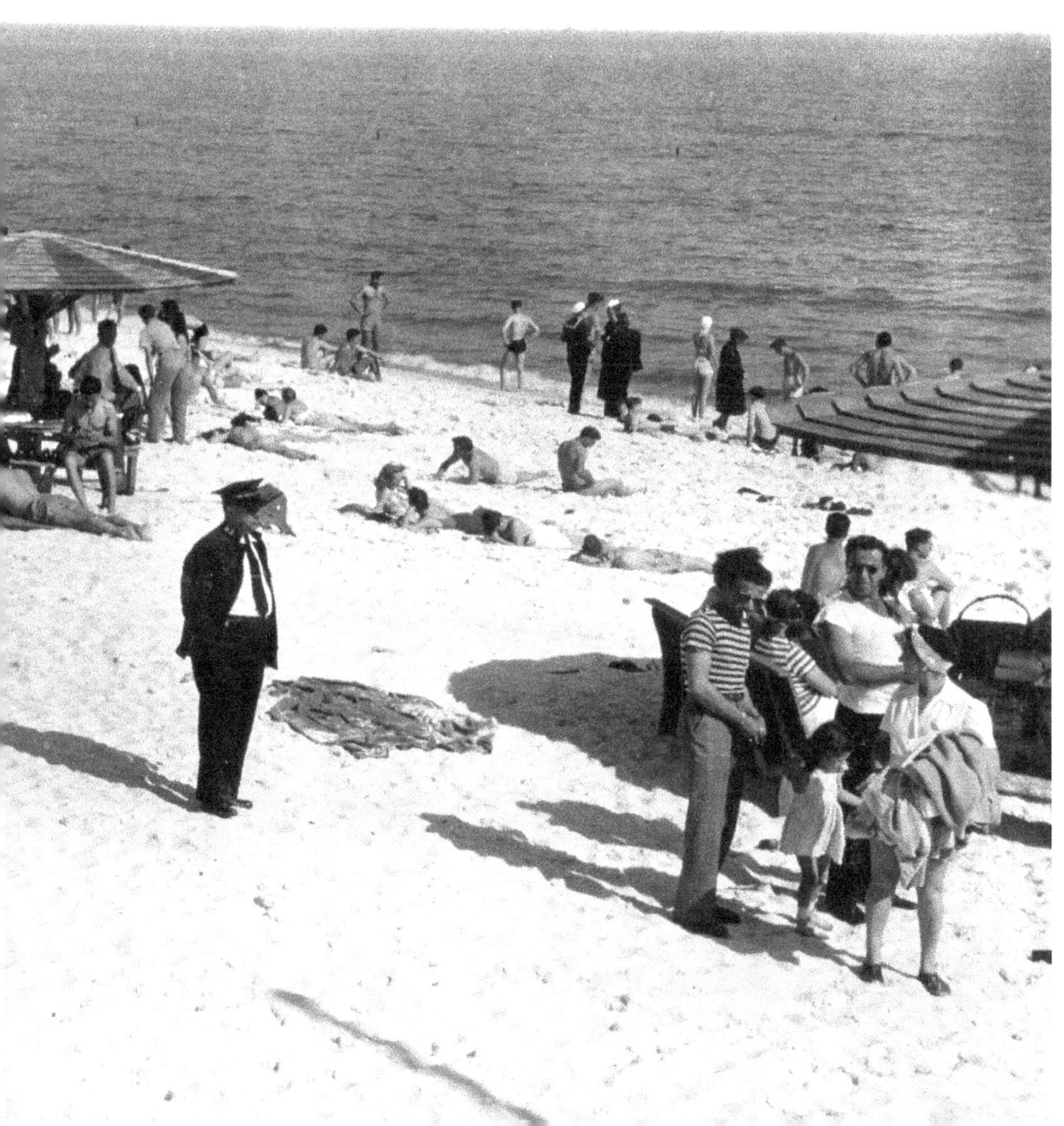

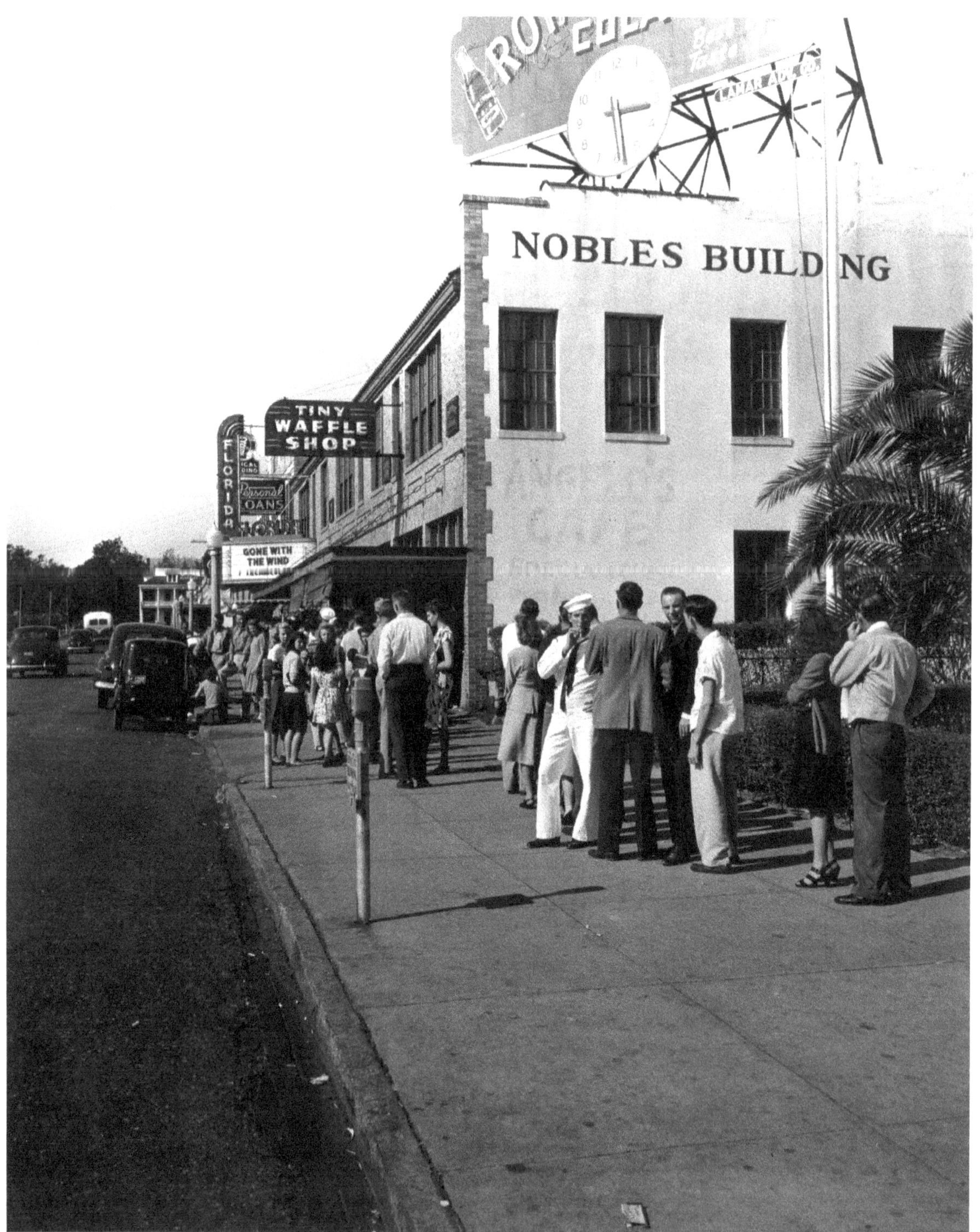

It was not unusual for lines of moviegoers waiting for tickets to the latest show at the Florida Theater to stretch beyond the Federal Building and wrap around the corner. This run of *Gone With the Wind* was no exception.

Downtown was still the main business and shopping district in 1948. The lack of available parking spaces reflects postwar development, which led many residents to move farther from the downtown area and drive into town.

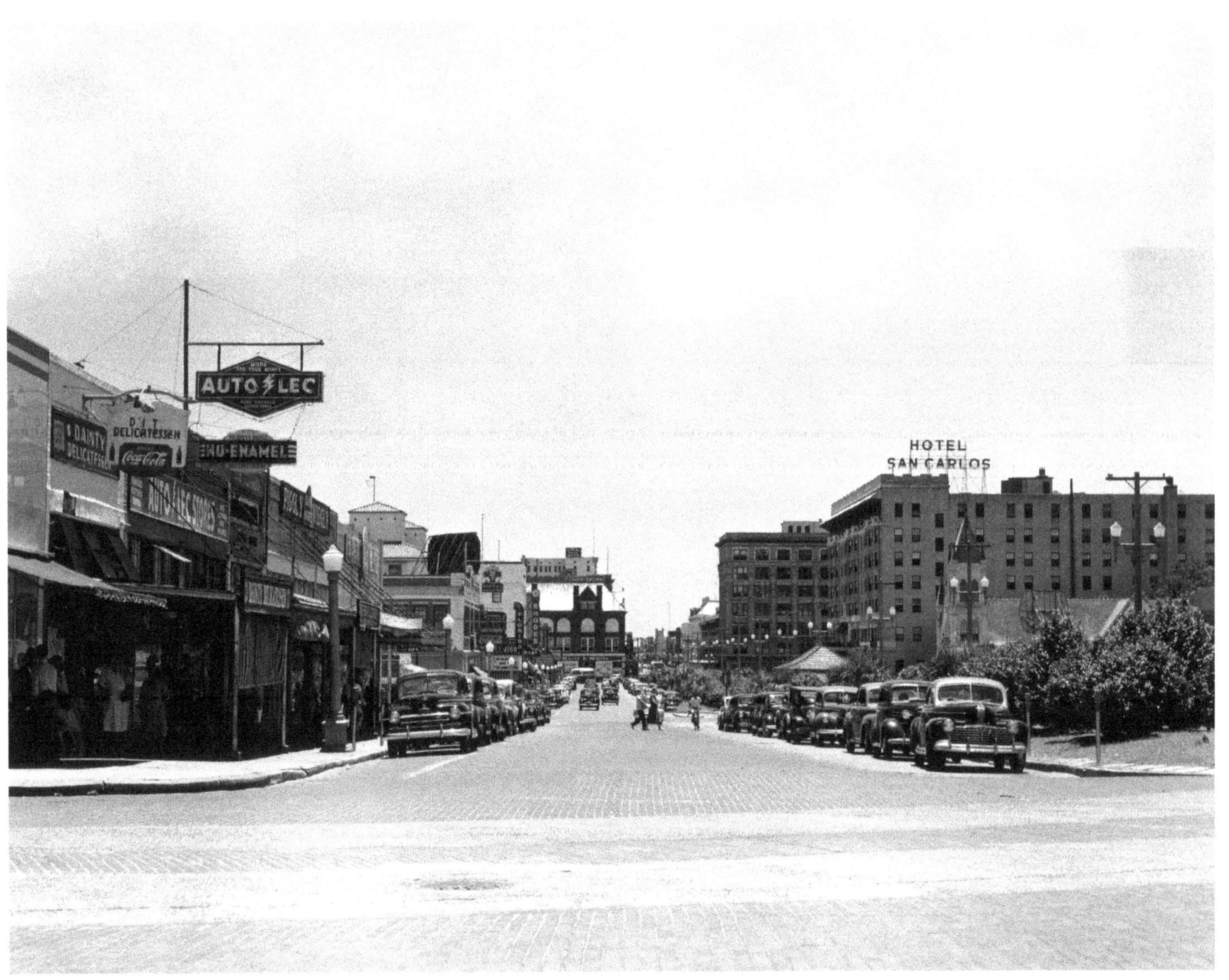

The Hotel San Carlos stands to the left in the foreground of this image from 1947, with the Rex Theater, Rhodes-Collins Furniture Store, the Federal Building, and the Nobles Building prominent on the right. The Scottish Rite Building is visible at the corner of North Palafox and Wright streets. A new, modern water tower is visible on the right in the background, replacing the old brick structure, which has been demolished. Alan Ladd and Gail Russell are starring in *Calcutta* at the Rex while a sign in the median announces "Dog Races Tonite" with a post time of 8:30.

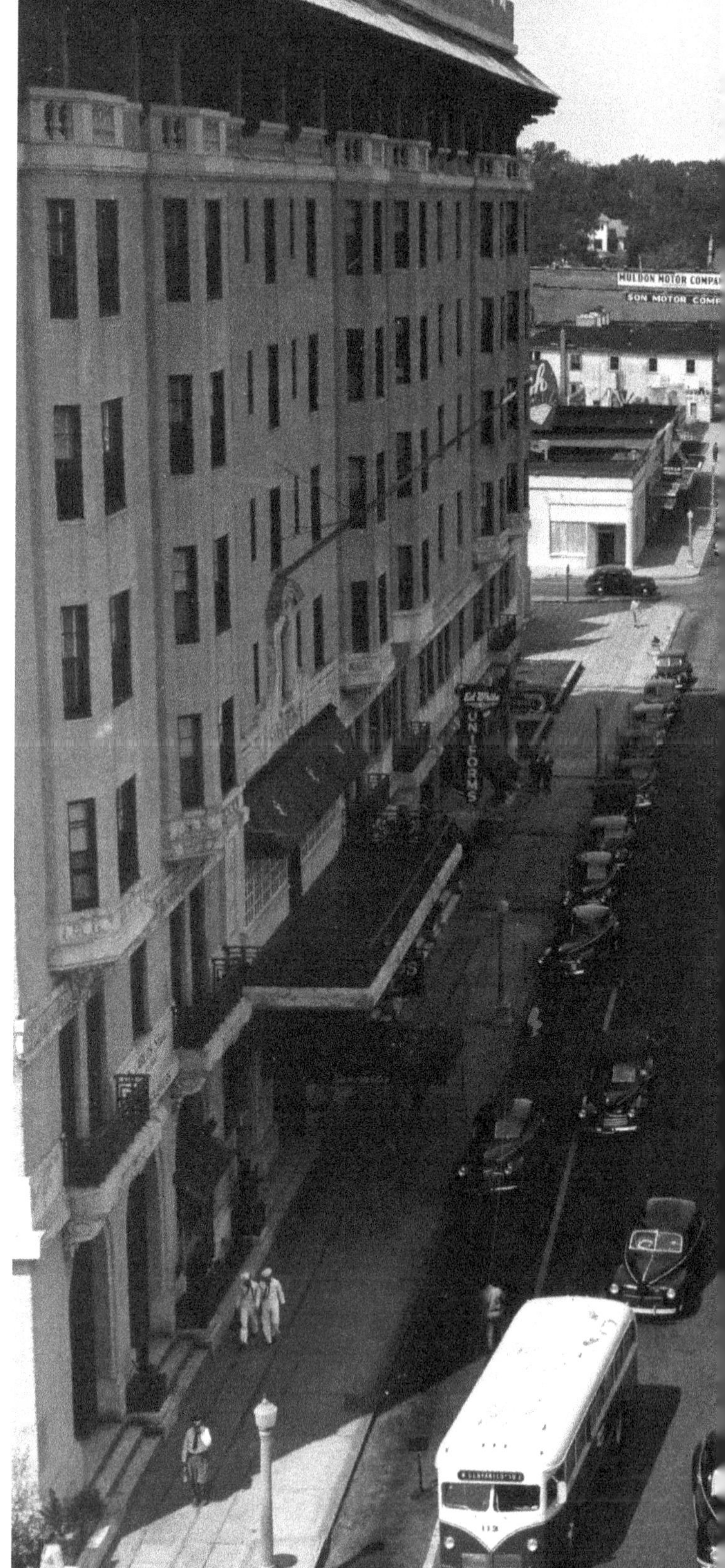

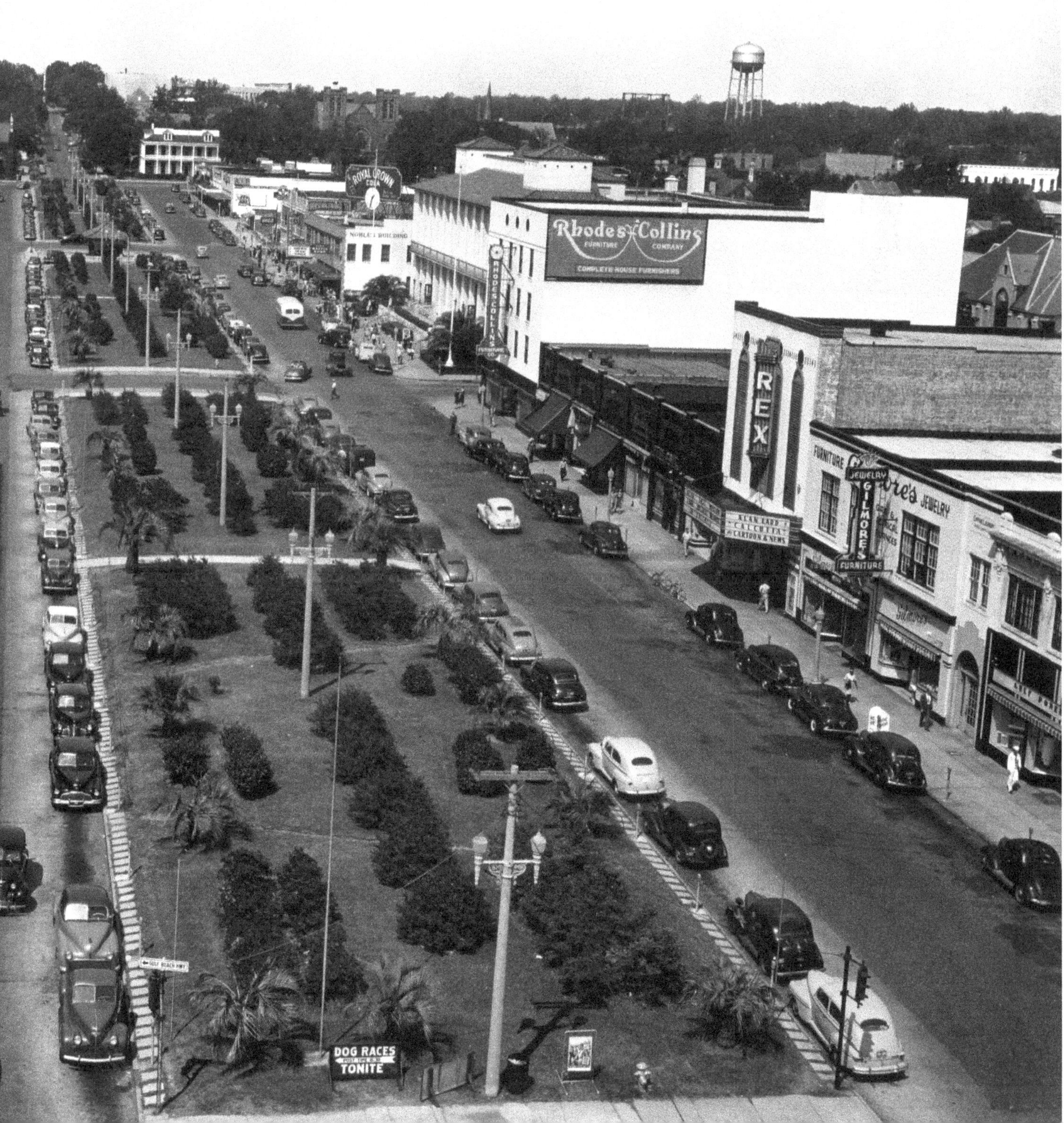

ROYAL CROWN
COLA
Rhodes Collins
FURNITURE COMPANY
COMPLETE HOUSE FURNISHERS
RHODES-COLLINS
REX
ALAN LADD
CALCUTTA
CARTOON & NEWS
JEWELRY
GILMORE'S
FURNITURE
JEWELRY
DOG RACES
TONITE

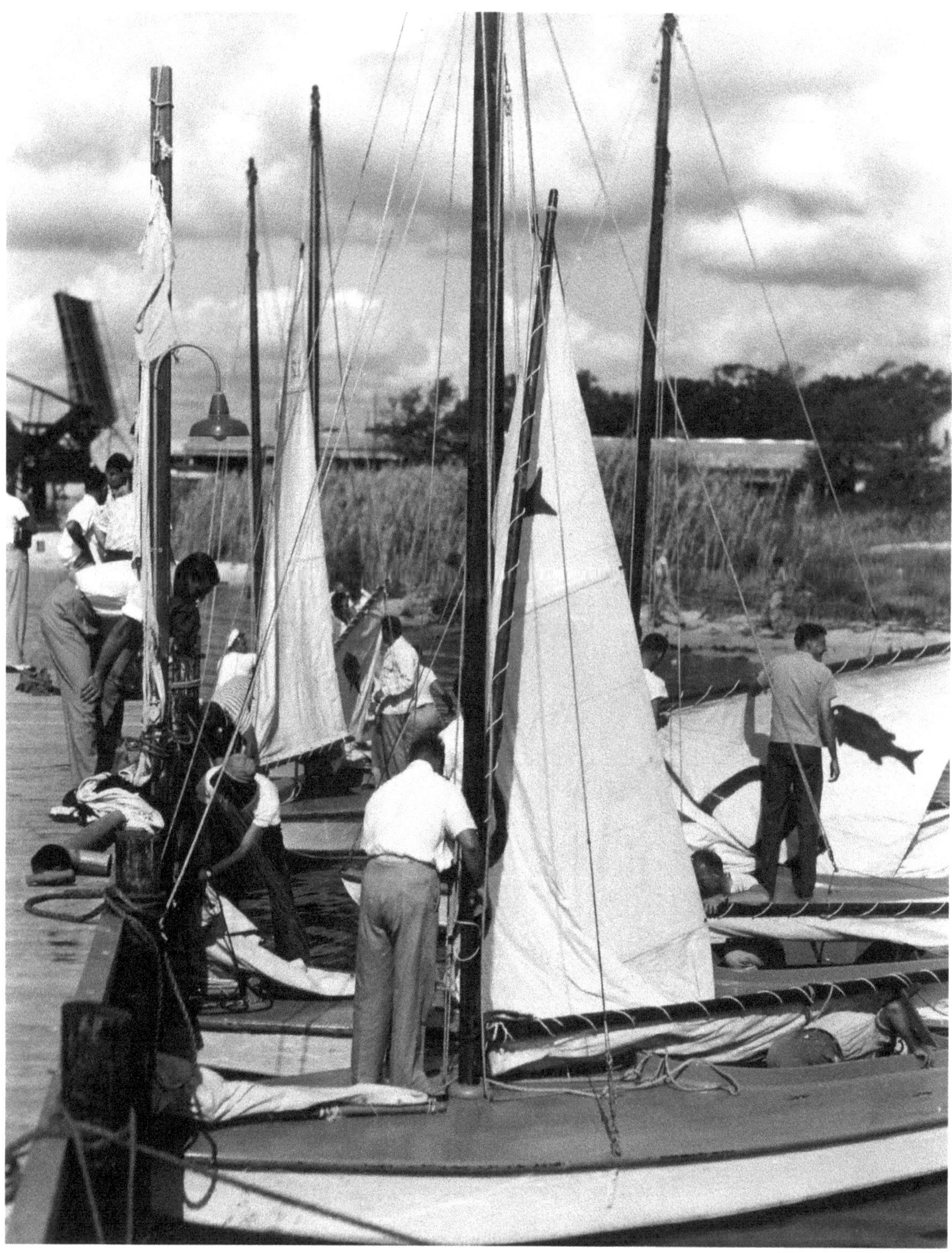

In 1920, British tea magnate Sir Thomas Lipton donated a silver trophy to the Southern Yacht Club in New Orleans. The trophy was to be presented to the winner of a regatta staged by the Gulf Yachting Association, which comprised clubs from New Orleans, Mobile, Houston, Biloxi, and Pensacola. Pensacola won the first competition in 1920 and was host for the 1921 competition.

This boat competed in the 1948 Lipton Cup Race in Pensacola.

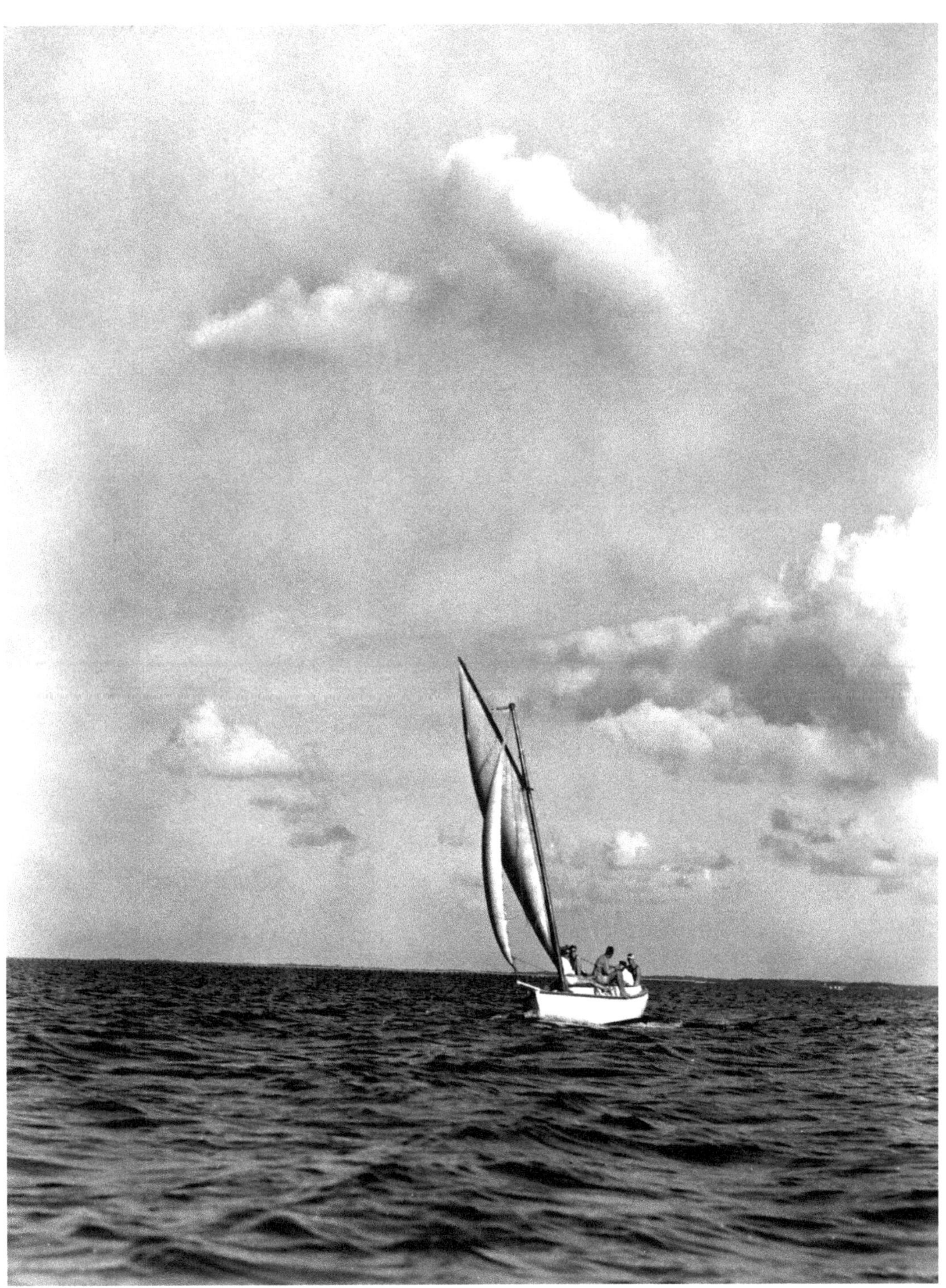

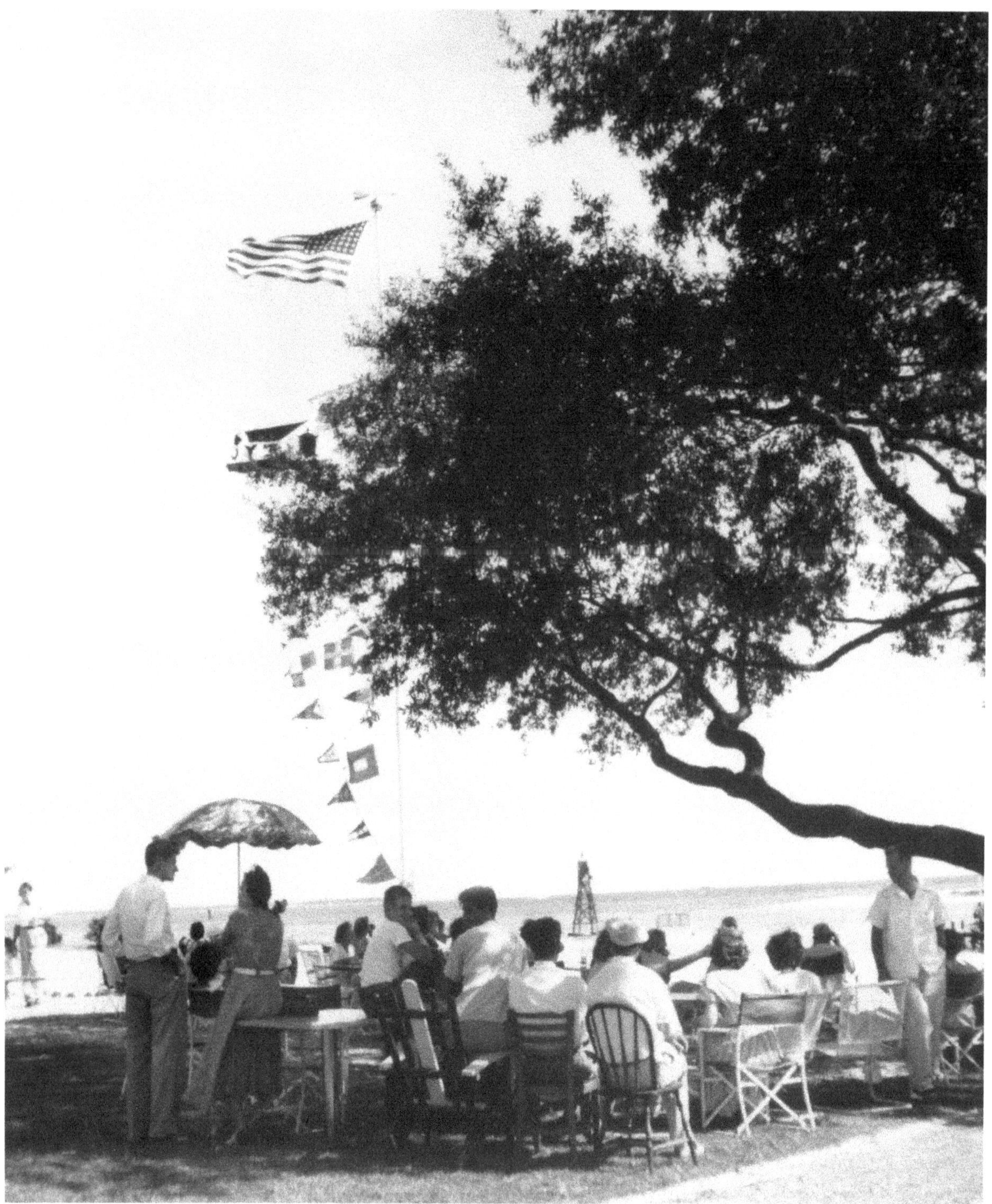

People gather to watch the 1948 Lipton Cup Race in Pensacola.

Andy Alphoso, captain of the winning team, the Gulfport, Mississippi, Yacht Club, accepts the Lipton Cup from George P. Hopkins, president of the Gulf Yachting Association, after the 1948 race.

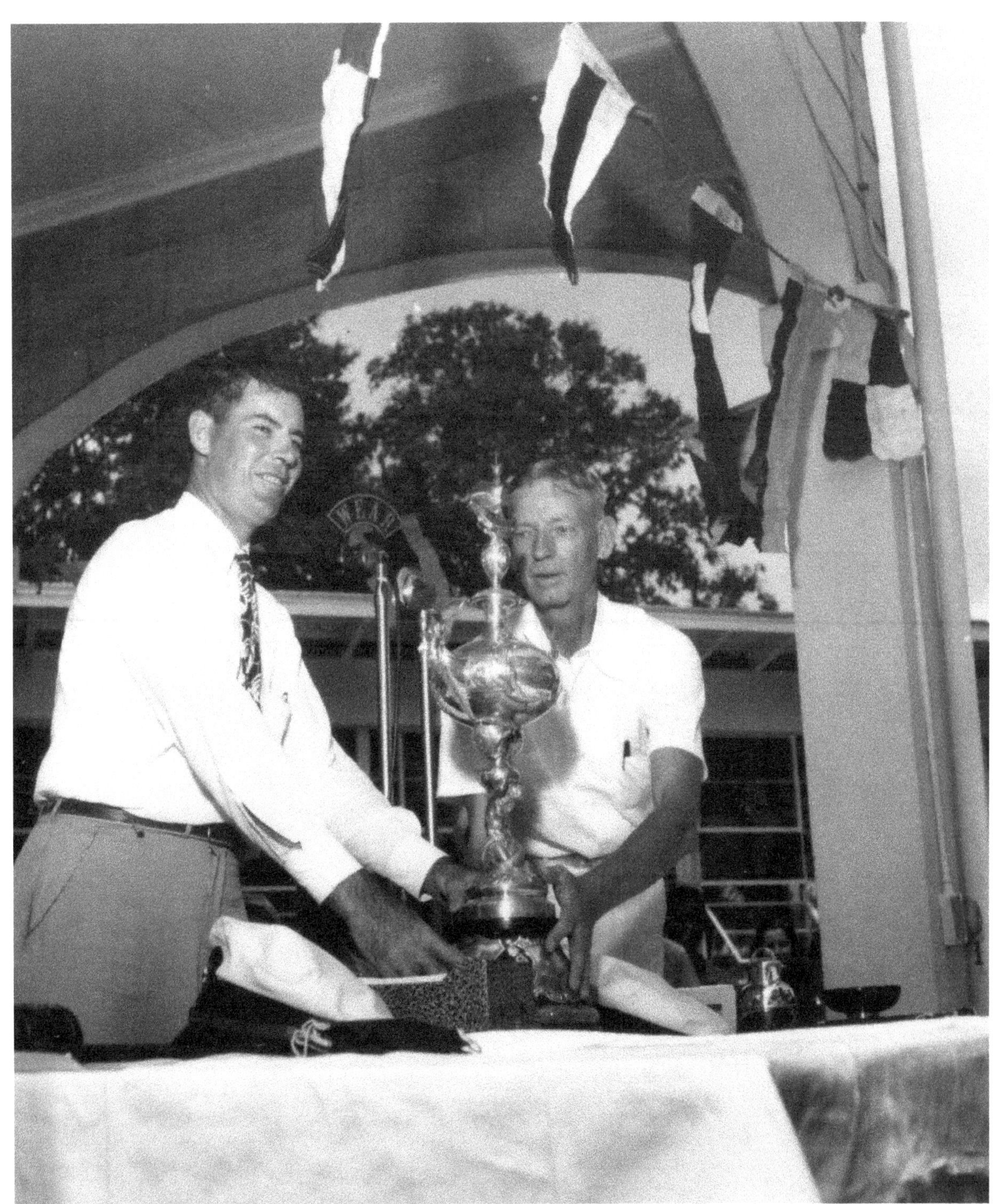

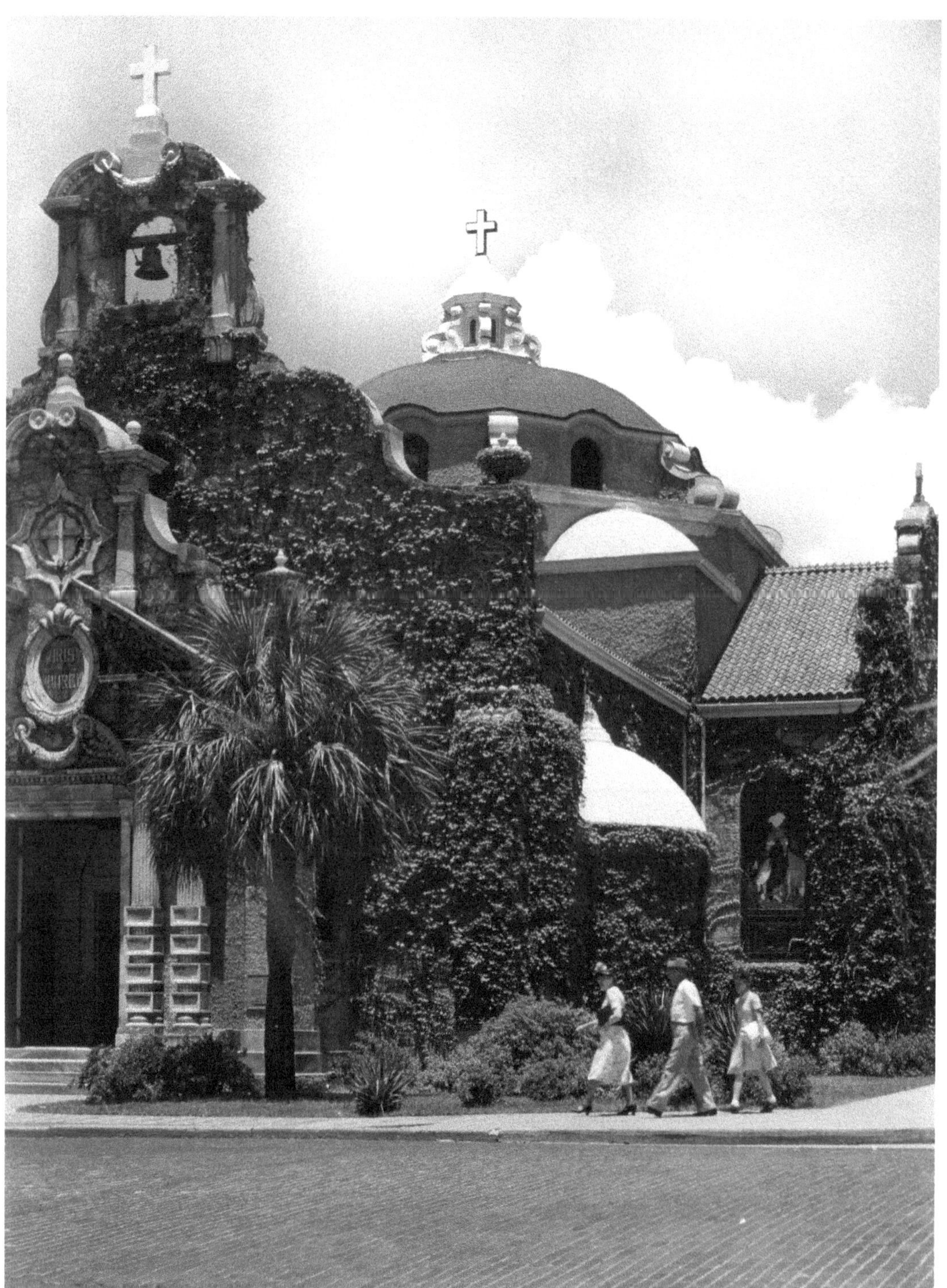

Ivy covered much of Christ's Episcopal Church in 1948, masking the distinctive architecture of the building.

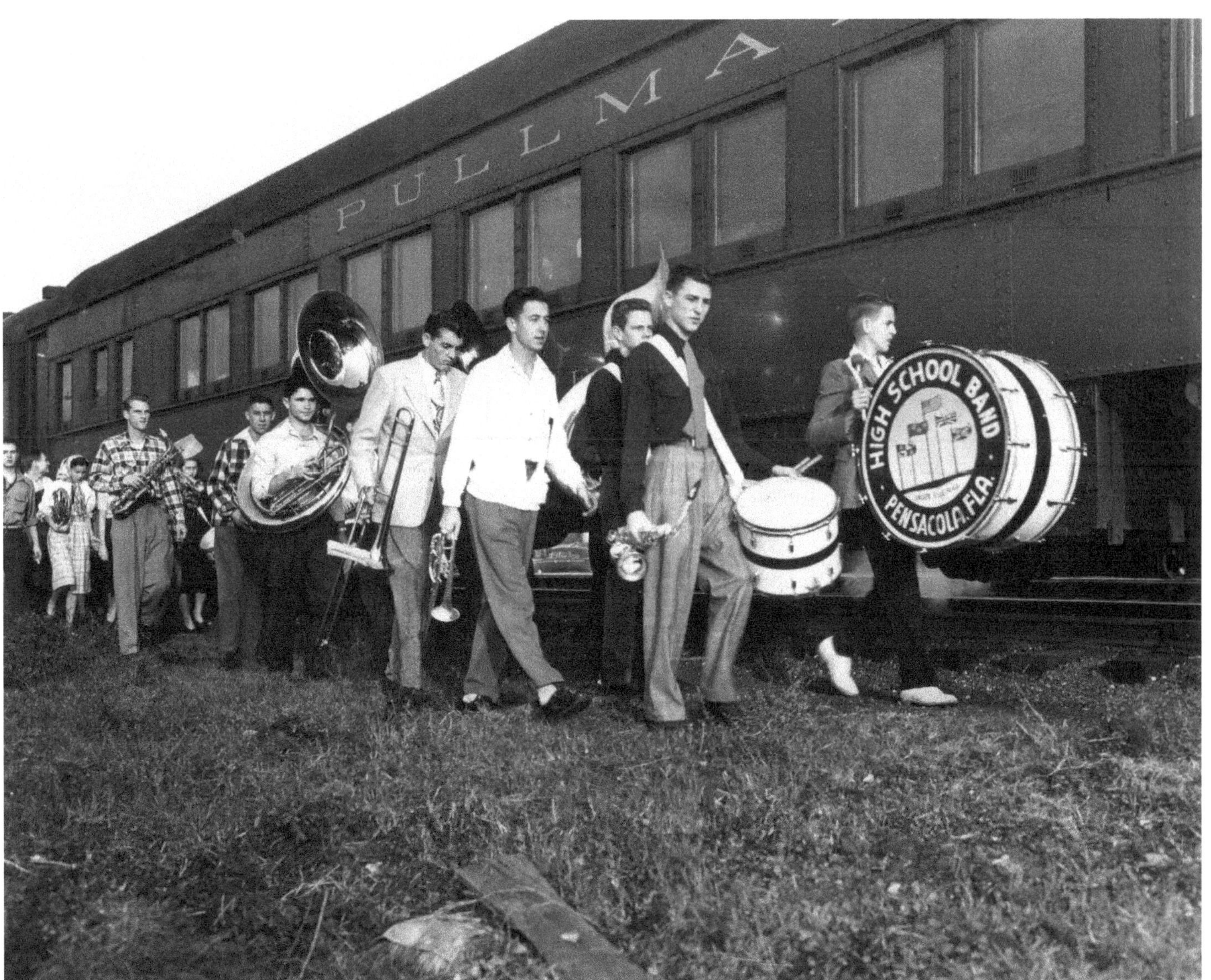

The Pensacola High School marching band played for the 1949 inauguration of Florida governor Fuller Warren. The band was led by director H. Vernon Hooker, captain Charles Hardin, and drum majorette Mary Frances Comstock.

Mrs. Barbara Warren, wife of Governor Fuller Warren, cuts the ribbon to open the new Gulf Breeze to Pensacola Beach bridge. Mrs. Mildred Pepper, wife of U.S. senator Claude Pepper, is to her right.

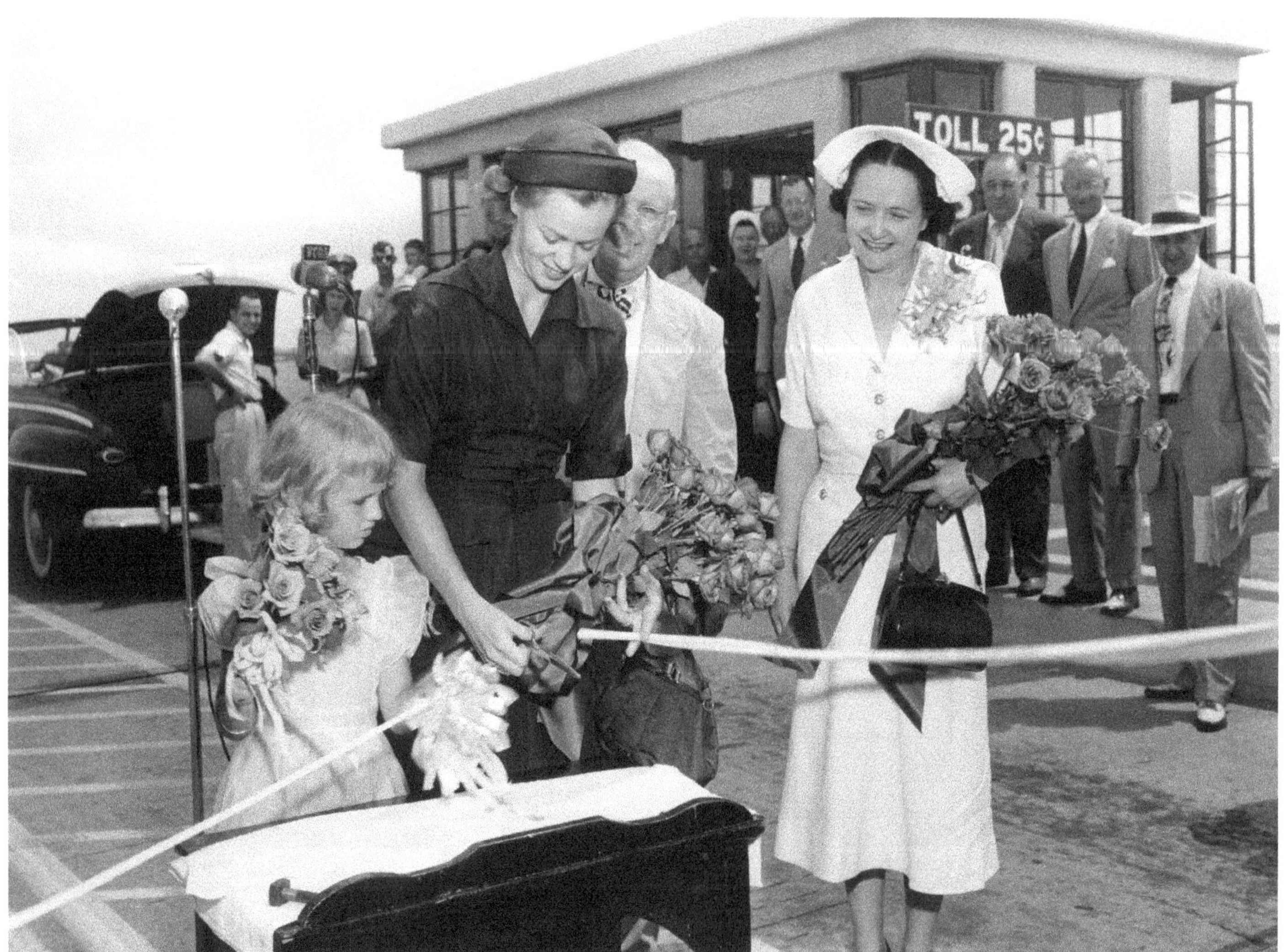

A boat passes under the open drawbridge of the new Pensacola Beach bridge.

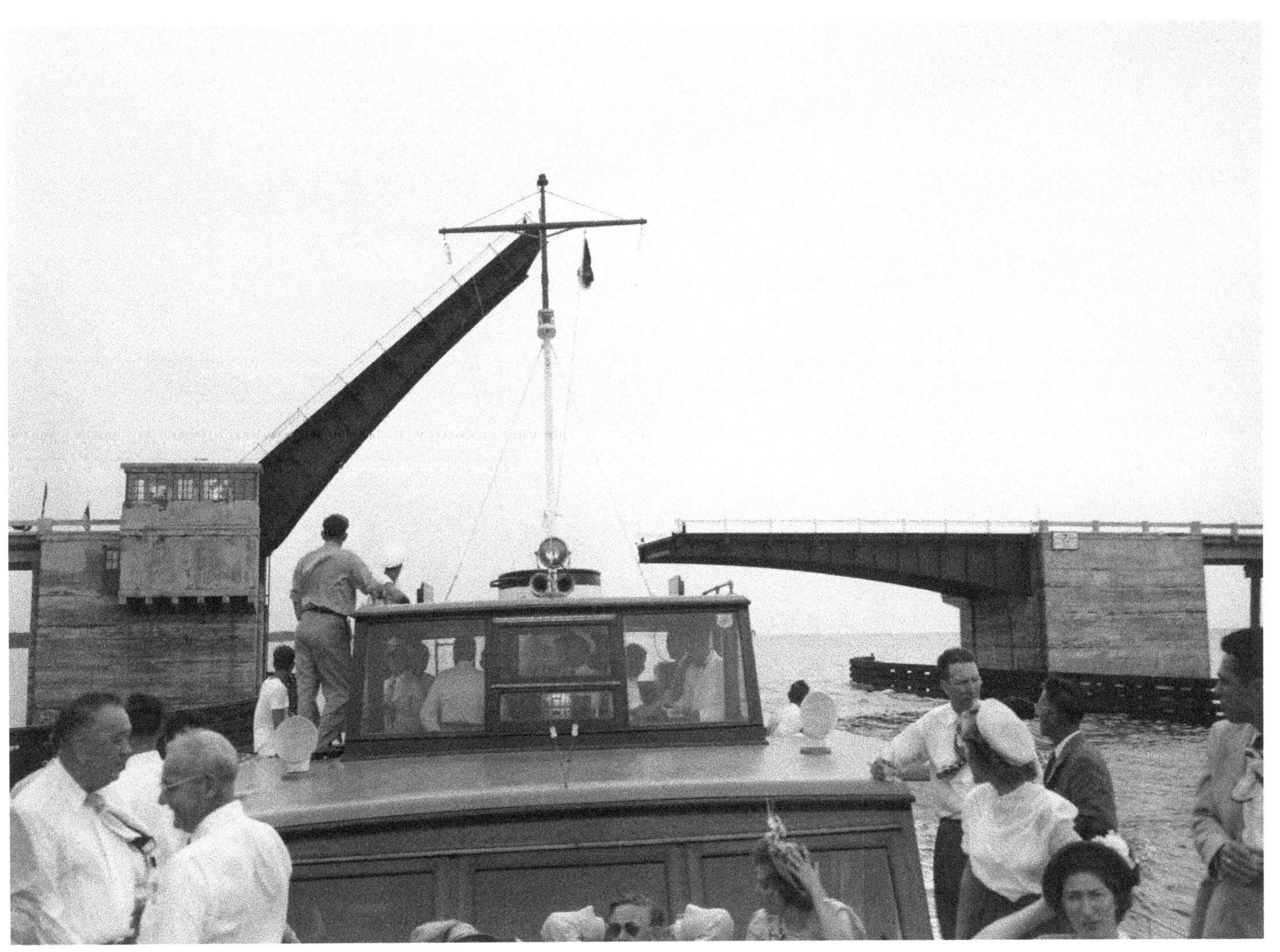

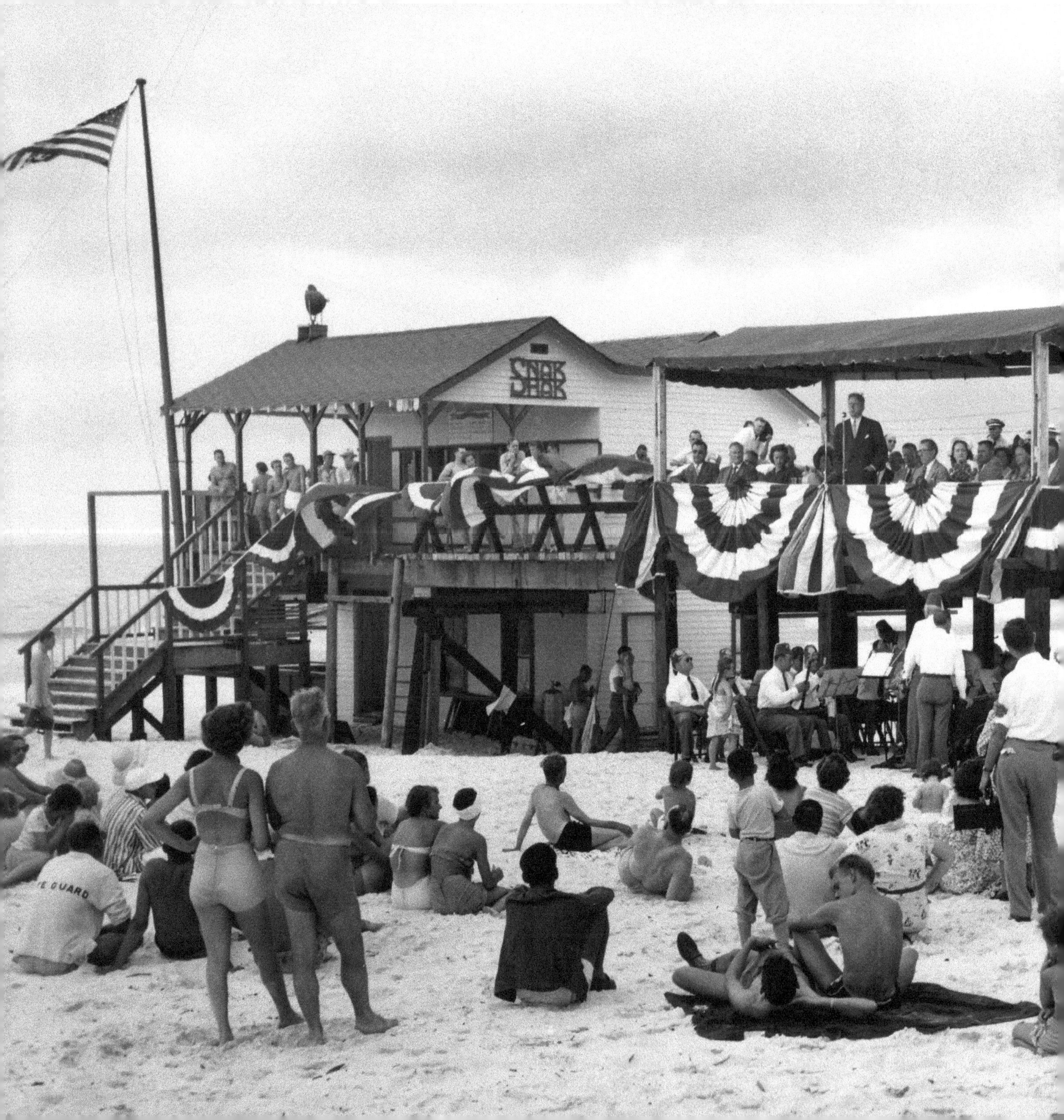
SNAK SHAK

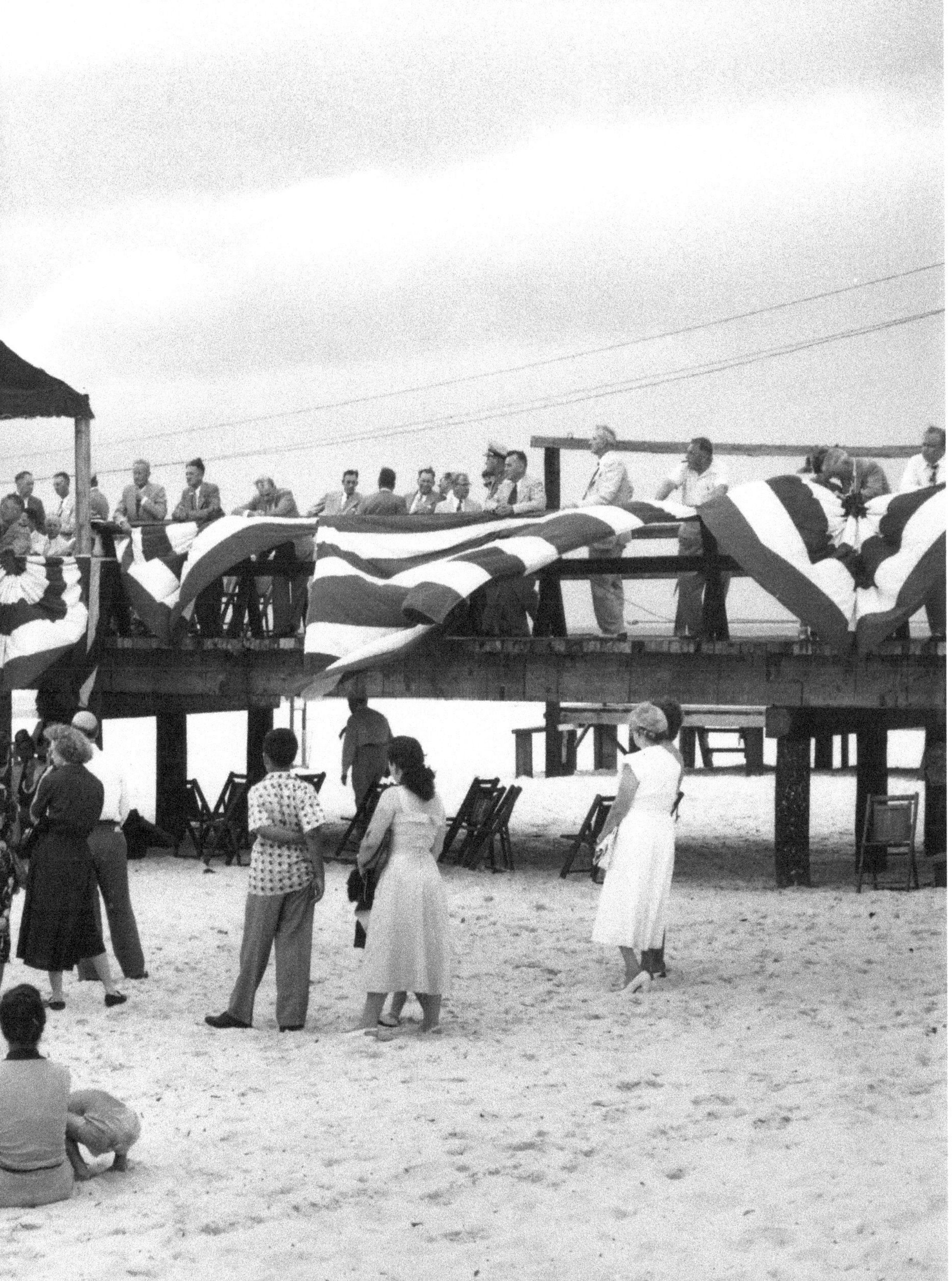

People gather on the beach July 16, 1949, for ceremonies to dedicate the new bridge from Gulf Breeze to Pensacola Beach.

The beach around the Casino was a popular area for swimmers and sunbathers, even naval personnel in full uniform.

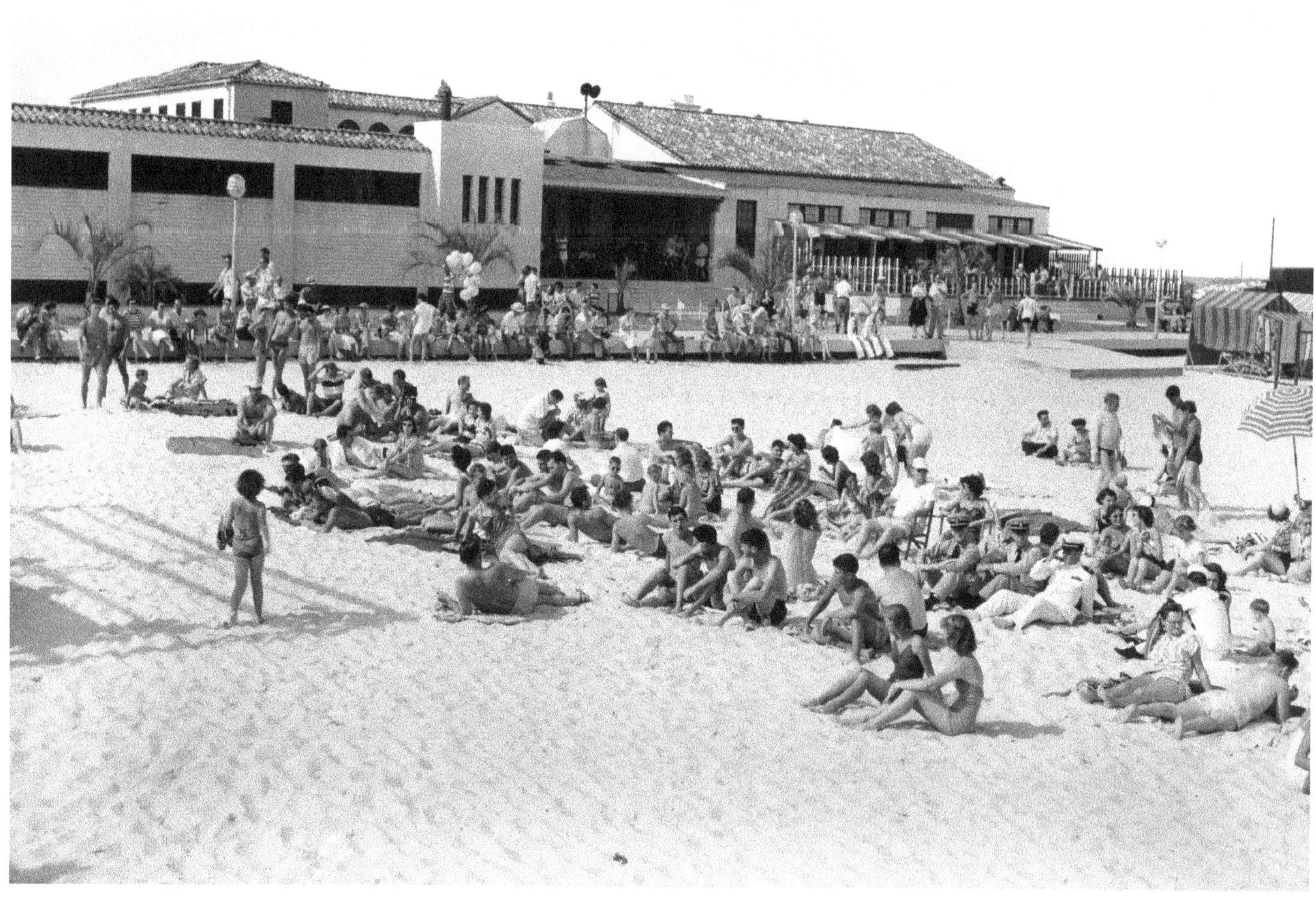

The lifeguard takes his eyes off the water long enough to speak with Rosalie Ivimey.

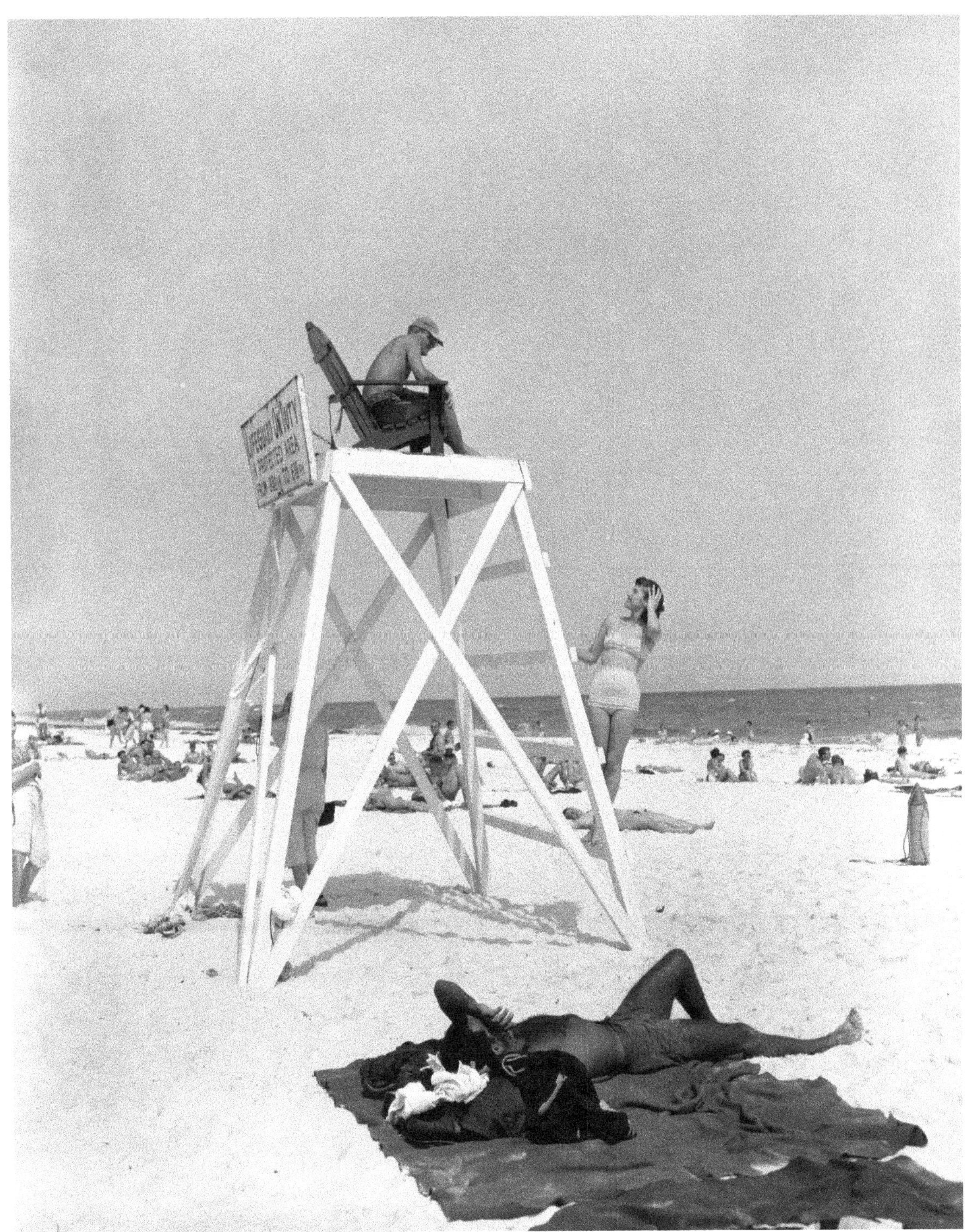

A yearly tradition since 1951, the Fiesta of Five Flags celebrates the 1559 landing of Don Tristan de Luna and the first settlement of Pensacola. Festivities include parades, treasure hunts, and dances.

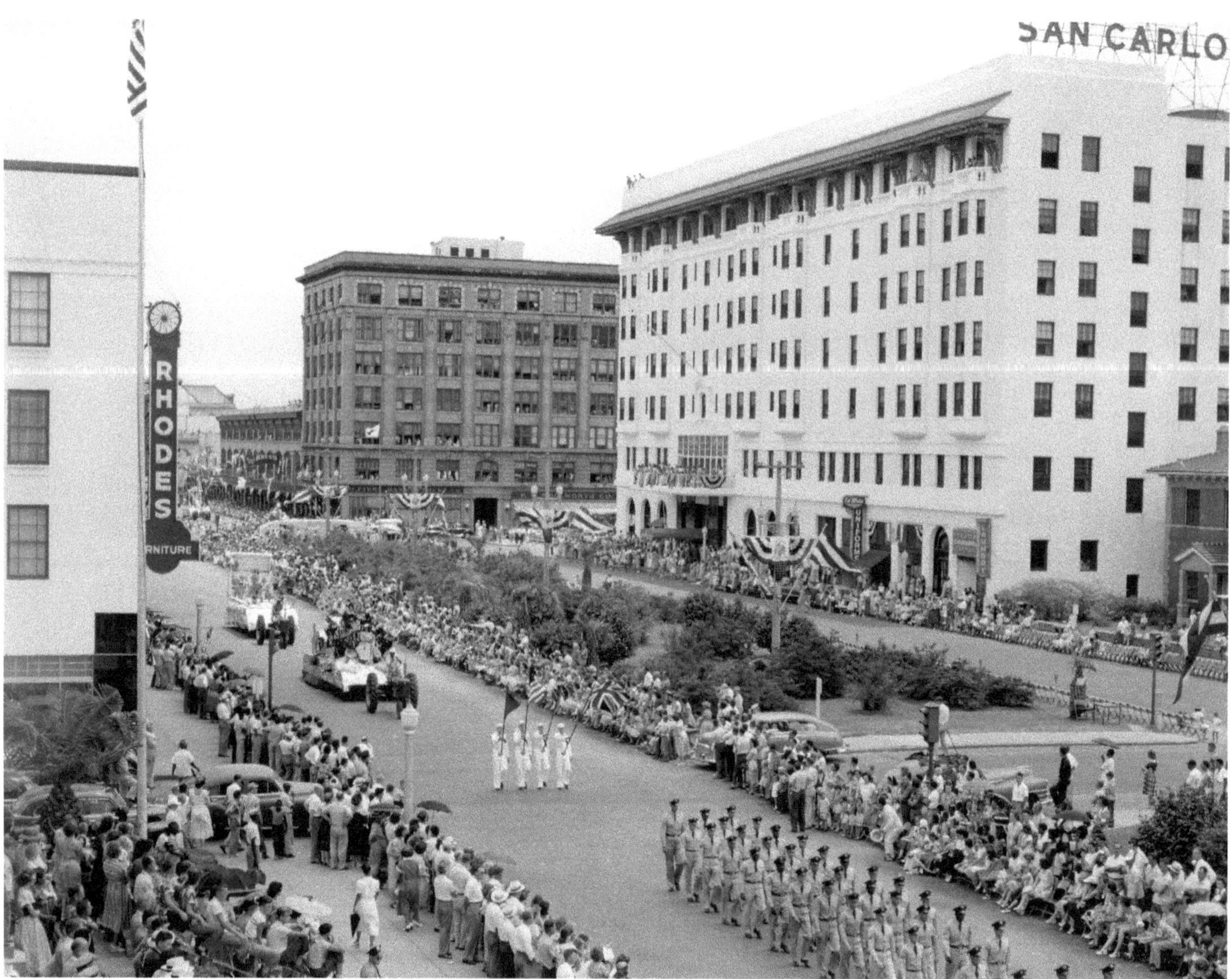

Miss America for 1951, Yolande Betbeze of Mobile, is greeted as she arrives in Pensacola to participate in the Fiesta activities.

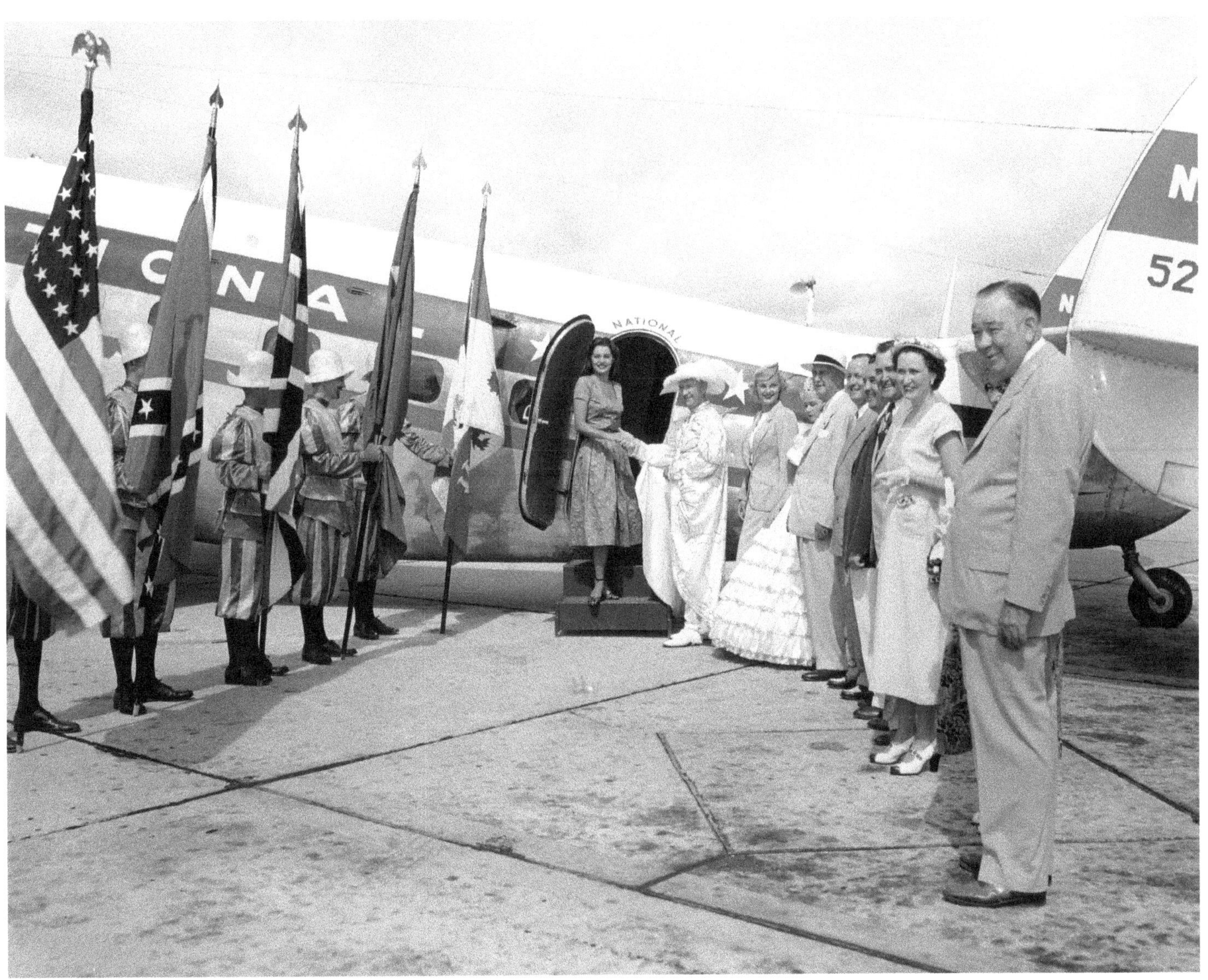

Revelers dance at the de Luna Ball, one of the highlights of the Fiesta of Five Flags.

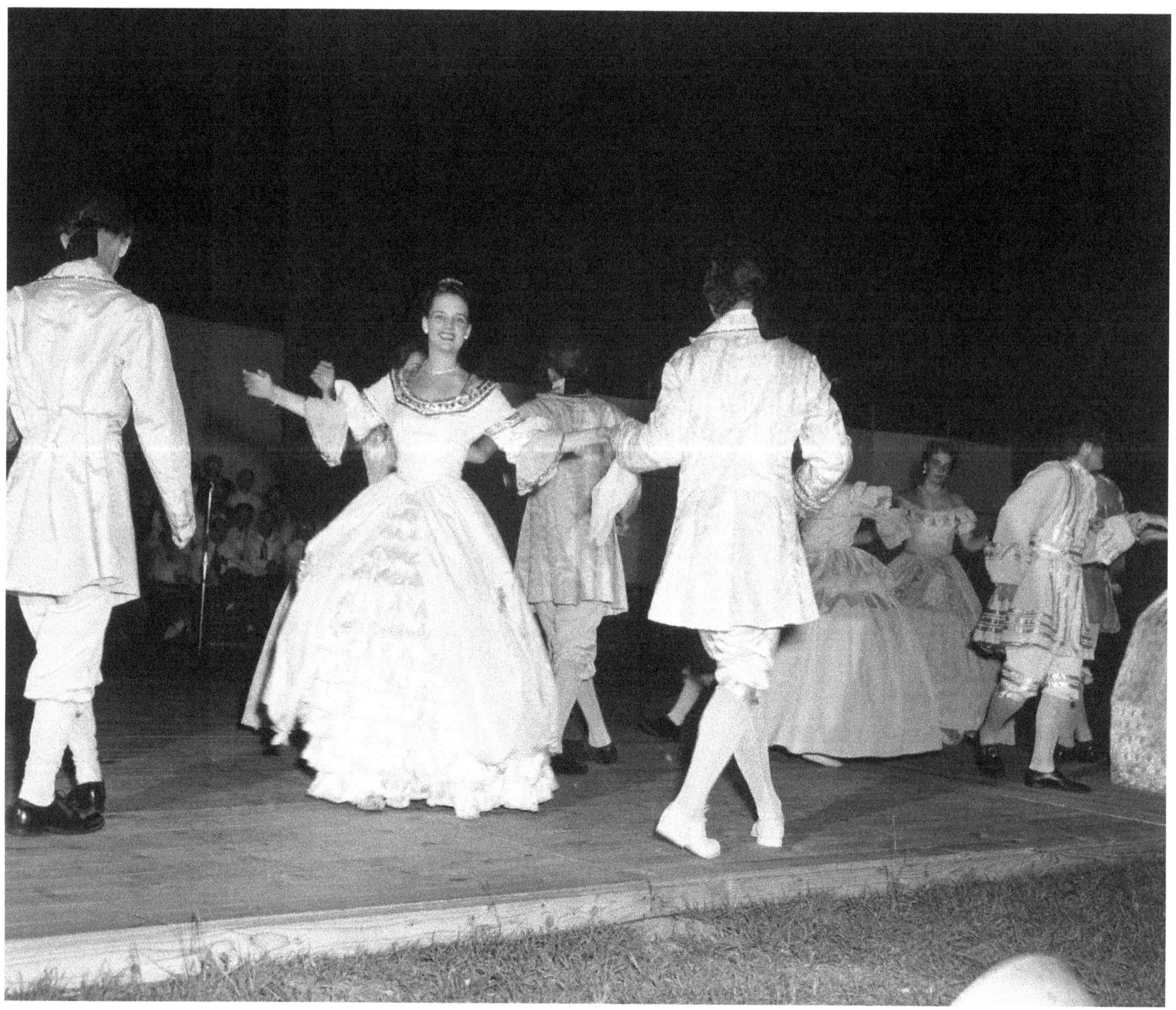

Doris Nettle is crowned Miss Pensacola in the 1951 Fiesta of Five Flags beauty pageant.

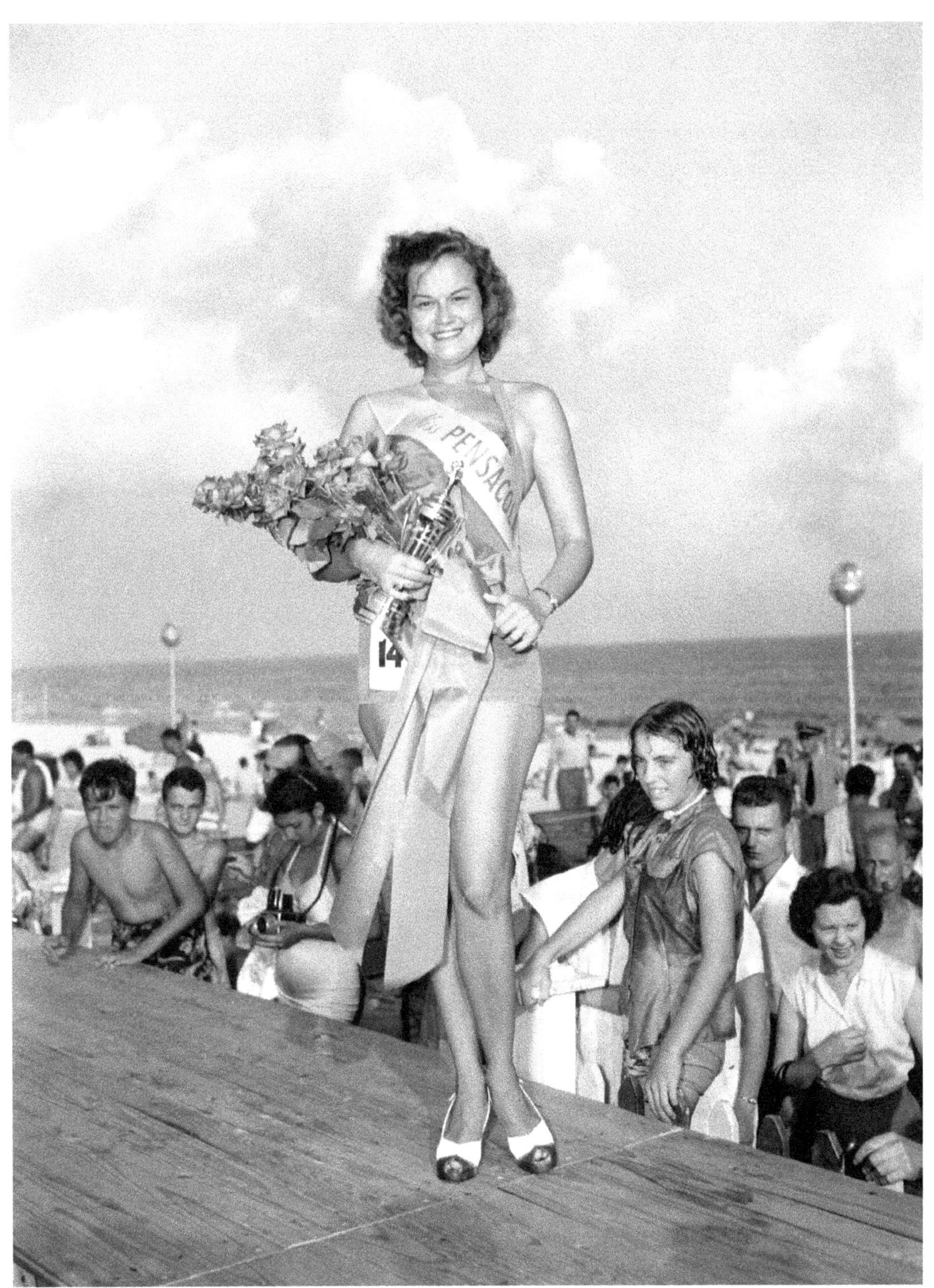

The Escambia–Santa Rosa Bar Association hosted a dinner June 15, 1951, at the Hotel San Carlos. Charles Thomas Henderson, a member of the attorney general's staff, was the guest speaker, and Secretary of State R. A. Gray attended as a guest of the association.

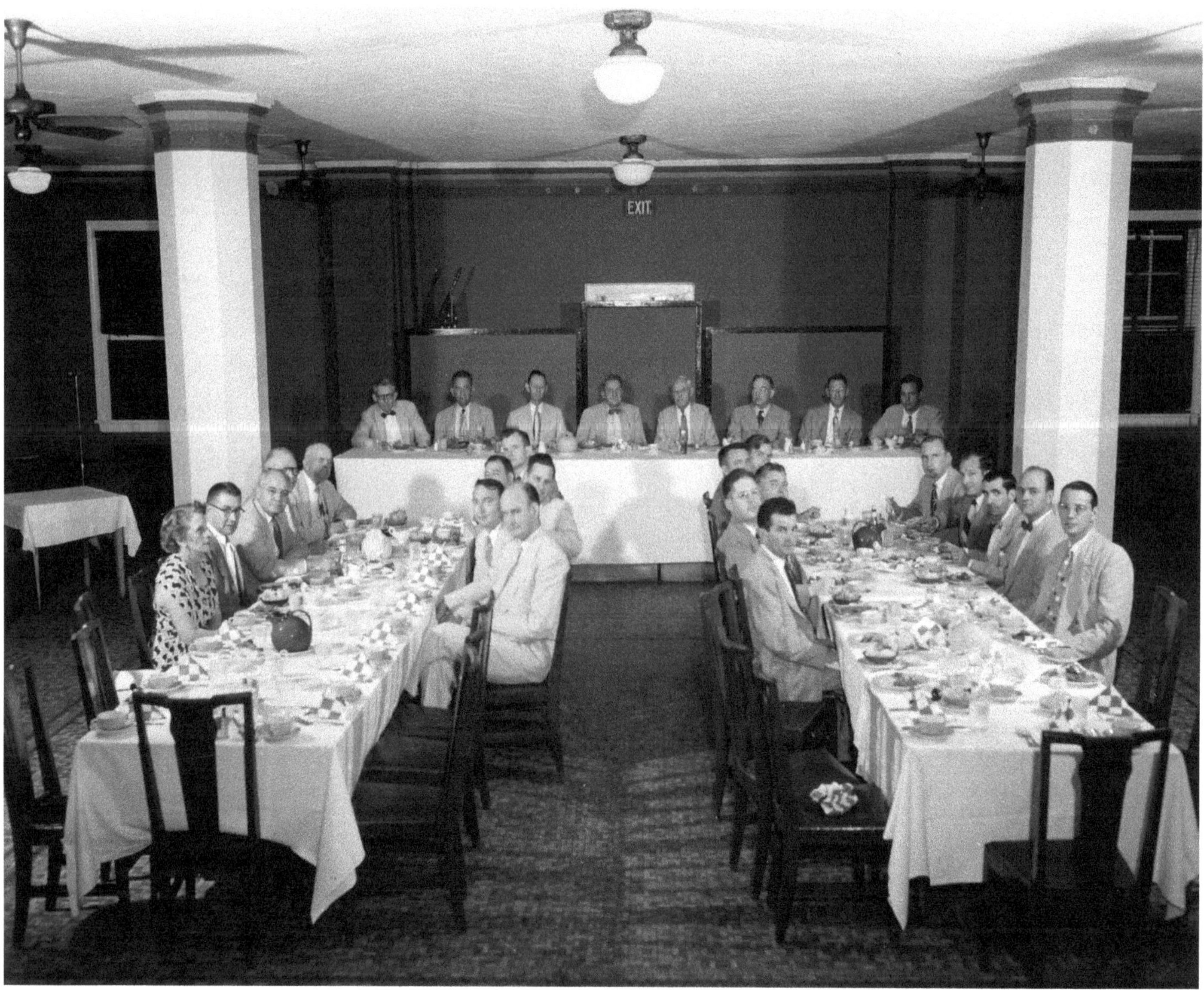

Israel Defense Forces Chief of Staff, Moshe Dayan, visited Pensacola in the 1950s. Pictured left to right are Yitzhak Rabin, Kiva Oberstein, Dayan, Anne Oberstein, Leah Rosenbaum, Chaim Herzog, and Modi Peled.

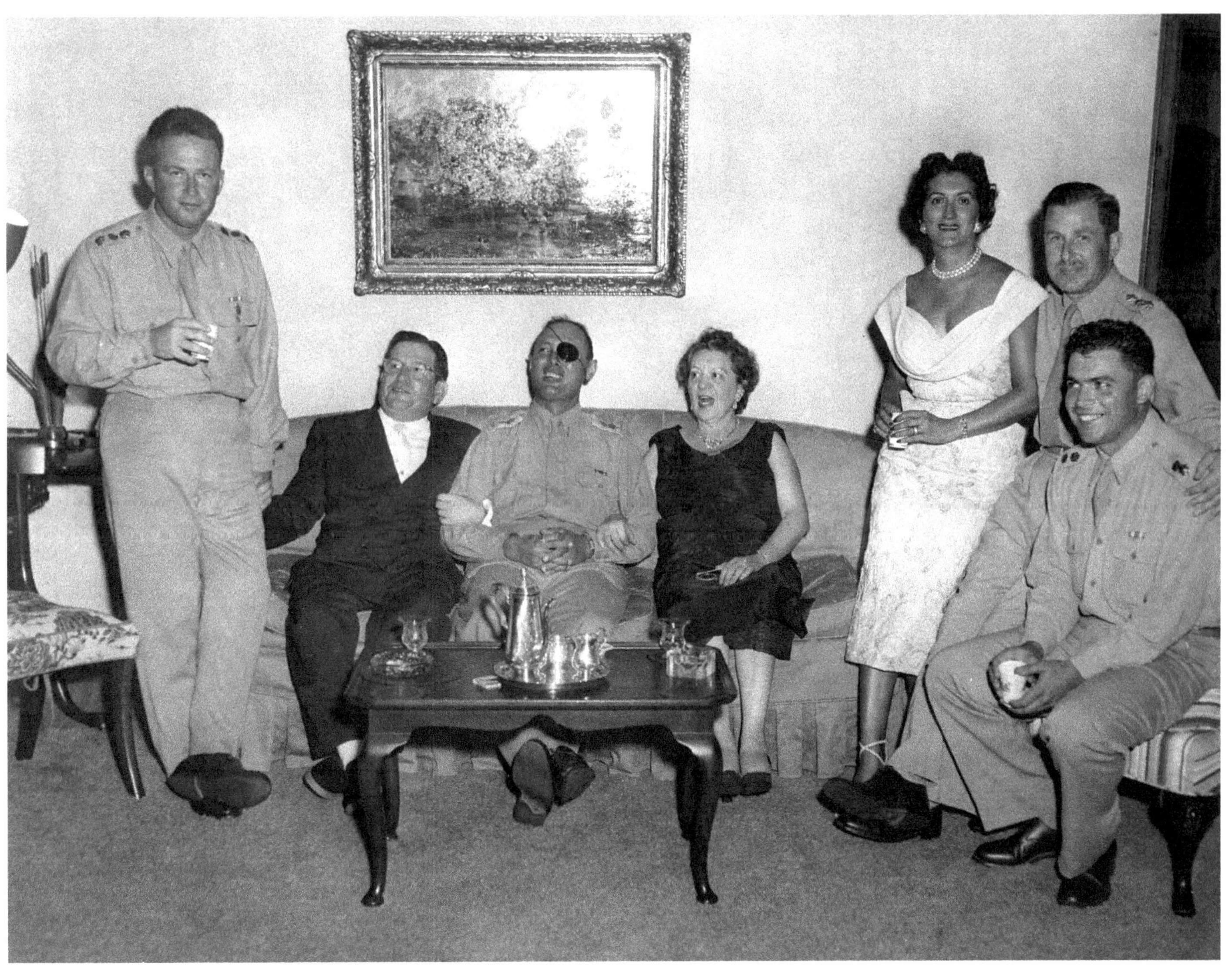

Parades celebrating the Fiesta of Five Flags are popular with children and adults.

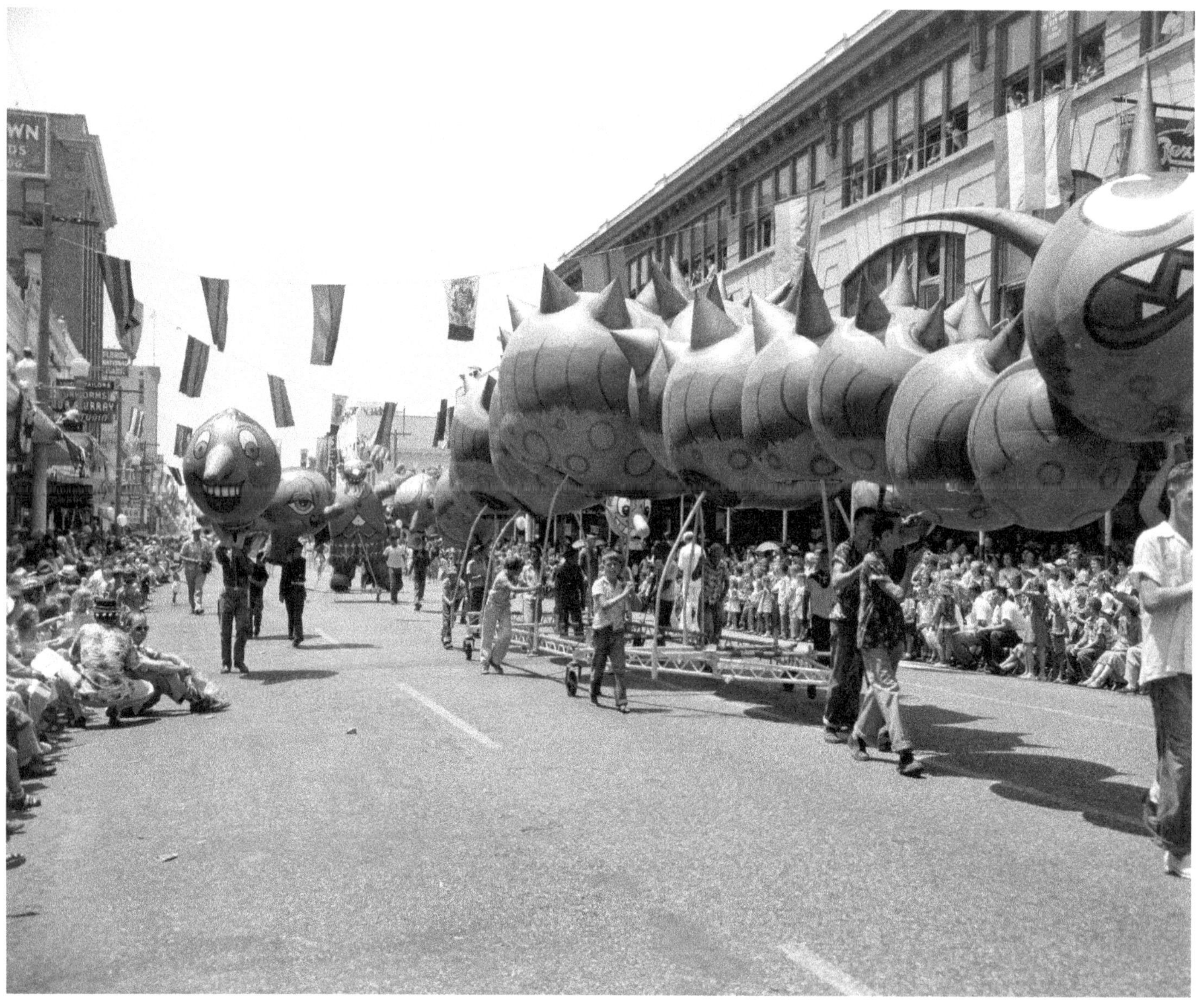

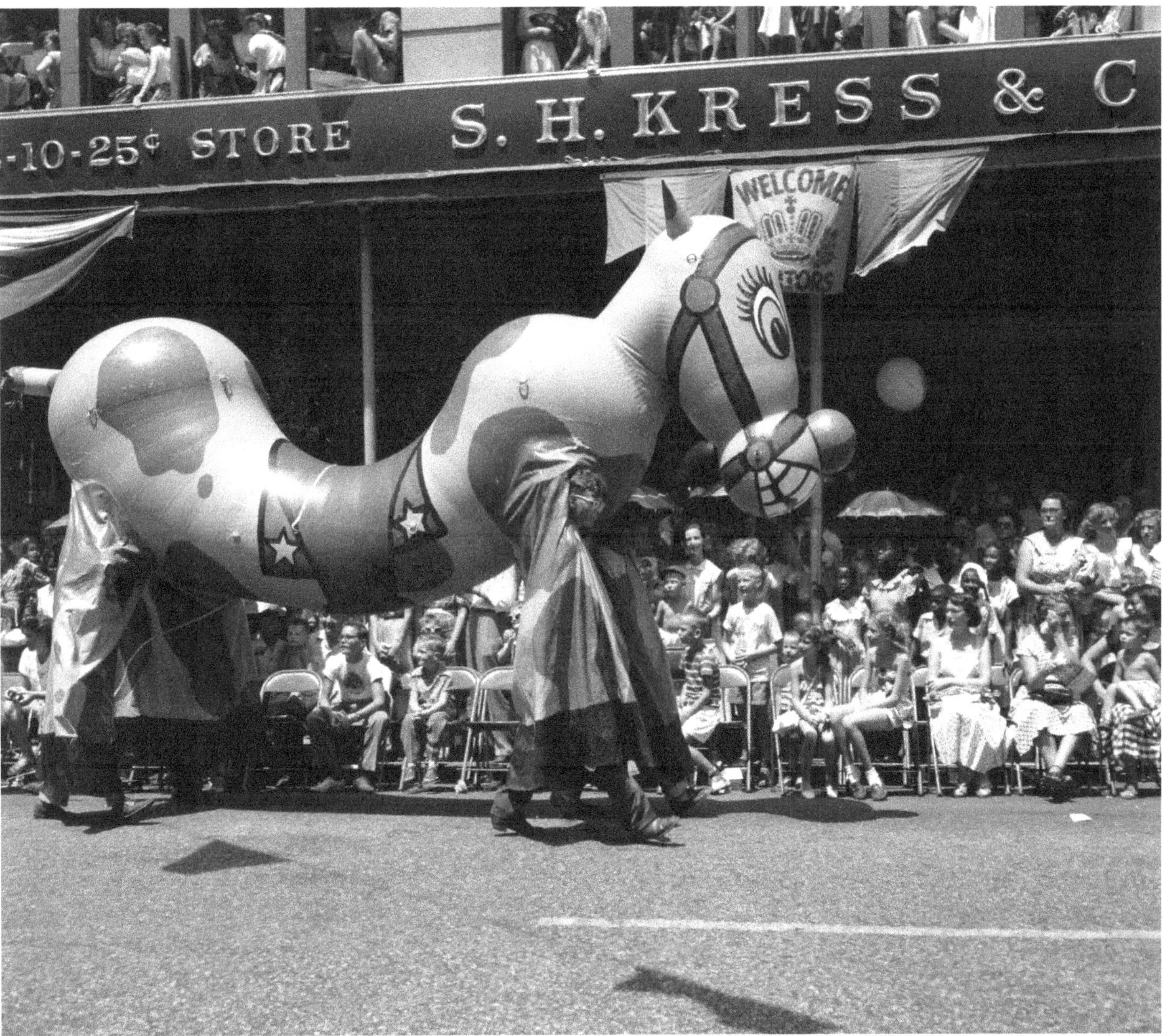

Some early parade watchers were lucky enough to find seats, others stood in the windows of S. H. Kress and Company as the parade passed down South Palafox Street in 1952.

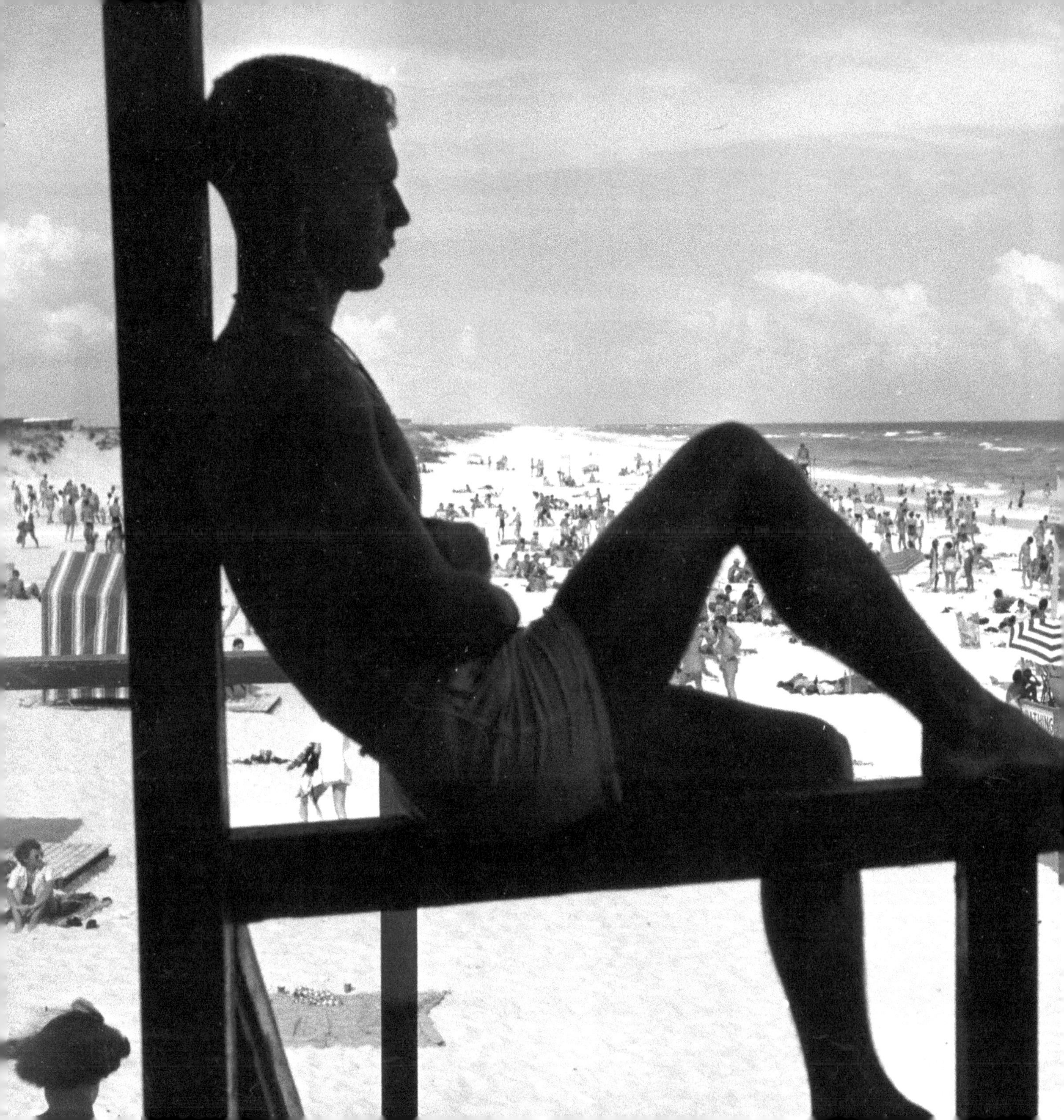

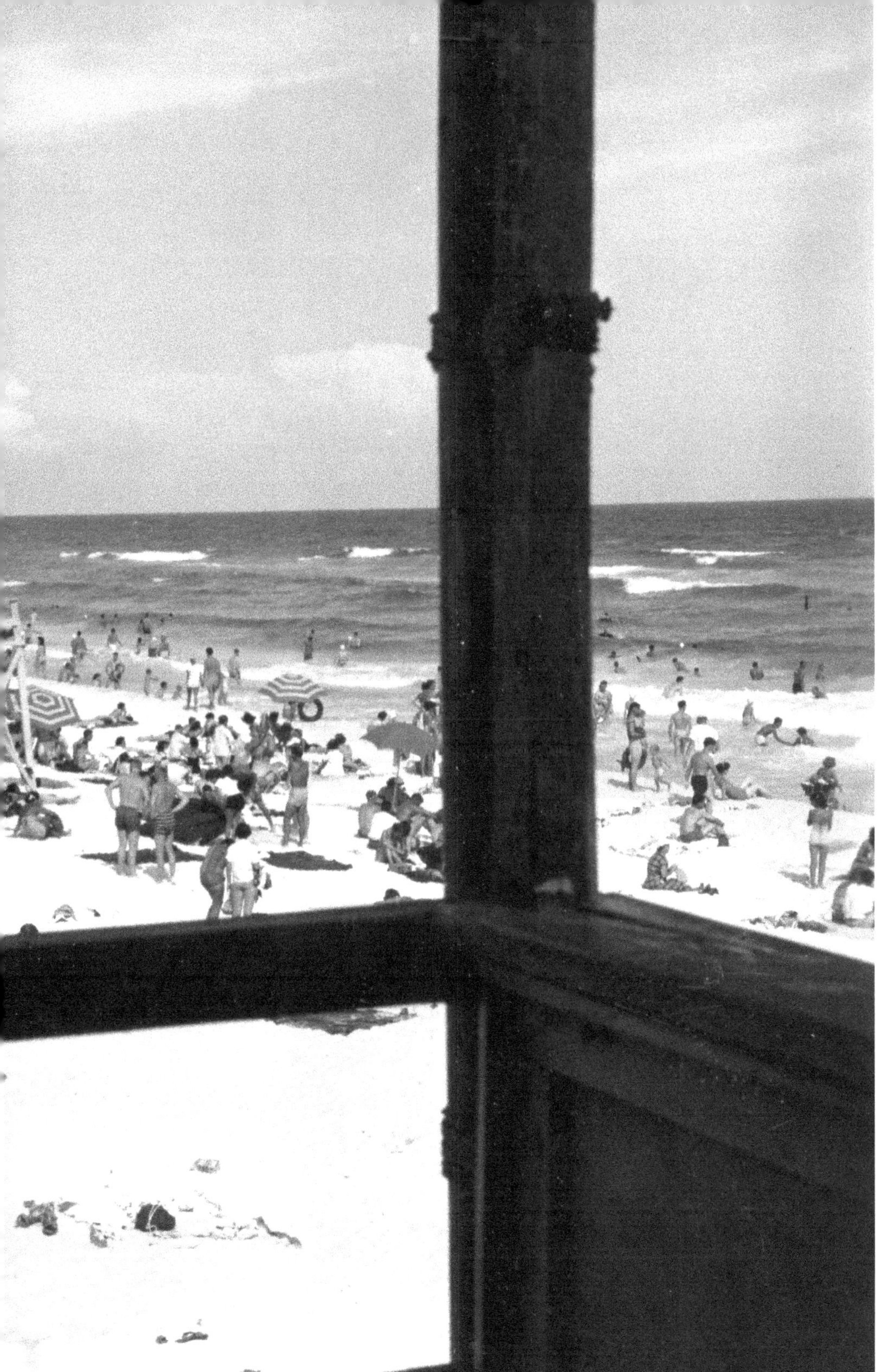

The railing around the Casino patio was a cool spot to relax and hide from the sun.

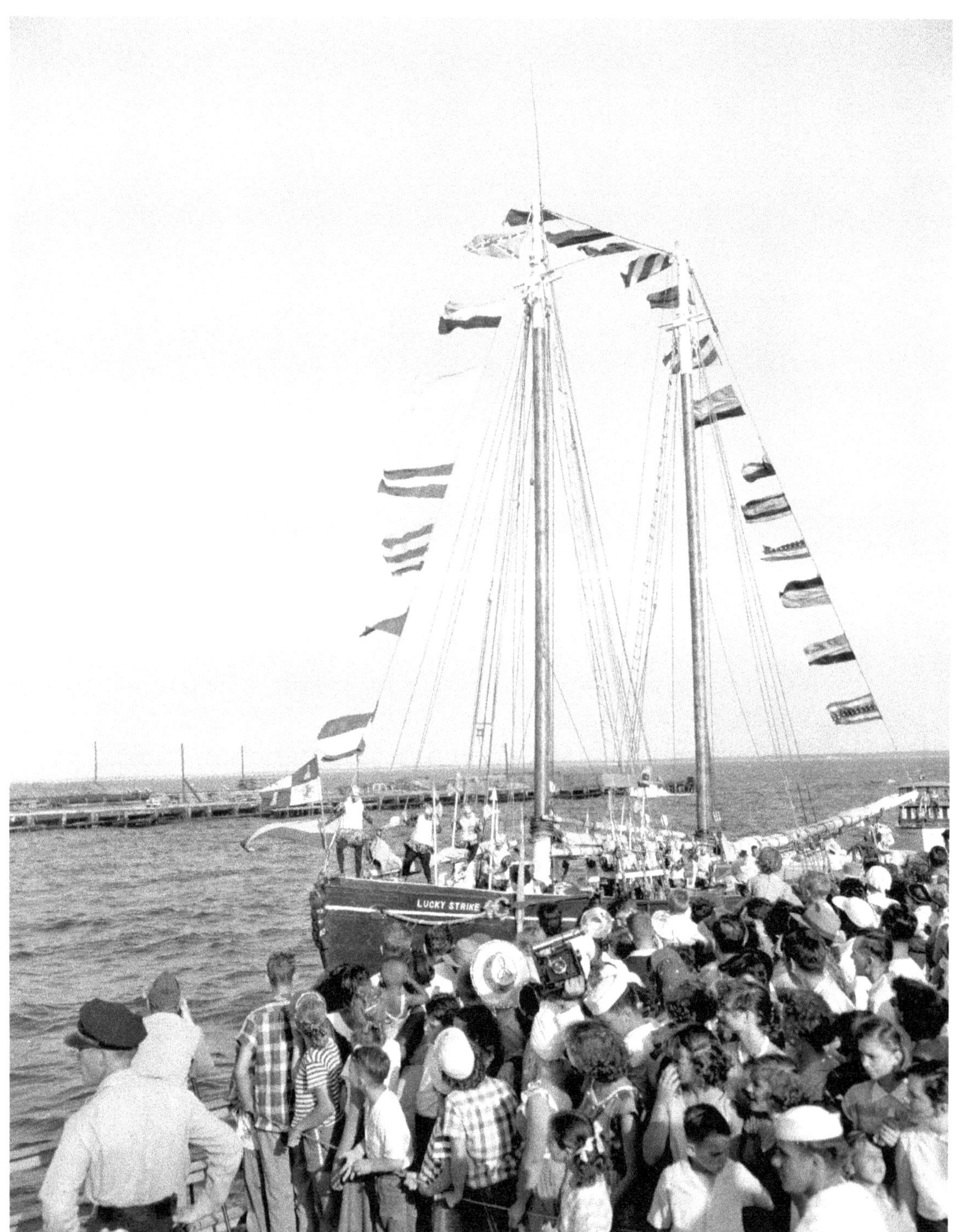

One of the high points of the Fiesta of Five Flags is the landing of de Luna. J. McHenry Jones, the 1952 de Luna, sailed to port in the *Lucky Strike.*

Contestants in the 1952 Fiesta of Five Flags beauty contest pose in their swimsuits.

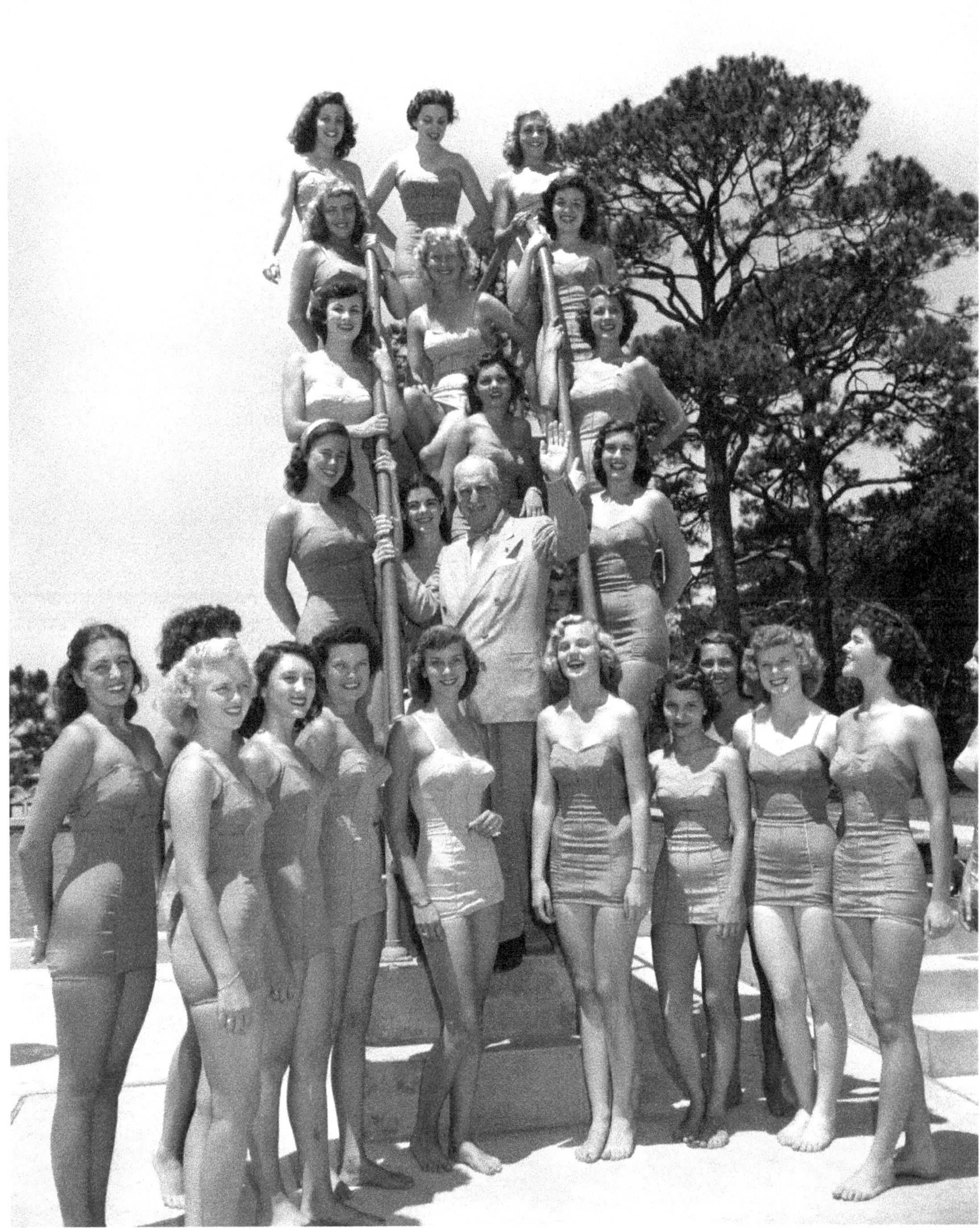

The Palafox Pier, with the Pensacola Municipal Auditorium under construction at the end, dominates this view of 1953 Pensacola. The auditorium opened in 1955 and hosted Elvis Presley for three shows on February 26, 1956. Later renamed the Bayfront Auditorium, the building was demolished in 2005.

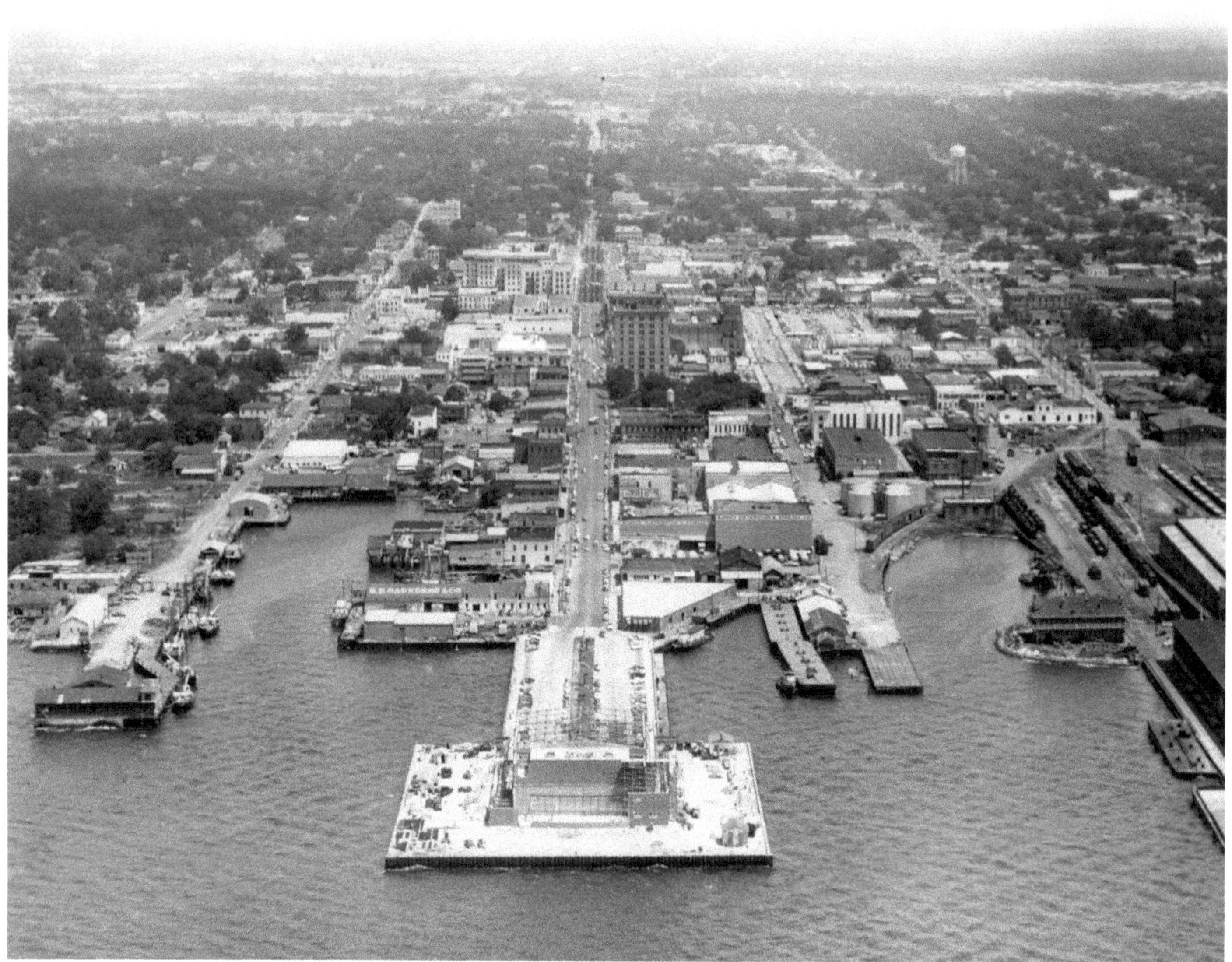

Carl A. Weis founded the Weis-Fricker Mahogany Company, which imported exotic South American woods. The firm operated in Pensacola from 1921 until 1979 and, at one time, was the largest importer of fine mahogany, importing 60 percent of the world's supply.

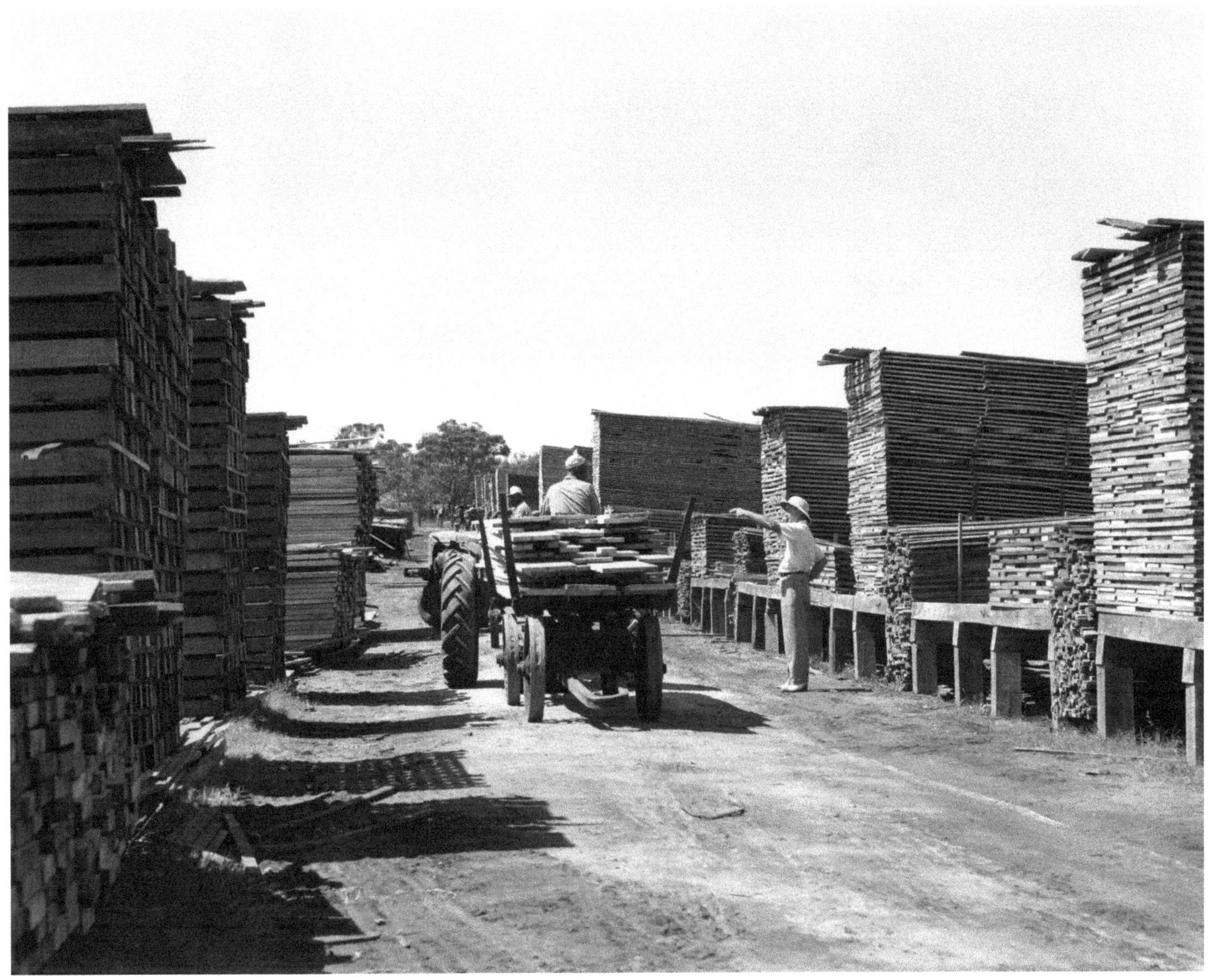

The 1954 Fiesta of Five Flags parade was the first local parade ever broadcast live to Pensacola homes. The scenes were sent from WEAR-TV cameras over Southern Bell Telephone Company lines to the central telephone office. The images were then beamed to the television station tower by way of microwaves.

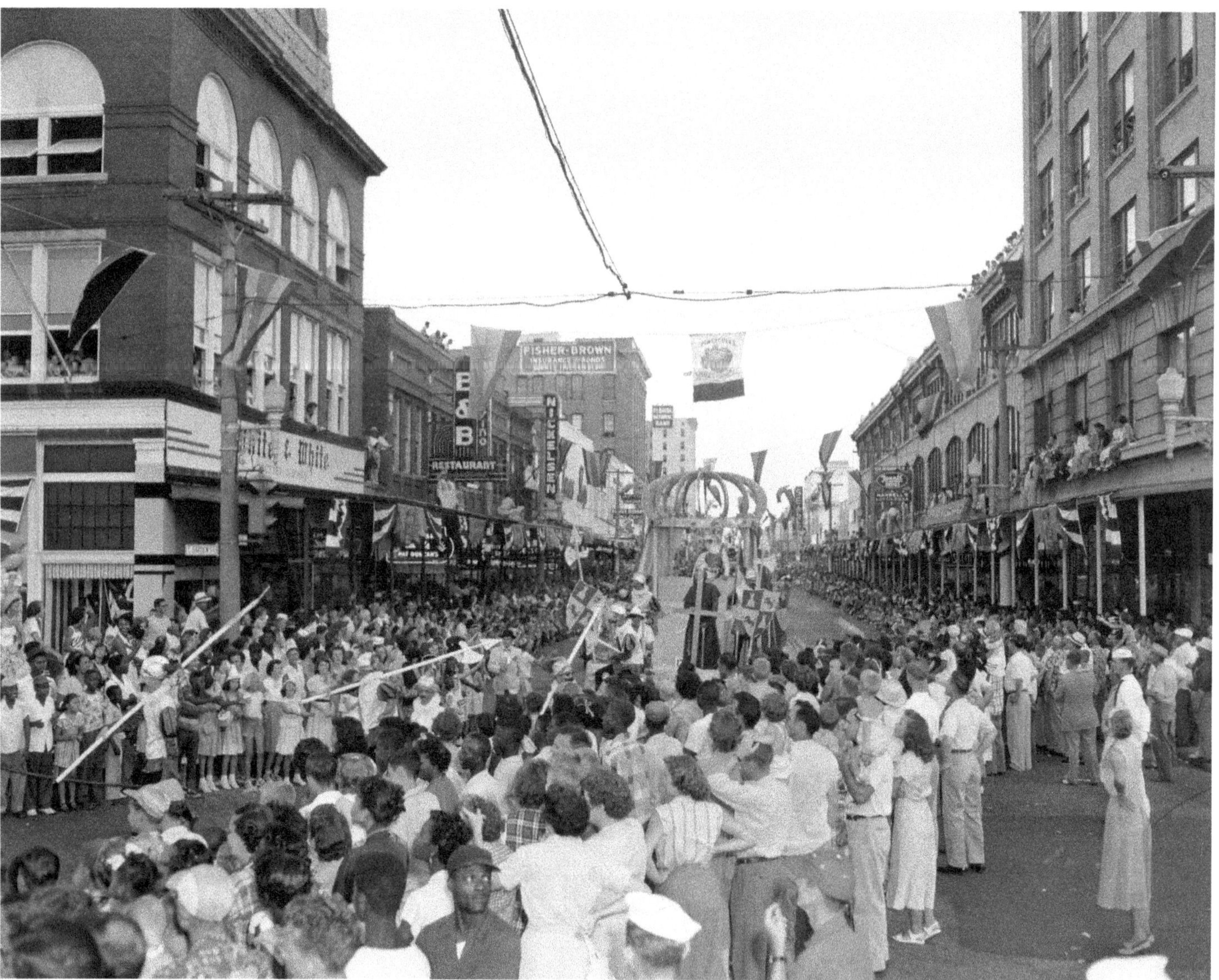

The new Chemstrand plant brought high-paying jobs to the Pensacola area when it opened in Cantonment in 1953. The first U.S. plant licensed to produce nylon, by 1963 the Cantonment site was the world's largest producer of nylon. The plant has undergone two name changes over the years. Becoming the Monsanto Company in 1962, the plant introduced Astro Turf in 1966. After a division of the company in 1997, the plant was renamed Solutia.

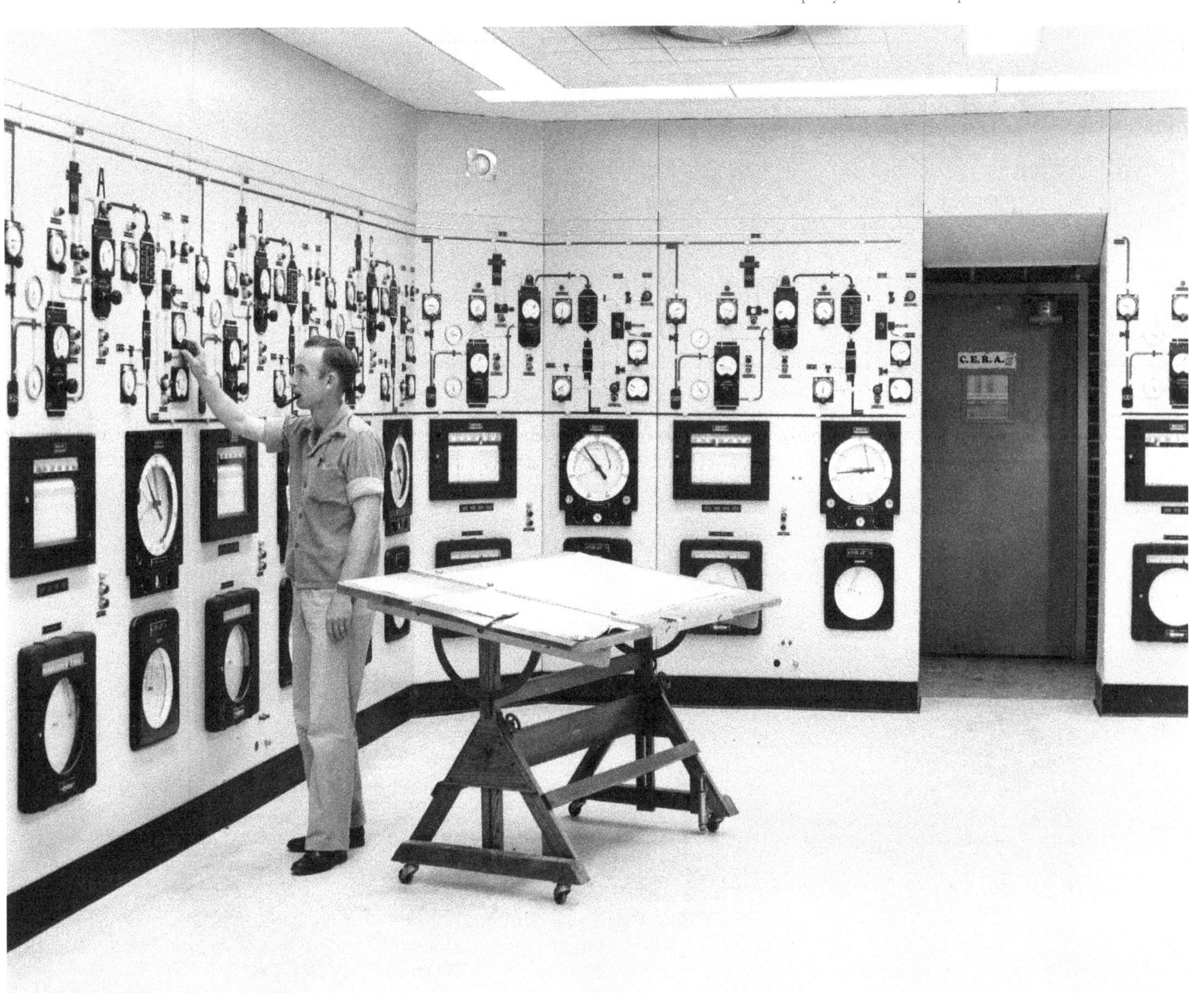

Joe Kingry, foreground, helps Nancy Beach land a red snapper she has caught on a 1958 fishing trip.

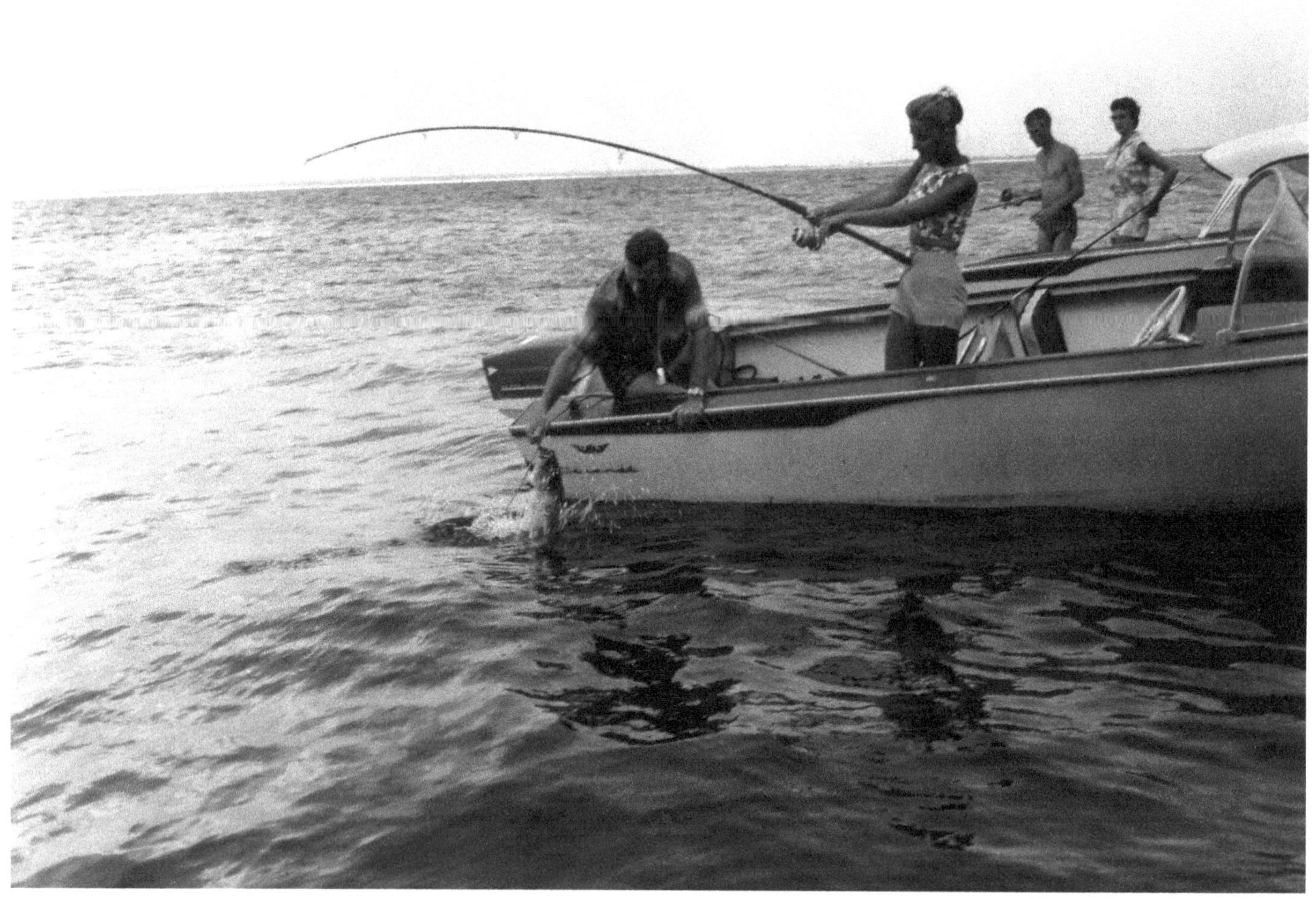

Raw bars have long been a favorite way to enjoy freshly shucked local oysters. This venue features the once-popular wall-mounted jukebox, an example of which is visible at upper-right.

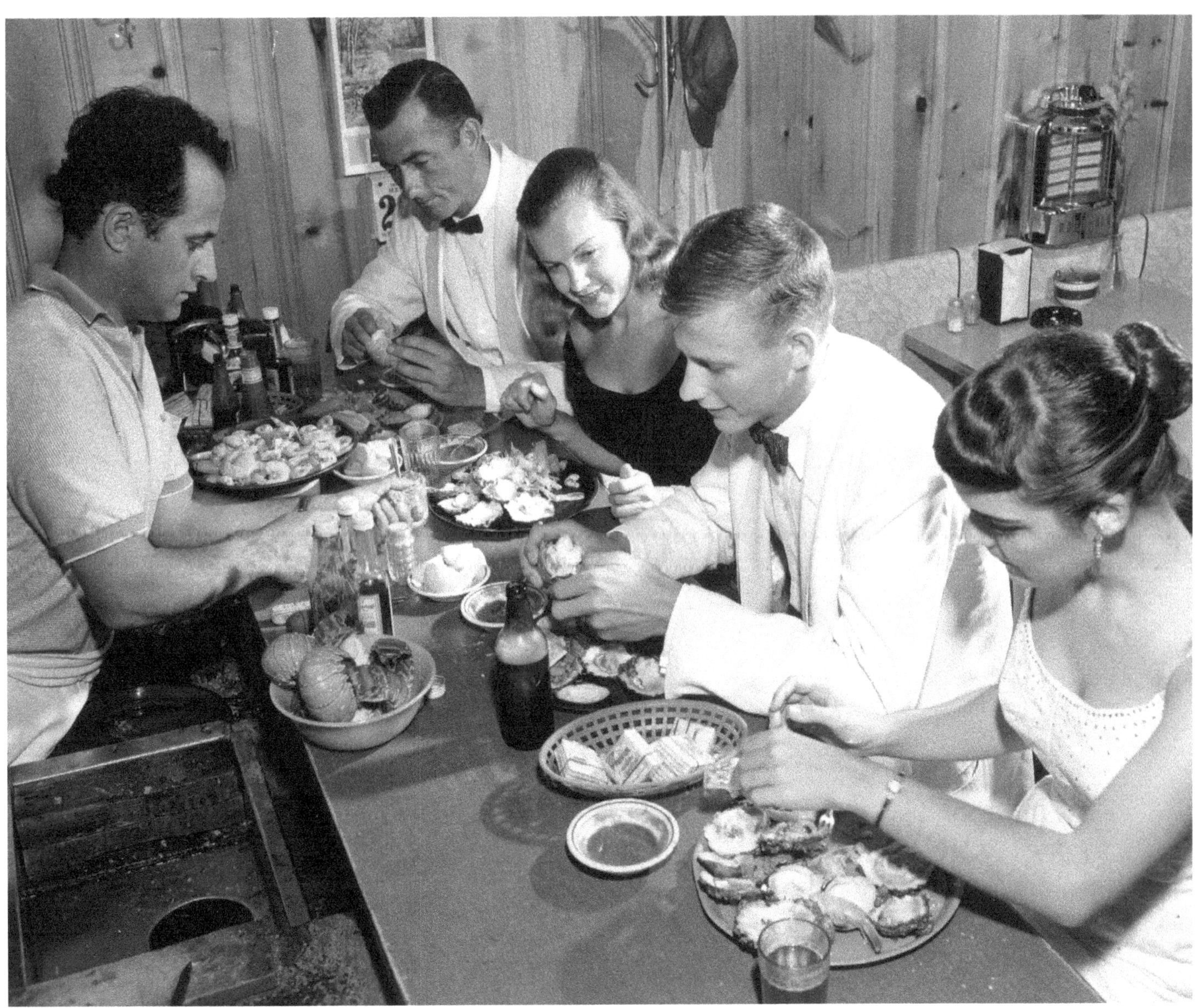

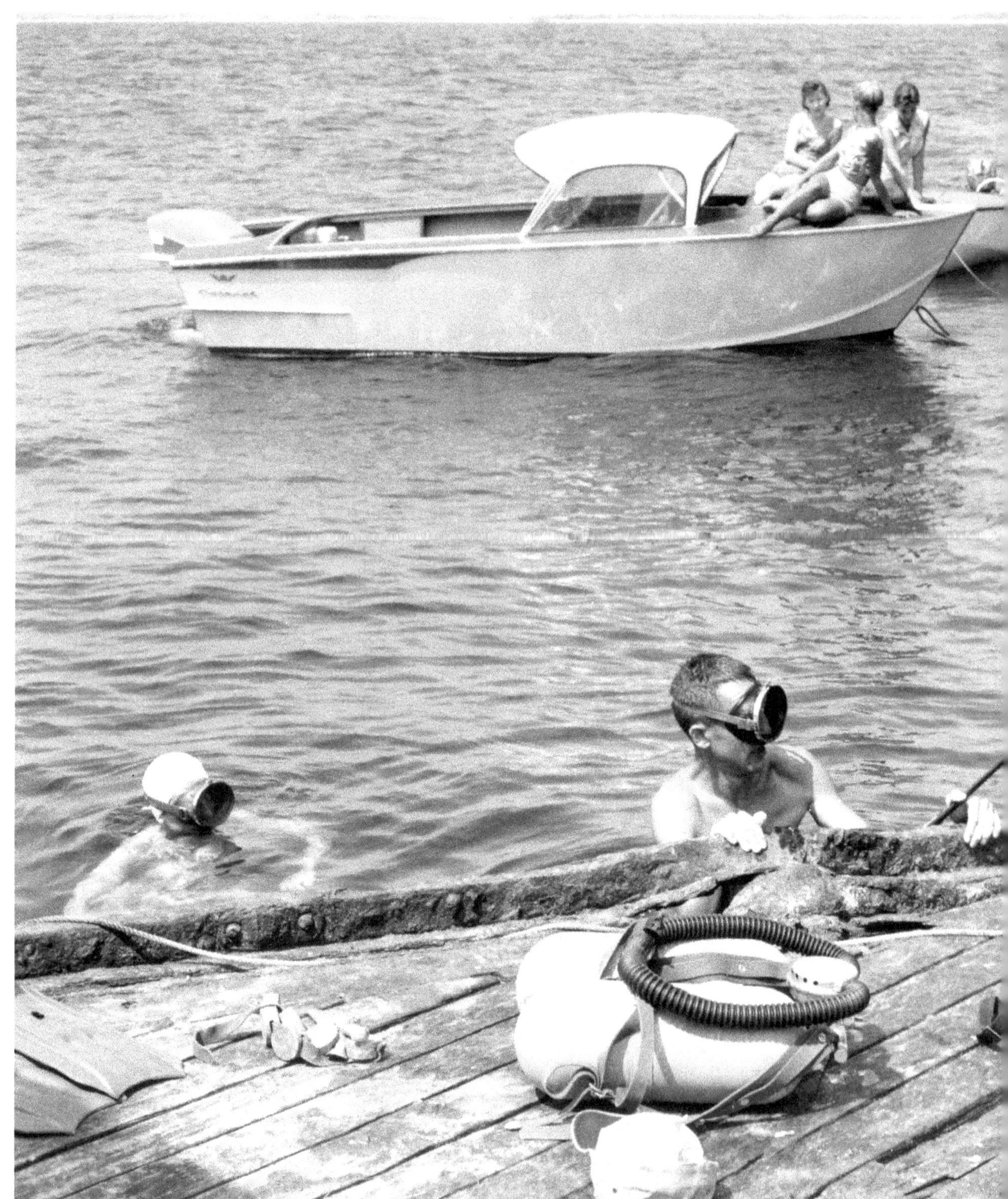

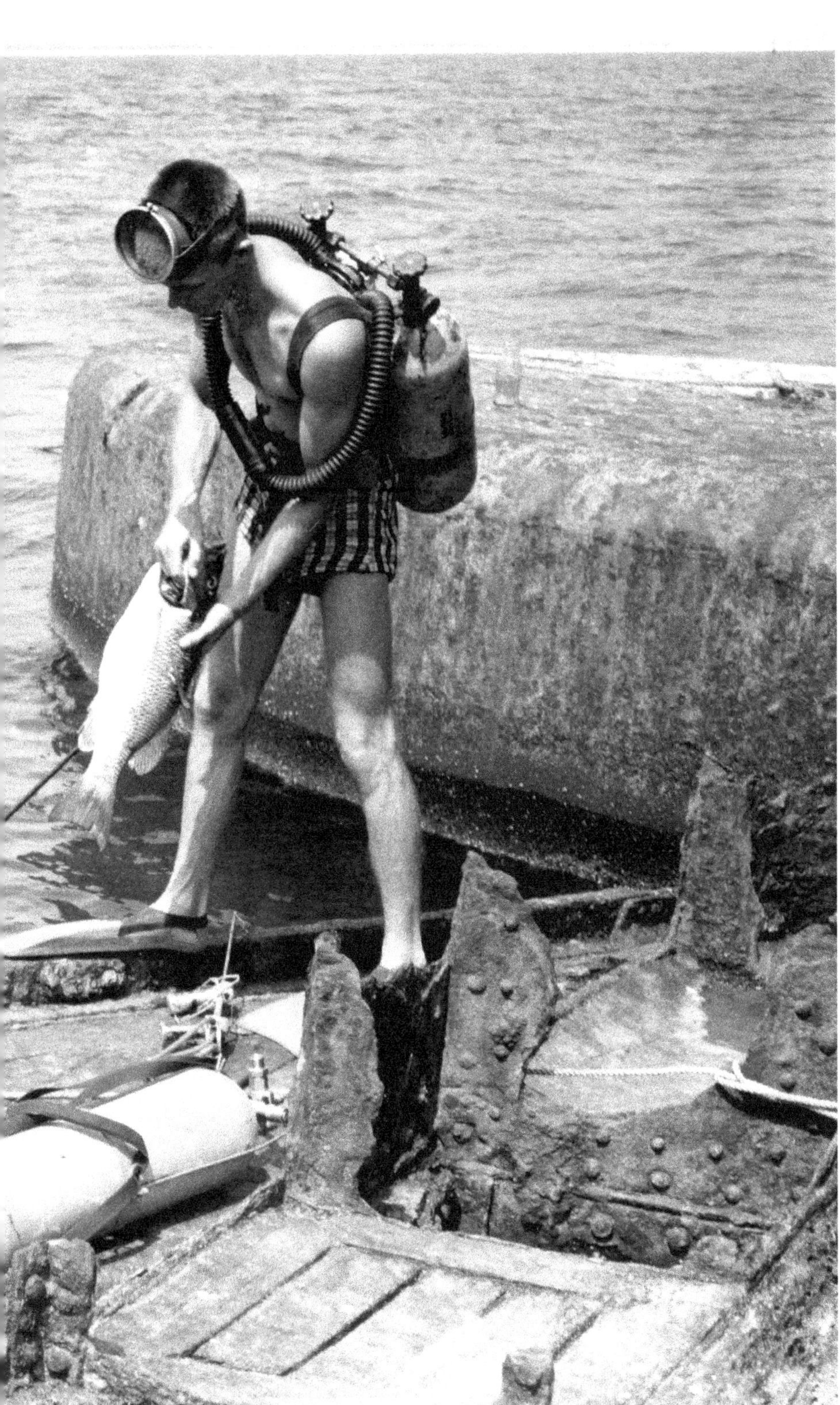

Scuba diving and spear fishing are popular area pastimes. These sportsmen were enjoying the fishing near the USS *Massachusetts,* which was sunk offshore after World War I and used for military target practice.

The Piasecki HUP was used for training naval pilots stationed in the Pensacola area.

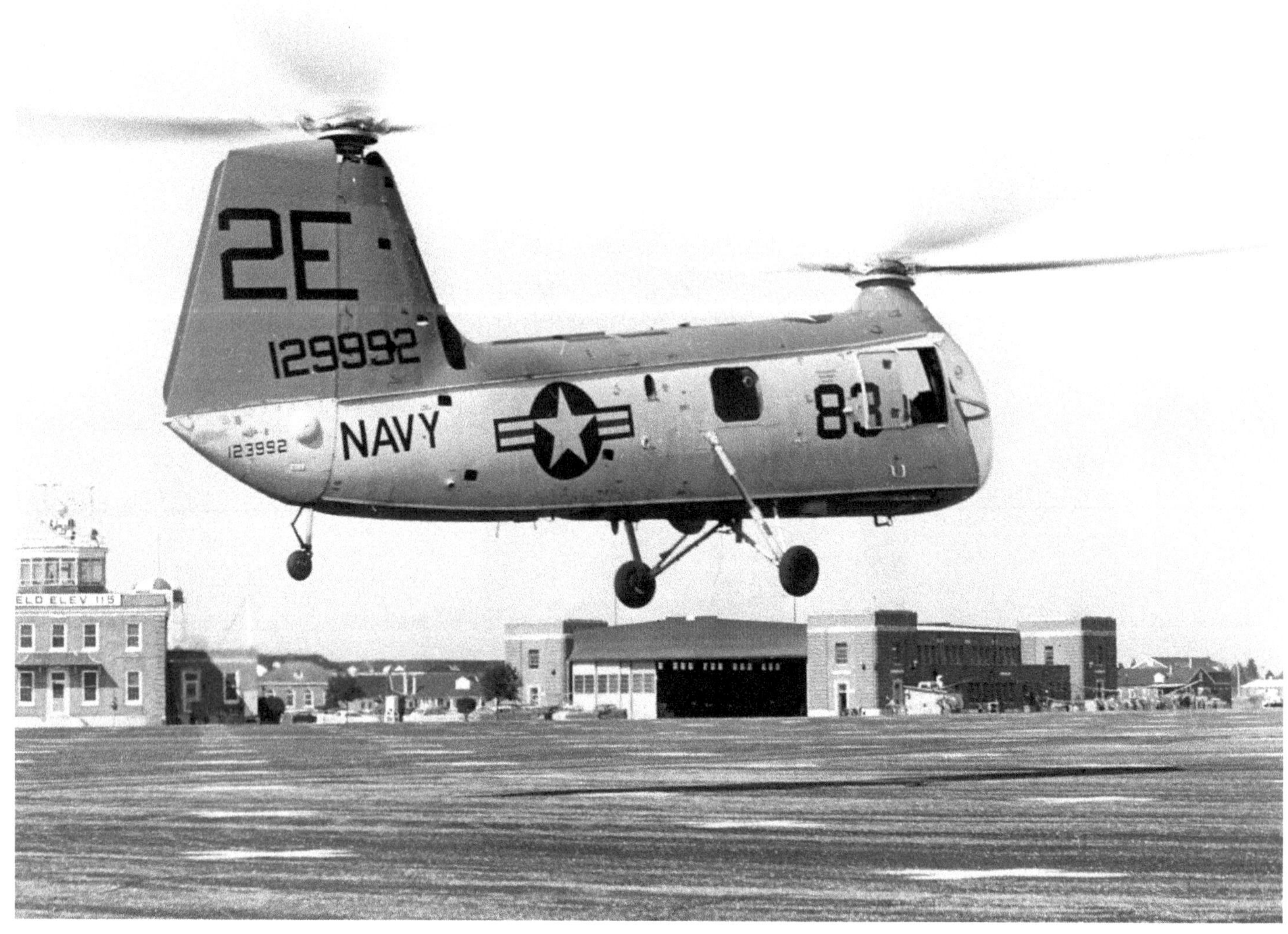

A replica of a colonial Spanish village was constructed on Pensacola Beach in 1959 for the Quadricentennial Festival, a celebration of the 400th anniversary of the first settlement of Pensacola. Archbishop Thomas J. Toolen of the Catholic Diocese of Mobile conducted consecration ceremonies of the village mission.

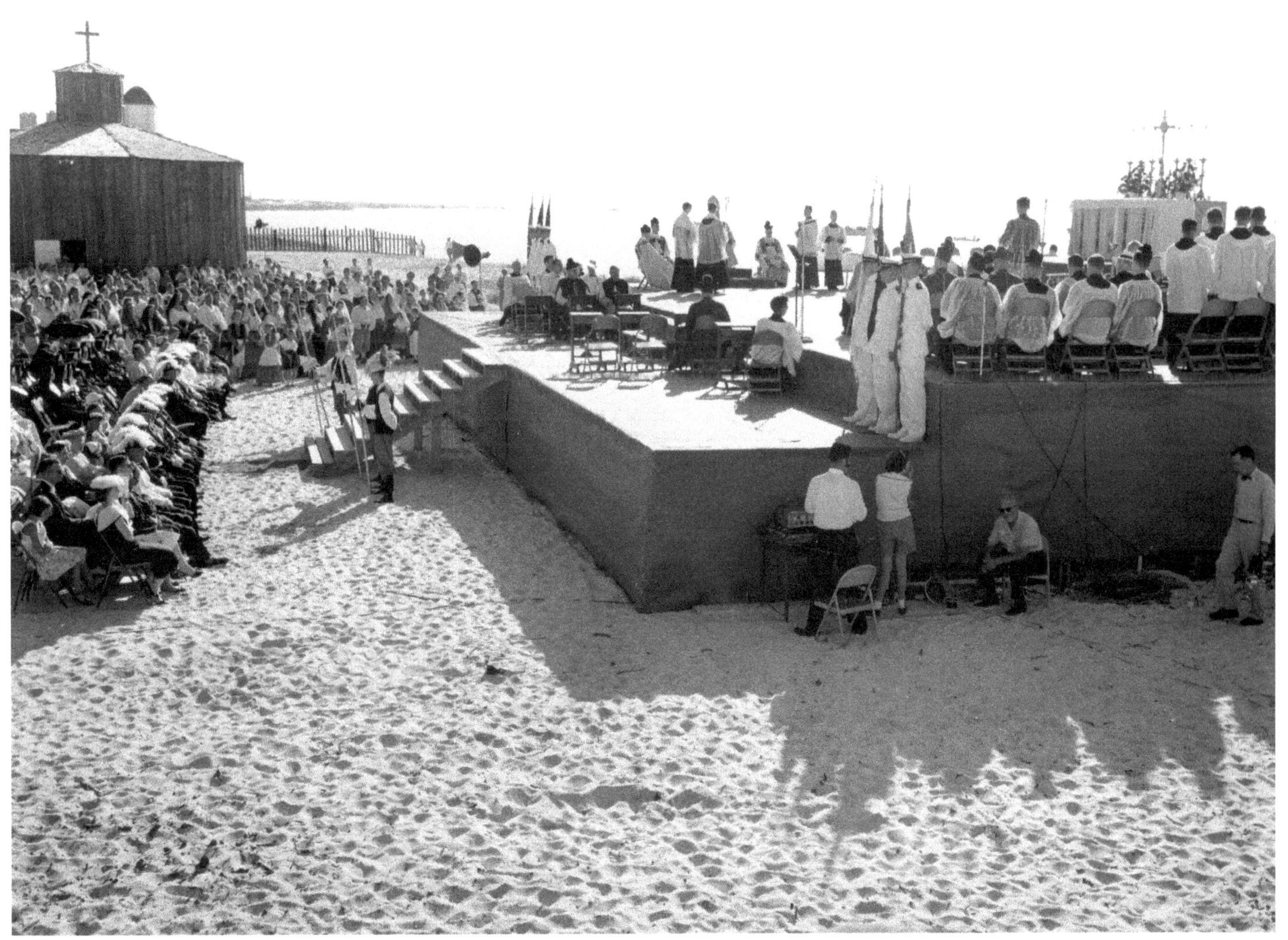

Dressed as a priest, a festival participant approaches the octagonal church that was part of the Spanish village erected on the beach to celebrate the quadricentennial of the first settlement at Pensacola.

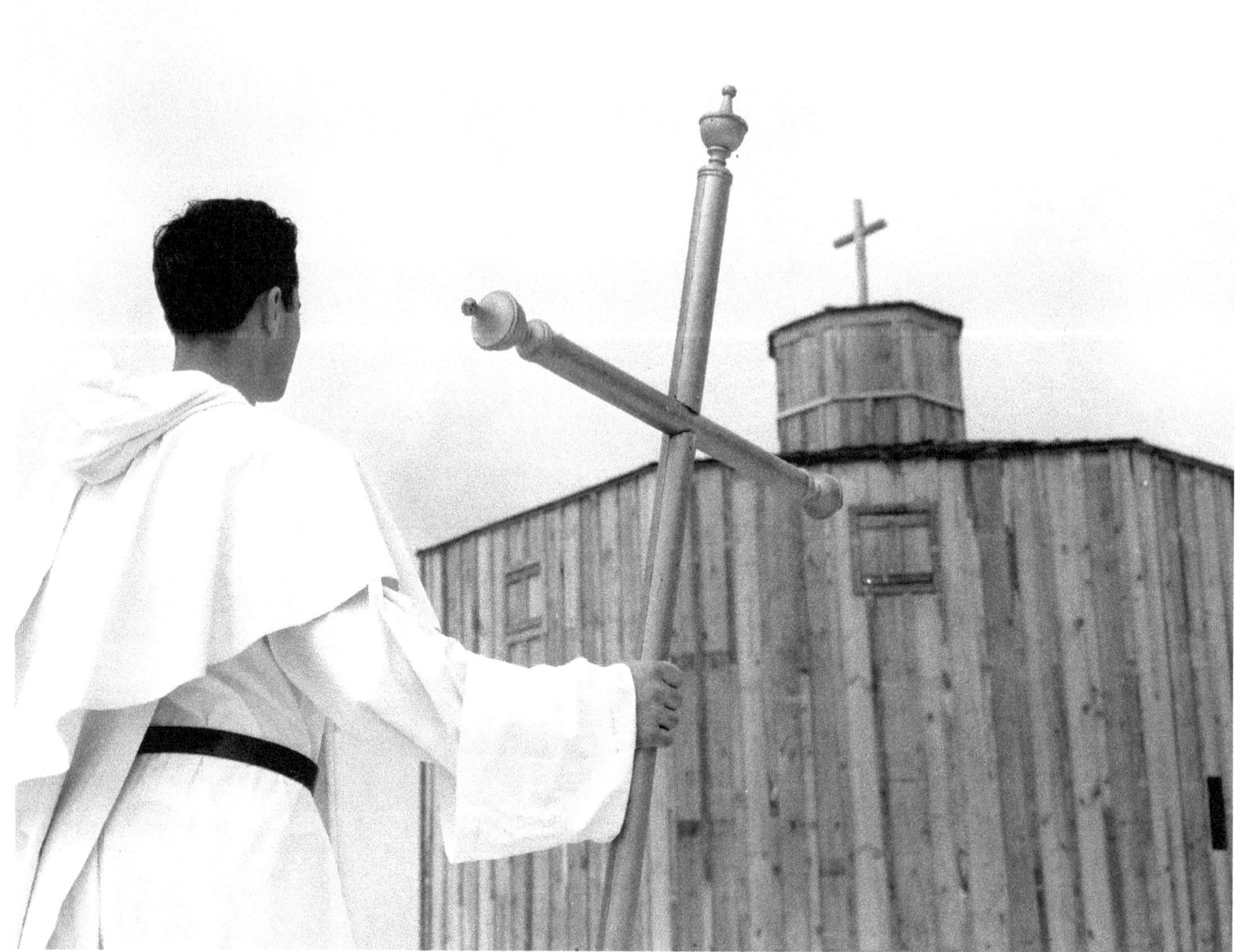

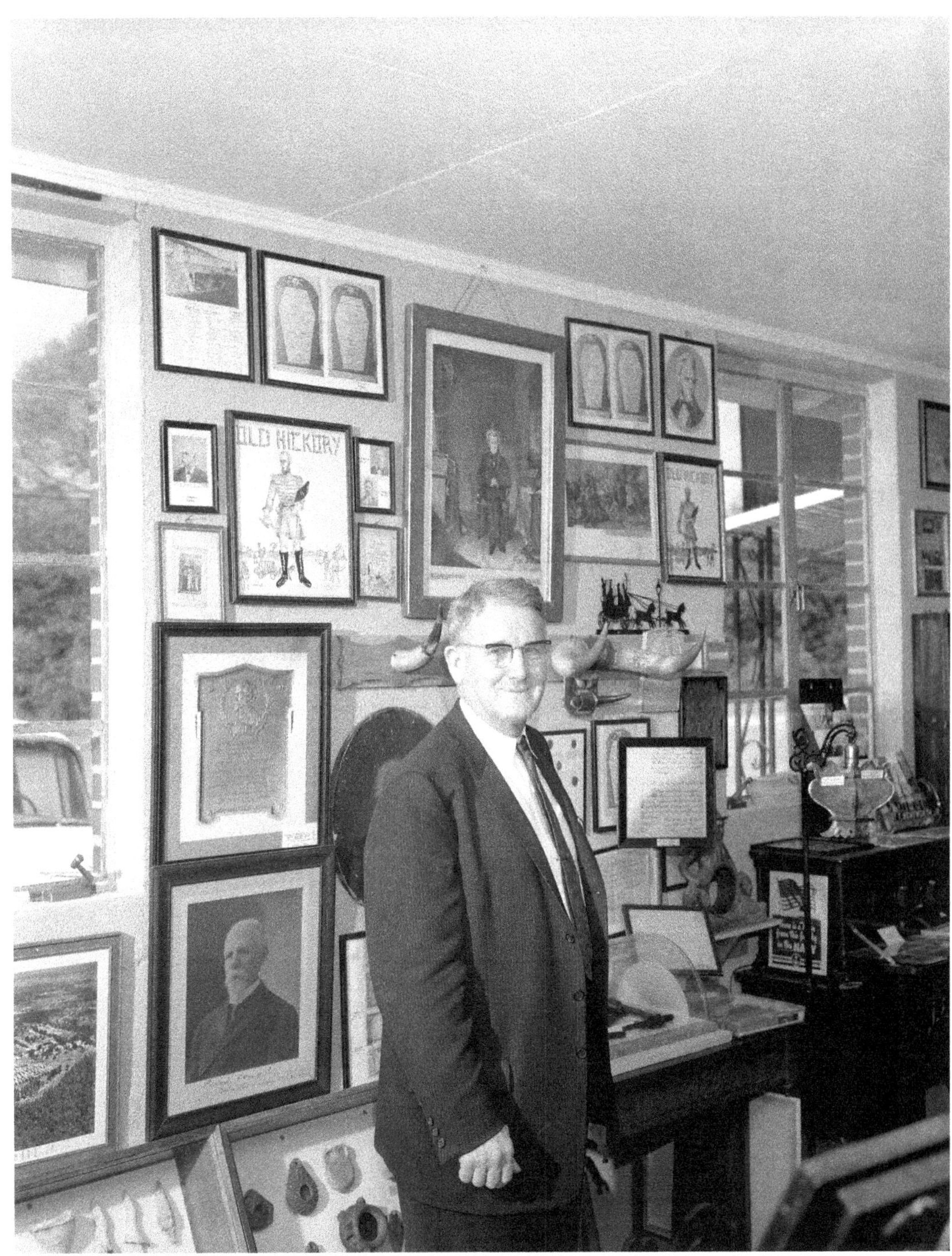

Mr. T. T. Wentworth, Jr., stands before a display in his museum on Old Palafox in Ensley. Wentworth donated his collection to the State of Florida, and the T. T. Wentworth, Jr., Florida State Museum on Jefferson Street, which now owns the artifacts, is named in his honor.

Sleek, modern streetlights line North Palafox in 1960. The Hotel San Carlos dominates the skyline, dwarfing St. Michael's Catholic Church and the Blount Building. An addition to the San Carlos closed the opening on the north end of the building.

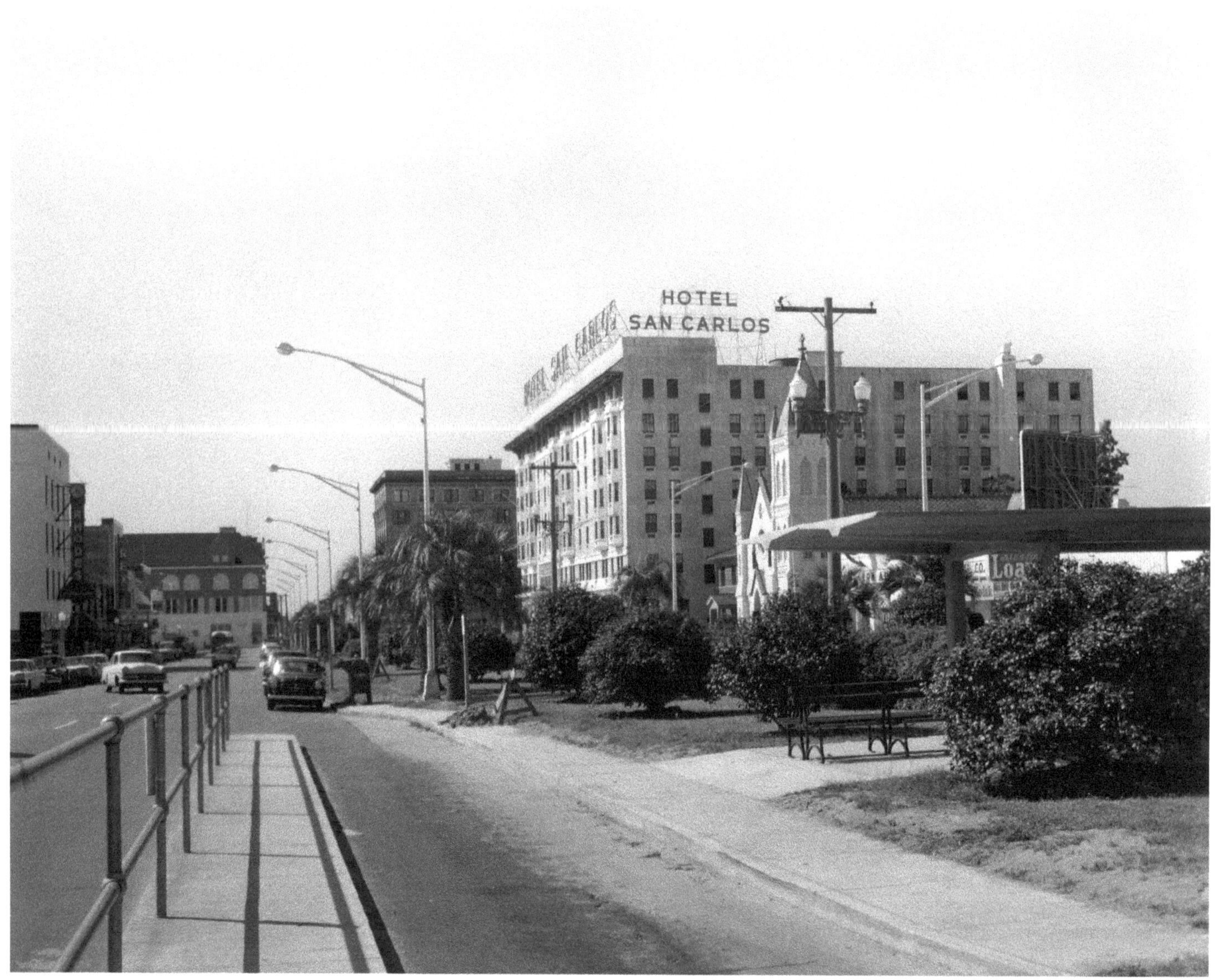

The Bay Bridge appears to stretch forever across the bay separating Pensacola and Gulf Breeze. The new bridge, constructed at a cost of $8,000,000, opened in 1960.

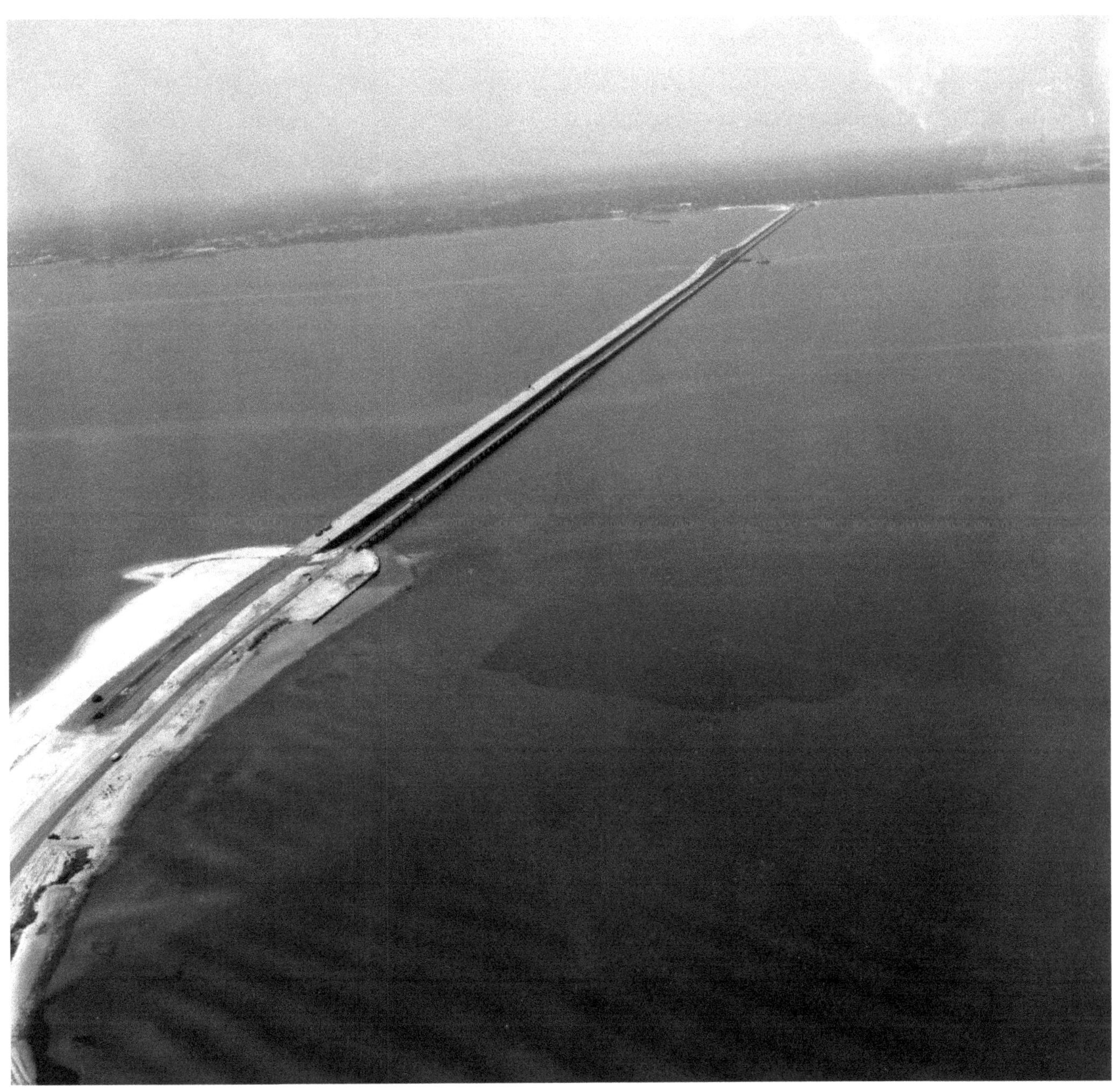

For many years, the Navy co-sponsored a national sports-car rally at Corry Field as part of the annual Fiesta of Five Flags. Ferraris, MGs, Jaguars, Triumphs, Austin-Healys, Mercedes, and Corvettes were some of the automobiles brought to the yearly event.

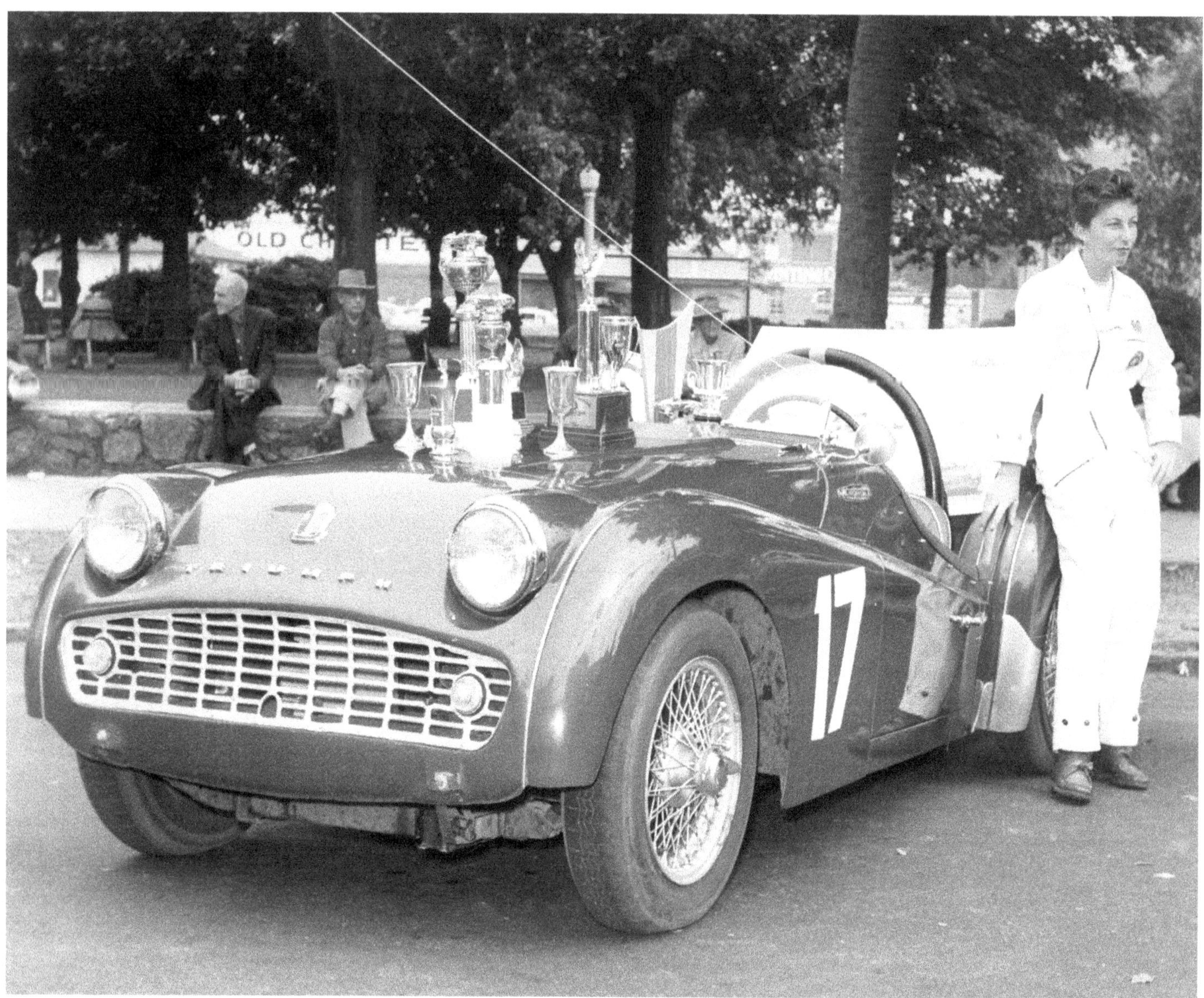

The Pensacola Beach pier has always been a popular place for anglers, offering them a chance to catch dinner as they enjoy the sun and water.

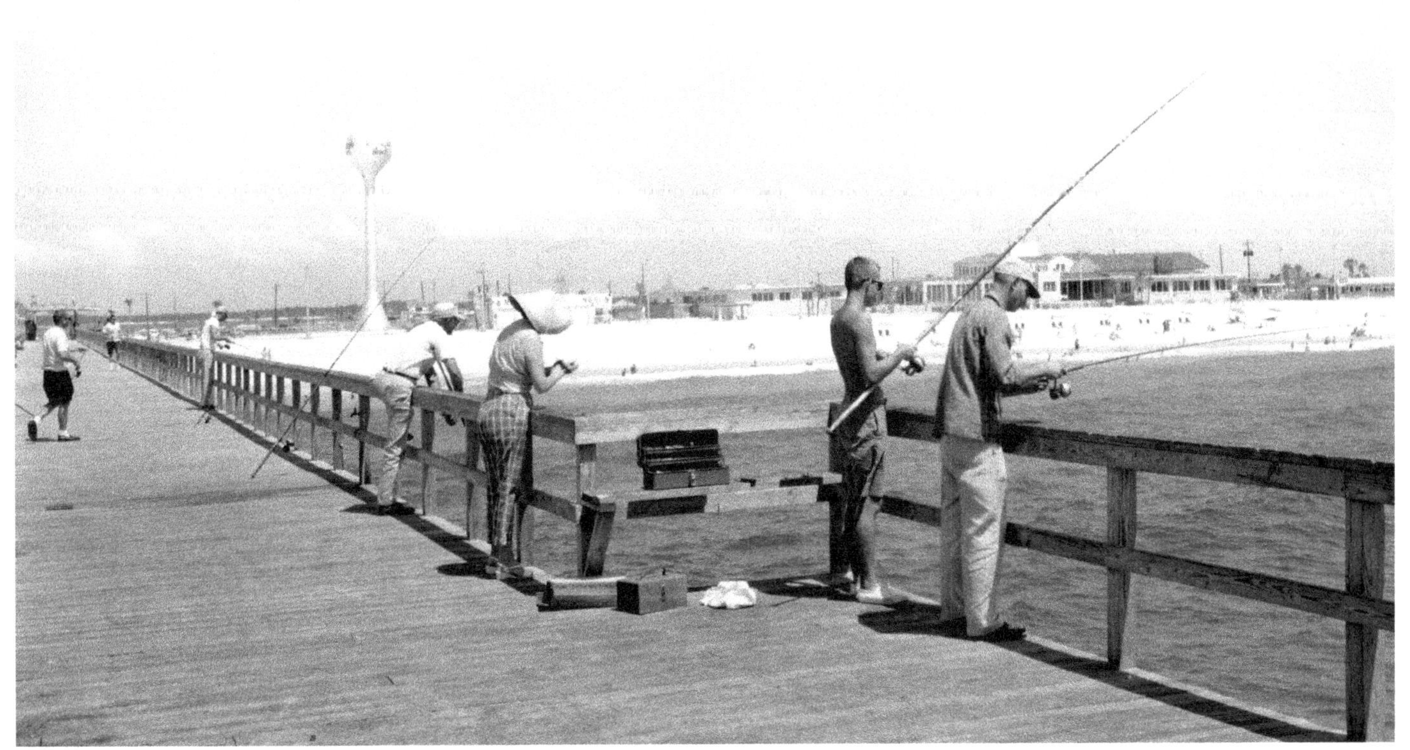

Vince Whibbs, owner of Vince Whibbs Pontiac, donated new convertibles for use in many of the Fiesta of Five Flags parades. Mr. Whibbs, known as the "Man of Integrity," was mayor of Pensacola from 1977 through 1991.

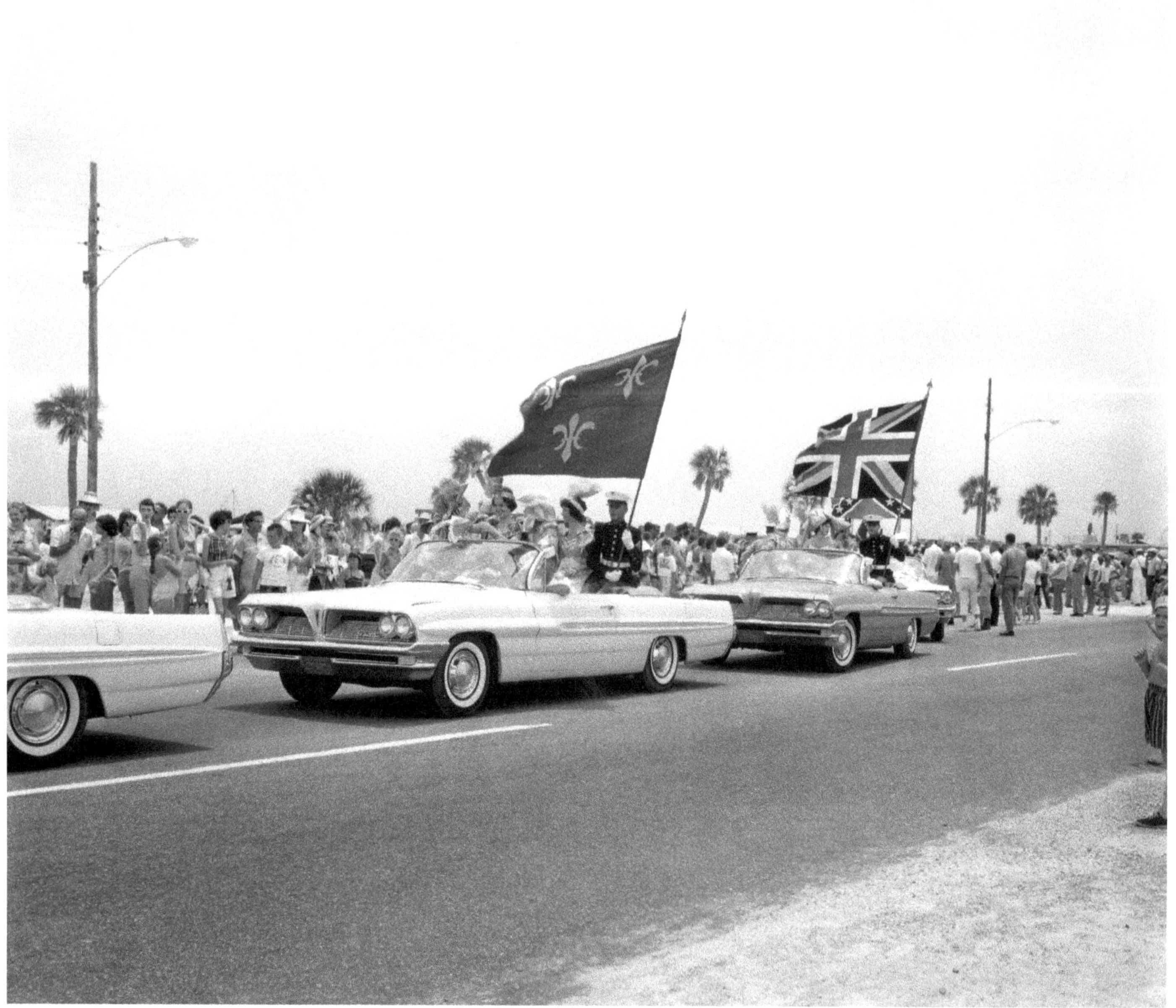

Pensacola's climate offers many warm days to enjoy boating.

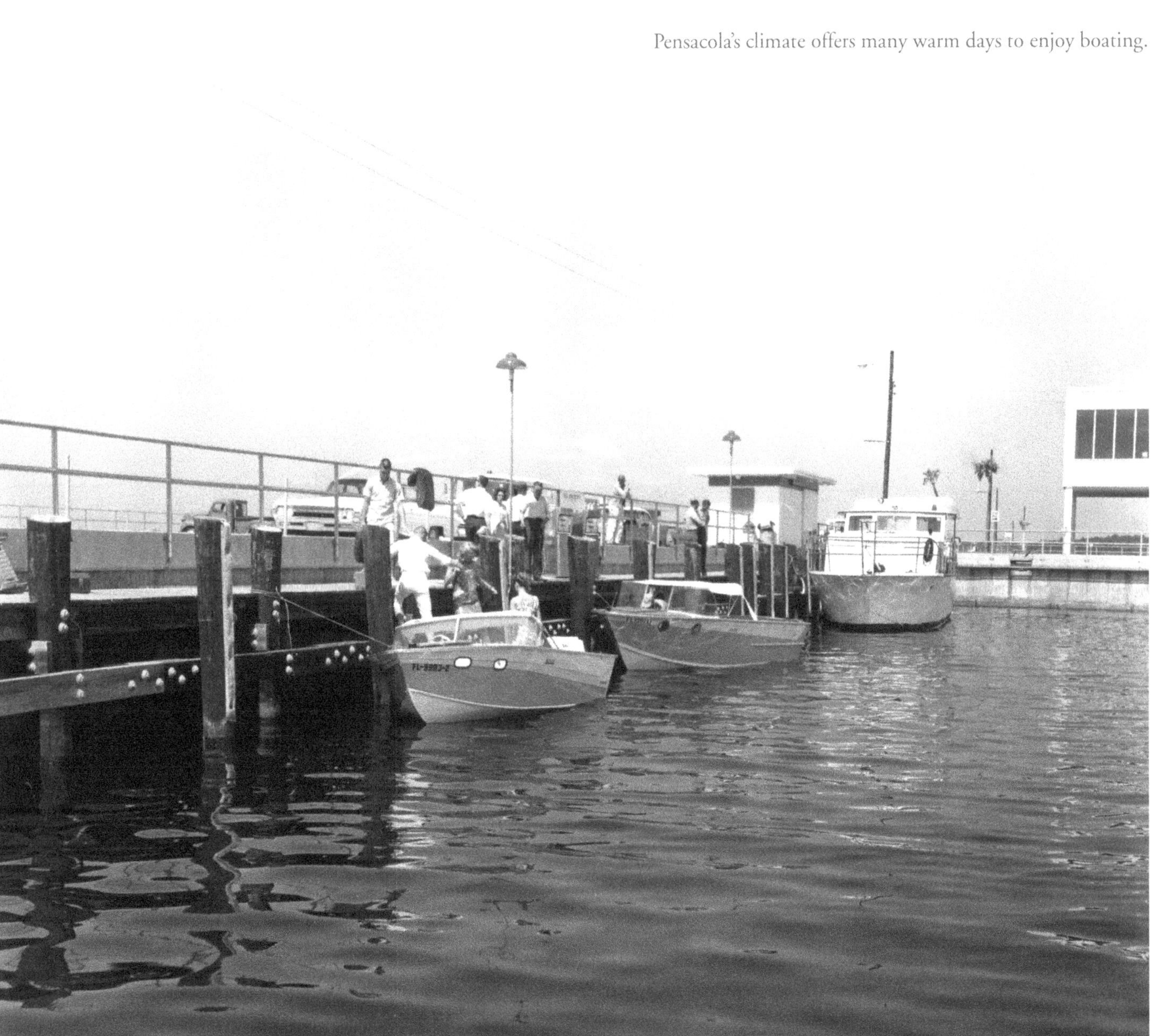

Pensacola was a stop in 1960 among candidates for public office. From left to right are U.S. representative Albert Herlong, Jr.; a pilot; U.S. representative Bob Sikes; Comptroller Ray E. Green; Superintendent of Public Instruction Thomas D. Bailey; a stewardess; gubernatorial candidate Farris Bryant; a stewardess; Agricultural Commission candidate Doyle Conner; Treasurer J. Edwin Larson; Secretary of State candidate Tom Adams; Attorney General Richard Ervin; Edwin L. Mason, campaigning for the Railroad and Public Utilities Commission; an unidentified man; and a pilot.

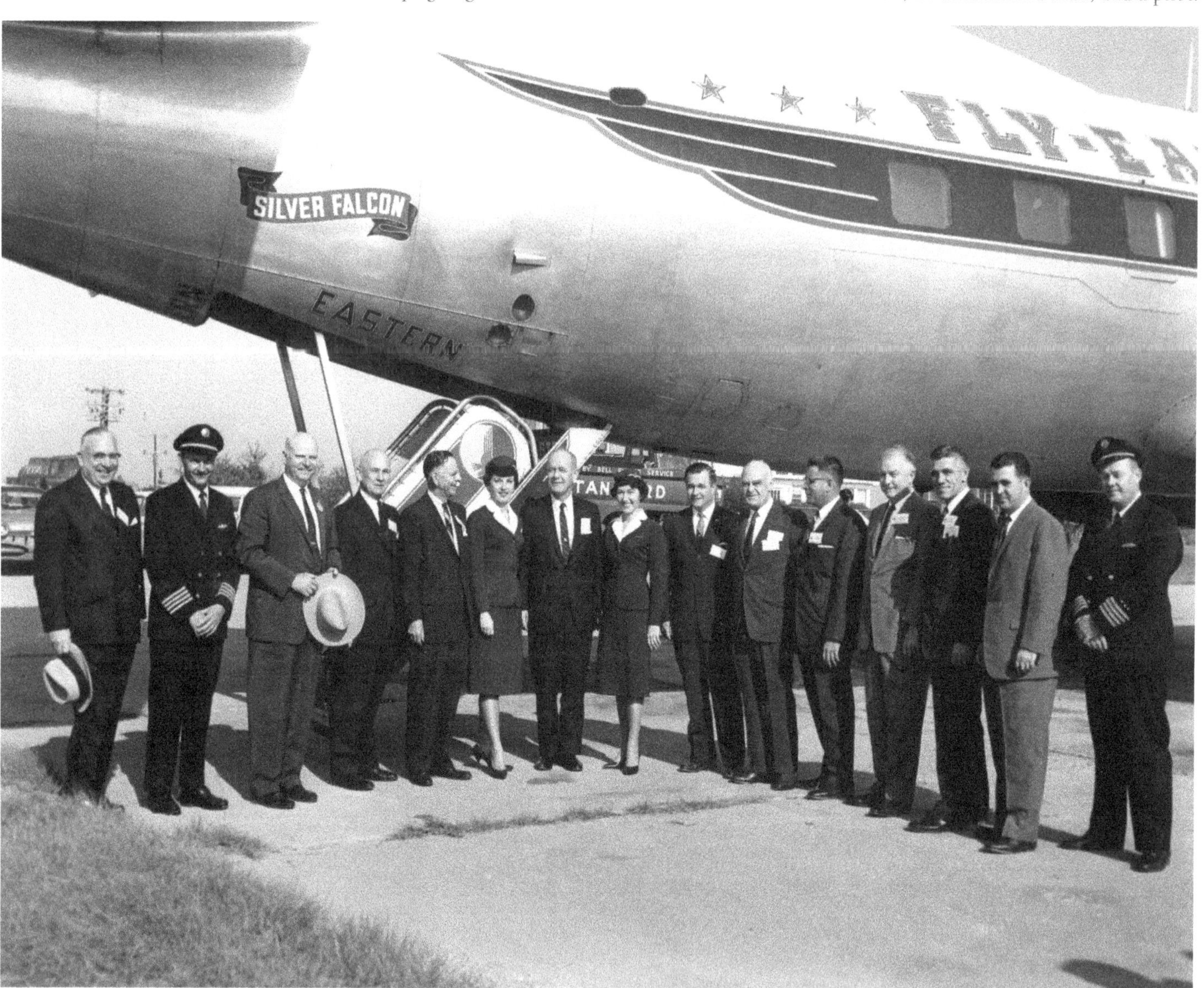

Casino Beach, with its lifeguards and amenities, continued to be a popular place to enjoy the sun and surf in 1960.

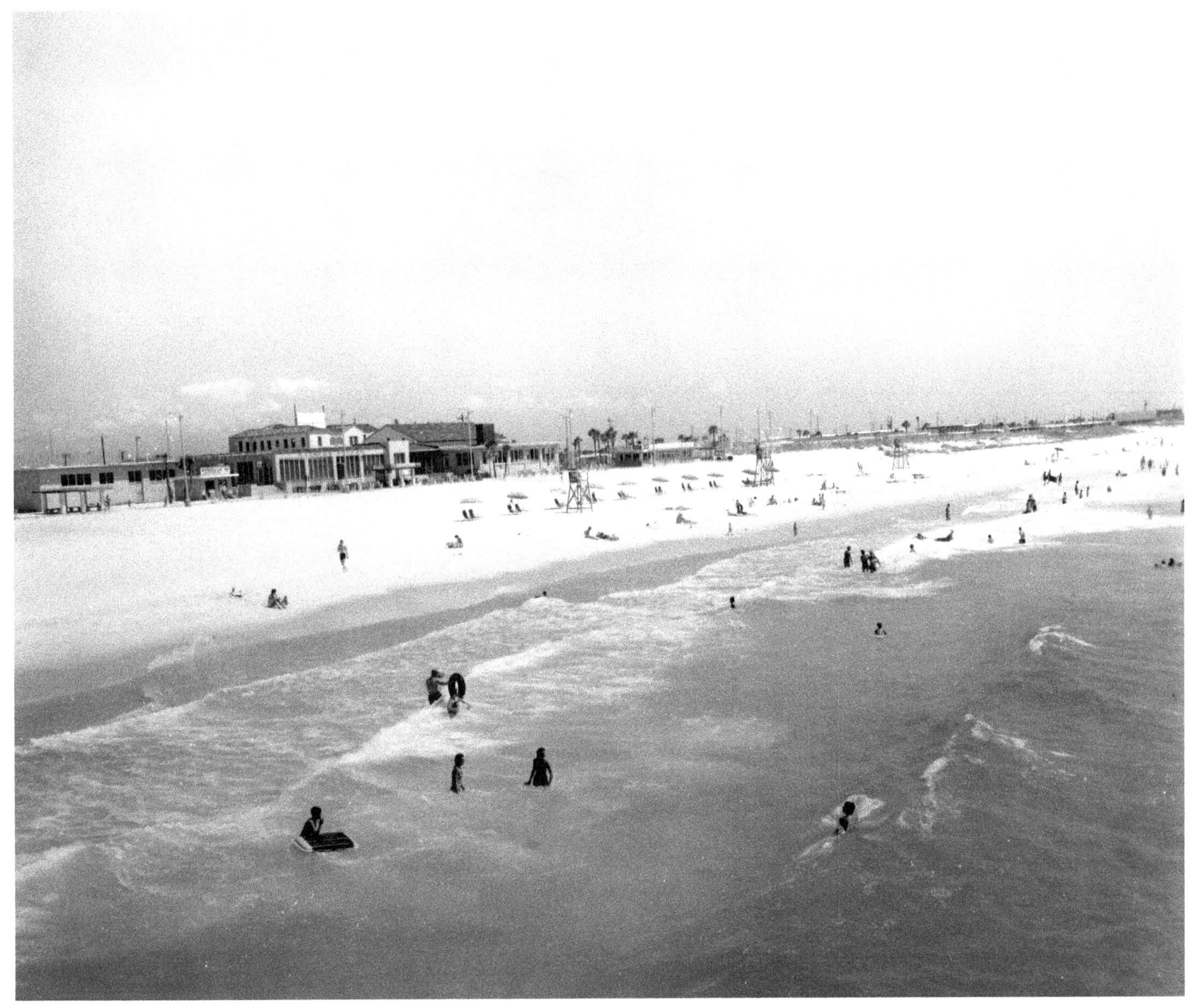

Notes on the Photographs

These notes, listed by page number, attempt to include all aspects known of the photographs. Each of the photographs is identified by the page number, photograph's title or description, photographer and collection, archive, and call or box number when applicable. Although every attempt was made to collect all available data, in some cases complete data was unavailable due to the age and condition of some of the photographs and records.

II **Chipley Monument**
Florida State Archives
Rc18956

VI **Blue Angels**
Florida State Archives
c035981b

X **Confederate Soldiers**
Florida State Archives
Rc02582

3 **Alabama Troops**
Florida State Archives
Rc15637

4 **9th Mississippi**
Florida State Archives
Rc02504

5 **Confederates**
Florida State Archives
Rc04842

6 **Navy Yard**
Florida State Archives
Rc05101

7 **Bayou Grande**
Florida State Archives
Rc02503

8 **Cannon Balls**
Florida State Archives
Rc07482

9 **Union Troops**
Florida State Archives
N030769

10 **Yellow Fever Victims**
Florida State Archive
N030766

11 **Kahn Home**
Florida State Archives
PR08497

12 **Base Housing**
Florida State Archives
N030770

13 **Downtown**
Florida State Archives
Rc18960

14 **Variety Store**
Florida State Archives
Rc03094

15 **Barrancas**
Florida State Archives
Rc06282

16 **Business District**
Florida State Archives
Rc04783

17 **Rome Engine**
Florida State Archives
N039300

18 **1880 Fire**
Florida State Archives
PR08414

19 **Chimneys**
Florida State Archives
PR08415

20 **Cadets**
Florida State Archives
Rc06181

21 **Brent Brothers**
Florida State Archives
Rc19204

22 **Plaza Ferdinand**
Florida State Archives
PR08445

23 **Harbor**
Florida State Archives
Rc18959

24 **Rebuilding**
Florida State Archives
Rc04785

25 **Customs House**
Florida State Archives
Rc06378

26 **Saunders Company**
Florida State Archives
Rc06179

27 **3rd Battalion Band**
Florida State Archives
FP83199a

28 **Fire Department**
Florida State Archives
Rc06214

29 **East Garden Street**
Florida State Archives
Rc19202

30 **Courthouse**
Florida State Archives
Rc03193

31 **Methodist Church**
Florida State Archives
PR08490

32 St. Michael's Church
Florida State Archives
PR08496

33 South Palafox
Florida State Archives
Pr08399

34 1894 Winter
Florida State Archives
PR08412

35 Masons Building
Florida State Archives
Rc00-16

36 Barkley Home
Florida State Archives
ms25785

37 Old Christ Church
Florida State Archives
Rc06369

38 Great Blizzard
Florida State Archives
PR09382

39 Garfield Guards
Florida State Archives
PR00848

40 General Chase Home
Florida State Archives
Rc19200

42 First National Bank
Florida State Archives
Rc07631

43 Train Wreck
Florida State Archives
Rc11255

44 Lumber Company
Florida State Archives
N036808

45 Fire Control System
Florida State Archives
Rc06370

46 Bath House Pier
Florida State Archives
Rc06216

48 Fire Control Towers
Florida State Archives
Rc06371

50 Center Avenue
Florida State Archives
Rc18995

52 Deepwater Port
Florida State Archives
Rc18965

54 Professional Firemen
Florida State Archives
PR08439

55 Showing Some Ankle
Florida State Archives
Rc03107

56 Palafox Street Pier
Florida State Archives
N036800

58 Spanish Church
Florida State Archives
Rc06099

60 Flooded Streets
Florida State Archives
Rc12633

61 East Main Street
Florida State Archives
Rc17084

62 Hurricane of 1906
Florida State Archives
Rc18964

64 Shipwrecked
Florida State Archives
Rc17085

65 Pensacola Lighthouse
Florida State Archives
rc05648

66 Consolidated Grocery
Florida State Archives
Rc19199

67 South Palafox
Florida State Archives
Rc03835

68 Pine Forest
Florida State Archives
rc01036

69 Strikebreakers
Florida State Archives
PR08429

70 Trolley Strike
Florida State Archives
Rc01670

71 Strike Camps
Florida State Archives
Rc01671

72 Militia
Florida State Archives
N036917

73 Strikebreakers
Florida State Archives
Rc01672

74 Brick Wall
Florida State Archives
Rc19201

75 Junior High School
Florida State Archives
PR08442

76 Fire Company #4
Florida State Archives
Rc04781

78 Methodist Episcopal
Florida State Archives
Rc18976

79 Bank Building
Florida State Archives
Rc06231

80 Crossing South Palafox
Florida State Archives
Rc06202

81 Big Parade
Florida State Archives
Rc04720

82 Scottish Rite Building
Florida State Archives
Rc04377

84 Parade
Florida State Archives
Rc04708

85 Airplane
Florida State Archives
N038791

86 Spanish Mission
Florida State Archives
Rc04373

88 County Courthouse
Florida State Archives
N036888

89 Fountain
Florida State Archives
Rc19191

90 Blount Building
Florida State Archives
Rc06124

91 Opera House
Florida State Archives
Rc06227

92 Star Laundry Company
Florida State Archives
PR08451

93 Richard Bingham
Florida State Archives
N036923

94 Paved Streets
Florida State Archives
Rc06125

95 New Pier
Florida State Archives
PR08468

96 Yacht Club
Florida State Archives
Rc05380

97 National Bank
Florida State Archives
Rc18962

98 Rail-Mounted Gun
Florida State Archives
Rc21495

99 Catholic Hospital
Florida State Archives
Rc19180

100 Seaplane
Florida State Archives
Rc06229

101 Obid Richards
Florida State Archives
N044764

102 Plane Catapult
Florida State Archives
PR08404

103 Naval Air Station
Florida State Archives
PR08402

104 Lt. Commander Corry
Florida State Archives
Rc03509

106 Free Balloon
Florida State Archives
Rc18992

107 Flying Boat
Florida State Archives
N036827

108 Family on Porch
Courtesy of the
Jernigan family

109 USS Huntington
Florida State Archives
Rc12787

110 DN-1 Airship
Florida State Archives
N036820

111 USS Pensacola
Florida State Archives
na10

112 Patriotic League
Florida State Archives
N036925

113 Naval Air Station
Florida State Archives
N036823

114 Twin Engine F5
Florida State Archives
PR00475

116 Automobiles
Florida State Archives
N038799

117 Officers Barracks
Florida State Archives
N030776

118 Ft. Barrancas
Florida State Archives
N030775

119 Group of Pilots
Florida State Archives
N047515

120 Ingham Dairy
Florida State Archives
PR08450

122 Vincent Vidal
Florida State Archives
ms25739

123 Wide Median
Florida State Archives
Rc06183

124 Roundhouse
Florida State Archives
Rc12963

125 Mother-in-Law
Florida State Archives
ms25749

126 Fire Ladder
Florida State Archives
PR08435

127 City Hall
Florida State Archives
Rc191892

128 Garcia Beck
Florida State Archives
ms25988

129 Corry Field
Florida State Archives
PR08410

130 Governor Sholtz
Florida State Archives
N036819

131 USS Pensacola
Florida State Archives
Rc20024

132 Students
Florida State Archives
PR08424

133 Mobile Sawmill
Florida State Archives
N032399

134 FERA Dock Builders
Florida State Archives
N036796

135 Bayview Park
Florida State Archives
PR08470

136 Mattress Factory
Florida State Archives
N034701

137 Bathhouses
Florida State Archives
N036851

138 Adult Education
Florida State Archives
PR00818

140 Pensacola Beach
Florida State Archives
N036805

141 17th Avenue Bridge
Florida State Archives
N036921

142 Band Playing
Florida State Archives
FP83200b

144 **UFO Event**
Florida State Archives
PR136512

145 **130 British Royal Navy**
Florida State Archives
PR13640

146 **War Effort**
Florida State Archives
Rc24106

148 **Esperanza**
Florida State Archives
c007425

149 **Pensacola Beach**
Florida State Archives
c005439

150 **USS Saipan**
Florida State Archives
C005578

151 **Passenger Depot**
Florida State Archives
c002316

152 **Casino Beach**
Florida State Archives
c006062

154 **Movie Lines**
Florida State Archives
c007738

155 **Downtown**
Florida State Archives
c010591

156 **Hotel San Carlos**
Florida State Archives
c0074022

158 **Southern Yacht Club**
Florida State Archives
c010673

159 **Lipton Cup Race**
Florida State Archives
c010656

160 **Watching the Race**
Florida State Archives
c010682b2

161 **Andy Alfoso**
Florida State Archives
c010688

162 **Ivy-covered Church**
Florida State Archives
c010589

163 **High School Band**
Florida State Archives
GV010758

164 **Ribbon Cutting**
Florida State Archives
GV035080

165 **Pensacola Beach Bridge**
Florida State Archives
PR15066

166 **Dedication Ceremony**
Florida State Archives
PR15067

168 **Enjoying the Sun**
Florida State Archives
c0135502

169 **Lifeguard**
Florida State Archives
c013192

170 **Fiesta of Five Flags**
Florida State Archives
c014995

171 **Miss America**
Florida State Archives
c014992

172 **De Luna Ball**
Florida State Archives
c013652

173 **Dorris Nettles**
Florida State Archives
c015097

174 **Bar Association**
Florida State Archives
c015010

175 **Moshe Dayan**
Florida State Archives
ms25754

176 **Fiesta Parade**
Florida State Archives
c0166622

177 **South Palafox Parade**
Florida State Archives
c016661

178 **Casino Patio**
Florida State Archives
c016844

180 **The Lucky Strike**
Florida State Archives
c016626

181 **Contestants**
Florida State Archives
c016672

182 **Palafox Pier**
Florida State Archives
Rc08097

183 **Lumber Company**
Florida State Archives
rc17652

184 **Broadcasted Parade**
Florida State Archives
c016658

185 **Nylon Plant**
Florida State Archives
Rc17375

186 **Catching Fish**
Florida State Archives
c027403

187 **Raw Bars**
Florida State Archives
c027264

188 **Scuba Divers**
Florida State Archives
c027660

190 **Piasecki HUP**
Florida State Archives
Rc18573

191 **400th Anniversary**
Florida State Archives
c030134

192 **Festival Participant**
Florida State Archives
c029506

193 **Mr. Wentworth**
Florida State Archives
c029527

194 **Modern Streetlight**
Florida State Archives
c034088

195 **The Bay Bridge**
Florida State Archives
c034141

196 **Car Rally**
Florida State Archives
PR08379

197 **Pensacola Pier**
Florida State Archives
c034109

198 Boating Days
Florida State Archives
c671915a

199 Vince Whibbs
Florida State Archives
c036533

200 Silver Falcon
Florida State Archives
Rc19254

201 Casino Beach
Florida State Archives
c034108

HISTORIC PHOTOS OF PENSACOLA

Pensacola is a city of many firsts. It was home to the first documented European settlement in North America, the first hostilities of the Civil War took place here, and it is the home of the first Naval Aviation training base. It was also the only natural deep-water port on the Gulf of Mexico.

Focusing on the downtown area, *Historic Photos of Pensacola* has captured the history of Pensacola from the Civil War to the 1970s. This walk through time documents Pensacola's move from a town of unpaved streets to a modern city. Unbeaten by a devastating fire in 1880, the city rebuilt and continued to grow.

In stunning black-and-white photography, this handsome coffee-table book details the historical growth of Pensacola from its early days up to recent times. Spanning two centuries and nearly 200 images, the book follows the building of this history-rich city, offering a compelling look into the past for any longtime resident and every history buff of Pensacola.

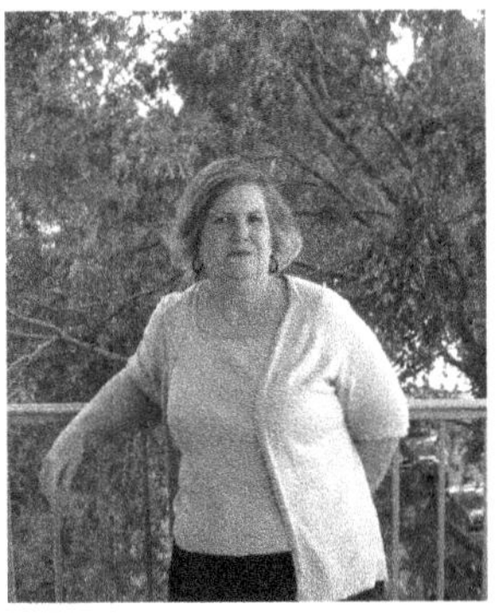

Jacquelyn Tracy Wilson is a fifth-generation Pensacolian and is fascinated with the history of the city. After a thirty-year career in the medical field, she returned to school and earned a bachelor of fine arts degree from the University of West Florida. She is currently finishing work on her master of arts in public history at the university. Employed at the Pensacola Historical Society, she continues to research the history of Pensacola.

WWW.TURNERPUBLISHING.COM

www.ingramcontent.com/pod-product-compliance
Lightning Source LLC
LaVergne TN
LVHW060612110826
845154LV00003B/75
9781684420032